COTTON DAVIDSON

THE LEGENDARY "RIFLEMAN" OF THE AMERICAN FOOTBALL LEAGUE

A biography by

Cotton Davidson

Cotton Davidson

As told to and developed by

Wayland Corgill

Wayland Corgill

Published by
Texas Book Publishers Association
Houston Texas

TEXAS BOOK
PUBLISHERS

The Rifleman is a memoir by Cotton Davidson,
NFL & AFL Quarterback, Baylor Player and Coach &
Coryell County, Texas Rancher, as told to and
developed by Wayland Corgill.

First Edition - First Print

13   12   11   10 9 8 7 6 5 4 2 1

 ISBN 978-0-87244-009-8 (hardback)
 ISBN 978-0-87244-010-4 (soft paper)

The Texas Book Publishers Association is committed to publishing
works of quality and integrity. In that spirit, we are proud to offer this
book to our readers; however, the story, the experiences, and the words
are the author's alone. The conversations in the book all come from the
author's recollections, not word-for-word transcripts. All of the events
in this memoir are true to the best of the author's memory. The author,
in no way, represents any company, corporation, or brand mentioned
herein. The views expressed in this memoir are solely those of the author.

Edited by Carole Corgill

Published by the
Texas Book Publishers Association
HOUSTON TEXAS

Dedication

From Coryell County and back has been a long, long journey. I couldn't have made it without the support of the folks who raised me, my invaluable partner Carolyn, and our family that I am so proud of. To them, I owe so much. The same is true for more friends than I can name who brightened my pathway.

Such things in life are of value beyond estimation. What can I do to show my appreciation? That question presents a problem, and I don't know the answer. Hopefully, this book will help tell both family and friends how important they are to me. This book and my story are for you.

Content

Preface

My parents and siblings, Back: Alyne holding Sandra, John Thomas; Front: Cotton, Anita, Hyram (Hy)
– courtesy of the Davidson family

The road from Coryell County, Texas, and back was a long and winding one for me. It was also a road lined with priceless memories and experiences. When I finished high school and left the rural environment of a cattle and goat ranch, I had no idea what might lie in store for me. I essentially had no knowledge of what life was like outside of the county. However, I immediately discovered that it sure was different from the place I had spent my growing-up years. There was more to learn than I could have ever imagined. Every day brought a string of new experiences. That initial circumstance didn't change very much as days progressed into months and months progressed into years. Throughout my whole life, new experiences have just kept coming. I have been exceedingly fortunate and successful all along the road from Coryell County and back. However, without the encouragement and support from notable others along the way, that story could well have been different. Those notable others include family, friends, co-workers, and people who gave me a chance. This book is not only about me, Cotton Davidson, but is also a tribute to those folks who were, and are, so important to me.

Foreword

Grant Teaff
Baylor's Head Football Coach 1971 - 1992
College Football Hall of Fame, Class of 2001

It was late December 1971. A job I never wanted and had not sought became mine. The job was head football coach at Baylor University, a struggling member of the storied Southwest Conference. Baylor did not seem to be anyone's dream job. I knew all 15 assistant coaches in the Southwest Conference that supposedly turned Baylor down. Numerous Head Coaches were offered and refused the job.

Upon accepting, the stark realization of my challenge hit me like a cold bucket of water. Floyd Casey Stadium, without a blade of grass, was not only the place where we played our home schedule but practiced every day in the fall and spring. The University had one basic universal gym for all sports. No weight room, no weights, no football dorm or cafeteria. The stadium bleachers were made of wood, placed there in the early '50s. To top all that off, my first day as a new coach found me walking underneath the stands when three young men approached me. The tall skinny one reached out his hand to try to introduce himself. It was Neal Jeffrey, the starting quarterback. Neal was a profound stutterer. I thought to myself, what have I done? Little did I know that I had just met my future All-American quarterback, who would lead us to Baylor's first Southwest Conference Championship in 50 years.

Just as pivotal was the phone call I received from Cotton Davidson the day it was announced that I would be the new coach at Baylor. I had, of course, heard of this Baylor and professional player. He informed me he would like to join my staff, and after spending time with him, I felt he was exactly what I needed to help restore Baylor to a championship football program. Coach Davidson coached Neal and many other all-conference quarterbacks in our 21 years together. I never had a finer coach, a better recruiter, and, ultimately, a better friend.

Coach Davidson taught me the spread passing game, and hopefully, I taught him a little bit about the run game. Together with our other offensive staff members, we created a powerful top-tier offense for the next 21 years.

Donell and I, and Cotton, Carolyn, and our families will always be friends. I will always appreciate Cotton Davidson for what he did for our university and for me.

In this book, readers will thoroughly enjoy the inspiring story of a young boy growing up in Central Texas, learning the hardships and the joys of ranch life, dreaming of playing in college and as a professional. With all of his achievements, his greatest remain his Faith, Family, and the Lives he touched and changed as a COACH.

Life in Pecan Grove

In the 1930s, in Coryell County, Texas, the rural community of Pecan Grove was an active place. The countryside supported more than a dozen families of Davidsons and almost that many families of Martins. A few other families lived in the community, but Davidsons and Martins were in the majority, by far. The Davidsons also figured prominently in nearby communities of Mound and Pulltight. All of the Davidsons were descendants of the first Davidson, James Madison, who arrived in the area in 1849. James Madison Davidson came to Texas from Tennessee by ox-drawn wagon. He married Vianna Moore in 1854, and their first child, Cordelia, was born in 1855. She was the first white child to be born in Coryell County. Three generations later, in 1931, I, Cotton Davidson, was born in a small four-room ramshackle house a few miles from the old frontier Fort Gates, where Cordelia was born.

The Davidson roots run deep in Coryell County. From those first roots, put down in the 1800s, five generations have grown. Prior to the youngest generation, not many Davidsons strayed to places very far from Coryell County. I am one of the exceptions. Many years were spent outside of Coryell County, but now I am back.

James Madison Davidson and Viann Davidson, paternal great-grandparents – courtesy of the Davison family

Parents of Coryell's First Child

Mr. and Mrs. James Madison Davidson, who were married the year Coryell was organized, hold the distinction of being the parents of the first white child born in the county. She was a girl, Cordelia, who was born in 1855 and later became Mrs. Z. W. Lemmond.

Mr. Davidson and Miss Viann Moore were married May 11, 1854, at Fort Gates in one of the county's first weddings. Davidson was born in Tennessee and came to Texas in 1849, settling near Fort Gates in 1852. He died in 1925.

As a young boy, I couldn't have dreamed of the unique places and extraordinary experiences I encountered during my career in the sports world. That career was a rare time for me, a young man raised on a cattle and goat ranch where trips to the nearest town, Gatesville, were once a week or less.

The Rifleman - Cotton Davidson

My family at the house where I was born.

Left front, Anita

Back (left to right): Hy, Alyne holding Sandra, & Cotton

-photo courtesy of the Davidson Family

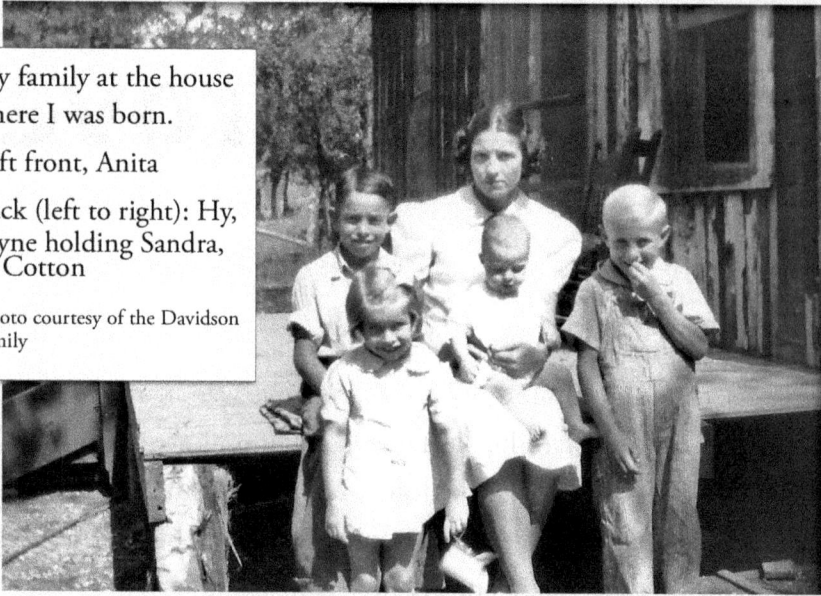

My experiences and memories, from the Coryell County ranch and football fields all over the U.S.A., are as different as day and night in many respects. However, they are surprisingly similar with regard to learning what it takes to be successful. I am fortunate for having a great deal of in-depth experience in both venues. However, without the lessons learned and total family support in my early ranch days, the second phase of my life in sports might have been very different. Those experiences in the Pecan Grove community are priceless.

The Pecan Grove community was located in the hills and wide valley along the lower reaches of Coryell Creek. This area is about ten miles southeast of Gatesville. Settlements started a few miles north of the creek crossing of present Highway 107 and continued south to the Leon River. From the mid-1800s until the mid-1900s, this rural community steadily grew, and houses dotted the countryside. Today, there is scant evidence that so many families once lived there. The homes of the early settlers are gone.

Although there are only a few families left in the Pecan Grove community, two prominent landmarks are reminders of the numerous families that populated the Coryell Creek valley in earlier times. One landmark is the Pecan Grove Baptist Church, and the other one is the Davidson Cemetery.

At the site where Coryell Creek crosses Hwy. 107, a small, gleaming white church building and a tabernacle stand out as the only structures visible in the surrounding countryside. They are nestled among the pecan trees by Coryell Creek on the north side of the highway. They have the unmistakable appearance of being established many years ago. Actually, this church building was erected in 1929, but the church was organized much earlier, in 1882. In earlier times, its name was Coryell Creek Baptist Church. In 1929, at the new location, the name was changed to Pecan Grove Baptist Church.

A Texas State Historical Marker at the entrance to the church grounds provides information about the church and its far-reaching influence. The church was important to many others in surrounding towns and communities as well as the civilization that once flourished in this fertile valley.

The Pecan Grove community church figured prominently in my family's life when I was growing up. It also set the stage for a totally unforeseen, unexpected, life-changing opportunity for me as I was about to take the big step of finishing high school and leaving home.

This small church was the focal point for community activities back in the community's heyday and is still active. The adjacent tabernacle is also in good condition and stands ready to host camp meetings, and revivals like it did one hundred years ago. However, those ten-day revival camp meetings are a thing of the past. The last one was held in the mid-1940s. A deep hole in Coryell Creek, a stone's throw from the tabernacle, was a perfect place for baptisms. It was also a great swimming hole when there was water in the creek, of course. Water levels in the creek could change quickly and dramatically, depending on the weather. The creek was often low or dry during the summer months. However, it quickly got out of its banks and flooded low-lying areas during heavy rainstorms. When that happened, the whole valley around the church would be flooded. Needless to say, camp meetings weren't planned during rainy seasons.

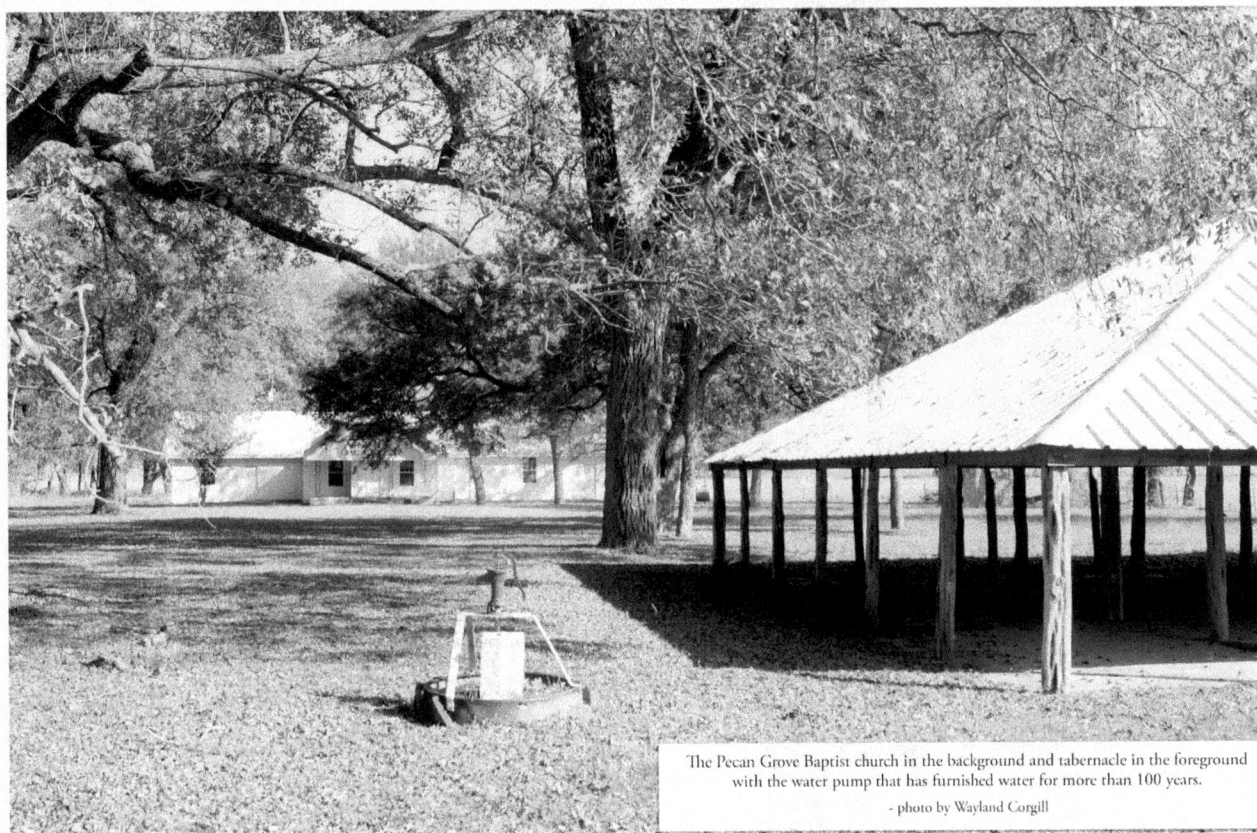

The Pecan Grove Baptist church in the background and tabernacle in the foreground with the water pump that has furnished water for more than 100 years.
- photo by Wayland Corgill

Another source of water, very important to the church, was located near the tabernacle. A pipe was driven down to the shallow groundwater table, and luckily, plenty of good water was found. The pipe was fitted with a hand pump that was extensively used during camp meetings. Over the years, that pump provided untold amounts of drinking water for people camped in tents close by the church. The pump still works, and the water is still as cold and sweet as it was a century ago.

The church had at least two homes before it was moved to its present location in 1929. From 1882 to 1891, church functions were first held in the Blackfoot School. From 1891 until 1929, the church home was the Davidson School. Those school buildings no longer exist, but they were located near the Davidson Cemetery, a couple of miles to the northwest of the present church location.

Students pose in front of the two-room BlackFoot school in 1926. The school closed just before I started the first grade.
- photo courtesy of the Davidson Family

10

Wayland Corgill

In the late 1800s and early 1900s, public buildings in rural communities were few. For many years, the only public building in the Pecan Grove community was the school building which served other uses as well as a school. Church services and community meetings were also held there. Two school buildings figured prominently in the community's early days. The first school was named the Blackfoot School. It was a one-teacher school and the first and only school in the area for several years. It was a one-room building. That building was replaced by a new building, also one-room, in 1891. The new building was named the Davidson School, although it was often referred to as the Blackfoot School. That was probably due to the new building being located a couple of hundred yards west of the abandoned Blackfoot School building.

How the Blackfoot School got its name is not definite. One theory is that it was named for Blackfoot Indians in the area. The more popular and more credible theory is that it was named for the man who donated land for the school. His name was Mr. Vandiver, and he had a business of making charcoal out of cedar and elm wood. Naturally, charcoal dust surrounded his charcoal-making works and stuck to his feet, hence, Blackfoot.

Land for the second school building was donated by Mr. J. Creg Davidson. Although the building was basically one-room, removable dividers were provided for configuring two rooms on school days. Dividers were withdrawn for church and community meetings. With two rooms, the school expanded to two teachers who taught grades one through eight. Teaching eight grades in one small building must have been a major accomplishment. Pursuance of higher education was possible in Gatesville. The Davidson School was closed in 1937. For several years prior to that time, children were bused to Gatesville for grades nine through twelve.

By one year, I missed starting school at the Davidson/Blackfoot School. I went to Gatesville for the first grade. However, my older brother, Hy, had the singular experience of spending his first three school years in that small, "two-room" school house.

Today, nobody lives on the Davidson land that once covered more than a thousand acres of hills and valleys along Coryell Creek. The little house in the woods where I was born is long gone. That house was also the birthplace of my older brother, Hyram (Hy) Alec, and younger sisters, Anita Blanch and Sandra Alyne. Being born at home was commonplace in the 1930s. Having the care of a doctor for the event was a major bonus. My parents, John Thomas and Alyne Davidson were of hardy pioneer stock. They were extraordinarily capable people who never neglected to take care of their responsibilities. Daddy took the precaution of having a doctor present for each birth, and they were all free of complications. Unquestionably though, my mother earned, and deserved, full credit for safely bringing four new lives into this world. She was of hardy stock and completely capable of handling any situation, including giving birth to a child at home.

The house where I was born had four small rooms and a screened porch. A wood-burning stove in the living room provided heat, and the wood-burning stove in the kitchen was for cooking. One of my jobs was to keep the wood supply stocked. As the family grew, cramped space inside the little house eventually caused Hy and me to be relegated to sleeping on the screened porch. That was fine during warmer times of the year and when rainwater didn't drip through the leaky roof. Finding a dry location for the bed was often a challenge during a downpour. Tolerating frigid winter nights always required special measures. A thick covering of blankets and quilts was a must, but specialized techniques for getting in and out of bed were also required. No time was wasted when getting under the cover. Once in bed, any excessive movement that would draw freezing air under the covers was to be avoided. Also, no time was wasted when getting out of bed in the morning and heading into the living room. Hopefully, a fire would have been started in the wood-burning stove at that time. On those cold nights, another not-to-be-forgotten precaution was to drink very little water, well before bedtime, and make a last visit to the one-hole, outdoor toilet before getting into bed.

About the time I became a teenager, Daddy had a much better house built. It was an attractive rock house and had plenty of room for a family of six. Hy and I didn't have to sleep on the porch anymore. That rock house is still proudly standing.

The house of my Grandfather Alex (PaPa) and Grandmother Charlotte (Little Grannie) Davidson

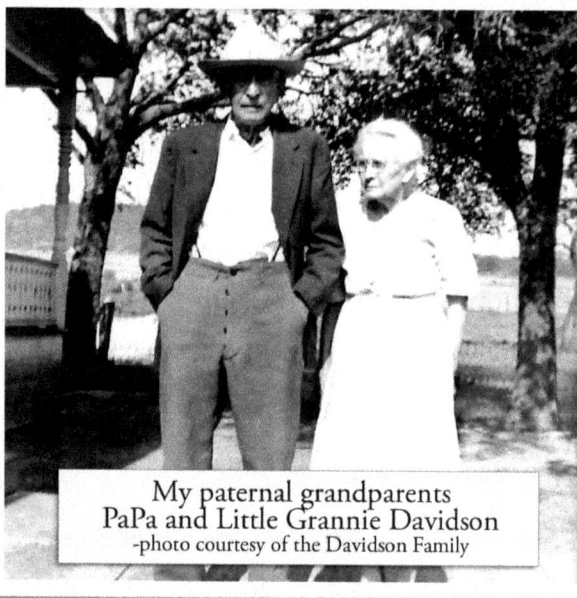

My paternal grandparents
PaPa and Little Grannie Davidson
-photo courtesy of the Davidson Family

is also standing. It is nearby to Daddy's rock house. PaPa's house is still fairly intact, even though it is more than eighty years old. However, it is no longer in very "proud" condition. Its tin roof doesn't leak, but dilapidated doors and windows have provided refuge for a few wild critters. A short path through the pasture between the two houses gave me easy access to PaPa. He was always entertaining and in good humor and was one of my most favorite relatives. Whenever I could spare time from working in the fields and tending to chores, I would go see PaPa. From my earliest years, I never got tired of being around him. Although he was unquestionably a good, responsible, respected man, some might refer to him as a "character."

Daddy never used tobacco or had a drink of liquor. I can't remember hearing him say more than one cuss word. He was pretty "straight-laced" and had a fairly narrow set of rules for proper conduct for himself as well as others. All of the Davidson clan in Pecan Grove was generally of that same character. PaPa was no different except for the tobacco thing. He chewed tobacco and smoked a pipe. His favorite brand of plug tobacco was Red Tag Tinsley. Chewing tobacco was considered to be an extravagance by many people. Money spent for that could be put to better use elsewhere. PaPa didn't share that view, but he sure got his money's worth out of a plug. When he finished with a chew, he didn't throw it away. He would put it up on a flat-top post in the fence of his mule corral. After a couple of days of drying in the sun, that chew would be just right for smoking in his pipe. The corral posts were taller than PaPa, and the tops were above his line-of-sight. No particular post was ever used, so, sometimes, a little bit of searching was required before the right post was found. When the dried-out chew was recovered, it went into his pipe in a peculiar way. PaPa's right index finger had been cut off at the first joint due to a blood poisoning incident in his younger days. That stub of a finger was a perfect tamper for mashing the dried, well-used wad of tobacco down in his pipe.

The smoke from PaPa's pipe did not agree with Little Grannie. She had asthma. An adequate distance between them had to be maintained when PaPa was smoking. Special measures were required when he lit his pipe at the house. In good weather, he would smoke on the porch. He would sit at the far end of the porch and lean his old chair against the wall. He would stay as close as possible to the corner of the house. In that location, the smoke was usually encouraged to trail around the house and dissipate in the pasture rather than drift back down the porch and filter through a screen door. During cold weather, with a fire in the fireplace, PaPa would sit as close to the fireplace as possible and exhale the smoke in the draft that was taking smoke from the fire up the chimney. He was a clever man and, evidently, believed in the bit of wisdom that says, "where there is a will, there is a way."

PaPa was not a farmer. He might help with a vegetable garden or help harvest a corn crop, but he had no interest in plowing or planting. His talents and capabilities were exceptional for handling and trading mules and horses. Like all of us who lived off of the land, he also had other animals that were essential for food supplies, not necessarily for trading. Everybody in the community had cows for milk and meat, chickens for eggs and Sunday dinners, and pigs for meat in the winter. Most people also had

My maternal grandparents
Left front: Hy, Hyram Davis, Laura Davis holding me
- photo courtesy of the Davidson Family

horses or mules for farm work. Tractors were just beginning to be fairly common by 1940. PaPa had none of that. He had mules and horses, but they were not for his farm work. They were for trading. That must have been a good business for PaPa. He always seemed to have money in his pocket, and that two-story, eighty-year-old house he had built was one of the best ones in the community. It was generously spacious for the time. It also had features that Little Grannie must surely have influenced. There was a bathroom with a claw-foot bathtub and a commode. For most people, bathtubs were #2 sized washtubs that were only big enough for small children to sit in. Grownups had to stand to bathe. The commode was a major step up from an outdoor one-hole toilet that most people had. Running water was even piped in from a windmill and storage tank near the house. There was only one water faucet in the house, but that sure was better than toting water supplies with buckets. PaPa did alright with his horse and mule trading business.

PaPa also liked to hunt and fish. I went with him on many of his trips to the Coryell Creek bottoms. He loved to eat squirrels. Having two people on the hunt had an advantage over just one person. PaPa would have me walk some distance ahead of him and "turn the squirrels." Squirrels are very smart critters and extremely adept at hiding themselves when in danger. As I would walk toward a squirrel, he would move out of my sight to the other side of the tree. PaPa, who was off to one side behind me, was far enough back to avoid alarming the squirrel. If the squirrel moved to the side of the tree where PaPa could see it, it took only one shot, and the squirrel would go in a bag. PaPa hardly ever missed with his trusty .22 caliber rifle. Squirrels

PaPa with a big Birthday Cake
- photo courtesy of the Davidson Family

were numerous in the creek bottoms, and we never failed to bring back plenty of them for supper.

Fish from Coryell Creek also supplemented PaPa and Little Grannie's diet. We usually caught perch. They weren't very big, but a small stringer of them made a tasty meal. PaPa loved to fish. He would say, "Cotton, let's go fishing," and I was always ready to go. After digging up a few earthworms from his worm bed, we would head to the creek. When the fish weren't biting, he would come up with an ingenious idea to change his luck. He would often say, "Cotton, sing those fish a song so they will bite." I would gladly comply and would often go through all the songs I knew before PaPa either caught enough or gave up. I am pretty sure the singing never helped, but he had me believing it would.

From my earliest memory, I was always called Cotton. It fit pretty well because my hair was just about the same color as cotton. Cotton was also convenient because it was a much easier name to say than the one on my birth certificate. That one, Francis Marion, was not a favorite with me, to say the least. To be sure, it is an honorable name, but, in my opinion, it didn't seem to fit a boy who was the trusted companion of a skilled hunter and fisherman like PaPa. Therefore, I encouraged the Cotton moniker as much as I could, and it stuck. Probably, not many people knew my given name in all my travels from Coryell County and back.

My siblings
Left to right: Anita, Hy, Sandra, & me
Photo courtesy of the Davidson Family

Wayland Corgill

When my great-grandfather, James Madison Davidson, came to Coryell County in 1849, he surely must have done a fair amount of hunting and fishing. At that time, he bought land in the area where the small town of Oglesby is now located. Stores in the area were few and far between. The nearest store of any size or kind was in the new town of Waco, 30 miles to the east. Waco was founded in 1849. Fort Gates, a frontier fort, was 10 miles to the west. Also, a small settlement, to be named Gatesville, was growing near Fort Gates. Gatesville was officially established in 1854. Waco was a good day's ride on a horse and more than a day's trip with a wagon. Gatesville could not be counted on for much more than a box of matches, much less food. Food during those early times had to be raised, grown, or hunted. Other sources of food were scarce, indeed. For a new arrival on the western frontier, hunting and fishing played a critical role in surviving.

In those early times, James Madison had more than food problems to contend with. Water was an immediate big one. Additional problems materialized later, but the water problem was the first one to be solved. The land he bought was good for farming if it rained enough, but it had no sources of water. Drinking water, for both humans and livestock, had to be hauled from Coryell Creek or the Leon River. Both of those sources were almost 10 miles away. There were no windmills in the area in 1849 or for several years thereafter. The water problem was just too much for James Madison to contend with. Shortly after the Civil War, he started looking for land elsewhere.

A pioneer named Oglesby owned a large tract of land nearby. His land stretched from the confluence of Coryell Creek with the Leon River and back north a couple of miles to what is now US Hwy. 84. Coryell Creek ran down through the middle of Oglesby's holdings. That land was not level and flat like the land James Madison had bought. Oglesby's land was heavily wooded and had small mountains, hills, and smaller areas of flat land along Coryell Creek. It was more suited for cattle and goat ranching than it was for full-scale farming. However, the land had water. James Madison and Mr. Oglesby arranged a land swap. That land swap suited both parties. On Mr. Oglesby's new holdings, a community was established that grew into a town named Oglesby. In time, James Madison's new holdings became a thriving ranch.

Developing the ranch required untold amounts of human labor and sacrifice by James Madison and his family. A house had to be built using materials at hand. A shed and corral were needed for animals. All of the wood for construction had to be cut from trees on the ranch. Rocks for a fireplace and chimney were hauled from the hillsides. Flat areas along Coryell Creek had to be cleared of trees and brush as soon as possible to make way for growing crops. A clear space for a vegetable garden was essential for providing food.

The work of clearing land was extremely back-breaking. Tools were no more than axes and saws. Methods were limited to men's muscle power and what a team of horses could do. After the trees and brush were cut down and burned, stumps and roots had to be removed before the land could be plowed. Stumps had to be dug out of the ground by hand if they could not be pulled out by a team of horses. The work was extremely hard, and progress was slow in developing the ranch, but the perseverance of James Madison and his family paid off. They built a place where they could grow and prosper, as well as for future generations of Davidsons. That is where I grew up. I still have a large part of that ranch, and those previous generations come to life in my mind every time I go there.

The Rifleman - Cotton Davidson

Walking around the old house that James Madison built a century-and-a-half ago brings back memories of when I used to play there in my earliest childhood. Surprisingly, parts of that house are still standing. The roof is gone, but the rock chimney is intact, most of the walls are erect, and the loft is still in place. The cedar posts used for wall studs are still as sound as the day they were cut. Even though construction techniques and materials were unbelievably basic, way back then, James Madison built a strong structure that endured and was the birthplace and home for not only his children but also grandchildren and great-grandchildren. His tools were limited to hammers, saws, and axes. Wood was limited to what could be cut from trees on his land. Nails were handmade. Those items, plus the ingenuity and ponderous labor of James Madison, created a dwelling that survived for generations.

Solving the water and shelter issues were major accomplishments, but those were not the only problems James Madison and his family had to contend with in this untamed land. Native Indians were one of those problems. Comanches, Kiowas, Apaches, Tonkawas, and probably other tribes roamed at will through the country that had been their hunting grounds for generations. Their ideas of civilized conduct and behavioral standards were nowhere close to the expectations of their new white neighbors. Clashes between those vastly different people were inevitable. James Madison and Vianna were on the front line in one of those clashes with unwelcomed Indian visitors.

In the 1850s, fences were difficult to build and, therefore, were not used except in special cases. Barbed wire had not been invented. Split rail or stockade/picket type fences, made with wood poles, were common. Corrals made with picket fences were popular for holding horses. Understandably, horses were a very valuable commodity for both Indians and pioneers on the frontier. In particular, Comanches and Kiowas

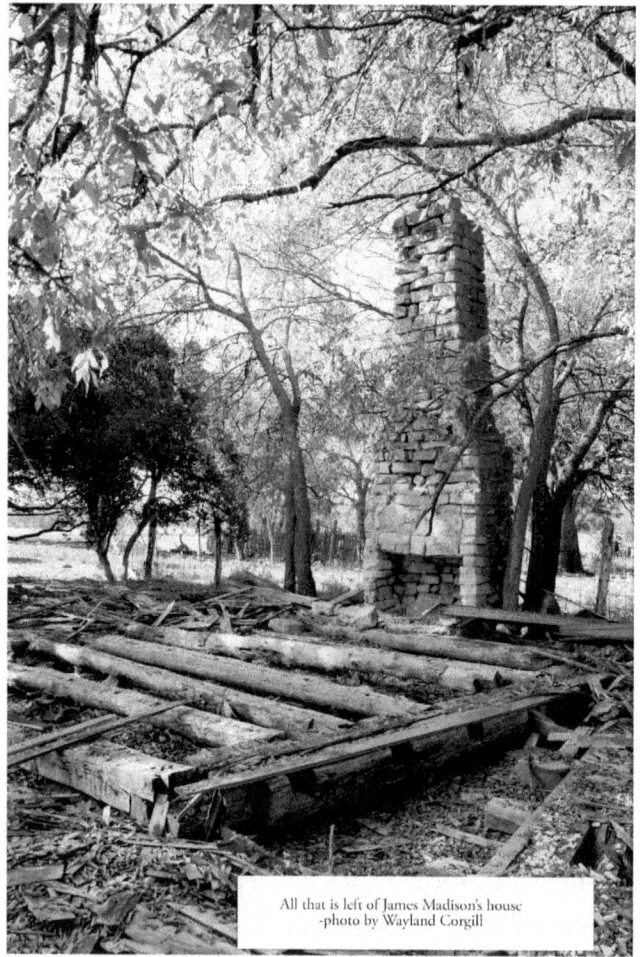

All that is left of James Madison's house
-photo by Wayland Corgill

placed great value on horses and had no reservations about stealing every horse they could. James Madison's horses did not go unnoticed by Indians for very long. They stole every horse in the corral one day. However, that raid turned out to be a deadly mistake for the raiders. It ended their raiding days.

James Madison and a couple of neighbors had a herd of hogs contained in a horseshoe bend of the Leon River. There were no fences there on the river. The wooded area encompassed by the tight bend in the river provided plenty of space for the hogs to roam and live off of acorns and pecans. The river banks were a natural barrier preventing the hogs from straying from the area. Also, the narrow mouth of the horseshoe bend made it easy to round up the hogs. James Madison and his neighbors were tending to their herd of hogs one day when they were alarmed by a young boy riding his horse into their midst at full gallop. His message was that Indians had stolen James Madison's horses. Hogs were immediately forgotten, and a "bee-line" was made to the house.

Eleven men on horseback were soon in pursuit of the Indians. The Indians were found encamped the next day, and a fight ensued. Fourteen Indians were killed or captured, and all of the horses were recovered. None of the settlers were injured.

The Indians had done a good job of scouting before committing their thievery. They knew that the men were a couple of miles away with their hogs at the Leon River. However, great-grandmother Vianna and her children were alone in the house while the noisy commotion with Indians and horses was going on. It is difficult to imagine the emotions she must have had. However, she did the best she could and hid herself and her children in the loft of their little house. Vianna was one strong and resourceful lady.

Indians weren't the only "bad actors" traveling throughout the sparsely populated countryside in the mid-1800s. During those times, a few white men had no compunction about helping themselves to corn from a crib, or a few chickens running loose, or a hog, or even a horse. Also, a smaller number of the white men posed a great danger of bodily harm to settlers. Such men had no "roots" in the area and, some had a fearsome mean streak in them. They might do much worse things than steal a chicken or even a horse. Therefore, strangers were viewed with a modicum of suspicion until it was determined that they weren't "up to no good." Minor acts of thievery were generally overlooked. However, stealing a horse was a very serious offense that was never overlooked. Punishment for horse stealing could be as harsh as being hung.

Some of the lawless strangers were very clever in their pursuit of criminal activities. James Madison experienced one of those clever attempts in a mysterious incident involving a cowbell. During a rainstorm one night, James Madison heard a cowbell incessantly ringing. The sound was coming from the direction of a large oak tree about fifty yards from the house and near the cornfield. The half-grown corn crop was an enticing bit of greenery for cows, so they had been kept in a separate pasture. The ringing cowbell might indicate that cows had managed to get into the cornfield.

According to the story that was handed down, James Madison stepped out of the house onto the porch, where he paused to survey the situation. In the darkness and rain, he couldn't see well enough to determine whether or not cows were in the cornfield but, apparently, something didn't seem right. The cadence of the cowbell was suspicious. It didn't sound like a cow that was slowly meandering through the field. The sound was too steady and regular. For reasons unknown, James decided to put off an investigation until the morning light. Perhaps he reasoned that cows wouldn't do much damage through the rest of the night. Likely, he would find them lying down in the morning. Perhaps, he thought, trying to chase them out might do more damage to the crop than leaving them alone until he could see what he was doing. Perhaps, he suspected that danger might await anyone venturing into the darkness in search of a strangely ringing cowbell. James Madison was a wise man who had survived by his own resourcefulness and was well aware of the threats that could exist in this relatively untamed country. He would not act rashly.

When James Madison took a look the next morning, he found a cowbell tied to the backside of the oak tree. Near the tree, a muddy plot of footprints indicated that a man had stood there. The assumption was that the man hoped someone would come his way to check things out. James Madison tracked the muddy trail of footprints until they were lost on hard ground. He never found out who had gone to the trouble of standing in the rain and ringing the cowbell or why the mystery man did that. However, that guy was surely "up to no good."

Great-grandpa might have found more than he could handle if he had started his search while the cowbell was ringing. In case the stranger had a deadly ambush on his mind, the damage to the family of great-grandmother and her children would have been a major disaster. In those days, a single parent, particularly a woman, had an almost impossible burden of providing even the bare minimum of support to keep a family together.

In matters of law enforcement and punishment for crimes, there were no sheriffs or marshals to call on. The only presence of law enforcement and protection was the military at Fort Gates. Soldiers could not be expected to get involved in minor acts of thievery or even major offenses, such as fatal gunfights between settlers. The settlers, largely, had to fend for themselves, and they did, with vigilante groups. Horse stealing was a hanging offense. One story that I heard from PaPa was about the demise of a young man who stole a horse. When a vigilante group caught up with him, he was hung in an unconventional way. A tree was bent over to the ground, and the hanging rope was tied to the tree top. The hanging noose did its job when the tree was turned loose. Such acts are almost incomprehensible today, but it should be remembered that civilization in the mid-1800s was a long, long way from what it is today. Back then, self-preservation often required extreme measures.

Even in the 1930s and 1940s, when I was growing up, minor acts of thievery occasionally happened in the Pecan Grove community. Lots of people still lived there. The neighborhood was peaceful, and there were never problems of crime amongst community members. Neighbors trusted neighbors. However, those were depression days, and Daddy had at least one problem with what was probably a dispossessed stranger passing through the country. Each fall or early winter, hogs were butchered for winter meat. Pork could be preserved and kept from spoiling in the winter months. We had no electricity and no other ways to keep meat except to cure it or can it. Much of the pork, such as bacon, hams, shoulders, and sausage, was cured and smoked in PaPa's smokehouse. The meat was also left there for the winter. One winter, somebody raided the smokehouse and made off with part of Daddy's stash of hams and bacon. Needless to say, he sure was mad. I don't know what he would have done if he had caught the thief. In the Pecan Grove community back in those times, nobody had a lock on any door. However, neighbors watched out for each other, and a thief had to be exceedingly stealthy and clever to commit a crime without being detected.

When I was a child, several members of the Davidson extended family would often gather on Sunday afternoon at one of the member's house. PaPa's house was a popular place. Sunday was a day of rest, and the afternoon was a good time for visiting. Memories of those times are so pleasant, especially in winter when we would sit around the fireplace and listen to stories from older days. There were barely enough chairs for adults, so children sat on the floor and quietly listened. PaPa's brothers and sisters, as well as my uncles and aunts, lived in the area. Therefore, enough representatives of the Davidson clan were always in attendance to give vivid life to an endless supply of stories from earlier days. I never got enough of hearing those stories as told from first-hand experiences.

The other six days of the week were certainly not days of rest. They were days of hard work for every family member. However, one annual exception was for the camp meetings. During the camp meeting time, daily chores of tending to livestock were not neglected, but all other work that could be put off was delayed. At all other times, ordinary work days started before sunup and didn't end until sometime after sundown. Daily routines included tending to animals, such as horses, cows, goats, pigs, and chickens, plus chopping firewood and filling water buckets. Seasonal work included vegetable gardening and growing corn and wheat crops. Cotton farming was tried in some years, but the soil wasn't suited for that crop, and it didn't do well.

Our fields were very small, as compared to most modern farming operations. However, those small fields required exorbitant amounts of manpower for plowing, planting, and harvesting. Daddy originally farmed with horses. One-row plows were pulled by a team of two horses or two mules. That was slow work. Early in 1940, Daddy bought an F-12 Farmall tractor, and that was a major labor and time saver. I could easily walk faster than the top speed of that tractor, but it more than doubled our capability to do field work. It pulled two-row plows and was faster than a team of horses.

Even with the advantage of a tractor rather than a team of horses, there never seemed to be an end to work that needed to be done or the lack of time to do it. There was so much other work that had nothing to do with a tractor. Just doing the weekly clothes washing, using wash pots, rub boards, and clothes lines was a time-consuming operation. Gardening was another example. Garden tending and canning, or preserving the produce still required the same amount of back-breaking attention. Mother, Little Grannie, and children were primarily responsible for that. Other grown-ups helped occasionally. The vegetable garden's importance was paramount. A well-stocked root cellar provided food for months when the growing season was over. Another essential in our diet was pork from hogs butchered in the fall. That meat was cured in a smokehouse near the garden behind PaPa's house. In effect, our "supermarket" was the root cellar and smokehouse.

Until well after World War II, nobody in the Pecan Grove community had much money and had few opportunities for making money. Effects of the great depression hung on through the 1930s and most of the 1940s. During World War II, those conditions worsened due to austere measures implemented by the federal government to support the war effort. Even Daddy's old F-12 Farmall tractor was impacted by the rationing of gasoline and tires. Families living in Pecan Grove generally "got by" without buying anything they couldn't grow, raise or make. Salt, pepper, baking powder, sugar, and syrup were food items that were normally purchased. Sugar was a luxury and used sparingly. Clothing articles that couldn't be made, or were difficult to make, were also bought. However, all clothing, whether handmade or purchased, was carefully used until it was totally used up. Probably, more than three-fourths of all spending was done for those basic items. Frugality was a word that our family, and our neighbors, probably never used but was a fitting assessment of our circumstance.

World War II had impacts that were markedly unique to the folks in Coryell County. In January 1942, a huge military base, Camp Hood, was established in the county. Camp Hood's original size was 64,000 acres. The north extremity of the base was approximately four miles south of Gatesville and also four miles south of Pecan Grove.

Some of those impacts of Camp Hood were certainly not looked on with favor by many people who were negatively affected. Those people, who were forced off of their ranches and farms, faced many hardships. However, the area's economy was materially affected, and a few extra dollars found their way into residents' pockets in totally unexpected ways.

By February 1942, base preparation was well underway. That required appraisers, surveyors, and engineers who were first arrivals in the area. They were soon followed by streams of soldiers, some with their families. Immediately, a gigantic problem materialized. Housing for those people on the base was nowhere near adequate. In early 1942, barracks didn't exist and were never adequate throughout the war. Also, tents were in short supply and weren't very pleasant abodes in the wintertime. Builders and building materials were in very short supply in and around Coryell County. The war effort required huge amounts of those resources elsewhere. Therefore, citizens in and around Gatesville were asked to help. Anyone, who had a spare room or could make a spare room, was asked to rent it. Spare rooms in Gatesville quickly filled up, as well as spare living quarters in communities like Pecan Grove. Renters weren't fussy. A roof over their head and a place to stay warm were the important things.

Daddy and Mother, as well as their neighbors, did their part to help with the housing shortage. In 1942, a soldier, Lane Moyer, with his wife and daughter, rented one of the small rooms in our little four-room house in the woods. They stayed throughout the war years. Hy and I were moved to the screened porch. A close relationship with the Moyer's evolved during those years, and they regularly corresponded with Mother and Daddy for many years after the war. How nine people managed to share the limited space in that little four-room house for those years is a remarkable example of what is possible by practicing good conduct. In 1944, Daddy and Mother's rock house was finished. It had much more living space than the little house in the woods. A room was rented in the rock house, but Hy and I didn't have to sleep on a screened porch anymore.

The housing shortage was so severe that spare rooms in houses were not enough. Barns were modified to make livable spaces. Daddy installed a wood-burning stove in our barn granary and rented that space too. Uncle Claude Sheppard modified part of his barn and rented it. Military personnel were almost standing in line to rent anything that was available. PaPa didn't have a suitable space in his barn, but he and Little Grannie made space in their house for two families.

So many things made permanent memories for me during those years, and, oddly enough, one that stands out is my first taste of raisins. A family we knew, who lived on the east side of the Pecan Grove community, also made space in their barn for a renter. Daddy and that family often helped each other when sheep-shearing time came around. We were over at that family's farm to do just that when I was introduced to raisins. A young boy, munching on something from a small sack, came to the sheep pen. I asked him what was in the sack, and he said, "Raisins." I didn't know what a raisin was and told him so. He gave me a handful and, from the first bite, I thought they were just about the best tasting things I could remember eating. Raisins were certainly not a common food item in Pecan Grove. I questioned where they came from and learned that the soldier, who rented a room in their barn, had brought them from the base. Our renters didn't have the same connections. Those were the only raisins I had for many years.

Renting rooms brought in a little money. I don't remember what the going rate was. I don't think it was over ten dollars a month and was probably less. That was the rate in the countryside. Rental rates in Gatesville were probably twice our rate. Renters in the Davidson household also got a bonus. Mother fed them too. Our lifestyle didn't noticeably improve from the rent income. In fact, I don't remember a change of any size. Daddy and Mother just did their part. There were no complaints. Neither did Hy, nor I complain about sleeping on the screened porch.

Although those depression and World War II times were hard for everybody in our community, in some ways, we fared better than many people in big cities. For us, luxuries were few and far between but, with our vegetable gardens, livestock, chickens, root cellar, smokehouse, and a lot of hard work, we didn't go hungry.

Daddy never had much time to take a rest, and vacations were unheard of. He worked all the time, and his clothes showed that. If he had three pairs of pants, only one pair would be good enough to wear to church. The other two pairs would be almost threadbare where they weren't covered with patches. Just "getting by" took the full-time effort of both Mother and Daddy. However, in the early summer of 1940, Daddy reached a limit. His back gave out. Multiple vertebrae were crushed. Not just one particular thing caused the problem. It was caused by too many years of heavy lifting. In those days, if something had to be moved, there weren't many options for moving it except by muscle power. Daddy could hardly walk and was in excruciating pain. There was no other remedy than an operation. He was taken to a specialist in Dallas. A large section of bone was taken from the fibula of his right leg. That bone was used to reinforce Daddy's back where the vertebrae were broken. He was put in a body cast from his armpits down to the middle of his legs above the knees.

When he came home from the hospital, he was bedfast for almost three months. Those three months happened to be the hottest part of the summer. How he tolerated lying there without even a fan is hard to imagine. We had no electricity. Not only was he totally immobile, but for some reason, he also had to keep a board wedged between his legs. The cast almost completely prevented Daddy from being in any position in bed except flat on his back. There was no way he could turn on his side. After a few days in that predicament, he asked for a pipe suspended from the ceiling in a trapeze fashion. When that was done, he could then move around a little bit. That made a world of difference in his ability to tolerate being bedfast in the cumbersome cast.

Those three months would probably have been unbearable for many people. However, Daddy never complained and did his part in accordance with the doctors' directions. He must have sincerely believed that he would be healed when he came out of that cast, and he was. He was eventually able to fully function in his normal routines on the ranch. I have often thought about that insufferable ordeal and marveled at Daddy's strength of character, patience, and tolerance.

During that summer, Daddy had a lot of moral support and many prayers from the citizens of Pecan Grove. Uncle Claude Sheppard visited one day, and he was asked to say a prayer. Everybody was pleasantly caught a little bit off-guard when he said it would be much better if someone would go get Little Grannie because God listened to her. I don't remember if that was actually done, but I expect that it was. She and PaPa's house was only a few minutes away by walking. Uncle Caude's opinion demonstrates the high regard that folks in Pecan Grove had for Little Grannie. I am sure that PaPa had the same opinion. She was recognized not only for her sensibility with delicate matters but also for being PaPa's understanding partner and for her spare-time handy-work with crocheting and knitting.

During that summer, Daddy also had a lot of support from kinfolk and neighbors who pitched in with their labor to help do work that was more than Mother and Hy, and I could handle. Mother was a hard worker too. She never ceased to do almost more than she was capable of during Daddy's recovery period. Daddy never hired a hand. There was no money for that.

I never knew where the money came from to pay for Daddy's medical bills. Every bit of money that had been saved was surely not enough. During those Great Depression Days, money was in very short supply for everybody in the Pecan Grove community. I expect that a large balance was left to pay, and it might have taken years to settle the account. Daddy never burdened his family with conversation or complaints about that. However, he always paid his bills, even though it might take a while to do so. He also did anything and everything he could to make a few extra dollars to put on those debts.

Cutting cedar posts was one way of making a few "quick" dollars. The work of cutting the posts was not very quick, but a wagon load of cedar posts provided a relatively quick supplement for a shortfall in a meager budget. A long day, or more, was needed to cut a wagon-load of posts worth approximately ten dollars. There was a market for cedar posts any time of the year. They could be sold at the little store in Pulltight, a couple of miles away. The Pulltight store could hardly be called a store. It was a small building and had a very small variety and quantity of things to sell. A trip to Gatesville was required for most things other than salt, pepper, sugar, and flour. However, my cousin, Gus Davidson, ran the store and was a fair man.

Ten to fifteen-foot-tall cedar trees grew in thick stands on much of the ranch. They seemed to thrive, even in the poorest soil. They grew well on the rocky slopes and tops of the hills and mountains. Those cedar trees were a nuisance. They starved grasses of water and crowded out desirable types of vegetation. The more cedar trees we cleared from the land, the better the ranch was. Making money by selling posts from our cedar clearing work was a bonus.

One of Daddy's favorite places to cut cedar posts was on top of a small mountain on the eastern edge of the ranch. Notably, it was not my favorite place. Just getting up there was a difficulty, but that was the relatively easy part of the trip. Getting down was another experience, entirely. The trail up the mountain was rough and steep. A team of horses pulling an empty wagon had to bow their backs and pull hard to power their way to the top, but it was doable. Successfully getting back down with a wagon full of cedar posts was the scary part for me. I wouldn't ride on the wagon for the downhill return. I would walk alongside. I would watch the straining horses with their hooves dislodging rocks and slipping on the hard-packed, uneven, rocky trail. I would wonder if this time would be "the" time that horses, wagon, posts, and Daddy would all wind up in a tangled mass at the bottom of the treacherous trail. There were no breaks on the wagon wheels. The only thing retarding the speed of descent was the horses. They set back in their harness with all their might while the wagon tongue was trying to push them off the mountain. That wagon tongue would be sticking up in the air as far as the straps, connecting to the horse collars, would allow. It looked like the wagon tongue was very close to lifting the horses' front feet off of the ground. Probably, that was not likely to happen, but if it had, disaster would have followed. Fortunately, none of the leather harnesses broke and caused a runaway. Daddy never gave any indication of uneasiness about riding that heavy wagon down the mountain. Obviously, he knew what he was doing because he always made it up and back. That might have been his favorite place to cut cedar posts, but I always thought there were several others just as good at lower levels.

Irrespective of all the efforts that went into being self-sufficient and the variety of all the mechanisms and activities undertaken to accomplish self-sufficiency, some amount of money was still required for things that could not be grown, raised, made or bartered. Money was required for the few things that were obtained from stores. Doctors were not likely to take payment with chickens or vegetables. Thus, cutting a load of cedar posts was one way to help get through a time when an infusion of a little cash was needed.

Besides the money made from cedar posts, most of the money that Daddy and Mother had, was made from other sources in small amounts at different times throughout the year. Produce from animals on the ranch and a portion of farmed crops were sold. Milk, butter, and eggs were generally sold throughout the year. Three or four litters of pigs were usually raised each year, and most of them were sold at livestock markets in nearby towns. Offspring from sheep and goats were also sold. In the fall, a little money could be made by picking up pecans, provided the trees produced that year. A small part of our corn crop was sold, but most of it was kept for our use on the ranch.

Corn was our most important crop. It was a staple food for both animals and humans. Hogs were fattened on corn. Many a bushel of corn was taken to the feed mill in Mound and ground into cornmeal for baking into cornbread. Cornbread graced our dinner table throughout the year. Raising, harvesting, and handling corn was hard work. However, our whole family gave it special attention because we knew that our existence depended on it.

Harvesting corn was particularly labor-intensive. A wagon was pulled along the corn rows, and the dried ears of corn (ear corn) were manually pulled from the stalks and thrown into the wagon. When the wagon was loaded, it was pulled to the corn crib. There, another exercise in physical strength and endurance began. From the time I was old enough to handle a grain scoop, I shoveled ear corn from a wagon into the corncrib. That was a challenge for a young, skinny boy. A scoop full of corn is not only heavy to lift but is awkward to handle. It was not easy to accurately propel a scoop full of corn through a small, high opening in the corncrib wall. A few of the ears always bounced off of the side of the opening. When I finished unloading a wagon, I usually had a small pile of corn on the ground under the portal to the crib. Later, as corn was taken from the crib, more work was required. Corn ears had to be shucked, and kernels had to be shelled from the cobs before feeding animals. Operating a hand-cranked machine for the shelling was another one of my daily chores.

Daddy was a resourceful man. He was always looking for ways to improve the ranch and better provide for his family. He knew that hard work would always be necessary, but he also believed in pursuing activities that had the potential for more lucrative results. His formal education only went to the eighth grade, but he was self-educated in many ways. He could do figures in his head faster than most people could using a pencil and paper. He was also a wise man. It took him several years to do it, but he developed a first-rate flock of registered Rambouillet sheep. That breed was noted for its large size and fine quality of wool. He judiciously managed breeding and selection processes to keep the flock healthy and productive. His sheep gained an impressive reputation in surrounding counties, as well as Coryell County. They were highly in demand, and Daddy never failed to sell all that he had available. Establishing that sheep herd became the most successful money-making venture that Daddy undertook.

PaPa, of course, made his money with horse and mule trading. The horse and mule business was his mainstay, but he also dabbled in smaller activities. He would occasionally take a pound of butter or a dozen eggs to Gatesville when he needed a few extra coins in his pocket. I think, if the truth were known, the main reason he went to town with a few items to sell was not for the money as much as for his desire to catch up on what was going on in Coryell County and maintain his contacts in the livestock trading business. PaPa was a gregarious man, and his presence was welcomed everywhere he went. No doubt, that personality trait was the key to his success in his horse and mule trading business.

PaPa had no formal education, but that was never a disadvantage or an impediment for his astute trading abilities. He always made money. He was also a wise and practical man who was well aware of the importance and benefits of education. When I was accepted at Baylor, his advice to me was to learn everything I could but to be sure and take a couple of courses in common sense. I always kept that in mind.

Probably, PaPa made more trips to town than was necessary. However, occasional trips were required to sell perishable items, like butter, before they spoiled. Electrical service was not available to us until the mid-1940s. Before then, in warmer months, perishables couldn't be kept cold, just cool, at best. One way to keep perishables cool was with an icebox, and another way was with a rack that employed an evaporative process. The evaporative rack didn't do much cooling but, it was that or nothing. An icebox was a well-insulated, free-standing, wooden cabinet with front doors and a metal lining. A fifty-pound block of ice would fit in the top of the ice box. Items to be kept cool were placed on shelves below. Ice could be bought in small sizes from a delivery man who knew how much ice was wanted by looking at a cardboard sign placed in a window. Daddy and Mother never even had an icebox before 1940. Their only option, for a tiny bit of cooling, was an evaporative rack. PaPa and Little Grannie's evaporative rack was a fancy one. It was made of angle-iron and was fairly large, about three feet square and three feet tall. It sat on a table on the shady part of a porch. It was covered with cloth that was periodically wet down. Evaporation from the cloth caused temperatures inside the rack to be a little lower than ambient. Often, additional cooling was provided by a pan of cool water from the well and placed inside the rack. Sometimes, chunks of ice were added to the pan when attempting to keep perishables cool for a longer period of time.

Children hardly ever had money in their pockets. When I got old enough to milk a cow, my largest source of income became PaPa. He would pay me a penny for milking a cow. He referred to a penny as a "copper." When he wanted help for milking, he would say, "Cotton, do you want to make a copper?" As a small boy, I thought that was a good deal, and I did a lot of milking.

I learned many useful things from PaPa, including how to make money. When our family's circumstances began to significantly improve, and Daddy built the rock house, I was almost a teenager. The rock house was an imposing step up from the tiny, four-room house where Hy and I slept on the porch and bathed in a #2 washtub. We thought the house was relatively magnificent, but its location was also a major improvement over our former abode. We weren't in the woods anymore. We had open spaces around the house. A baseball field was laid out in the front yard. Baseball games with friends and family became lively sporting events on Sunday afternoons. Those gatherings gave me another opportunity

Daddy (on right) with his Rambouillet sheep
– photo courtesy of the Davidson family

to employ PaPa's influences for making money. In the summer heat, both players and spectators would welcome a drink of water a few times before a game was finished. That was my opportunity. I made sure I had a couple of gallon-jugs of water handy for sale by the cupful. A cool drink of water from a wet-burlap-wrapped jug would fetch a few pennies. I think I made more "coppers" from that than by milking PaPa's cows.

From the time I was old enough to pick up a rock, I had a pretty strong arm for throwing. I had lots of practice too. Daddy often told me that I could hardly pass by a marble-sized rock without scooping it up and throwing it at something. I loved to be the pitcher at our Sunday baseball games. When hunting squirrels or birds, I could do just about as good with well-aimed rocks as with a .22 caliber rifle. I tried using different types of slingshots for hunting and target practice but soon gave them up. I was accurate enough with thrown rocks. Besides, I never quite mastered the use of the type of slingshot that David used when he battled Goliath. One day, while practicing with that weapon, the rock I was whirling around came out in the opposite direction I intended and broke a window of our house. The slingshot was retired, and I went back to hand-thrown rocks.

No doubt, all that throwing as a kid helped later on when I was throwing footballs while at Baylor and in the NFL.

By the mid-1940s, money, or the lack thereof, became a little less of a problem for Daddy and Mother. They often had enough spare funds to pay for a movie in Gatesville on Saturday evenings. Daddy also had enough money to buy a 1936 Ford, two-door sedan. That was a fine car. Mother learned to drive it, and she was usually our chauffeur to the Saturday evening movies. At that time, Gatesville had four movie theaters. I always patronized the one that specialized in Westerns. Tom Mix, Johnny Mack Brown, Lash LaRue, and others of that genre were good enough for me. The movie cost ten cents. On the street near the theater, a Mexican man had a pushcart from which he sold delicious, fresh-roasted peanuts for a

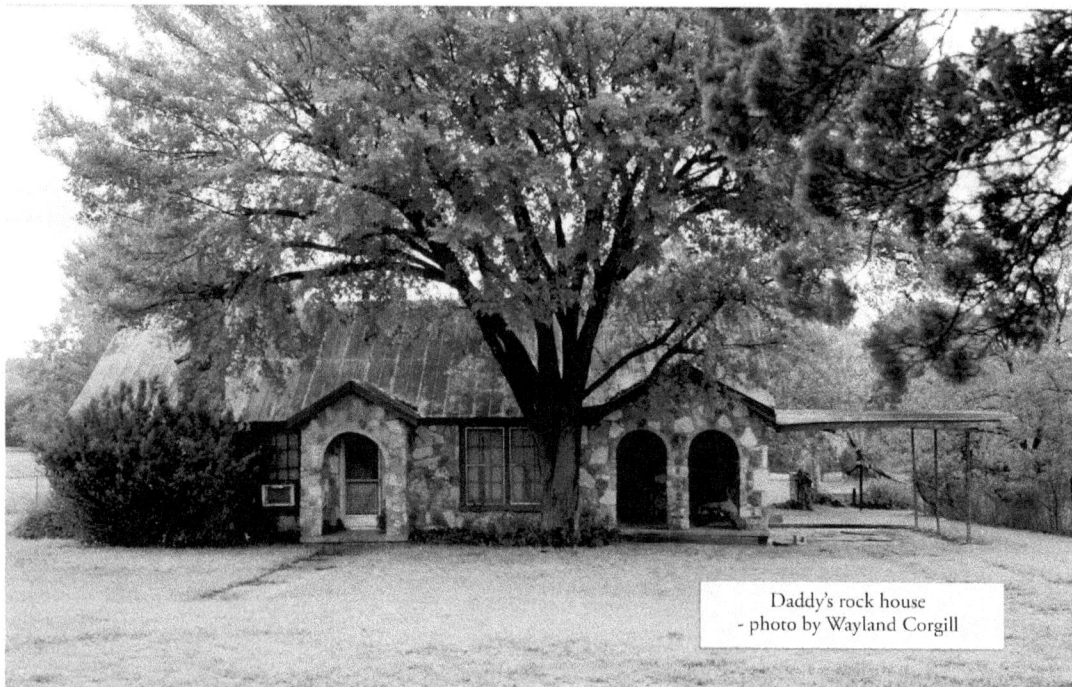

Daddy's rock house
- photo by Wayland Corgill

nickel. There was no better way to spend a Saturday afternoon than with a small sack of those peanuts in a movie theater. I didn't want anything else. That was fortunate because the movie and peanuts totally used up our budget, and there was no money for anything else.

The 1940s were years of rapid changes in social and economic conditions for the world and the whole United States, including the citizens of the Pecan Grove community. By the mid-1940s, one of the community's most notable changes occurred. The annual camp meetings were discontinued. Those camp meetings had gone on for generations. Their termination signaled the end of a rare time period in the history of the westward progression of civilization across Texas. Camp meetings had certainly been important to the community. They had promoted friendships and reunions of neighborly bonds between community residents. In addition

I had an early start with baseball
Photo courtesy of the Davidson Family

My practice partner - Hy
Photo courtesy of the Davidson Family

to spiritual aspects, they had provided entertainment and an enjoyable diversion from the constant grind of long days of hard work for all those who made their living off of the land. However, times were changing. The outside world had invaded Pecan Grove "big time." World War II, cars, radios, commerce, industry, and so many other things all had their effect on Pecan Grove. People moved away. Money could be made by working at easier jobs than the demanding ones of farming and ranching. Spending a July week-and-a-half in a tent by the little Pecan Grove Baptist Church no longer had the same appeal as it did in the horse-and-buggy days, not that long ago.

As a young boy, my recollections of those camp meetings are exceptionally pleasant. Those were the days when tents and wagons dotted the grounds near the tabernacle and church building. People would come from the surrounding towns and communities of Gatesville, Oglesby, McGregor, Eagle Springs, Mound, and Turnersville. Some came prepared to stay for the full ten-day period, which ended on the last Sunday in July. Others would drive over whenever they could spare the time or on those days or nights when special services were held. Music and singing were always an enjoyable part of the services. Also, dinner on the ground gatherings of all attendees were such pleasant times of comradery. A large gathering was always present for baptisms that took place in Coryell Creek on the last Sunday afternoon. Two hundred, or more, people under the tabernacle was a common attendance for nighttime services.

Families that came prepared to stay on the grounds for the full ten days came with everything they needed to be self-sufficient during that time. They brought wagons loaded with tents, bedding, cooking equipment, food, and a change or two of clothes. The trusty well and hand pump near the tabernacle supplied plenty of water. A dozen, or more, tents were usually set up. Those families had an extra measure of visiting and togetherness during the camp meeting. Nights were dedicated to services at the tabernacle, but days were filled with visiting and taking care of all the necessities associated with living in a tent. Most men would go back to their farm or ranch during the day to take care of work that had to be done.

However, women and small children stayed in the camp. Camp-life activities for them included all the things they would do at home, but without the conveniences, they had at home. Children were cared for. Three meals a day were prepared. Wardrobes were not extensive, and measures for clothes washing were done. Women's days were busy, but they also found time to make the most of visiting opportunities with neighbors.

Mother enjoyed those camp meetings. Living out of a tent and a wagon for ten days was not a problem for her. She relished the interchange with fellow campers and the preachers who stayed among us. She would send me on errands just to help promote personal contacts between campers. Even when she didn't need salt, she would send me to borrow some from a neighbor. She was an excellent cook, and we could count on hosting a preacher, or two, a few times during the meeting. One year, a preacher, who was new to our group, let it be known that he did not like deer meat. To get better acquainted, Mother and another lady teamed up to provide an evening meal for the new

John Thomas Davidson (Daddy)
& his mother Little Grannie
Photo courtesy of the Davidson Family

man. One of Mother's contributions was a large deer roast that she cooked to perfection using her camp gear equipment. Their guest ate that meat and commented numerous times on how good it was. Mother could hardly contain herself from laughing. He was not enlightened about the subterfuge that night but was told a couple of days later after Mother and her friend were through amusing themselves with what they had done. When they finally confessed, the preacher said he was ready any time for another meal with deer meat if Mother cooked it.

The Davidson Cemetery
-photo by Wayland Corgill

As a young boy, I thought those ten-day camp meeting revivals were great. It was a time of freedom from chores and a golden opportunity for playing with other boys in the camp. We kept the Coryell Creek swimming hole busy. I could hardly wait to jump in the creek early in the morning. However, boys will be boys, and a little skullduggery sprang up on occasion. After a few days of doing the same things over and over, the fertile brains of the older boys were very clever with figuring out how to prevent boredom. One year they hit on the idea of mixing up babies of families who put those babies to bed in their wagons. A wagon was considered to be a safe place for a baby. It was away from insects and critters on the ground. Tent dwellers usually slept on pallets directly on the ground. Late at night, the soundly sleeping babies were interchanged in the wagons. Needless to say, the next morning, consternation reigned throughout the camp until the babies were matched up with their parents. I don't remember any of the boys getting into trouble over that episode. No harm was done, so the affected parents evidently decided to avoid creating a fuss. However, there might have been a special segment added to the revival services that night. For the record, I wasn't involved in any baby swapping.

After the days of those ten-day camp meeting revivals, shorter, non-camping revivals were still held at the Pecan Grove Baptist Church. Often, Baylor ministerial students came to preach at those revivals. Also, they often came to preach at regular Sunday services. My exposure to Baylor through those preachers had a profound effect on my career and much of my life as well. After finishing Gatesville High School in 1949, I was bound for Baylor. However, that is another story and that story wouldn't have happened without the little Pecan Grove Baptist Church.

In addition to the Pecan Grove Baptist Church, there is one more salient reminder of where the Pecan Grove community was. That landmark is the Davidson Cemetery. It is an old, old cemetery and the only one for miles around. It is located on the upper part of a hill on the west side of Farm Road 1829, about one mile north of Hwy. 107. The cemetery is oriented, long-wise, in a north-south configuration, with all graves arranged in an east-west direction.

More than six hundred graves are marked with headstones. However, there are, surely, more people than that buried there. In the mid-to-late 1800s, opportunities for burials with chiseled grave markers were often slim to none. How many of those earliest burials were marked with no more than stones is anybody's guess. After decades and decades of weathering and traffic, poorly marked graves became indiscernible. Hopefully, the number of those is few.

If you are looking east, from the cemetery, the view is across gentle slopes of the valley down to the Coryell Creek bottom and beyond to the bordering line of mountains in the east. In 1834, a young frontiersman, James Coryell, accompanied a group of men surveying land in the area along the Leon River and up what is now Coryell Creek. The survey party was lead by a prominent, early-day Texan, Capt. George B. Erath. The impressive view from the hillside location of the future Davidson Cemetery surely must have inspired James Coryell to claim a homestead in the beautiful countryside he gazed upon. James was also a member of a group of men called Rangers. Those men helped protect settlers from Indian depredations. For their service, Rangers were rewarded with land by the Mexican government. Texas independence was still two years in the future. James' survey party measured and staked a quarter-league of land, approximately 1,100 acres, for him. That survey encompassed the lower-western part of the Coryell Creek valley and extended down to the Leon River.

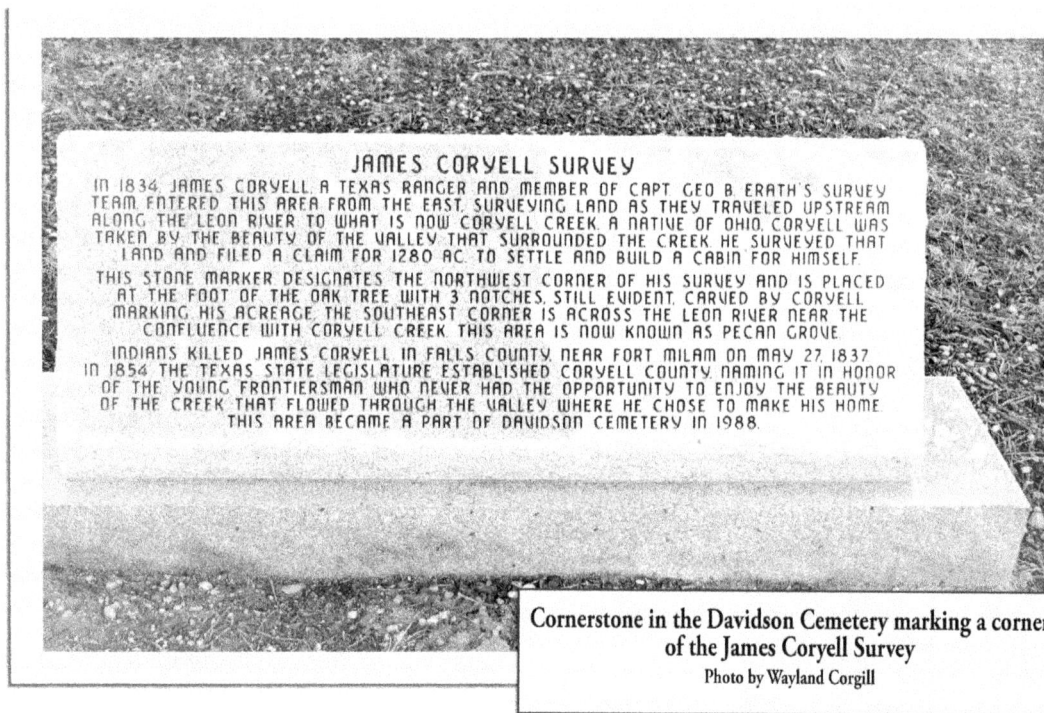

Cornerstone in the Davidson Cemetery marking a corner
of the James Coryell Survey
Photo by Wayland Corgill

The Mexican government granted James the homestead he wanted. It was the first homestead in what became Coryell County several years later. Surely, James never had any idea that that land claim would set in motion events that would cause his name to be permanently ingrained in Texas history. Tragically, he never settled on the land he was so taken with. In 1837, he was killed by Indians at Fort Milam on the Brazos River a few miles to the east.

Wayland Corgill

At the north end of the Davidson Cemetery, a large, old live oak tree marks an interesting spot. That tree has three faint, slash-marks that were cut into it in 1834. Understandably, the marks are a little difficult to make out so many years later, but they are unmistakably there. James Coryell blazed those cuts on the tree to mark the northwest corner of his homestead survey.

Visiting the Davidson Cemetery brings back to life family members and friends buried there. I have such pleasant memories of those remarkable people from my formative years in our close-knit community. While passing by their graves, I can almost hear their voices and smell the smoke from PaPa's old pipe.

Standing with my back against the old oak tree with James Coryell's blaze marks, and looking east across the valley, always stirs up a flood of memories about growing up there. The landscape is extraordinary but, for me, the memories are better. Gazing along Coryell Creek's winding contours reminds me of countless squirrel hunts, fishing trips, and dips in my favorite swimming holes. With field glasses, I can easily pick out the spot on the mountain where Daddy cut cedar posts. The rock house that Daddy and Mother built is a stone's throw away, across the highway to my left. A couple of hundred yards behind the rock house, a small patch of the roof of PaPa and Little Grannie's house is visible through the trees. The Blackfoot and Davidson school buildings once stood nearby. Their structures are gone now, but not their memory. In the bottom of the valley on the east side of Coryell Creek, the site of great-grandpa's house is visible. The top rocks of the chimney of that old house barely show above the big trees that I used to play on as a kid. Fields in the valley, where we sweated over growing corn and wheat, are still being cultivated. However, not one mule or plow horse is to be seen. That work is much easier these days with air-conditioned tractors. The location of the Pecan Grove Baptist Church is out of sight, a couple of miles to the southeast. However, just looking in that direction revives countless memories of so many things that happened there.

I can easily understand why James Coryell was determined to own a piece of the beautiful valley that stretched in front of his viewpoint at the old oak tree. Regrettably, he never had the chance to make memories of living there.

Life in the Pecan Grove community was many things. It had all of the elements of gentle, simple, complicated, easy, hard, trying, rewarding, satisfying, neighborliness, and character building. The people were great, and so is their legacy.

The oak tree in the Davidson Cemetery with three faded slash marks made by James Coryell in 1834 as a survey boundary marker.
- photo by Wayland Corgill

Gatesville School & Sports

September 1938 – First Grade

The school bus from Leon Junction picked me up from the roadside, and I was on my way to Gatesville for my first day of school. I had walked from our little house, back in the woods, to the roadway near the Davidson Cemetery. As I waited for the bus, I tried to imagine what school would be like. My only exposure to school had been the Blackfoot School that had closed in the spring. I had never even seen the Gatesville school grounds. Would Gatesville schools be similar to the Blackfoot School, with several grades taught in one room? How many kids would be going to school? Would kids ride their horses to school and tie them to a hitching post during the day? There was no kindergarten or preschool in those days, and I was totally in the dark about what to expect. Prior to this first day, my "world" didn't extend very far outside the bounds of the Pecan Grove community. Everything was new and unknown from that moment when boarding the bus, and I was eager to finally be on my way to find out what school was all about.

Except for the annual camp meetings, I had very little experience in socializing with other children. Besides my brother, Hy, there were no other boys my age in the neighborhood. Also, opportunities for trips to neighboring communities were limited. Even as young boys, Hy and I were kept busy with work on the ranch. Daily chores and seasonal work with crops left little spare time for ranging very far from home. However, a cousin, David Davidson, lived about six miles away in Mound and, whenever I could, I would ride a horse over to see him. I rarely did that. Hy was virtually my only playmate. For us, playing consisted of little more than throwing a baseball back and forth. School changed all of that. My meager social experience was immeasurably improved from the very first day.

From that first day in elementary school, a whole new world opened up for me. This was something I couldn't get enough of. I would have walked the ten miles to school if I had to. There were almost ninety students in that first grade. Getting to know and make friends with them and other kids were more pleasurable than anything I could have imagined. Hy and I still played catch at home but, at school, I had dozens of playmates and opportunities for playing more than just catch.

Socializing with other kids was the most exciting part of elementary school for me, but activities in the classrooms also were enjoyable. The teachers were great. We behaved ourselves, and teachers had our undivided attention. They were generally regarded as unquestionable figures of authority, just as our mothers and fathers were. That easily kept order in the classrooms and provided a good learning environment. However, in the early grades, while the teachers were concentrating on more important things, I often had thoughts of what I would be doing during recess. For me, the playground and my friends were a delightful bonus of school.

In those early years, recess activities for little boys included playing marbles, spinning tops, and playing softball. The girls played hopscotch and skip-rope.

Most boys carried marbles in their pockets. Among those marbles was a favorite one, a shooter called a taw. The game consisted of each contestant putting a few marbles in a circle that was drawn in the dirt and then trying to shoot them out by flipping the taw using a thumb. Game rules weren't simple and had many variations. In general, whoever shot the most marbles out of the circle, and didn't lose his taw, was the winner. Special rules applied to the taw. A taw left in the circle, without shooting another marble out, was "fair game." If that taw was shot out of the circle by anyone other than its owner, the game was over for the taw's owner. One variation of the game was "playing for keeps." That is, whoever shot a marble out of the ring, kept it. However, on the school grounds, "keeps" was forbidden.

Rules for playing with tops were similar to rules for marble games. One objective was to knock fellow contestants' spinning tops out of a ring drawn in the dirt. This was attempted by a person aiming his top at another one in the ring. In case of a miss, the person, who had just launched his top, had to stand by while others took aim at it. One high mark of skill in playing tops was to split another person's top with a direct hit. A top's metal spindle was usually kept sharp for the possibility of accomplishing that feat.

Organizing a softball game during recess time was my favorite. I had an advantage in playing that game. Accurately throwing a ball was easy for me after all the rock-throwing I had done and playing catch with Hy. In those early grades, I had no inkling of the importance of ball throwing skills in my future. However, by the ninth grade, that began to be apparent.

In 1938, Gatesville school buildings were located on a hill overlooking Raby Park on the south side of Gatesville. Grades one through twelve were divided into three groups with a separate building for each. The elementary school was grades one through six. Junior high was grades seven through nine. High school was grades ten through twelve. A large gym building also occupied part of the hill. During my eleven years there, I got very familiar with all of those facilities.

Due to limited space, the playground was common for all children. That feature of the campus had a small disadvantage for little boys who came in contact with high school boys. At that time, an occasional practice by older boys was to tightly grip a younger boy's hair and scalp with one hand and then jerk upwards. Naturally, that would "smart" more than a little bit. Therefore, I quickly learned to avoid those encounters when at all possible. Other than that, I don't remember any other objectionable issues among students on the playground. We all got along very well and entertained ourselves with substantially no playground equipment. A few swings were the extent of playground equipment.

Part of the two-story elementary school building extended over the edge of the hill. A cafeteria was constructed under the overhang. I didn't spend any time in the cafeteria. Mother packed a lunch for me, as well as for Hy. When Anita and Sandra started school, Mother packed their lunches too. She packed them in paper bags that were used over and over until they were worn out. I was responsible for keeping a bag useable as long as possible. Those lunches were usually a sausage or ham biscuit and a piece of fruit. Often, the fruit was an apple, but it was no ordinary apple. Mother would remove the core and pack the cavity with peanut butter. Those apples were the best.

Many students brought their lunch. Bologna sandwiches were common in the city kids' lunches. When I started the first grade, I had never seen bologna, and it really looked good. I just had to try it. For a few weeks, I easily found classmates who would swap their bologna sandwiches for my sausage biscuit. However, before too long, bologna lost its appeal. I realized who was getting the better deal, and it wasn't me. Bologna looked great, but it didn't compare with sausage or ham. I never swapped my special apple for anything.

Those were great years in elementary school. I had no problems with other kids or any of the teachers. However, when I was in the sixth grade, I did get a bit of criticism from my homeroom teacher, Mrs. Maude Alice Painter. That one-way exchange was stimulated by what I thought was an insignificant, innocuous incident on a fire escape. She didn't share my opinion. My classroom was on the upper floor of the building. The back window of that room opened onto a landing from which a metal slide extended to the ground. When a fire alarm sounded, the boy nearest the window in the back of the room knew that he was the one to open the window and lead the class down the slide. This drill was all to be done in a serious, orderly manner. Those fire drills were practiced often enough to make sure everybody knew what to do. One day, the fire alarm sounded, and I happened to be the boy nearest the window. I, dutifully, opened the window and stepped onto the landing. Just before I got on the slide, I had a spontaneous idea for adding a little levity to this drill. As I zipped down the slide, I hollered, "Hi-ho Silver, away!" Mrs. Painter didn't think that was even a little bit funny. When she caught up with me outside, I was properly chastised for my lack of seriousness.

To this day, I have no idea why I thought about shouting the Lone Ranger's trademark instruction to his horse, Silver, as I lead the charge down the fire escape. Perhaps it was because I had recently listened to a Lone Ranger episode on the radio. His adventures were fascinating, but I never listened to very many of them. Evening chores and weekend work got in the way of that. Also, the radio reception out in Pecan Grove was poor, most of the time, and static was constant. Whether or not Mrs. Painter was a fan of the Lone Ranger, I never knew. However, I didn't think so that day.

For me, elementary school was one year shorter than normal. When I started in 1938, the Gatesville school system was an eleven-year program. In 1940, the program was expanded to twelve years. Adjustments were made in the elementary grade levels, and I had to skip the third grade.

Those five years in elementary school were great and, had I spent another year there, that would have been fine with me.

Junior High School 1943 - 1946

As the 1943 school year began, I wondered what new experiences lay in-store by moving up to junior high school. Surely, I would like that as well as elementary school. I wasn't concerned about possible challenges ahead with new teachers and new classmates. I just didn't waste time thinking about that. However, one thing I took note of was that the junior high building was one story with no fire escape slide. I was also aware that Mrs. Painter would remain in the elementary school. For the next three years, I wouldn't have to be concerned with proper etiquette on a fire escape slide.

Although I generally looked forward to each and every school day, the first two years of junior high were not very exciting. There were no big changes in the regimen that had prevailed in elementary school. Basic courses continued in the subjects of reading, writing, and arithmetic. There were no organized team sports. Except for softball, I had outgrown most of the playground activities that were fun in earlier years. The game of marbles had lost its allure. For those reasons, I don't remember much about the seventh and eighth grades. However, the ninth grade brought a very welcomed change.

My satisfaction with school took a leap forward in the ninth grade when I joined the ninth-grade football team. That was my first opportunity to get involved in football, and I was eager to give it a try. I knew very little about the game. Growing up on our ranch in the Pecan Grove community had kept me somewhat isolated from experiencing many things happening in the "outside world," including football. Demands of our day-to-day ranching and farming activities left very little time for venturing outside our rural environment. There were very few days that were not filled with work that had to be done. If I had grown up in town, many things would have been different for me, and I would have had a head start in knowing something about football.

Ninth-grade football proved to be a sport that I could really get interested in. I knew very little about the game, but it was a challenge that I welcomed. I had watched a few varsity games when Hy was the quarterback. Now I had a keen interest in watching him more closely and also seeking his advice. Like Hy, I wound up in the quarterback position. Although passing was not such an important part of game plans back in those days, as quarterback, I was able to put to use my rock-throwing skills developed from years past.

Coach Lloyd Mitchell was the only full-time coach in the Gatesville school system. However, Mr. Oran D. Bates, the elementary school principal, provided some assistance. Coach Mitchell was responsible for all sports, including football, basketball, baseball, tennis, and track and field. He also taught a couple of classroom subjects. Understandably, he had very little time to spend with the ninth-grade football program. Mr. Bates helped out with that. Coach Mitchell's principal focus was on the varsity teams.

Our ninth-grade team played only a few neighboring schools. We played more for practice than anything else. However, Coach Mitchell did manage to spend enough time with us to start us on the fundamentals of football. Hy also helped me a lot. Remarkably, Coach Mitchell treated ninth-grader team members as though our performance was important to the school, and he earned the full respect of every team member in the process. He was always even-tempered and never raised his voice. He taught teamwork and made the game of football exciting. Without fail, Coach Mitchell's conduct was exemplary in all situations. The Gatesville school system was lucky to have had him as a coach.

The practice field for football, baseball, and track was downhill from the school campus and adjacent to the sewage treatment plant by the Leon River. We kept our football gear in the gym. The gym was on the school campus high-ground. We suited up in the gym and walked down the hill to the practice field. Going down was not so bad but going back up after practice was a long, hard climb. With our football gear on, hiking back and forth from the gym to the practice field was like a workout, particularly when ascending the hill after a sweaty practice. The practice field was a good one, but it had a couple more complications. It would flood when the Leon River got out of its banks. That problem was minor because flooding seldom happened. The other problem was fairly offensive and happened often. Noxious odors from the nearby sewage treatment plant were strong when the wind blew in our direction. Breezes out of the southeast would gag us. That practice field separated the boys who were serious about football from those who were not.

As our football season wore on, the number of boys in the program often dwindled to less than what was needed for two teams for scrimmage. To work around that, the local State School for Boys would get our attention. That institution often referred to as "the boys' home," housed homeless boys and boys who had been in trouble and needed corrective supervision. The boys' home had a football team, and they were ready to play at any time. We ninth-graders often scrimmaged with those kids at the boy's home, and they were worthy opponents.

Our football equipment was very basic. Pads were adequate, but helmets left a little to be desired. They were leather. We didn't have plastic helmets in Gatesville until 1948. There was also a shortage of footballs. We only had one. That required some interesting workarounds to avoid losing the football during games at the football field in Raby Park.

The Raby Park football field was "shoehorned" into a space that was barely large enough to play on, plus provide the space for bleachers. The park is a beautiful landscape due mainly to the extremely rough terrain within the park boundaries. Steep hills slope down to creeks that run throughout the park. As nature created the park, there was no place flat or level enough for a football field. Therefore, thousands of tons of fill dirt were hauled in to create a surface that was minimally big enough for a football field. The north end of the field was near a street with an apartment building across the street. The south end of the field was near the edge of an acutely steep slope that ended fifty feet below in a grove of oak trees. Those dimensional and geographic features figured prominently in playing with only one football. That football often landed outside the field of play, and special measures had to be taken to get the ball back without excessive game delays.

The goal post at the north end of the field was near the street. Kicking extra points and field goals often projected the football into the yard or on the roof of the apartment building. The goal post at the south end of the field was near a sharp drop-off, and kicks at that end would put the football in the oak trees at the bottom of the slope. Therefore, throughout the game, a student equipment manager was stationed at the apartment building, and another boy was stationed in the oak grove. Their job was to get the football back on the field as quickly as possible so the game could continue. The south end slope to the oak grove was a particular problem. The climb from the trees up to the field was so steep that it took a few minutes to ascend that rigorous path. Concrete steps with a handrail were eventually installed on the slope to help the young man retrieve the football and help reduce game delays.

The Raby Park football field is long gone. A swimming pool now occupies part of that space. However, the concrete steps going up the slope from the oak trees are still there.

Wayland Corgill

Steps installed in 1948 at the Gatesville football field to help get the football back in play when kicked beyond the end zone, we only had one football.
- photo by Wayland Corgill

The Raby Park football field had a good surface. The fill dirt provided a good foundation for growing grass. With proper maintenance, the field could be kept in very good condition for football games. Rodeos were also held on the football field. Even after those events, it was not an excessive problem to keep the field surface in good shape.

The football field surface always looked good. That was due to a man who, over the years, became a "fixture" at the Gatesville school campus. Everybody called him Sarge, but his name was Sam Smith. He was the custodian for school properties, including the football field. He took a special interest in keeping the field fertilized and watered. His favorite fertilizer was goat manure, and it sure kept the grass green. Sarge knew what was best for the grass and didn't worry too much about the smell.

Sarge had an unusual and interesting life long before he became the school custodian. He was adopted from the Gatesville boys' home by Uncle Claude and Aunt Vergie Sheppard. Their small boy had died, and Sarge filled the void. When Sarge finished public school, he joined the Army and retired from there after thirty years of service. During his military service, he had been to many places all over the world, but there was no other place he considered settling down except with his friends in Coryell County. He and my father were the same age and were very close. Sarge lived with us and worked for Daddy a few years before becoming the school custodian. That job became open one year when Daddy was on the school board and, of course, Daddy recommended Sarge. The school board made a good decision.

High School 1946 – 1949

I was too busy in the ninth grade to pay attention to what was going on in the high school building next door, except for one bit of high excitement. One day, the fire alarm rang out in that building, and the evacuation process took place in a hurry. Those fire drills that many students had thought were a nuisance paid off. The upper floor fire escape slides were well-used pieces of equipment that day. Fire trucks soon arrived with sirens blaring. The whole campus was startled into alert mode, and classes came to a halt. The fire was on the second floor, and fire hoses were immediately routed through upper windows. Luckily, the fire was quickly extinguished.

Later that day, the cause of the fire became known to everybody in Gatesville. Floor sweep granules had been dribbled through a small hole in the upstairs floor. A little pile of that combustible material collected on the ceiling of the floor below. A lighted match was then dropped through the hole, and results desired by the prankster(s) were instantaneous. It was well known that the fire was intentionally started, but who started it was never revealed to the general public. No doubt, the identity of the fire-starters didn't remain unknown to key people for very long, and, surely, the perpetrators got a stern scolding, as a minimum. Also, the punishment was very likely worse. It might have even included an appropriate paddling by Uncle Sid Pruitt, the high school principal. He always kept a suitable instrument handy and was very adept at using it.

If I had been in the high school building when the fire alarm sounded, I probably could have been helpful with the evacuation. Mrs. Maude Alice Painter's thorough instruction for the proper use of a fire escape slide in elementary school would have paid off. I was an expert on that.

High school was an extraordinarily exciting, memorable, and formative time for me. All three years were filled with incessant learning experiences that were satisfying and challenging. I was introduced to a variety of activities that I could never have imagined as a kid growing up on a remote ranch in Pecan Grove. My world constantly opened up as I participated in school functions. The sports program was particularly appealing to me. However, I also found great enjoyment in everything that high school had to offer, including extracurricular activities. All of it suited me, even choir and homemaking. I was voted the junior class favorite. In a way, that showed how much I enjoyed the camaraderie of my classmates.

1949 Gatesville high school yearbook -photo courtesy of Gatesville ISD

Cotton put Gatesville on the map by winning all-state honorable mention in football.

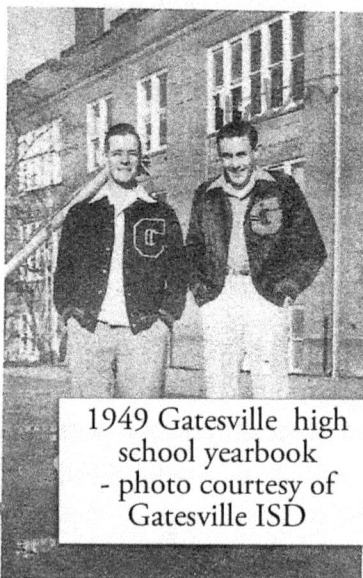

1949 Gatesville high school yearbook - photo courtesy of Gatesville ISD

When the all district team was announced, Bill David and Cotton had reason for big smiles.

As a sophomore, I really got excited about football. Traveling with the varsity team to their games was a thrilling treat for a kid who had rarely been outside of Coryell County. However, the most stimulating elements of the game were interactions with my teammates and the conscientious coaching supervision. Coaching for tenth-grade football was altogether more intense than it had been in the ninth grade. Coach Lloyd Mitchell took his job seriously. I could not have had a better coach. His presence on the field gave our workouts a whole new meaning. He had an extraordinary ability to motivate kids to do their best. We had a lot to learn, and he was an excellent teacher. He intended to get us ready for winning games on the varsity team. Unlike football in the ninth grade, football was now getting serious, but it was fun, and I welcomed the challenge.

Coach Mitchell put me in the quarterback position. I quickly discovered that, perhaps, I had more to learn about football than most of my teammates. The realization that this was not a simple game was somewhat shocking. The more I learned, the more I became concerned about what else I needed to know. However, Coach Mitchell always put me at ease with his temperate guidance and instruction. He really knew the game. He was patient and extremely effective in his methods of teaching. Also, his corrective instructions were always given in a calm, respectful voice. That went a long way in moderating my apprehension about being successful in learning the game. Coach Mitchell made the whole process fun, and I always looked forward to showing up for practice. In time, he became almost like a "father figure" and was more than a friend throughout his life.

Football practice, before the school year started, coincided with our August corn harvest on the ranch. Without question, corn had to be gathered when the time was right. Our livelihood depended on it. Daddy, Hy, and I were the harvest crew. By August, the ears of corn had thoroughly dried on the stalks and were ready to be broken off and loaded in a wagon. Nothing about the corn harvest was particularly easy, and one part was more laborious than the rest. The wagon was too wide to go between the rows of corn. It had to be driven over a row which left the corn stalks bent over on the ground. Working those "downed rows" required a strong back for bending over at every stalk. That was often my job. Understandably, I sure was grateful that Daddy would give me a reprieve from the corn patch when it was time to go to football practice. He would even loan me his car. The support I continually got from Daddy had as much to do with my success in sports as anything else.

Coach Mitchell's interests in the Gatesville community are worthy of recognition. He was much more than a coach. He had a wide-ranging influence beyond the sports fields. His presence touched many more lives than those involved in boys' athletics. Although his primary interests were in sports, they were certainly not limited to that.

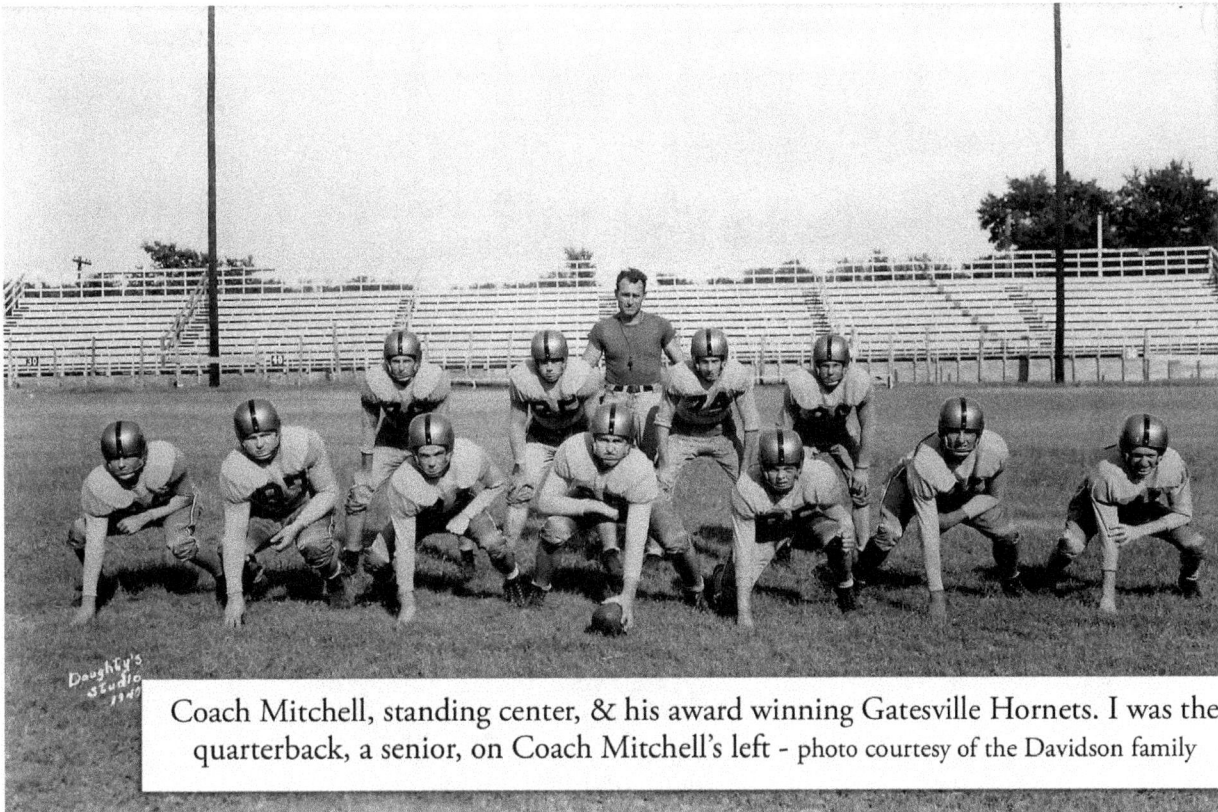

Coach Mitchell, standing center, & his award winning Gatesville Hornets. I was the quarterback, a senior, on Coach Mitchell's left - photo courtesy of the Davidson family

Coach Mitchell was a star athlete during his years at Baylor. He earned numerous honors and was selected as a member of the All-Southwest Conference Team in both football and track. He participated in just about every sports program that Baylor had to offer. That experience served him well as coach of boys' athletics in Gatesville. He even found time to occasionally follow the rodeo circuit and help with officiating "bronc-riding" events. He was a time-keeper at several big rodeos. Coach Mitchell was probably a cowboy at heart. Gatesville had space for his horses, boots, and saddles, which might have had a lot to do with his selection of Gatesville for a coaching job. However, according to his daughter, Mary Catherine Mitchell, he was very favorably impressed with the interview he was given by the fine people in the Gatesville school system. That, plus the beautiful countryside of Coryell County and relatively close proximity to Baylor, helped him make his decision to move an easy one.

Coach Mitchell's interest in cowboy life was definitely a dominant factor in his most well-known legacy in Gatesville. While he was enrolled at Baylor, he spent his summers working for the U.S. Forest Service as a fire-spotter in Yellowstone National Park. He had no car. Getting there and back was done by hitchhiking. While standing on the roadside waiting for a ride on one of those trips, he noticed something metallic sticking out of the ground. He dug it out. It was a spur for a cowboy's boot. That one spur was the start of a collection that eventually numbered over six thousand. That collection is now one of the main attractions of the Gatesville museum. In order to adequately publicize the collection and honor Coach Mitchell, the museum petitioned the Texas State Legislature to declare Gatesville as the Spur Capital of Texas. That was done and, thanks to Coach Mitchell, Gatesville now has the distinction of an unmatched official title.

Why would anyone consider collecting spurs? According to Mary Catherine, her father's answer to that question was, "After I found that one spur, I kept looking for its mate but never found it."

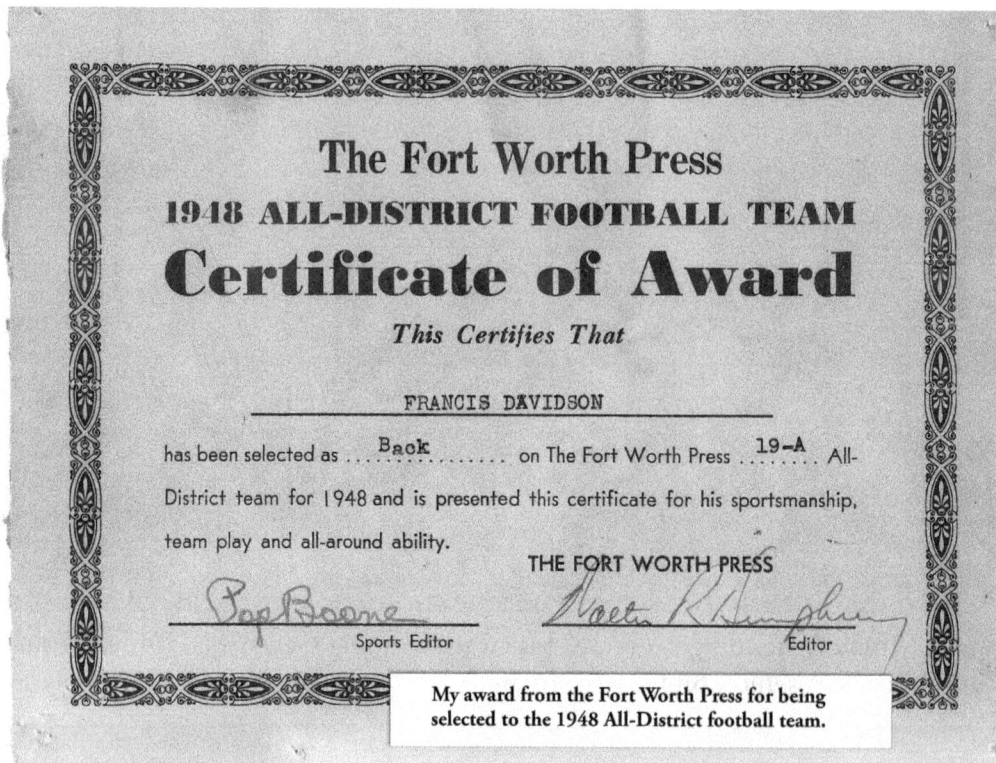

The Fort Worth Press
1948 ALL-DISTRICT FOOTBALL TEAM
Certificate of Award
This Certifies That

_____ FRANCIS DAVIDSON _____

has been selected as .... Back .... on The Fort Worth Press .... 19-A .... All-District team for 1948 and is presented this certificate for his sportsmanship, team play and all-around ability.

THE FORT WORTH PRESS

Pop Boone
Sports Editor

Walter R. Humphrey
Editor

My award from the Fort Worth Press for being selected to the 1948 All-District football team.

Wayland Corgill

How could anyone amass a six-thousand spur collection? Mary Catherine shed some light on that question too. In addition to Coach Mitchell's keen searching for old spurs everywhere he went, many of the spurs were brought to him by soldiers who were stationed at Ft. Hood. Coach Mitchell taught at the Gatesville schools from the mid-1940s to the mid-1950s. For a summer job, he often managed the Gatesville swimming pool. Soldiers were his best customers. Even if they didn't swim, they would visit the pool just to talk to the friendly man who managed the place and made them feel at home. Coach Mitchell's quest to build his spur collection soon became common knowledge throughout Ft. Hood. Before long, spurs from all over the world were winding up in the hands of the soldiers' friend at the swimming pool. For years, the spurs kept coming.

Coach Mitchell's friendly personality and winning ways would have made him successful in whatever he had chosen as a career. He was a great example of living a respectable, responsible life. Everybody liked him. Daddy and Coach Mitchell had a lot in common as well as Mother and Madge Mitchell. They all became the best of friends and often spent summer vacation trips together. Driving trips to Colorado and Yellowstone were their favorites. The final resting place for all four of those old friends is the Davidson Cemetery in Pecan Grove.

I have never encountered very many people like Coach Mitchell. His methods for dealing with troublesome situations and keeping his athletes in line were admirably unique to his character. For example, during basketball season in my junior year, one of my buddies thought it would be fun for us to go downhill from the gym and smoke a cigarette. We did. When I got back to the gym, Coach Mitchell was on the far side of the basketball court. His attention was fixed on me as I walked through the door. I walked over to the bleachers and sat down. He strolled over and joined me. In a calm voice, he said, "Do you need some money to buy cigarettes?" I am sure that I turned as red as a beet. I don't remember what else, if anything, that Coach said, and I don't remember saying anything. Needless to say, I was embarrassed and probably speechless. Also, I don't remember exactly how that episode on the bleachers ended, but that was my last cigarette. Coach never mentioned it again.

Although Coach Mitchell was responsible for the entire boys' athletic program and did most of the coaching, he had part-time assistance from one of the teachers, Mr. Oran Bates. Also, during my three high school years, a former Gatesville football player, Dan Edwards, occasionally showed up on our practice field. He was four years ahead of me and was now playing college football at Georgia. During his infrequent, short trips back home to Gatesville, Dan was usually on the football field when we were. He sure knew a lot about football, and getting to know him was my good fortune. Our association didn't end after I graduated from high school but continued for many years.

How Dan wound up at Georgia had an interesting twist. Several soldiers at Fort Hood were from Georgia. They were football fans and attended the Gatesville home games. Dan impressed them, and they convinced the Georgia coaches to come to Gatesville and check Dan out. The coaches were also impressed, and Dan went to Georgia on a football scholarship. Those soldiers were good friends of Gatesville football. Due to their recommendations, three more Gatesville boys became Georgia Bulldogs.

The Rifleman - Cotton Davidson

After college, Dan had a successful career in pro football. That is where he and I crossed paths again. In the 1948 NFL draft, Dan was the 1st round, 9th pick by the Pittsburgh Steelers. However, he didn't go with the Steelers. Instead, he took an odd route of playing five years for teams no longer in existence. He got to the Baltimore Colts in 1953, a year before I arrived. We had one year of playing together before I was drafted into the Army in 1955. Dan helped me a lot during that first year with the Colts. I could never have imagined such a connection during those days in high school. At that time, football was just a fun game for me, and it never crossed my mind that I would be involved in that sport beyond high school.

In my junior year, I started as quarterback for the varsity team. The number on my jersey was 74, which I thought was a little high for a quarterback. However, there were no numbers below 70 on anybody's jersey. I thought that was a little unusual too. Most of the team was composed of seniors. It took some time before I became comfortable with being their quarterback. However, our win-loss record was predominantly on the winning side, and, under Coach Mitchell's direction, we all settled into being a very effective team. My teammates became my good friends.

Only a few football games in those junior and senior years stand out in my memory. Our biggest rivals were always Hamilton and McGregor. McGregor was the most competitive of all. We could count on really tough games every time we played those two schools. However, one game I won't forget didn't have anything to do with either Hamilton or McGregor. In my junior year, we played our annual junior-senior exhibition game for the home crowd. I was the quarterback for the junior team. We had a strong team that year. Although none of us were very big, we had several outstanding athletes. I weighed about 160 pounds. We were well matched with the senior team. However, during that game, I got hit so hard that I was effectively "out on my feet." In the huddle, I would ask one of my teammates what I should do next. After a couple of plays, Coach Mitchell realized something was wrong and took me out of the game. He was so concerned about my condition that he took me to the hospital. I spent the night in the hospital and was totally out until shortly after midnight. That was about the hardest hit I ever got in my football career, but it didn't dampen my enthusiasm for the game.

When I left the hospital the next morning, I was still groggy. I didn't fully come to my senses until later that day. When getting dressed to go home, I kept looking for my boots. I had a new pair of boots that Daddy had brought to the hospital. I wouldn't put them on because I was certain they were not mine.

I was discharged from the hospital with a bit of strong advice from the doctor who had attended me. He said that there should be no more football for me. However, after a few days, the effects of my concussion went away, and I never looked back. Luckily, so many years later, there are still no lasting effects of that severe "bell ringing." Obviously, the doctor's analysis didn't factor in the hardness of my head.

Another game that stands out is the last game of the season in my senior year. Gatesville played La Vega for the district championship. With only a few seconds left in the game, I threw a pass to a teammate in the end zone, and he dropped it. La Vega beat us by one point: 20 to 19.

When each football season ended, I enthusiastically looked forward to the basketball season. As with football, my classmates were also very good at basketball. In my junior year, we were bi-district champions. The most memorable game that year was the last one when we played Nocona for the regional championship. We lost that game, but it was more memorable for another reason.

Wayland Corgill

Nocona was, by no means, the friendliest opponent we had that year. Actually, we were not treated well at all. When our bus arrived in Nocona, there was no one to meet us, and the gym was closed. We sat on the bus for quite a while until the Nocona team started arriving. Even after we got inside the gym, the "welcome mat" was still not out. Our bench had been set up directly in front of the Nocona band, and they began tuning up just as we started warming up. That band was really loud. When we were near the band, we could hardly hear each other. A tuba player in the front row was particularly effective in cranking out the decibels. After enduring that for a few minutes, I got an idea. I asked one of my teammates to stand near the band. I told him that I was going to throw him the ball but do not catch it. My aim was accurate, and that tuba player wound up with a basketball lodged in his horn. My plan didn't permanently put a damper on noise from the band. Still, I did get some satisfaction out of giving those offensive musicians something to think about besides music.

In addition to the Nocona team getting help from their band, they also appeared to have an advantage in the ages of their team members. Most of them looked like they had been shaving for several years. In my junior year annual, Coach Mitchell wrote the following note, "Hope we can play Nocona again."

The Gatesville 1949 basketball team. I am #54, 4th from left
- photo courtesy of the Gatesville ISD

BASKETBALL SQUAD OF '49

As with basketball, I eagerly awaited the baseball season. My throwing arm worked well with a baseball, and I was the pitcher. All those young years of practice at targeting squirrels and birds with rocks continued to pay off. I really liked baseball. It was just about my favorite sport.

The Rifleman - Cotton Davidson

Baseball was a popular sport throughout Coryell County. Many communities had their own baseball team. Matches between community teams were numerous on Sunday afternoons. I could always find a team that needed a pitcher, and I spent many Sunday afternoons on the mound.

Gatesville also had an active track program, and we did very well in most events during my junior and senior years. We won all-district honors in both of those years. Coach Mitchell's experience from participation in Baylor's track program paid off for the Gatesville team.

In my senior year, I qualified for State competition in low hurdles and discus throwing. I didn't win first place in low hurdles, but I was in the top three finishers. I don't remember whether I was number two or three. In discus throwing, I didn't place. There were some brawny lads throwing the discus at state. My 160 pounds couldn't quite match their much larger size.

In my junior and senior years, I won all-district honors in football and basketball, as well as track. My senior year was an exceptionally good one for both me and Gatesville. I won all-state honors in football and our season record was 6-1-1. If we had avoided that unfortunate, one point, loss to La Vega, we would have had an excellent year.

The Gatesville 1949 Bi-District baseball championship team. I am 4th from the left in the back row – courtesy of the Davidson family

Wayland Corgill

For me, the high school boys' athletics program was more exciting than anything I could have imagined. I participated in every sport that I could work into my schedule, and that schedule was a full one. School wasn't the only agenda that competed for my time. At home, everyday chores, plus extra work at harvest times, could not be neglected. I can't overstate the value of Daddy's interest and encouragement in everything I was doing. He realized how important sports were to me and his support was crucial in allowing my participation.

No doubt, my focus on high school sports had an effect on my record as a scholar. The "scholar" part of my high school experience could have been better. However, sports were higher on my priority list.

Even though I wasn't the best student, I enjoyed most of the classroom studies too. Agriculture class was just about my favorite due to the excellent teacher, Mr. J.J. Bates. Mr. Bates had a friendly way about him that was almost like sitting down and talking to Daddy. Growing up like I did on our ranch, I knew a lot about agriculture already. I knew how to take care of animals and what it took to grow crops like

corn, wheat, and cotton. However, Mr. Bates did teach us many more things that were new to me. I enjoyed learning new things, but my main interest in going to his class was just to be around him and hear him talk. He sure made the topics interesting.

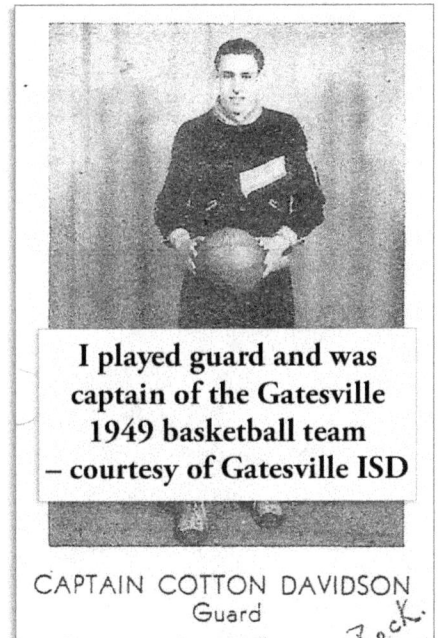

I played guard and was captain of the Gatesville 1949 basketball team – courtesy of Gatesville ISD

CAPTAIN COTTON DAVIDSON
Guard

I took agriculture classes in both my junior and senior years. At the end of my junior year, Mr. Bates organized a treat for about twenty boys in his class. We made an unforgettable trip on a Gatesville school bus. It was quite an adventure for a boy like me who had not made many trips outside Coryell County.

Our first stop was Galveston, where we spent time on the beach. That was my first look at a body of water larger than one I could throw a rock across. Most of us donned swimsuits and tested the water, and got a crusty coating of salt. I preferred the clear, cold water in our Coryell Creek swimming holes.

After a night in Galveston, we went over to Del Rio and walked across the Rio Grande River Bridge into Mexico. Many of the poor little dwellings on that side of the river reminded me of similar ones that could have been found in rural Coryell County not very many years in the past. After a healthy meal of tortillas and beans, we walked back across the bridge to prepare for spending the night and getting an early start the next morning.

From Del Rio, we headed northwest to Carlsbad, New Mexico. Our plan was to visit the caverns. Soon after leaving Del Rio, the countryside became more barren with each passing mile and stayed that way through Ft. Stockton, Pecos, and all the way to Carlsbad. That type of scenery was something new for me and reminded me of how Coryell County was a Garden of Eden in comparison. The caverns were an unbelievable sight. There was no way that I could take it all in on a short visit. It was too big for that. I wondered if anybody could ever spend enough time in that place to become familiar with its labyrinth of passages and rugged, warped contours.

The Rifleman - Cotton Davidson

The two-day trip from Carlsbad back to Gatesville was a long, uneventful ride except for several stops in small towns. There was very little outstanding scenery. However, the changes in vegetation, geographical features, and appearance of small towns that were so different from familiar sights around the home, did add a measure of interest to the trip. After a week on the road, though, we were all glad to get back home, even though it had been a rare, memorable trip. Mr. Bates had, once again, exceeded what would normally have been expected of him.

Why I took a homemaking class in my senior year, I am not really sure. I was probably looking for an easy course that would allow me to concentrate more on sports. Also, that was where the girls were, and I probably thought that might be interesting. Four or five of my teammates had the same idea I did. We had no idea about how the teacher, Mrs. John O. Potts, would react to having boys in her class, but, surely, homemaking would be a "snap," or so we thought.

Mrs. Potts accepted a group of athletes in her class without the least bit of concern. Actually, she seemed to enjoy our presence. However, she saw to it that we stayed busy doing the same things the girls were doing. My main project was to make a shirt. I had in mind to make a long-sleeved cowboy shirt with snaps. Using a pattern, I cut the parts and pieces and struggled with sewing them together in the prescribed manner. Needles, thimbles, and thread didn't exactly fit hands that were practiced at husking corn and milking cows. After finally getting Mrs. Potts' approval of my sewing job, I was ready to install the snaps. That should be easy. At this point, I hit a snag in my plan. Mrs. Potts would not approve snaps. She required buttons and buttonholes. Wow! I could imagine how hard that would be, but I had no choice. The buttonholes really "gave me fits," but I eventually got it right after a lot of practice. I was proud of that shirt, and I even got a compliment from Mrs. Potts.

This might be the western shirt I made in high school homemaking class - photo courtesy of the Davidson family

Wayland Corgill

Mrs. Potts made us work, but she also took care of us. She was really a "sweetheart." I am sure that she got a kick out of having boys in her class. We enjoyed it too, even though it was not a "snap."

Choir was another activity I experimented with, in my senior year. I had little interest in learning the finer points of singing, but I had an ulterior motive for joining. Miss Mamie Sue Halbrook directed the choir. She was also the American History teacher. The rumor was that joining the choir would almost guarantee passing her history class. That got my attention.

I quickly learned that being a "stand out" in the choir was not going to happen for me. My singing might have suited PaPa and the fish in Coryell Creek, but it left something to be desired for Miss Halbrook. I did my best to follow her instructions, but practice as I might; my voice was just not suited for blending with the other choir members. I was more suited for barking instructions on the football field.

Just before Christmas, the Gatesville Lions Club invited the choir to present a program. On the scheduled day, I dutifully went along and lined up with the others on a stage behind closed curtains. Right before "showtime," I guess Miss Halbrook was having second thoughts about my vocal contribution. She walked over and quietly asked me to stand by the curtain draw-rope and open and close the curtains. The curtain operator would be my part in the choir's performance. Even though Miss Halbrook quietly spoke to me, most of the choir heard what she said, and a little ripple of laughter went through the lineup. Probably, the club members on the other side of the closed curtains thought that they were about to be entertained by a very happy group.

I was quite happy to have been the curtain operator that day and, later, I was even happier to have passed Miss Halbrook's American History class with flying colors.

As the final days of my senior year approached, I thought less and less about sports, making shirts, and singing, and more about what would be happening next. The realization was gradually soaking in that a big change for me was on the horizon. Consideration of that fact had been obscured by my intense preoccupation with all the activities I enjoyed in school. As graduation day neared, the unavoidable question of "what next" loomed large. I began to seriously think about what I might do after marching across the stage. My first thought was to follow a path similar to one that Hy had taken. He had always done well in rodeo roping events and was now working on a ranch in southwest Texas. My roping skills were also good, and I loved the cowboy aspects of rodeos and ranch life. Whatever I did, the realization that my life was about to dramatically change, and I had some decisions to make, was a sobering thought.

I didn't follow the cowboy way of life. From high school, I went to Baylor on a football scholarship. Why and how that happened had a lot to do with advice from Hy and help from friends at the little Pecan Grove Baptist Church. Hy minced no words when he told me to get myself into Baylor. Regarding the church, it was very fortuitous that one of the preachers was on the Baylor football team. I was lucky, and Daddy and Mother sure were glad about how things turned out.

Me (left) and one of my Baylor teammates - courtesy of The Texas Collection, Baylor University

Baylor Sports

The days after graduating from high school were an extremely confusing time for me. I had very little advice and was unsure about how to react to potential opportunities for scholarships in sports. Soon after graduation, I was surprised to get an invitation to visit Rice University in Houston. I didn't know what prompted their interest in me, and I had no idea about the recruitment process. From childhood to high school graduation day, my life had been totally wrapped up in activities very close to home. I had had absolutely no experiences that would prepare me for understanding how to handle something like dealing with a scholarship offer. Coach Mitchell did say that I should think about going to Rice. However, there was not much for me to think about, except the fact that I knew very little about what to do or say once I was there. I had no knowledge of my options. Also, it didn't occur to me that Rice might not be the only university interested in me.

Since I had no offers from other universities at the time, I decided to visit Rice. I didn't know what to expect, but I figured that I would learn something by going there. Also, I believed that I was doing what my family and Coach Mitchell would have wanted. One of my teammates, Joe Daniels, also had an invitation and accompanied me. I don't remember how we got to Rice, but we hitchhiked back. I remember that return trip very well. Catching a ride from Houston to College Station was easy but from there to Pecan Grove was anything but easy. It seemed that half of the Aggie student body was also hitching. It took almost all day to get a ride to Waco and then home.

At Rice, we were escorted around the campus by Vernon Glass, the quarterback for Rice's football team. Vernon did a good job of showing us around, but of course, he was non-committal about scholarship details and what it would mean to become a Rice Owl. Vernon introduced us to the coaching staff, where one of the coaches talked to us about some of those issues. I don't remember that conversation being overly informative. When I left Rice that day, I still had about as many questions as I had when I arrived. I didn't have a firm understanding of anything beyond Rice's assurance of a scholarship offer. Many details of the offer, as well as what my responsibilities would be, were still unclear. Rice personnel talked to me as if they were confident everything would work out fine, but I was far from being sure of that.

Back in Pecan Grove, after a couple of days of consideration, I accepted Rice's offer. At the time, my options were either that or get a job. The very next Sunday, everything got turned upside down.

Sunday evening services at the Pecan Grove Baptist Church were conducted by a young man, Ray Mayfield, from Baylor. Ray was a theology student, but he was also an offensive guard on the Baylor football team. He played football on Saturday and preached on Sunday. Ray and I had known each other for a couple of years. When I told him that I had accepted a scholarship from Rice, he immediately said, "You don't want to do that." Ray then said that I should consider Baylor and mentioned a few obvious advantages. I told him that I had not heard anything from Baylor. Not only that, I had never been on the Baylor campus and knew nothing about Baylor. I had no way to compare Rice to Baylor. Ray asked me to be patient for a couple of days and give him a chance to talk to the Baylor coaches. He also said that he would try to arrange for a couple of coaches to come to talk to me and Daddy and Mother.

Before the week was out, Ray and the Baylor coaches showed up at Daddy and Mother's house. They came with an offer of a football scholarship. They took time to be thorough in their explanation of what a scholarship entailed and the economic advantages of staying closer to home. They also pointed out various benefits, such as Mother and Daddy being able to easily keep up with my activities and attend all the Baylor home games. By the time Ray and the coaches left to go back to Waco, my parents and I were convinced that Baylor was the best option for me.

I now had a big problem. I had committed to Rice. How could I get out of that? I couldn't think of any other way around that difficulty except to not "beat around the bush" and tell the folks in Houston that I had changed my mind in favor of an arrangement much better for me. That is what I did, clearly and to the point. I really didn't know what I was doing when I committed to Rice, but I didn't tell them that.

The response I got from Rice was unexpectedly harsh. That bothered me for a long time. I shouldn't have been surprised, but I was. I thought, surely, those Rice officials would not consider that the absence of a Coryell County boy's name on their roster would ever be noticed. However, someone did notice and took the time to pen a letter that respectfully but effectively admonished me for backing out of my commitment. Their main point was something like the following: "You should not start your life by not living up to your commitments and not keeping your word."

Surely, Rice never missed me. Surely, I would have handled the entire recruiting experience in a professional manner if I had known the first things about how to go about it. I might have successfully adapted to life in Houston, but that sure was far from Coryell County. That separation might have been

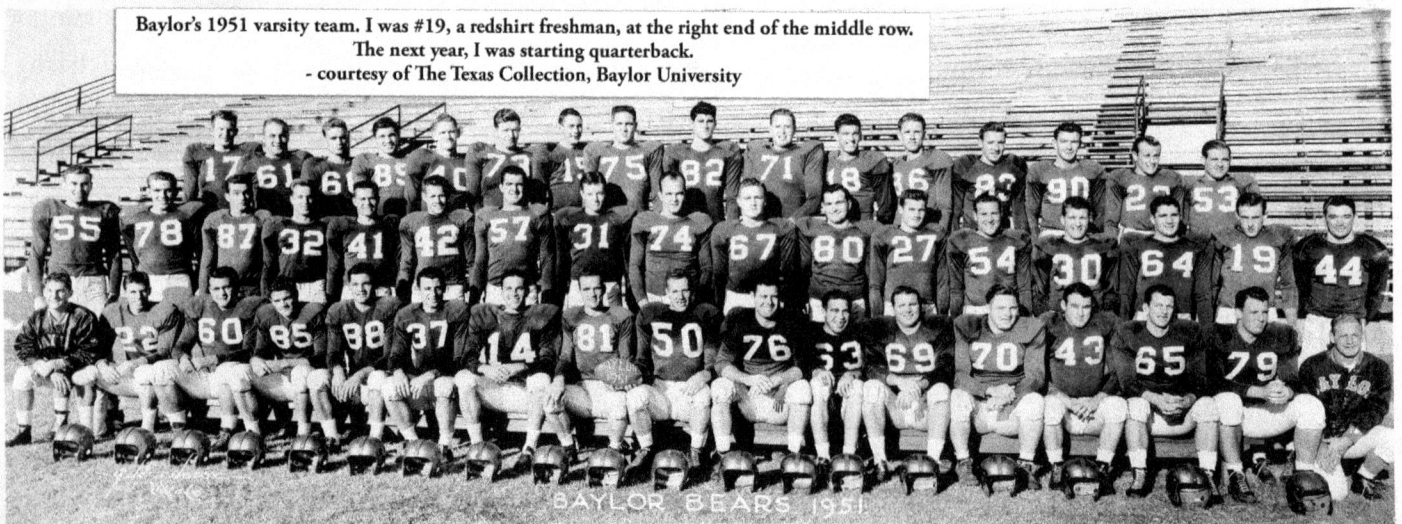

Baylor's 1951 varsity team. I was #19, a redshirt freshman, at the right end of the middle row. The next year, I was starting quarterback.
- courtesy of The Texas Collection, Baylor University

1951

a little too much of a drastic change for a boy that hadn't ever been very far from home. In the final analysis, my backing out of the Rice commitment might have been the best decision for both parties. I know that it was for me.

Interestingly enough, a few years after my ill-fated visit to Rice, I learned that Vernon Glass had a brother named Bill, and he was at Baylor on a football scholarship.

Being acquainted with Ray Mayfield was my very good fortune. Regarding the recruiting process, he knew everything I needed to know and shared his knowledge with me. He also had a thorough understanding of what would be in my best interests. His trustworthy advice and guidance were invaluable. By encouraging me to go to Baylor, he helped me make one of the best decisions I ever made. Ray and I remained friends and kept in touch with each other until his death. I was honored to be one of his pallbearers.

I signed the commitment with Baylor in the early summer of 1949. Big changes in my life started immediately. The athletic department asked me if I needed a summer job. I told them that Daddy always had a job for me, but I needed a job making as much money as I could to support myself when school started in the fall. I understood that Baylor would provide food and rooming plus ten dollars a month

Baylor's 1953 varsity team. I am still #19, second from left in the front row - courtesy of the Davidson family

Front row, left to right: FORDERHASE, L.; DAVIDSON; SULLIVAN; WENTWORTH; MURRAY; LUCKY, B.; BLACK; BRISTOW; ERBEN; KNOWLES; HOPKINS; REID; JONES, C.; SHERMAN; BARNARD; TALBERT; HOOPER; RADFORD.
Second row, left to right: HOLLEY; COWLEY; PESCHAL; RICHIE; CLARK; DIERKING; DAVIS; SMITH, J. R.; TAYLOR; ROBINSON; JONES, A.; SMITH, C.; DUPRE; GREMMINGER; BARNETT; COODY; BAILEY (Mgr).
Back row, left to right: ANDERSON; TALAMANTEZ; CULVAHOUSE; JACKSON, AMYETT; DUPRE, C.; LUCKY, W.; LETBETTER; GREEN; MILLER; LISTON; HARRIS; HILTON; RUTHERFORD.

for laundry, but I had to provide everything else. Summer earnings would be important. I was told that there was an opening for a ranch hand at Brackettville in South Texas. That sounded like a good job for me, and I immediately accepted.

The bus ride to Brackettville was long and hot. Brackettville is 125 miles west of San Antonio. I lost count of all the little towns where the un-air-conditioned bus stopped along the way from Waco. We finally arrived in Brackettville late in the day. I stepped out of the bus into a setting that was totally foreign to me, a seventeen-year-old who had virtually no experience outside of Coryell County. A Baylor student named Jitter McKinney was supposed to be there to meet me but, no luck. There were few people at the bus stop, and I didn't see one friendly face among them. I began to wonder what in the world I had gotten myself into. I wondered how much trouble it would be to catch a bus back to Waco if things didn't get better soon. Jitter finally showed up before dark, and that put some of my apprehension to rest. However, this was such a strange and different place for me, and I was apprehensive about adjusting.

Jitter was a senior at Baylor and also on the football team. He turned out to be a great guy, and we really "hit it off." That was fortunate because we were around each other for just about twenty-four hours every day that summer. We worked together, bunked together, cooked together, and ate together.

On the way from the bus stop to the ranch, Jitter filled me in on a few things. The ranch was a 30,000-acre spread owned by a man named James T. "Happy" Shahan. He had over 1,000 head of Angus cattle. Breeding season was over, and our immediate job would be gathering bulls out of the mesquite thickets and separating them from the herd. Those animals were scattered far and wide, and we would

Me holding the ball for one of my Baylor teammates
- courtesy of The Texas Collection, Baylor University

have our work cut out for us. The bulls liked where they were and did not want to be chased back to a cattle pen. I could see that my cowboy skills would be tested. Along with gathering the bulls, we would also do cattle spraying and other miscellaneous work needed to keep the herd healthy. We expected to have a full summer of cowboying.

Our quarters would be at the ranch foreman's house in a remote area of the ranch. It was a little four-room house with bare necessities. We did have electricity but only one bulb in the kitchen ceiling. Otherwise, electricity did us no good since we didn't have a radio or any electrical appliances. Water had to be toted from a gushing spring a mile away. That water was so good. Jitter observed that the three of us would get to know each other very well before summer was over. We would be several miles from town, and visits there would be few. We wouldn't see another person for days. We would cook for ourselves, and the bill-of-fare would be simple. Usually, whatever was cooked in the early morning hours would provide enough leftovers for lunch and supper. Standard practice would be to cook a big pot of beans and a couple of skillets of cornbread. Virtually all of our daylight hours would be spent in the saddle with little time for gourmet meals.

Happy Shahan was a man of action and with unlimited imagination and talents. Throughout the summer, I kept learning about so many more of his credits besides managing a ranch. He had played basketball for Baylor back in the 1930s. He was currently the mayor of Brackettville. He was the president of the Angus Breeders Association of Texas. He continually applied his enormous creativity in pursuing any avenue or activity that would keep the little town of Brackettville from dying. One of his ideas was to entice moviemakers to use the countryside around Brackettville and his ranch for western venues. He was working on the prospects of making a movie about the Alamo at least a decade before it was actually filmed on his ranch.

While I was there that summer of 1949, I saw the beginnings of some of Happy's plans to prepare for a movie. About a mile north of the foreman's house, Happy picked out an area for a replica of the Alamo. The site was thickly infested with mesquite. The first order of business was to get rid of it. Two huge bulldozers, with a blade on the front and a giant, rotating cutter on the back, made war on that mesquite. The foot-long teeth on that rotating monster of a cutter made small pieces of big trees and tore the ground up so bad that it was difficult for a horse to walk across it. However, the mesquite, roots and all, was obliterated after the bulldozers passed by. Graders and rakes removed debris and smoothed the ground, making it suitable for future construction of a full-scale model of the Alamo. Sure enough, it was built a few years later. Clearing an area large enough for the Alamo and surrounding grounds was a big task. It went on for many days.

Our "brush-popping" work of chasing bulls out of the rough country went on for many days too. The country was not only rough, but everything that grew down there seemed to have thorns. Those were long, hot days too. We were up well before daylight and finished eating supper after dark. Jitter and I didn't need any encouragement to "hit the hay" as soon as we could each evening.

Bathing accommodations were somewhat primitive. When coming back to our quarters late in the day, we would stop by a large, metal water tank that was big enough to swim in. That tank sat on the ground and was about six feet high and at least twenty feet in diameter. It was kept "topped up" by a nearby windmill. The water was warm from soaking up a day's worth of sun rays, and it sure felt good to strip down to our birthday suits and dive in. We didn't worry about anybody seeing us because the nearest human being, other than the foreman, was several miles away. After a short soaking, we would climb out and let the last of the day's sun rays dry us off. We couldn't dawdle because our horses had to be tended to, and supper was waiting.

Our schedule that summer was repetitiously rigid, but there were a few bright spots. Three or four times, we finished work early on Saturday and borrowed the foreman's pickup to go to town. After talking to horses and cows for days on end, we longed for a chance to talk to human beings. The foreman wasn't much of a conversationalist. Prospects for talking to a cute Mexican girl in Brackettville seemed pretty exciting. Those Saturday excursions left me with a totally different opinion of that little town than when I first stepped off of the bus.

Two weeks before time to enroll for the fall semester at Baylor, I got word that Mother and Daddy were planning a driving trip to New Mexico. They would visit the Carlsbad Caverns, White Sands and take a circuitous route home through Fort Sumner. They asked if I would like to go with them. Boy, was I ready! They picked me up in Brackettville, and I didn't look back as we headed north. I had had a summer to remember, but I was ready to move on.

When the 1949 fall semester started at Baylor, I was there. I was ready to face the challenges that surely lay in store, even though I had no idea what many of them might be. Plainly, I would have more to learn than how to blend in with the sports programs. The distance between Baylor and home was not very far, about thirty miles. However, that short distance took me to another world. So many things were new and different from anything I had ever experienced. I had rarely ventured outside Coryell County, and this was my first time to live away from home. I could hardly comprehend the giant step I had taken.

I had never seen the Baylor campus before Daddy drove me there and dropped me off with my suitcase in hand. While standing there looking around, I was surrounded by magnificent brick buildings and manicured grounds. It was a scene that was more beautiful than any picture I had seen in a book. Every direction revealed a unique view. Each building was different and designed as a work of art. Some buildings stood out with gold-colored steeples. All were huge and multistory. The lush and green lawns were accented with strategically placed flower beds and shrubs. Some shrubs were flowering. Walkways and roadways were lined with perfectly shaped trees. The whole area was an intricately organized display of beautiful structures and landscaping. Nothing was out of place. I never had any idea that such a place existed in Texas, let alone thirty miles from Pecan Grove.

The scene I beheld couldn't have been more different from the surroundings familiar to me in the Pecan Grove Community. There, I was used to seeing misshapen trees and shrubs being located randomly as Mother Nature had placed them. Also, in the whole Coryell Creek valley, there was not one brick building. How unbelievably different Baylor was from the Blackfoot two-room schoolhouse and school buildings in Gatesville. For several minutes, I lost track of time and all thoughts of why I was in the place I now stood. The overwhelming beauty of the Baylor campus absorbed my undivided attention. I just couldn't take in everything I was seeing in a short time.

Wayland Corgill

Finally, my thoughts came back to my present situation. While setting my suitcase down and taking in my surroundings, I hadn't moved one step since Daddy had driven off. Now, all alone in this strange place, I began to wonder, with a touch of apprehension, what I had gotten myself into and what to do next. I could almost count on one hand the number of times I had been outside of Coryell County. I knew no one at Baylor except Ray Mayfield and nothing about Baylor except what Ray had told me. I had never encountered a situation like now. Before making another move, I suddenly remembered PaPa's words: "You go down there and get a good education but be sure to take a couple of courses in common sense, and you will be better off." For some reason, that advice was comforting as I was embarking on this first giant step away from home. PaPa believed in me, and so did many others. They believed that I could make it and that sure boosted my confidence at this juncture of a new beginning. If others could fit in, surely, I could too.

If it hadn't been for Ray Mayfield, I would have had a much more difficult time at Baylor during my first days there. He had told me where I should go and what I should do upon arrival. From Ray, I knew that Kokernot Hall was the dormitory building where I would be staying. As Daddy's car faded into the distance, I picked up my suitcase and set out to find my new home.

After following directions given by a couple of people I met while walking, I located Kokernot Hall. I wondered about the name Kokernot and learned later that it was the name of a ranch family whose large ranch was in West Texas near Alpine. Kokernot Hall was the freshman athlete dormitory. It was near a larger dormitory building where all the other athletes stayed.

When I arrived at my dorm, I found that I had a roommate named Joe Elam. He was a country boy like me. Also, he seemed to be feeling out of place like I was. We were both away from home for the first time and in very unfamiliar territory. Neither of us knew what to say to each other. There was no conversation between us that first night. However, as we got to know each other, each day got better. Joe turned out to be a friendly young man, and we were compatible. During that first year at Baylor, there were numerous times when we helped each other through the ups and downs. We had so many things to learn, and it sure helped to have a friendly roommate to discuss the events of the day. Also, until we learned to think less and less about home, both of us would have an occasional tinge of homesickness, and we leaned on each other during those times. Joe was a good roommate, and he became a good friend.

My life at Baylor improved rather quickly. Settling into my new surroundings and regimen was easier than I expected. Also, I easily made friends with my teammates. They were great guys and good company. Most of the freshmen athletes were like me: new to the program and required a lot of guidance. We had to be shown the location of everything from the cafeteria to the locker room. However, in just a few short weeks, I had settled in and begun to really enjoy being at Baylor. No doubt, my association with Ray Mayfield helped with that transition. He had made a special effort to tell me so many things about Baylor and what to expect during my first days there.

I grew up a lot in my freshman year. It was a great experience that I could never have imagined while sitting on the creek bank fishing with PaPa.

The Rifleman - Cotton Davidson

Freshmen athletes had more to contend with than following coaching instructions on the football field. They also had to endure a few indoctrination practices by upper-classmen. None of it was harmful and actually added a measure of interest to the life of a freshman. At least, we knew we weren't forgotten or ignored. All athletes ate together. Standard dining hall "etiquette" included "special rules made by upperclassmen" for freshmen. Freshmen often had to be waiters for upperclassmen. One advantage of that was that freshmen quickly learned the names of upperclassmen who were routinely adversaries or teammates on the practice field.

The 1949 freshmen athletes were a talented group. Freshmen football was mostly practice, practice, practice. We played only four other university freshman teams that year. There were enough freshmen to make two teams, and we spent our time on the field going at each other. Freshmen played on a separate field from the varsity. However, once in a while, freshmen and varsity players had a skirmish to test each other. As a freshman quarterback, I really faced a challenge at those times. Claude Kincanan was also a freshman quarterback, and we had plenty of practice trying to outdo each other. Unfortunately, Claude dropped out of the program after that first year and was replaced by Billy Hooper.

As freshmen, we had two coaches: one offense and one defense. They did their best to teach us the finer points of the game. I got plenty of practice as quarterback and was encouraged to find that Baylor placed a lot of emphasis on their passing game. Currently, Baylor had three quarterbacks who excelled with passing. They were Adrian Burk, Hayden Fry, and Larry Isbell. They were outstanding athletes and led Baylor to record-winning seasons. Watching them was inspiring. They would all be gone from Baylor when the 1952 season started. When that time came, it would be great if I were the starting quarterback.

Watching the varsity team reminded me that I had much to learn to effectively lead a varsity team. I knew I had a strong arm and could throw accurately. However, there is so much more that is required for a successful passing game. Hopefully, I could learn those things from the Baylor coaches. In Gatesville high school football, little importance was placed on the passing game. Generally, the only passing that was done was on third-and-long situations. It was usually a "last-ditch" effort, and in most games, no more than a hand full of passes were thrown.

Early in my experience with high school football, I realized how important a passing game could be to winning. However, when throwing a football, minimizing the bad outcomes requires a lot of practice. Quarterbacks and receivers must work together for a long time to make it effective. Also, coaches must design game plans that support a few pass plays. Not many are needed. Having two or three good pass plays and working the "dickens" out of them can make a world of difference. I did what I could with that in high school, but I had a big problem with the practice part. I rode a school bus ten miles to school and, if I missed the bus in the afternoon, I had to walk home. I tried to never do that. Therefore, I had very little time to work with receivers at school, although I did what I could. In my senior year, I began to concentrate more on my passing game in hopes that it would help me get a scholarship. Now, I was at Baylor, the varsity was throwing the ball and, maybe, I could be ready to do the job when my chance as quarterback came. As a freshman, I was impressed by what I had seen of the Baylor coaching staff. I would do my part.

Wayland Corgill

Soon after arriving at Baylor, my schedule got so busy that I thought about home less and less. I not only played football but also joined the baseball team. Again, I have to thank Ray Mayfield for opening doors for me at Baylor and encouraging Baylor's interest in me as a baseball player. Through Ray's duties as pastor of the Pecan Grove Baptist Church, he had learned much about my community, its people, and what we did for entertainment. He knew I loved baseball and that I had been a pitcher on various teams in Coryell County. Also, he had seen me play. Ray didn't tell me what he told the baseball coaches about my pitching experience, but it got their attention. Right away, I was given a chance to demonstrate my pitching ability and, the next thing I knew, I was on the team. All that rock-throwing I did as a kid was paying off in ways that were unimaginable. Having Ray for my friend sure paid off too.

In the 1940s, baseball was a very popular pastime in Coryell County. Most communities and towns, even the small ones, had a baseball team. Nearby places like Flat, Mound, South Mountain, and Blackfoot all had a team. The Blackfoot team even competed in a big tournament in Waco one year. There was a lot of pride in a community's team, and the competition was serious. I stayed busy as a pitcher whenever I had the time, and I probably pitched for all of those teams at one time or another.

I played baseball at Baylor for four years and didn't miss a game. Luckily, I didn't have any serious injuries. During spring training, the football coaches would let me have enough time off to also train with the baseball team. I stayed busy.

One of the most rewarding baseball experiences I had didn't happen on the baseball field. It happened in the athletes' dorm when I started my sophomore year with a new roommate, Ty Newton. Ty was at Baylor on a baseball scholarship. Since we both played baseball and were roommates, we sure spent a lot of time together during my years at Baylor. I couldn't have had a better guy to spend time with. We quickly became the best of friends. We had a lot in common due to sports, but our friendship went far beyond that. Today, he is as close to me as a brother. Over the years, that extraordinary friendship has never wavered. Ty was my best man when Miss Carolyn Mabrey became my bride in 1954. Also, ten years later, we chose "Ty" as our newborn son's name. Those are just a couple of examples of how important Ty's friendship has been to Carolyn and me. Being assigned to a dorm room with Ty Newton was one of the most fortunate things that happened to me at Baylor.

Due to my busy schedule with baseball and football, I didn't get back home on weekends as often as I would have liked. I missed my family and Mother's home cooking. However, when I could get away on Friday, I would hitchhike to Pecan Grove and hike the last mile to Daddy and Mother's house. I never had a car until my senior year, so I got really good at hitchhiking. Back in those days, getting a ride from Waco going in the direction of Gatesville was not a problem. Waco was a much smaller city in 1949. There was nothing built west of where Highway 6 crossed Franklin Avenue. That point was about three miles from the Baylor campus. I would walk there if I couldn't get a ride. That is where I would stand with my thumb out for a ride toward Gatesville. I might have looked a little suspicious with my bag of dirty clothes for Mother to wash, but I always got rides. I rarely had to wait more than a few minutes.

Getting a ride back to Baylor on Sunday evenings was a bit of a problem unless I could connect with Ray Mayfield. That was usually the case. On Sundays, Ray would drive over from Baylor to Pecan Grove to conduct services at the Pecan Grove Baptist Church. Ray helped me in so many ways during my early days at Baylor.

I pitched for the Baylor 1952 NCAA National Champion Baseball Team. I am in the middle with Raymond Fitzpatrick and Chuck Deveraux on my right and Jo Mac Gresham and Milton Isenberg on my left.
- courtesy of the Davidson family

Sunday mornings were usually spent roping calves. That was my way of relaxing. Several young men in the Gatesville area were interested in calf roping and were very good at it too. The group that would get together for Sunday calf roping practice often included: my brother Hy, Jack Fry, Kenneth Fry, Jack Saunders, and two Baize brothers. Those guys were quite competitive and had numerous rodeo awards at home to vouch for their skills.

Even with my bag of dirty clothes, Mother was always so glad I could make it back. No doubt, there is a special place in heaven for mothers. She always did more than was expected of her. On Sunday evening, when I got ready to go back to Baylor, I would leave with a fresh set of clean clothes neatly folded and orderly arranged in my bag.

On those weekends when I could get home, I had a pretty good deal for rides plus good food and a fresh wardrobe for the coming week. I was the only one in my family to go to college, and perhaps, that got special treatment for me.

I didn't get back home more than a couple of times during the summer of 1950. I spent that summer in south Texas playing baseball for the LaGrange city team. One of my teammates and I were hosted by his family, who set us up with upstairs quarters in their home. It was a great summer with lots of competition, playing teams from surrounding towns. Also rewarding was the experience of getting to know the family I was staying with and learning about an area of Texas that was new to me. My world was quickly expanding from what I had known in the little Pecan Grove community. I would occasionally think of Daddy there and his routines of taking care of the ranch. I sure appreciated that he didn't insist on my helping with work during the summer months. Life was good for me. So many changes had come my way in the last few months since Daddy had dropped me off at Baylor.

I was red-shirted in my sophomore year of 1950. A couple of factors played into that decision. One factor was associated with my age. I was eighteen at the beginning of the school year. A year as a red shirt would help me mature a lot. The more significant factor was that Baylor had a couple of exceptionally talented quarterbacks ahead of me. They were Hayden Fry and Larry Isbell. With those two athletes, the quarterback position for 1950 was well covered, and I was not needed. However, Hayden would graduate in 1951 and leave Baylor's football program. Larry would follow suit in 1952. I was in line to back up Larry in 1951, and being red-shirted gave me an extra year to get ready. Hopefully, I would be the starting quarterback in 1952 and 1953.

In the late 1940s and early 1950s, Baylor had several very talented quarterbacks. Adrian Burk was one of those stand-out athletes. He was the starting quarterback in 1949. That was his last season and my first year at Baylor. In 1950, he was drafted as the second pick in the first round by the Baltimore Colts. After one year with the Colts, Adrian played for the Philadelphia Eagles for six years, where he had an award-winning performance. After retiring as a player, he went on to pursue an NFL officiating career.

Hayden Fry never secured the starting quarterback position at Baylor, but he was a very able backup to Adrian and Larry. Hayden, a native Texan, had an outstanding record as quarterback for the Odessa High School. In 1946, Hayden's high school senior year, he led Odessa to the Texas State High School championship. After graduating from Baylor in 1951, Hayden didn't go to the NFL. Instead, he started on a path that eventually took him on a long and distinguished career of coaching football. He is most noted for his coaching successes at numerous universities throughout the southwest.

After Adrian graduated in 1950, the way was cleared for either Hayden Fry or Larry Isbell to be Baylor's starting quarterback. Larry was selected for that position in both 1950 and 1951. He was an exceptional athlete. While at Baylor, he not only excelled in football but also in baseball. He received All-American honors in both sports. In 1952 he graduated from Baylor and was drafted by the Washington Redskins in the first round. However, he never played for the Redskins. Instead, he decided to give up football and go the baseball route. He signed with the Boston Red Sox. Later, after two productive minor league seasons, he gave up baseball and went back to football. He signed with the Canadian Football League, Saskatchewan Roughriders, and finished his career in sports by playing there for five seasons.

My redshirt sophomore year was a great one for advancing my knowledge and skills as a quarterback. Most of those improvements came from scout teamwork. Scout teams were made up of those players who were red-shirted and juniors and seniors who weren't going to play on the varsity team. We practiced against the varsity and specialized in executing plays that opposing teams might use in upcoming games. We analyzed films of opposing teams and spent lots of time with coaches to learn plays and execute them. A good scout team can really help a varsity team. It surely helped me too. When the 1951 football season rolled around, I was much more ready to back up Larry Isbell at the quarterback position.

The Rifleman - Cotton Davidson

In the summer of 1951, I was back at LaGrange again for more baseball. Three of my teammates and I rode a train down there, and that was another new experience. I had only seen one train and had never ridden on one. As expected, our summer playing schedule was a busy one, and I had a full slate of pitching. We had spirited games with Brenham, Weimar, and a few other city-sponsored teams in the area. We were really busy that summer. In addition to baseball, we attended another activity when time permitted. We measured cotton acreage. Little time was left for seeing a movie or visiting an ice cream parlor that summer.

As another great summer of playing baseball ended, I looked forward to making a start on the Baylor varsity team. Playing on the varsity team for the first time was a novel experience for me. Oddly enough, I had seen only one college game before I played in one.

In 1951, our Baylor Bears football team had an outstanding season. My participation was on both offense and defense. I was not only the backup quarterback but also played as a defensive back and safety in the secondary. I was also the punter. Our overall win-loss record was 8-2-1, and we were ranked #9 in the final AP poll. We beat all of our Southwest Conference rivals except for the loss to TCU and a tie with Texas A&M. Our other loss was to Georgia Tech in the Orange Bowl. Larry Isbell also had an outstanding season and was instrumental in making the Orange Bowl game one of the most exciting of all time. He was awarded All-American status. Three other players, Stanley Williams, Bill Athey, and Ken Casner, also earned All-American status.

Losses are often much more memorable than wins, and that was our experience for the 1951 season. The loss to TCU was particularly painful because it was in front of a Homecoming crowd. The Baylor stadium was filled with Baylor fans confident that their award-winning team would continue its remarkable winning streak. After all, Baylor was a two-touchdown favorite. TCU certainly had a different opinion. They came to Waco with a game plan and a determination that was a match for the Bears. TCU knew that any chance for a win required combating Baylor's exceptional passing game strength. Throughout the evening, TCU put up a stunning pass defense that saved the day for them. Interceptions and blocked passes were the chief causes for the final score of TCU 20 and Baylor 7. Baylor never slacked up or quit pressing with all their might until the final second, but it was just not to be. For many days, that game was discussed in locker rooms, coffee shops, business lunches, and other gatherings of all kinds.

On January 1, 1952, Baylor faced off against Georgia Tech in the Orange Bowl. It turned out to be a game for the record books. Sportswriters later touted it as one of the greatest games in Orange Bowl history. Georgia Tech's rambling wreck had a national ranking of number 6 while our ranking was number 9 but, for most of the game, we could feel victory. However, it was not to be. We dominated in all of the game stats throughout the evening, but penalties and interceptions at critical junctures took their toll. With the game tied at 14 and 14, Georgia Tech kicked a field goal to give them a three-point lead in the last three minutes of the game. Even so, a win was still in our grasp. We were deep in Georgia Tech territory and threatening to tie the game or make a touchdown when time ran out. The game ended with the 17 to 14 score and "wrecked" our chance to have a near-perfect season, except for the TCU shocker.

Wayland Corgill

My participation in that Orange Bowl game was as a defensive back as it had been in other games that season. I was a backup quarterback for Larry Isbell, but he led the Green and Gold for the whole game. However, the entire experience of just being there was something I could never have imagined. Life was getting to be more exciting for me by the day. The Miami metroplex and the huge stadium filled with more than 65,000 people were so different from anything familiar in my experiences. I couldn't help but think about my folks at home in the Pecan Grove community and what they might think if they were with me in this setting. They might have difficulty believing that the boy down there on the field in jersey Number 19 was really the kid they knew who used every fence post on his father's ranch as a target for throwing rocks.

For me, 1952 was another year of change and challenge. Three years prior, my world was limited to a small corner of Coryell County. Since then, I had been constantly confronted with new experiences, and there was no end in sight. However, I thoroughly enjoyed what I was doing, and my major concerns were about "measuring up" to expectations. I often thought about family and friends at home and how they never quit or gave up in the face of extreme difficulties. Their examples of success through hard work and perseverance were always a source of inspiration. Also, I frequently remembered PaPa's advice about common sense. As time went on, that bit of wisdom seemed to be more significant than when I first heard it.

As the summer of 1952 approached, I had another offer to play baseball. I was really pleased about that. This time, I would be in the south Texas town of Weimer. I would be playing for a team owned by the Weimer Herder Trucking Company. It was good to be back in familiar territory and re-connect with people I had come to know in previous years. Most of the young men on opposing teams were competitors that I had pitched against when I played for the neighboring city of LaGrange. Even LaGrange was now my competitor. Every last one of those guys I had played for or against was remarkably pleasant to be around, and we had lots of fun.

It was another outstanding summer that was capped off by a very large surprise when the season was over. Mr. Herder was an avid baseball fan and a very likable gentleman. He also had a ranch near Weimer, where I helped with ranch work whenever I had time. Mr. Herder and I were together a lot that summer, and we became good friends. My surprise was his gift of a two-year-old mare that I had ridden several times. Needless to say, his generosity caught me totally off-guard and left me almost speechless. That was the first horse I ever owned. Mr. Herder was another great addition to a growing list of fine people I had come to know in just a little over three short years since leaving home.

With summer baseball behind me, I now looked forward to starting the 1952 Baylor football season. Larry Isbell had graduated and moved on to the pros. Billy Hooper and I were now the Bears' quarterbacks. I had to win the starting position, but it was a sure thing for me after our second game. In our first game, we beat Wake Forest with a score of 17 to 14. The second game with Washington State was a rout at 31 to 7. I had a good showing in both games and held onto the starting quarterback position in both the 1952 and 1953 seasons.

The Bears' 1952 football season was not as good as the previous year. Our conference win-loss record was 1 – 3 – 2, and our overall standing was 4 – 4 – 2. We still had a strong team but had lost valuable experience of seasoned players who had graduated. However, I thought our performance was better than the win-loss record indicated. For example, our loss in a game or two was a real "squeaker" that we could have easily won if only one or two developments had gone our way. The games were that close. Although it was no consolation for us, I noted that our rival Longhorns ended their season with a worse record than ours.

For several years, Baylor coaches had had a significant interest in the passing game. In 1952, I thought our passing was very good and better than most of the teams we played. If we hadn't lost so many graduating seniors from the previous season, our won-loss record would, no doubt, have been much better. Our coaching staff was great. Each coach had very extensive experience and impressive sports records. Head coach, George Sauer, was an inspirational leader. I really appreciated the backfield coach, Jack Wilson, who worked with me and the receivers. The other coaches, including an assistant coach, "Uncle Jim" Crow; line coach, Mike Michalske; end coach, Bill Henderson; and freshman coach, Sam Boyd, were also exceptional in working together as a team to promote teamwork among the players. Teamwork wins games. As a quarterback, I understood that very well. No quarterback can consistently look good without the rest of the team doing their part. We all got along great, and football was fun.

Those coaches sure taught us a lot. Very importantly, they helped me learn how to read offenses and defenses and take advantage of developing situations on the field. That knowledge paid off so many times when the opposing team's defense made adjustments a second or two before the ball was snapped. In those cases, I would call an audible and change the play to compensate. Often, we could turn such a situation to our advantage. Many times, I could avoid a sack by a defensive back and pick up good yardage by sending an end around to the opening left by the charging back. There were so many things for the whole team to learn and execute with precision on the field. However, the coaching staff realized that it was important to keep things as simple as possible. With that approach, costly mistakes during a game were reduced. I always believed that it was enough to have three or four running plays and a couple of pass plays that were practiced until they were executed most of the time, flawlessly. We had a few more plays than that, but I think the coaching staff shared my opinion. That surely helped build our confidence and performance on the field.

Baylor's football coaching staff was exceptionally talented when I arrived in 1949 and remained that way during the years I was there. Proof of their coaching capabilities and effectiveness was demonstrated by the successes of so many outstanding Baylor players who were drafted by the NFL in the first rounds. Baylor quarterbacks stood out in that regard. I believe that Baylor's attention to the passing game played an important part in that outcome.

One of the most memorable games for me in 1952, and perhaps all of Baylor, was with Texas A&M. That was our homecoming game, and we won it. It sure felt good to make our fans happy. It was a totally different outcome than the previous year's homecoming game when TCU had put an unexpected beating on us. That embarrassment was hard to live down. Also, this year's win over Texas A&M had extra satisfaction because the previous year, we could only tie them.

Wayland Corgill

The final score of that homecoming game was Baylor 21 and Texas A&M 20. It was another "squeaker" of a game, and Baylor's winning points came in the last three minutes. For most of the game, it looked like Baylor was headed for another very disappointing homecoming evening. The fans were quiet. Tension was heavy in the air. I was the quarterback, and the gravity of the situation was not lost on me. With time running out, we were down on the Aggie 12-yard line, third down, and seven yards short of a first. It was just about "now or never" for getting a win. We had to have a touchdown. I don't remember thinking about anything else. We called a pass play. The ball was snapped, and I searched the field, but no one, absolutely no one, was open. There was a small opening along the sideline, and I knew that was my only option. I headed for that spot and broke a tackle just before crossing the goal line. The fans were no longer silent. Pandemonium, not tension, was now in the air. However, we had not won yet. We were tied with 20 points each. That condition was quickly remedied by our extremely reliable field goal kicker, Cosimo Brocato, and the game ended with our one-point lead. That sure felt good.

Members of the 1922 Baylor championship team had been honored at half-time and were in the stands. They were especially elated at the dramatic and unexpected finish of another "heart-pounding" Baylor game.

Our sensational homecoming contest with Texas A&M made sports news headlines in several Central Texas newspapers. Throughout the game, numerous unexpected outcomes and unpredictable events caught the attention of a large number of sportswriters. They were particularly complimentary of my performance as quarterback. So far this season, I had occasionally seen my name in sports columns, but I never expected that and paid no attention to it. However, after that homecoming game, the favorable comments bordered on being excessive and were difficult to ignore. I was uncomfortable with that. After all, the win was a team effort.

The homecoming win was enormously satisfying, but that was our last time to celebrate in 1952. Unfortunately, we didn't have another win during the rest of the season. Of the five games left to play, we lost three and tied two. All of those games were tough, and we had a fighting chance to win at least three of them. Notably, one of the tied games was with TCU. That tie was somewhat satisfying since it was so much better than the previous year's anguishing loss to them at our homecoming game.

Our 1952 football season ended in front of a hometown crowd on November 29 with a loss to Rice. That loss of 20 to 14 was particularly exasperating since we had the game well in hand until Rice managed to come from behind late in the fourth quarter. We sure wanted to end the season on a high note and capitalize on our last chance for a conference win. That sure would have helped our season win-loss record look better. That record ended up being markedly worse than the one for the previous year. However, we had given all we had in every game, and we took our losses hard. The season did have several "bright spots," though. One of those was having four of our players receive All-Southwest Conference honors. They were: Jerry Coody, back; Robert Knowles, tackle; Bill Athey, guard; and Jack Sisco, center.

Bill Athey and Jack Sisco were among the twelve seniors on our team that would graduate in the spring of 1953. Losing so many experienced players was a little concerning for those of us who would be on the front lines when the 1953 football season started. That would be my last year of playing for the

The Rifleman - Cotton Davidson

Green and Gold. I sure wanted it to be a good one. When practice started for the 1953 season, I resolved to do everything I could to put more games in the win column. However, at this point, the season was over, and I could look forward to another delightful summer of playing baseball somewhere.

For summer baseball in 1953, my Baylor teammates and I went west rather than south. Four or five of us, including Bobby Benge, Mike Sullivan, and Wayne Hopkins, wound up in Paducah, Texas. Paducah is way out on the West Texas plains. Amarillo is just a little bit farther west. The countryside around Paducah was as different as day and night from the LaGrange area. It was hot, dusty, dry, and thirty miles to Childress, the only sizeable city in the area.

Our living quarters were on the second floor of the Paducah Fire Department building. Those accommodations provided an extra measure of excitement. As we settled in the first night, I pulled my bunk next to an open window to try and catch whatever breeze might stir. However, there was very little breeze, the night was hot, and it was near midnight before I dozed off. My siesta didn't last long. About two or three o'clock in the morning, the siren on the outside wall under my window cut loose with a screeching sound that rattled my bed. Needless to say, for a few moments, I had a major problem with collecting my thoughts. Where was I? What was the siren all about? Was I in a life-threatening situation? Should I get out of the building? So many questions. This surely was a new experience for me. The Gatesville schools' fire drills and using the fire escape slides had, in no way, prepared me for this. When the siren quit blaring, and things settled down, I happened to think that maybe my bunk might be better in another location, breeze or no breeze.

That summer at Paducah turned out to be one of the best. We played really good teams in Childress and surrounding towns, plus Sheppard Air Force Base in Wichita Falls and Fort Sill in Oklahoma. The tournaments were well organized, and the competition was good. When we played on the Paducah diamond, baseball took on a little different look. There was not one blade of grass on the whole field. To keep dust from offending spectators and clogging noses and eyes of players, our friends from the fire department would graciously use a fire truck to wet the field before game time. The whole experience was a lot of fun, even with the challenging climate and ever-present threat of a super loud siren startling me out of bed.

As my 1953 summer baseball schedule wound down in the dusty West Texas town of Paducah, departure time approached. It soon became time to say goodbye to my friends at the fire department. Unexpectedly, that turned out to be a little bit of an emotional event. Without thinking about it, something like a kinship had developed between the folks, who had welcomed me into their lives, and me. Not knowing when I would ever return, I realized that I was going to miss those friendly people. However, immediately ahead was the serious business of preparing for a winning 1953 Baylor football season. Baylor sure needed a better record in the upcoming season, and it would be my last chance to help with that objective. It was time to get started.

I really enjoyed baseball at Baylor. Also, those summer experiences with city leagues were nothing short of pure pleasure. It was a delightful time of my life. I played with great team members and made a lot of friends. I would have been satisfied with specializing in baseball. However, the primary reason I was at Baylor was football, and I was determined to do the best I could with that.

Wayland Corgill

Our 1953 football season was so much better than the previous year. From the beginning, I just knew that we should have a very good season. I felt confident that I could do my part. Also, I had talented receivers to work with, the backfield was great, and our offensive linemen were among the best in the Southwest Conference. I could depend on every one of those guys to get every yard possible. The whole team roster was loaded with outstanding players, and the coaches had prepared them very well.

The talented coaching staff consisted of five members from the previous season and two new ones. They were all outstanding with their experience, knowledge of the game, and leadership skills. The five coaches, who had been so effective in the previous season, were Head Coach George Sauer, Backfield Coach Jack Wilson, Offense Coach Sam Boyd, Assistant Coach "Uncle Jim" Crow, and Assistant Coach Bill Henderson. The new coaches were Line Coach Jack Russell and Assistant Line Coach Bulldog Turner. It was a very strong coaching staff. Each member had remarkable credits in his resume. Coach Sauer was an All-American halfback at Nebraska and was a starting halfback for the Green Bay Packers for three seasons. Coach Wilson was an All-American halfback at Baylor and played a couple of seasons for the Los Angeles Rams. Coach Boyd was an All-American end at Baylor and played three seasons for the Pittsburgh Steelers. Coach Crow had been a Baylor student and had coached every sport on the Baylor campus for more than three decades. Everyone knew Coach Crow. Coach Henderson was actually the head coach of Baylor's basketball team, but he loved all sports, and his contributions to the football team were valuable. Coach Russell was an All-American end at Baylor and, after World War II, he played seven seasons of professional football in the All-American Football Conference, NFL, and CFL. Coach Turner was an All-American center at Hardin-Simmons University and played thirteen years for the Chicago Bears. He had just retired from the pros and was embarking on a coaching career. He had earned a very long list of awards in the pros, and more would come his way in the future, including induction into the Pro Football Hall of Fame.

Practice got off to a serious start and continued that way throughout the year. It paid off. Our Southwest Conference win-loss record was 4 – 2 – 0, and our Overall record was 7 – 3 – 0. Some of those games in the win column were so satisfying; particularly, the homecoming game with TCU.

When the season was over, I, and two of my teammates, received honors and were also invited to play in post-season All-Star games. James Ray Smith was selected as an All-American and also All-Southwest Conference player. Jerry Coody and I were selected as All-Southwest Conference players. In the East-West post-season game, I was the West team co-captain and played quarterback. Jerry Coody played halfback for the West. Jerry also played in the Hula Bowl. Our teammate, Wayne Hopkins, played as wide receiver in the North-South game.

Our 1953 performance on the field left our fans with many exciting memories. We nudged Baylor football back into sports writers' headlines and created positive conversations wherever a few people gathered. For me, it was a year loaded with rare opportunities, and I was extremely fortunate to be able to take advantage of them. Indeed, those kinds of years don't come by very often.

From the first day in practice, it was apparent that coaching had undergone a few changes. One new member of the coaching staff was particularly motivating. That was Clyde Douglas "Bulldog" Turner.

The Rifleman - Cotton Davidson

I had never heard of Bulldog, but we quickly got well acquainted. Bulldog worked with our centers. According to him, the center should deliver the ball like a bullet. I found that out the hard way when I took my first snap from a center that Bulldog had been coaching. I was standing in position with my hands out to receive a snap and, when the ball came, I never touched it. It zipped right through my open hands and gave me a resounding thump in the middle of my chest. From that moment on, I had to quickly make adjustments necessary to coordinate with Coach Turner's techniques. I suppose his methods did save a nano-second or two, and that could be important.

Bulldog was one of those rare, super accomplished, amazing individuals that a person could never forget. He began as a tough West Texas kid that excelled in high school football in Sweetwater and went on to set records at Hardin-Simmons University in Abilene. The Chicago Bears drafted him in the first round in 1940, and he played with them for thirteen years. While there, he continued his awesome performance on both sides of the line and racked up accolades of all kinds along the way. He was selected on the All-Pro first-team eight times and helped the Bears win four NFL championships. He retired from the Bears in 1952 and came to Baylor to teach us a thing or two. He was at Baylor only one year and then went on to coach a few years for the Chicago Bears and the New York Titans. After retiring from coaching, Bulldog continued to be awarded honors for his outstanding career as a player and coach. We were lucky to have him.

It was my good fortune to have been at Baylor during Bulldog's one-year coaching stint there. Our relationship lasted much longer than that year of 1953. We crossed paths over and over during our NFL careers, and, years later, we often visited each other after Bulldog bought a ranch near Gatesville. Bulldog made unforgettable impressions on people.

I was the starting quarterback again in 1953. It was a season of incredibly satisfying experiences and successes for the team and me. I still showed up at Mother and Daddy's house with my dirty clothes on weekends but, in just a few short years away from the ranch, my life had evolved into something I could never have imagined. I was so fortunate to be part of a Baylor Bears team that had jelled into a hard team to beat.

Every team we played knew they had a contest on their hands. It sure felt good to be in the winning column most of the time. We shocked the University of California with a 25 to 0 victory. It was the first time that California's Coach Waldorf had lost a season opener in more than six years. It was a very good game for me, and I hit several big passes. Our next game was on the other side of the U.S., where we beat the Miami Hurricanes with a score of 21 to 13. Arkansas succumbed to a score of 14 to 7. Vanderbilt was tromped with a score of 47 to 6. Texas A&M was edged with a score of 14 to 13. At our homecoming game, we drubbed the TCU Frogs with a particularly satisfying score of 25 to 7. SMU lost a thrilling game with a score of 27 to 21.

Until late in the season, it looked like Baylor might be able to have a "clean sweep." However, that was not to be, and we wound up with three losses for the year. Our first loss was to Texas, with a score of 21 to 20. That was followed the very next week with a loss to Houston with a score of 37 to 7. Our third loss, and last game of the season, was with Rice and a score of 45 to 20. Each one of those games was crucially important to us in our conference standing and national ranking.

Wayland Corgill

The game with Texas was a heated rivalry. That loss was particularly disappointing because it took us out of a commanding position for a shot at a Southwest Conference title. Before the game, we had a national ranking of number 3, which was better than the ranking for Texas. We had every expectation of winning. Apparently, Texas was really worried about that. Prior to the game, all of Austin was roused into a fever pitch of excitement. We had planned to go to Austin the day before the game so we would not have to hurry our preparations. That didn't happen. One of our representatives in Austin called to advise us to stay in Waco and travel down on the game day. He said that chants could be heard all over Austin saying, "Beat the pee out of number 3." Our man in Austin was worried about passions being intense enough to spawn violence if we were in town early. We took his advice.

That Texas game was a "nail-biter" all the way and gave everyone an evening to remember. The memorial stadium was jam-packed. Our one-point loss was such a big disappointment since the game could easily have gone the other way. We would have at least tied the game if we hadn't missed a point-after kick. Also, we could have easily won by a touchdown if one official's call had been different. I was directly involved in the play where the official's ruling was disastrous for Baylor.

The ruling in question happened when a Texas receiver caught a pass on our end of the field and charged for the goal line. I was on the field as a defensive back. The pass play developed on the opposite side of the field from me. However, I recognized what was happening when the football left the Texas quarterback's hand. At the same time, I immediately headed toward the intended receiver. I tackled him and knocked the ball out of his hands on the two-yard line. The ball rolled into the end zone, and I recovered it. I was feeling really good about what had happened until I was shocked by what the official said. He ruled that the Texas player had crossed the goal line before the ball was knocked loose. Wow! That was that! In those days, with no video corroboration of an official's ruling, there was nothing to do but grumble.

The reason I was on the field as a defensive back was related to a new rule in 1953 having to do with a player's time on the field. The rule required a player to "sit out" a specified number of plays every time he came off of the field. Therefore, to avoid having to do that, I played every play in the game. I was the quarterback on offense and defensive back when Texas had the ball. Playing both ways like that was just a little bit of a workout.

That one-point loss to Texas turned out to be crucial to our standings for the year. It was an extraordinarily good year in many ways, but our number 3 ranking evaporated, and we wound up un-ranked. Without the loss, we had a chance of being number 1 in the nation.

Following the loss to Texas, we had our second loss for the year when we played Houston in Waco. We were hurting. Our All-American, James Ray Smith, had missed the Texas game due to an injury, and he was still out for the Houston game. Also, during the game, I left with an injury, and so did our starting tackle, Robert Knowles. It was an agonizing loss.

Although the Houston game was non-conference, the loss knocked us out of a chance for the Southwest Conference title. However, that was not the only regrettable outcome. It was the worst defeat that the Bears had suffered in a half-dozen years.

Coach & Athlete

THE MAGAZINE FOR COACHES, PLAYERS, OFFICIALS AND FANS

NOVEMBER
1953
25¢

Volume XVI
Number 3

Campus
Close-Up:

AUSTIN
COLLEGE

Sherman, Texas

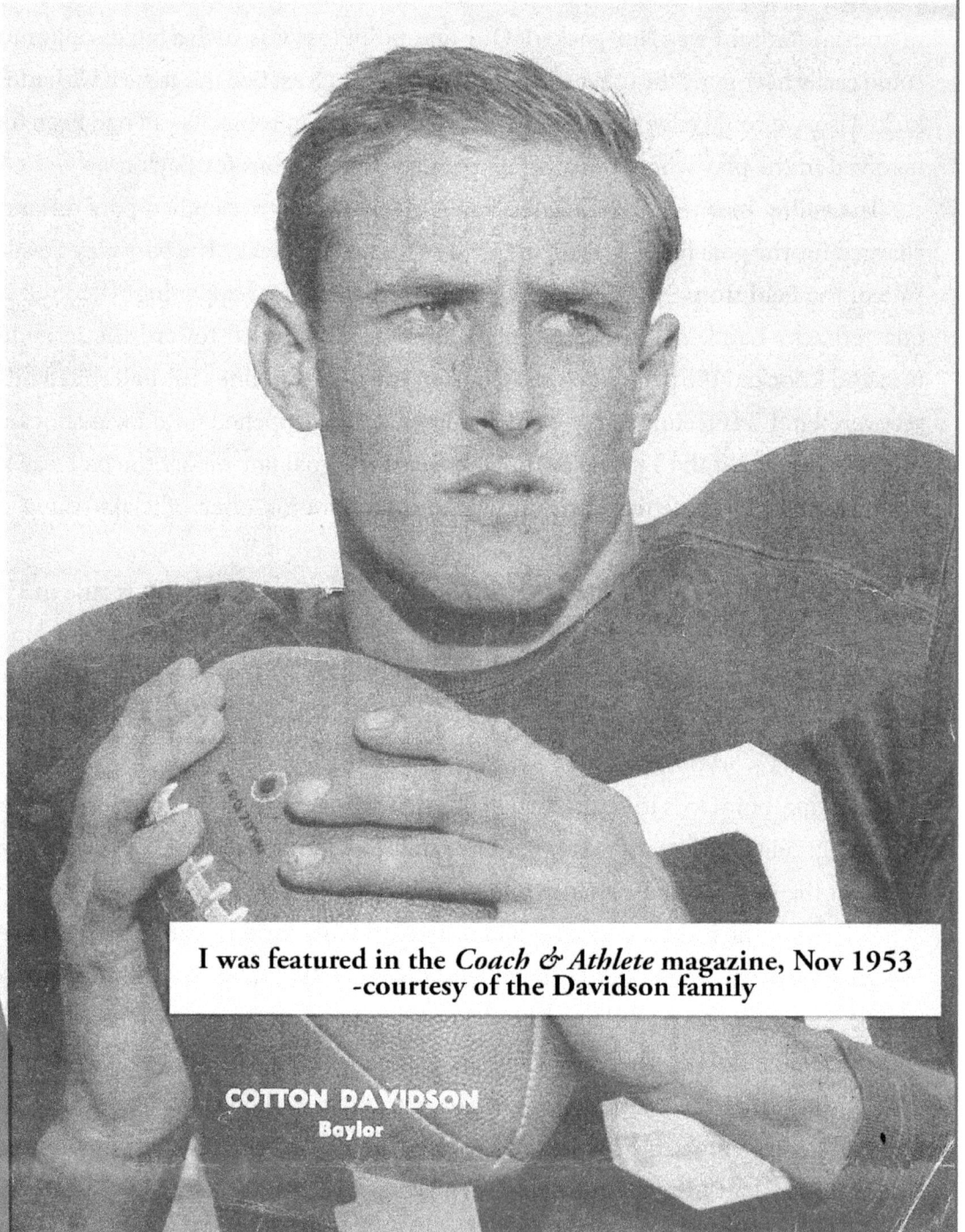

I was featured in the *Coach & Athlete* magazine, Nov 1953
-courtesy of the Davidson family

COTTON DAVIDSON
Baylor

Wayland Corgill

Our third loss for the year was to Rice. It was another distressing defeat and my last game as quarterback for Baylor. Also playing their last game were my teammates Ronnie Black, Charles Bristow, Wayne Hopkins, Dickey Murray, Jack Wentworth, Jack Reid, Robert Knowles, Bill Lucky, Pete Erben, Charles Radford, Bill Bernard, Clint Chambers, Charles Jones, Billy Sherman, Mickey Sullivan, and Jerry Coody. We had traveled many roads together, and I was surely going to miss them. Undoubtedly, the Green and Gold would miss them in the next season too.

Most of the games we won were extremely satisfying. Of those, avenging our previous homecoming loss to TCU two years ago was exceedingly sweet. That loss was never supposed to have happened. This year, it was homecoming time again, and, as it turned out, the Frogs didn't stand a chance. I was particularly gratified to have had one of my best days in the passing game.

Two of our most exciting wins in 1953 were with Texas A&M and SMU. Both games were talked about for a long time after the final play, but the SMU contest was a "barn burner." Those were two of the best, most satisfying games that I played while in college.

Our one-point edge over A&M was hard-earned by epic defensive battles and attacks through the air. As in the 1952 matchup, the outcome was highly questionable throughout the game and only decided in the final seconds. It was a fair and well-played contest by both teams. It was one of my better games as quarterback. Also, I think it was the best game I ever played as a punter. I made the best punt of my football career, and I made it at a highly crucial point in the game. With a couple of minutes left in the game and the score at 14 to 13, we had the ball close to our goal line. A&M's defense held, and we could not get a first-down. I had to punt from our end zone, and I knew it had to be a good one. If the Aggies got the ball within field goal range, that might lose the game for us. Everything worked in my favor beginning with the snap of the ball. My foot hit the ball just right. Before I even looked up, I knew I had made a good punt. Hopefully, it was long enough. As I watched the ball, I felt better with each passing second. I thought it went past the 50-yard line, and sure enough, it did. That punt was at least 60 yards. I was so glad, especially when we stopped the Aggies where the ball came down. Now, we had a chance to hold onto our one-point lead. However, we couldn't let up. The Aggies were very capable of advancing into field goal range, and there was enough time for them to do that. If we could hold them for just four more plays, we would go home with a win. Stopping them would be up to our defensive team. Those tough guys did their job, and Baylor put win #5 into the 1953 record book. So far, Baylor had not lost a game.

The Aggies were honorable in defeat and, after the game, I was surprised by the compliments I heard from those guys who had done their best to pound us into the turf all evening long. They openly praised the "fearsome foursome" as the best backfield they had faced and had extra kudos for James Ray Smith, me, and Bill Lucky. They credited Bill as the best defensive lineman they had come up against and James Ray as a virtually unstoppable tackle. Someone even said he thought I was a better all-around ballplayer than some of the quarterbacks getting top ratings by sportswriters. Needless to say, those Aggies' comments were totally unexpected. Perhaps, their favorable remarks indicated that they considered we had beaten them fair and square. From the game that day, I took away an opinion of the Aggies that fit with a banner in their dressing room defining a champion: C – condition; H – hustle; A – attitude; M – manliness; P – patience; I – intelligence; O – obedience; N – nerve; S – sacrifice.

Sportswriters dubbed the Baylor – SMU game as a climax of one of the greatest weeks Waco ever had. We were coming off of a two-game losing streak and really needed to beat SMU. They were on a winning streak and ranked number 11 in the nation. All week before game day of September 21, the whole city got involved with pep rallies, and a high level of excitement was in the air everywhere in Waco. The pressure was on and, when game time rolled around, the extraordinary, spectacular excitement in the crowd packing Baylor Stadium was clearly an indication that our fans expected a win. We had a reasonable chance for that, but we would be playing at reduced strength. There was just a "little" apprehension on our side of the field concerning injuries. Our co-captain, Robert Knowles, was out with an injury. Also, for a few days leading up to the game, I was questionable most of the week due to a minor injury. However, I was able to play. In one of the wildest and most exciting games Baylor had had in a long time, I had what was probably the best game of my college career. That 27 to 21 win was a thriller and sure felt good.

Something else that felt good was the publicity and kudos that continually sprang up for the "fearsome foursome" throughout the 1953 season. That foursome was composed of three of my teammates and me. My teammates were Jerry Coody, L.G. Dupre, and Allen Jones. That was the best overall backfield that I ever dealt with. Of course, our offensive line was great too. The term "fearsome foursome" immediately caught on with every sportswriter who penned a few lines about our games. Our expectation was that our opponents would be intimidated by such a moniker. However, I am not sure that worked in our favor as well as we hoped it would.

After all the years that have passed since that SMU game, a couple of things are still as fresh in my mind as if they happened yesterday. One is a big play perfectly executed when I hit our tight end, Charlie Smith, with a pass he took for a touchdown. It was beautiful. Charlie looked great as he made a skillful move on a defensive back and raced fifty yards to the goal line. Another memorable event was when our halfback, Jerry Coody, blocked an SMU defensive tackle, Tiny Goss. He hit him so hard that Tiny's teeth and blood went flying. Tiny was actually huge, and Jerry wasn't all that big. He only weighed 185 pounds. However, when those two collided, Tiny was on the ground and spent the rest of the game being cared for by the medical staff.

After watching Jerry Coody play for even a short time, his membership in the "fearsome foursome" was understandable. He was a tough athlete and played hard. Also, he was an extraordinarily fierce blocker. Much of his blocking was done with his helmet. That was referred to as butt blocking. Such blocking is not permitted by today's rules. Notably, Jerry's high energy collisions did have serious detrimental effects on his health later in life. While at Baylor, Jerry's contributions on the football field won several honors. He set records for rushing in 1952 and was voted the best blocking back in the Southwest Conference that year. Presently, he is also a member of the Baylor Athletic Hall of Fame.

That last year at Baylor was the highlight of all my years so far. Football had been unimaginably satisfying. By far, it was my best year on the field. I loved the team atmosphere and associating with the hard playing, talented guys that had made our 1953 season one to remember. They were competitors that I was proud to call friends. I would be leaving with a wealth of knowledge pounded into my head by the first-class coaching staff. Also, I would be leaving with priceless memories of so many things that had happened in training rooms, locker rooms, and on football fields near and far. My Baylor experiences had far exceeded all my expectations since the day that Daddy dropped me off there. While thinking about those things, I couldn't forget the sage advice and help along the way from people like PaPa, Ray Mayfield, and so many others.

The years of 1953 and 1954 were major milestone years for me, not only for football but also for one particular additional reason. On a November day in 1953, I wandered over to the Student Union building during a break between classes at midmorning. The building was packed with students, and a large group was gathered around someone who was singing. As I made my way through the crowd, I saw a gorgeous girl sitting on the lap of my friend, Bill Lucky. This girl was singing the song, "It Had to Be You," and looking at Bill like she meant it. Bill was not only my friend; he was my teammate and suitemate in the dorm for athletes, Brooks Hall. The girl was Carolyn Mabrey. I had seen her around the campus a few times but didn't know her.

I went right up to that duo and congratulated Bill on his good fortune. That started a series of events that I certainly never expected. Before Carolyn could finish her performance, Bill got up from his chair with Carolyn in his arms. He motioned for me to sit down and then deposited her in my lap. I could feel the warmth rising up my neck, and my face was surely turning red. I don't remember whether or not Carolyn finished the song or anything I might have said. I was tongue-tied.

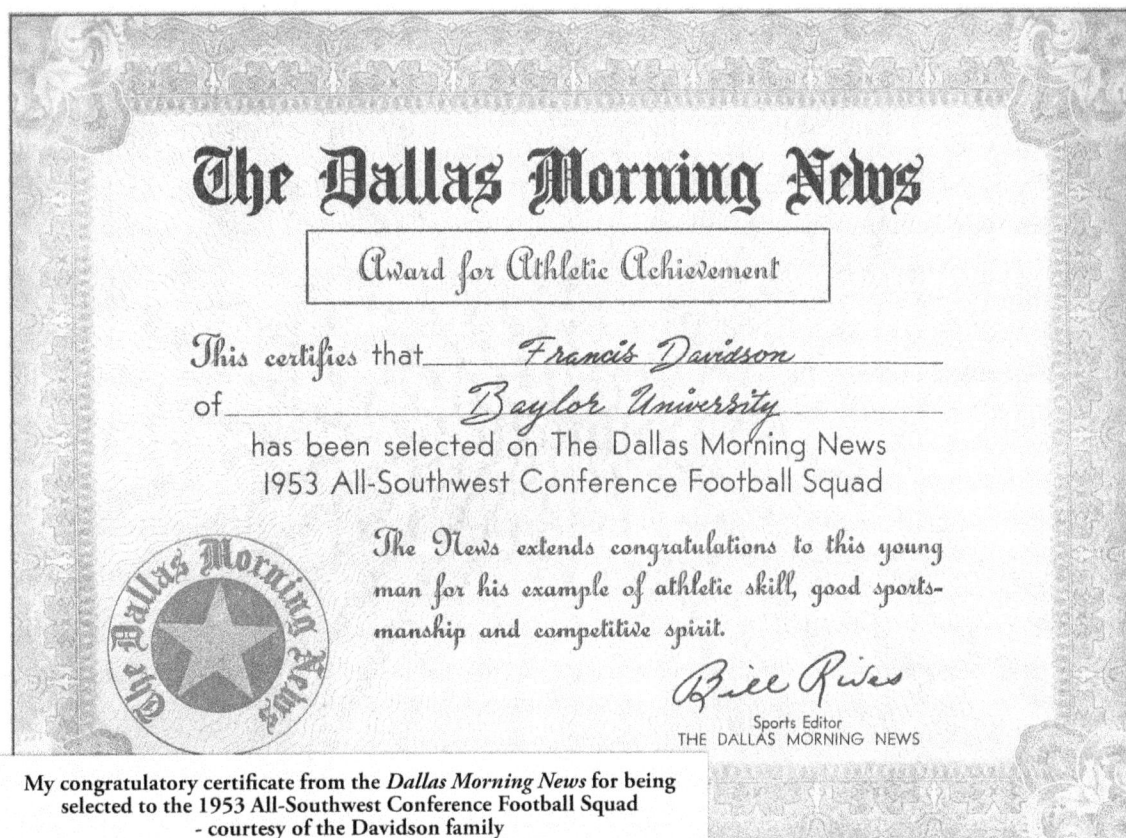

The Dallas Morning News

Award for Athletic Achievement

This certifies that ___Francis Davidson___
of ___Baylor University___
has been selected on The Dallas Morning News
1953 All-Southwest Conference Football Squad

The News extends congratulations to this young man for his example of athletic skill, good sportsmanship and competitive spirit.

Bill Rives
Sports Editor
THE DALLAS MORNING NEWS

My congratulatory certificate from the *Dallas Morning News* for being
selected to the 1953 All-Southwest Conference Football Squad
- courtesy of the Davidson family

The Rifleman - Cotton Davidson

After the "show" was over, Carolyn clued me in on what her public performance was all about. She was pledging the Pi Phi Sorority, and singing to Bill was part of the initiation proceedings. Bill was her friend and classmate. He had agreed to help her fulfill the task that had been assigned.

As the crowd melted away and Carolyn and I had a few minutes to talk, I quickly got over being tongue-tied. During that short conversation, I must have had one of my better performances because a beautiful relationship was started that day.

Carolyn and I started dating right away. We had three or four dates before Christmas when I left for the East-West Shrine game in San Francisco. After I returned in January, dating continued into the new year and, before long, we began to feel like we belonged to each other. I spent a weekend with Carolyn and her family in Breckenridge, Texas, and that went great. By March, we were engaged, and a marriage that has lasted through thick and thin, the rest of our lives, took place on June 5, 1954.

While I was in San Francisco, Carolyn and I wrote to each other often. She even sent me a Christmas package. I opened that package one morning at breakfast with my West teammates. Boy, was I surprised! While finishing my bacon and eggs, I removed the Christmas wrapping paper and gently opened the box. The only thing I saw was a note on top of a dried "cow patty" wrapped in cellophane. Stating that my interest was piqued would be a huge understatement. Also, I immediately had the undivided attention of my teammates. The note stated, "Displaying this memento from the life you love on the ranch will help to keep you from getting homesick while you are way over there in California. Merry Christmas."

It took me a while to absorb the humor and thoughtfulness of that unique gift. Also, lengthy conversations with my teammates were started. Those, who were not from a rural background, needed explanations. When I finally got around to inspecting the box contents a little closer, I found another gift: a beautiful pair of cufflinks. What else could I want?

Notably, I heard later that Carolyn's mother did not share Carolyn's enthusiasm about the unusual Christmas gift and didn't consider that the cufflinks made up for the other part of the present. That event gave me something to remember, and I thought it was great.

I didn't hang onto that cow patty very long. A nice little tree had been planted in front of the motel I was staying in. It soon had a boost in its chances for growing by application of a bit of Texas fertilizer. Surely, that is a beautiful tree by now.

The Rice game was the last one while playing for Baylor. However, I still had one game to play before I left the college scene. That was the East-West Shrine Game. Maybe I could go out with a win there. Three Baylor players had been invited to play in post-season All-Star games. Jerry Coody and I would be playing in the East-West game and Wayne Hopkins would play in the North-South game. The East-West game was played in the San Francisco Kezar Stadium on January 2, 1954. I was the quarterback and co-captain for the West team. We handily won with a score of 31 to 7. It was a really good game, and I made a good showing. That game turned out to be an extremely important one for me. At the time, I never expected that. However, when Weeb Ewbank of the Baltimore Colts came calling a few weeks later, it dawned on me that their interest had a lot to do with the East-West game.

Carolyn and I on our wedding day, June 5th, 1954
-courtesy of the Davidson family

Since leaving Daddy's ranch in 1949 and until Christmas 1953 in San Francisco, I had encountered a steady stream of new challenges and experiences along the way. Now, I was confronted with several more new ones. In the East-West game, I would be playing with coaches and teammates I had never seen before. The only person in the group that I knew was Jerry Coody. As quarterback, I knew that I needed to be a fast learner and a fast achiever to get a team of strangers functioning like they had played together for years.

TWENTY-NINTH ANNUAL SHRINE

EAST WEST

ALL STAR FOOTBALL GAME

With my #19 jersey, I was featured on the cover of the program for the 1954 East-West Shrine game
-courtesy of the Davidson family

KEZAR STADIUM • SAN FRANCISCO • SATURDAY, JANUARY 2, 1954

Our head coach was from Stanford, and he and his staff did a good job. They realized that there was only so much we could learn in four or five days of workouts. That was all the time they had to get their system installed. However, the coaches put in long hours with us, and practice on the field was just part of our training. Training sessions continued in the evenings in our motel rooms, too. Those coaches were serious about getting us prepared to win.

During our intensive training schedule, there was very little time for pleasure. Nearly every day was filled with study, practice, and more study. However, we were taken on a trip to the redwood forest one day. It was a staggering sight to see how big those trees were. The tallest tree on Daddy's ranch in Coryell County wasn't more than forty feet. We drove through miles and miles of giants that were over 200 feet tall and more than a dozen feet wide. The roadway even went through one of those trees. Needless to say, those amazing trees put my mind to wandering far away from the reason I was in California. However, back in San Francisco, the coaches quickly took care of getting us back to business.

From the beginning, it was obvious that the coaches would be working to keep the game plan as simple as possible. They stressed their objective of avoiding beating ourselves by making mistakes. Our general approach was to have repetitive series of three running plays and two pass plays. Our running plays were predominantly based on what was referred to as the Green Bay sweep. With options of the Green Bay sweep, we didn't need a dozen or more running plays. That approach was very effective for us. Our running game was very good, and our passing game was too. Keeping it simple worked.

Much of what I had to learn in those few days of practice was different from what I had been used to at Baylor. Our Baylor offense was basically a running offense. For the game I was now preparing to play, the game plan would put me on the spot for passing. I was delighted to have an opportunity to show what I could do. As the game developed, I didn't disappoint the coaches or my teammates. I had a great day throwing the ball and that had a lot to do with my being voted offense MVP for the West.

The stands were full for the East-West game. There were many California kids on both teams, and the California fans turned out. Also in the crowd were NFL scouts. A scout from the Baltimore Colts was there. I didn't know that until after the game when I was approached by scouts on a couple of occasions. I didn't know anything about the NFL or what was meant when they said they were interested in me. Except for a very few times since I left home in 1949, I had listened to a radio. We didn't have a radio in the dorm, and our radio at home was almost useless in the low-lying Coryell Creek bottom. What reception we got was loaded with static and faded in and out. The best chance for reception was from a Waco radio station, and it didn't cover professional football games. Television was unknown in our part of Texas at that time. There were no professional teams in the south. Needless to say, I was in the dark about what professional football was all about. I had no idea what part the scouts played.

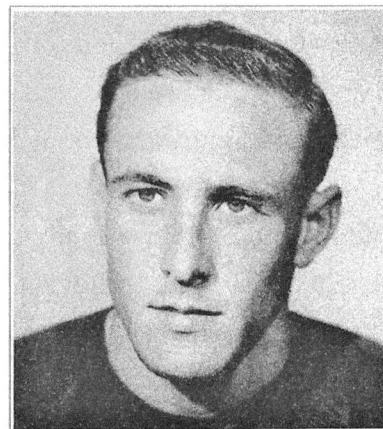

FRANCIS DAVIDSON, qb
BAYLOR. One of game's finest T formation quarterbacks, Davidson is a fine passer and punter and a magician at ball handling. Also is one of country's fine defensive backs. All pro teams have eyes on this sparkling Bear.

Information in the Program for the East-West Shrine Game- Courtesty of the Davidson Family

During the game, my concentration was totally on executing our game plan to the best of my ability. I had no thoughts about those people in the stands who were watching. I didn't even know the scouts were there. I wasn't trying to impress anybody. I was just trying to win.

Years later, after I had done some scouting myself, I thought back about that game and tried to put myself in the shoes of the Colts' scout. What did he see in my performance? I know what I would have looked for and, probably, the scout had the same objectives. How did I do with leading and coordinating with a group of players I had known for just a few days? How effectively did I adapt to a game plan that was quite different from what I was familiar with? How successful was I in reading and dealing with defense formations? How did I move on my feet? What did my passing capabilities look like? Also, in addition to evaluation of game management and ball-handling skills, what were attitudes like, both on and off the field?

After watching our workouts for four or five days and seeing the game, scouts had a very good idea about those players of interest. Unbeknownst to me, the Colts' scout must have seen something about me that he liked.

About a month after I returned to Baylor, head coach George Sauer called me to his office one day. He told me that a man from the Baltimore Colts was waiting to talk to me. He was Weeb Ewbank, the Colts head coach. After Coach Sauer introduced us, Coach Ewbank and I walked over to the Student Union building, where we sat for a while and visited. I learned that Coach Ewbank had used his first pick to select me in an NFL draft that had just been completed. He said that I was the fifth pick in the first round. Wow! I didn't even know the NFL had such a thing as a draft. He was there to talk to me about the terms and conditions of a contract, including salary. Coach Ewbank was friendly and seemed to be genuinely interested in working out an agreement that would satisfy me. However, I had a problem. I didn't even know the basics of what to expect or what to ask.

Coach Ewbank knew a lot about me and my record, but I knew nothing about him or the team he represented. My first impression was that he was a reasonable man. He told me that he had just taken the job of head coach for the Colts. The team had been struggling, and he needed to shore up the quarterback position. Due to age, his two quarterbacks were expected to retire in a couple of seasons. He said that I could really help the team, and he would do his best to work up a contract that would satisfy me. All of that sounded great, but I didn't know enough to judge whether or not an offer was good or bad.

I was in a predicament of unfamiliar territory! Coach Ewbank had me at a real disadvantage. I sure could have used advice from anybody who had even a minimal amount of experience with professional football. I hadn't even listened to a professional football game on the radio, much less seen one. I knew absolutely nothing about the organization. I didn't know what my options if any, were. I had no way to evaluate a salary offer. I sure wished that my old friend, Dan Edwards, was available to ask for advice. Dan was playing for the Colts and, since the 1953 football season was over, he was back at home in Gatesville. Unfortunately, he was out of town on a job and didn't get back until after I had already signed a contract.

Coach Ewbank left me with a contract proposal, and I promised to give it due consideration. The only person I knew, who knew anything about the NFL, was Dan Edwards. Since he was not available, I would have to make a decision on my own with my other consultants: Daddy and Mother. Of course, they were not knowledgeable of the NFL either, but it helped to be able to talk to them. PaPa's "common sense" philosophy also played a part in my deliberations. I didn't have any other offers, and what would I do if I didn't play for the Colts? The only other option readily available to me might be to help Daddy on the ranch until I could figure out what else to do. Since I might be getting married in the near future, the salary offer was very important to me. Also, I had no way to judge whether or not that was a fair offer.

When the coach with the unusual name left Baylor to return to Baltimore, he left me wondering about many things. Should I trust this man? Unquestionably, he appeared to be honest, honorable, and concerned about telling me things he thought I should know. What was he not telling me? He struck me as being a good man. Maybe, I could trust him to do the best he could for me. His calm demeanor and pleasing personality were very similar to those characteristics of the people in Pecan Grove that I had grown up with and respected. However, what kind of a person would have a name like Weeb? I had never heard of a name like that. I wondered what country it came from. It didn't sound like an American name. Maybe he got that name in unusual circumstances like I got the name of Cotton. My puzzling over the strange name was only a fleeting thought that didn't come up again for a long time. From our first meeting, I always called him Coach; never, Weeb. However, many years later, by chance, I learned where the name came from, and it was a surprising, interesting story. I wondered why I had not asked about it earlier. Weeb's given name was Wilbur Charles. His younger brother's pronunciation of Wilbur sounded like Weeb, and that became a nickname that stuck with him for life.

CONGRATULATIONS
FROM BAYLOR ATHLETICS

COTTON
DAVIDSON

2015 SOUTHWEST CONFERENCE HALL OF FAME INDUCTEE

I was inducted into the Southwest Conference Hall of Fame in 2015 following
induction into the Baylor Hall of Fame in 1982
-courtesy of the Davidson family

The Rifleman - Cotton Davidson

After a couple of weeks, I decided to accept Weeb's offer and take my chances with the Colts. I signed the contract assuming that I was being treated fairly and in line with other players. If those players could make it, surely, I could too. As it turned out, the salary was just enough to get by on, with very few extras. Perhaps, that was the best the Colts could do. I had no way of knowing. No doubt, Dan Edwards could have helped me with that. As one might expect, pro football players' salaries in 1954 were nowhere near those of more modern times.

Soon after I graduated from Baylor, Carolyn and I were married and headed north. Things began moving fast for a Coryell County boy who had rarely been out of Texas. Going to the pros was another milestone leading to a career full of unexpected opportunities taking me to places I could never have imagined. It would be a long time before I got back to familiar territory around Gatesville.

Baltimore Colts

In June of 1954, Dan Edwards, Bulldog Turner, and I headed north for the startup of football training camps. The three of us rode together in my car. Dan and I were going to the Colts in Baltimore. Bulldog was bound for the Chicago Bears, where he had taken an assistant coaching position. Our route went through Indiana, where Bulldog left us to take a bus to Chicago, and Dan and I turned east toward Baltimore. Carolyn and Dan's wife, Joyce, drove up later in her car. They pulled a one-wheeled trailer packed with belongings needed to support two families through the rest of the year.

That trip with Dan and Bulldog was a great experience. Riding with those guys was interesting and educational for me. Of course, football was the main topic of discussion. Since I had never even listened to a professional football game on the radio, I was eager to learn everything I could from my companions. Both Dan and Bulldog were a wealth of information. Importantly for me, both of them knew something about the Colts' new head coach, Weeb Ewbank. They told me he had a reputation of being a very good coach, a fair man, and they thought he was very much in favor of developing the Colts passing game. That sure sounded good to me. I felt like I knew what I had to do to fit into that program. Throughout the trip, Bulldog added an extra measure of interest to our discussions with his dry humor, and we had a lot of laughs. It was such a pleasant trip and one I often reminisced with Bulldog many years later when both of us resettled in Coryell County.

We were also amused by a few highly unusual sights along the way. The most bizarre sights were encountered in Indiana. We passed by several areas with large crowds of people gathered in roadside parks. Those people looked like they had brought everything they needed to camp there for a long time. As we motored by, they would wave and cheer in a friendly manner. We wondered what in the world was happening. Something was going on that was definitely out of the ordinary. Maybe they thought we were fellow participants in whatever they were involved in. If so, maybe our Texas license plates prompted their enthusiastic welcome of partners from down south. We would certainly try to find out about those strange, large gatherings at the first opportunity.

After arriving in Baltimore, we found out why those throngs of campers were gathered. A Chicago woman had predicted that the world would be coming to an end later in the year. She claimed to have direct knowledge that the Supreme Being was going to "clean up" a world that had gone off of the "straight and narrow." Her prediction was that all existing landmasses were going to sink and, eventually, new ones would rise from sea depths. A few influential people believed her enough to effectively spread the word through social media. The desired results were achieved. Astonishing numbers of people became believers and followers. Perhaps, those groups were looking for higher ground. Maybe, they hoped to hang on to their precarious positions long enough for new ground to poke up through the waves.

Training camp began the very next day after our long drive up from Texas. The camp was located in a town near Baltimore. We were quartered in dormitories at a small college, and we worked out on its football field. Coach Ewbank and his staff were there and ready to get started.

Weeb was a good, solid, hands-on coach. I had a lot of respect for him. He had spent time under other good coaches and was exceptional by effectively applying his broad experience. Also, he was very competent with organizing and managing a talented coaching staff. There was no question about his knowledge of the game and ability to get consistent results. In addition, he was a gentleman and treated the team members with respect.

I had learned a lot about the passing game at Baylor, but I learned a lot more from Coach Ewbank. If you don't have a good passing game, you will get whipped. The passing game consists of so much more than just throwing the ball. A quarterback needs to be aware of everything happening on the field and know how to appropriately react in fast-changing situations. Also, to make pass plays work, the whole team had to be "clued in" on what to do. That took a lot of practice and close coordination with coaches.

Coach Ewbank and I worked together well. He was always calm, collected, reasonable, and willing to listen to me even when I didn't agree with him. If I could convince him of my assessment of a situation, he would change his. He gave me the plays, but I always had the option to change them. Both of us had the same objective, and that was to win. Generally, we were always "on the same page" with our approach to the passing game. He was satisfied with my performance and rarely had suggestions or instructions for fundamental changes in that regard. I kept on doing things the way I knew how and, generally, Weeb was satisfied with that. In fact, the only thing I remember Coach Ewbank telling me to do differently was to not throw the ball so hard. However, I didn't stop doing that, and he never mentioned it again. The main reason I didn't stop was that Raymond Berry, our star receiver, heard the conversation and later told me to throw the ball the way I wanted to, and he would catch it the way he wanted to.

Many years later, thinking back to that time in 1954, I wondered how things might have turned out for me and the Colts if the U.S. Army hadn't come into my life early in 1955. I only had one year with the Colts. Interestingly, that turn of events had not only far-reaching effects on me but also had major impacts on the career of at least one more quarterback. It gave a young man named Johnny Unitas a chance to show what he could do in the pros as the Colts quarterback, and he excelled. What would the future have held for both me and Johnny if I had not been drafted into the Army? Considering that eventuality leads to interesting speculation. In 1955, Johnny had been drafted by the Pittsburgh Steelers but didn't make the cut and was released before the season started. In 1956, I was still in the Army when Johnny walked on at a Colts' tryout and was picked up. The rest is history, but would my presence have made any difference in his getting that chance with the Colts? However, even if it would have, I am confident that Johnny would have found another team to lead to spectacular heights just like he did with the Colts.

Wayland Corgill

Training camp got off to a good start for me. Coach Ewbank was helpful from the first day, and I really appreciated having Dan Edwards on the team in those early days. I can't say enough about how valuable his friendship was. He had explained many things to me during our trip and was particularly helpful after we arrived at camp. Without his companionship, I wouldn't have had a clue about what to expect when I got there. I learned so many things from him. However, one of the most significant things he did for me was to introduce me to the players. Since he had played for the Colts the year before, he knew all of them very well. Getting to know my team members as quickly as possible was hugely important to me. On the field, Dan's support continued. He was a tight end, and he and I worked out together. Knowing Dan was one of the best pieces of good fortune for me.

Dan was five years older than me and was almost like a father figure. He had been playing football ever since he had graduated from Gatesville High School. He played college football at Georgia. He was drafted by the Pittsburg Steelers in the first round of the 1948 NFL draft. He played for the All-American Football Conference (AAFC), Brooklyn Dodgers and Chicago Hornets, and the NFL's New York Giants and Dallas Texans. The Texans folded after the 1952 season, and Dan joined the Colts. He had played for the Colts one season before that day in 1954 when Bulldog and I rode up north with him to begin the football season.

Training camp started in June, at least a couple of weeks before the exhibition game season started. From the first day in training camp until the start of the regular season, two-a-day workouts continued on a daily basis. The exhibition game season started in early July and continued on a weekly basis until the regular season started.

From my first day with the Colts in 1954, so many things were new to me. It was a year of new things for the one-year-old Colts organization too. A couple of the more significant firsts were Coach Ewbank's first year and the first year for a Colts' cheerleading team. They made history by being the first cheerleaders in the NFL. However, I don't remember ever seeing them. Perhaps they performed during the games, but my attention must have been entirely focused on football.

In early August, my training in Baltimore was interrupted for a few days. However, training would continue in Chicago, where I went to participate in the 1954 College All-Star Football Classic game. I would be training with a team of star college players who would play the NFL champions, Detroit Lions, on August 13 in Soldier Field.

It was quite an honor for me to have been selected to play in the All-Star Classic. Before I graduated from Baylor, I knew I had been chosen for that. I don't remember who relayed the information to me, but I wasn't told very much about the event. Only after I arrived in Chicago, I learned details of what the All-Star game was all about. The game was started back in the 1930s as a promotion of the Chicago Tribune. The competition would pit a team of star college seniors against the reigning NFL champion team. The original intent for the game was to benefit Chicago-area charities. Surely, the game did a very good job of making money because over 93,000 people attended this 1954 contest.

I had more than a little bit of concern about what kind of a "fix" a bunch of college kids would be in when facing professional champions. My apprehension grew considerably after I got a good look at the Detroit players. One of my coaches in Baltimore kept telling me that he was certain the college boys would "kick the stuffing" out of those Detroit guys. No problem. After my first look at those "Detroit guys" on the field, I knew we had a problem. They looked like they could eat us alive. They were a tough-looking bunch.

Sid Gillman was the head coach for our college team, and his assistant was Al Davis. At the time, I had no thoughts about much of anything except to learn the offense system they were working to install. However, the consequences of those few days affected my future football career more than I could have imagined. We got to know each other pretty well during that intensive, short training time. Al Davis concentrated on quarterbacks. His knowledge of the game and his techniques for designing and implementing effective plays was very impressive. He and I got along very well. We agreed on virtually every element of his approach to pull together a group of college boys from different parts of the country. Years later, I had several opportunities to reflect on how beneficial the experience with those two coaches was. The connection with Al Davis played a particularly large role in the later years of my pro football career.

Even though preparing for the All-Star game was a lot of work, and we were handily beaten, I really enjoyed being there and getting to know my teammates and coaches. I played about a quarter and did okay. However, we were no match for those Lions and were probably lucky the score wasn't worse than 31 to 6.

Carolyn came up from Texas and sat in choice seats on the fifty-yard line with other team family members. No doubt, the game was more exciting for her than it was for the college boys getting mauled by seasoned opponents. It was a memorable event for her. However, the excitement didn't end with the final play of the game. A different type of confrontation was in store before the evening was over.

After my teammates and I exited the locker room, all cleaned up and with scrapes and bruises treated, we boarded a bus with our family members and headed to our hotel. The bus was reserved for us, but there happened to be one man in the crowd who ignored that. He elbowed his way onto the bus. No one paid attention to him at that time. However, a few minutes after the bus got underway, everybody started paying attention. Perhaps the game had not suited him. Perhaps he bet on the wrong outcome. Perhaps someone stepped on his foot. For some reason, he started sounding off in an extremely loud and vulgar tirade that was hardly understandable. He was a very unhappy drunk. He wouldn't stop.

After a couple of minutes of listening to that wild man, I became an unhappy passenger who was still recovering from a pounding by a bunch of Lions. I made my way to the loudmouth, grabbed him by the collar, and hauled him to the front of the bus. The driver stopped, as I asked, and I gently helped the drunk off of the bus. That incident ended our excitement in Chicago. It also gave Carolyn another story to tell her friends in Breckenridge.

I was on a tight schedule in Chicago. The next morning after the game, I was headed for Hershey, Pennsylvania, and Carolyn flew back to Texas. The Colts President and General Manager Don Kellett had flown from Baltimore to attend the All-Star game. He and I flew together to Hershey. The Colts team was already in Hershey and preparing for an exhibition game with the Eagles that day. I suited up for that game too. I didn't play as a quarterback. I was a punter. Beginning in high school, I always got plenty of punting opportunities throughout my football career.

From that first time I played the Eagles, I always looked forward to a return trip. All those varieties of chocolate in nearby Hershey were like a magnet.

Coach Ewbank's first year, 1954, at Baltimore was not his best, by far. He ended the season with a 3-9 record. However, he was very effective by turning things around. Weeb was respected as an exceptional coach and teacher. He was one of three of the best coaches in the pros that I was fortunate to play for during my career. His expertise began to pay off the next year, which was much better with a 5-6-1 record. Unfortunately, I wasn't there to celebrate. I was in the Army.

Conversely, 1954 was a good year for me, even though I didn't get much playing time as quarterback until well into the season. When I arrived in Baltimore, there were two quarterbacks on the Colts roster, Gary Kerkorian and Fred Enke. Gary was the starter. Both men were not expected to stay with the Colts over a couple more years. Possibilities for my future with the Colts looked very bright. I just needed enough playing time to prove myself and stay free of injuries.

As the season progressed, my time on the field increased. Toward the end of the season, I was getting plenty of playing time as quarterback. I played in the last three games of the season. Two of them were particularly important for me. Both games were wins, and I did well. Those games gave me the boosts I needed for a serious start of a career in professional football. One game was with the San Francisco 49ers and the other with the Los Angeles Rams. The games were played on consecutive weekends, and we stayed in California during the week. My passing game made a difference in both contests. The 49ers game was a great one for me. By the time we played them, we had won only one game, and it looked like another would be in the loss column. However, near the end of the game, I hit Dan Edwards with five or six passes in a row to make a touchdown, and, soon thereafter, we kicked a field goal to win with a score of 17 to 14. That win was enormous for me. It was our second win for the season and the first win after a string of seven losses. I was accused of being partial to Dan, but I think everybody was so happy with the win that, even if true, they approved.

The next game was with the Rams and was another big game for me. It was a "nail-biter." We won by one point, 22-21. We got the ball with two minutes left in the game and 80 yards to go for a touchdown. We were down by two points, and we had to, at least, make a field goal. I completed seven consecutive passes to get us within field goal range. With 12 seconds left, our kicker put the ball through the uprights, and celebrations began. I was elated.

Our last game of the season was with the 49ers. I was the quarterback. We didn't win that one but at least we came close to tying it. We were down by a score of 10 to 7 late in the game when we got the ball on our 25-yard line. With time running out, we advanced to within field goal range. The kick failed, and our season ended with a loss. However, it was another exciting game that could have easily gone our way.

Those last three games of the 1954 season were an intensive challenge for me to find out how I might do in the pros. Even though we only won two, I sure felt good about being able to make a significant contribution.

Almost on a daily basis, my first season in the NFL was another learning experience. I had had a constant string of those since graduating from Gatesville High School. Early in the season, I got a few important lessons from a game with the Chicago Bears in Wrigley Field. The rainy weather in Chicago was terrible that day. We had occasional heavy downpours throughout the game. Our dugout caught a couple of feet of water from a roof drainpipe, and we had to find a place in the stands that would shelter us from being drenched. Also, uneven places in the field had standing water deep enough to float a football. The weather didn't hold up the game, though, and I learned a few things about handling a slippery ball. I was certainly not used to playing in those miserable conditions. However, the Bears must have been accustomed to heavy rain and a saturated field because they beat us 28–9.

When I was sent into the game as quarterback for that soggy contest, I also learned a bit of a self-preservation technique from my halfback, Buddy Young. It was my first time to face the Bears. I knew very little about their team members. I certainly didn't know anything about their right-defensive-end, Ed Sprinkle. He was the subject of Buddy's advice. Buddy said, "Don't let that end get behind you. Don't stand around and watch the ball after you throw it. Get out of there. If he can, he will bulldoze you into the sod, even after you get rid of the ball." I took Buddy's advice to heart and stayed alive during that game. His advice came in handy for many future games, too.

When the Colts' 1954 football season ended, Carolyn and I headed back to familiar territory in Texas. Her parents lived in Breckenridge. We rented an apartment there, and I took a job to tide us over until football started again in 1955. Life was good, and under control, we thought. However, there were changes headed our way that we had not considered. A letter from the U.S. Government arrived one day. I opened it up and immediately wished that the postman had lost it. The letter said that Uncle Sam needed me in the Army.

Since leaving Coryell County, my life had been an endless string of new experiences and, surely, another one was in store. I wondered what PaPa would have to say about that. Hopefully, this turn of events wouldn't be too difficult to handle.

Army Sports

When Uncle Sam's letter found me in Breckenridge, Texas, on that fateful day in 1955, it gave me a short notice to pack my bag and show up in California for processing into his Army. Naturally, I complied. After completing the processing formalities, I reported to Fort Carson, Colorado, for eight weeks of basic training. My next stop was Fort Bliss in El Paso, Texas, where I was scheduled for eight more weeks of basic training. I got very familiar with Fort Bliss since it turned out to be my home for the next two years.

Needless to say, that two-year sabbatical at Uncle Sam's expense was costly for me too. It cost me in several ways. One way was with money, but the largest impact was on my career in professional football. After one year with the Colts, I was confident that I had a very good chance of being their starting quarterback in the next season. After a two-year absence, that might be highly questionable.

My salary with the Colts was nothing to brag about, but Uncle Sam's stipend was really slim. My starting salary at Fort Bliss was $100 per month. I could get by on that as long as I stayed in the barracks on base. However, when Carolyn joined me, things really got tight. For privates, there was no family status housing on base and no allowances for living off base. The only way we got by was for Carolyn to take a job so we could rent an apartment off base.

My career was turned upside down. With the Colts in 1954, I had a clear shot at being their starting quarterback for several years, provided that I avoided serious injuries. Reportedly, both of the Colts' quarterbacks planned to leave in a relatively short time, perhaps in a couple of years or less. Weeb Ewbank had a big problem with his quarterback position for the 1955 season, with me in the service and out of the picture. That year, he drafted George Shaw, and in 1956, Weeb picked up Johnny Unitas, who was playing for a semi-pro team in his spare time. Johnny's initial performance with the Colts in 1956 was unimpressive but, by the end of that season, he had everybody's attention with his passing skills and mastery of the game. Also, the 1957 season was very much better for Johnny. It was a record-setting year, and he was voted the NFL's most valuable player. With Johnny on board, Weeb had solved his quarterback deficiency problem.

When I was inducted into the service, I was unsure how the next two years would affect my career. When I got back to the Colts in 1957, I knew my prospects of being their starting quarterback were not only questionable but virtually impossible. As it turned out, those two years in the Army couldn't have come at a worse time. A car wreck wouldn't have hurt me more.

The Fort Bliss baseball team had outstanding talent.
Sharing in the pitching game was a great pleasure.
– US Army photo

Wayland Corgill

Before I received Uncle Sam's greetings, I hadn't seriously considered the possibility of being drafted into military service. That proved to be a mistaken notion. For a couple of reasons, I thought I had a good chance of being exempt. One reason was related to my physical condition, and the other was based on my service in the National Guard.

From birth, I have, what my family called, a hole in my chest. It is not really a hole, but a deep depression where my sternum had buckled back. I had no idea how serious that might be, if serious at all. I never detected that it had any effect on my physical ability. However, doctors always took consequential note of it when I had a physical. I thought that imperfection might disqualify me. That was on my mind when I reported to the draft board in Gatesville with draft notice in hand. The doctor administering my physical examination took note of my chest deformity but was noncommittal about what he thought. Whatever his ruling was, it stayed with the draft board agent in charge. He made the final decision. He emphatically said, "If you can play in the NFL, you can make it in the Army."

While at Baylor, I joined the National Guard. Several of my friends did that too. We thought that service in the Guard might help avoid being drafted into the military. Of course, that didn't work. However, being in the Guard for three years did have other advantages. I was designated as a truck driver. To me, that assignment seemed a little bit odd since I had never owned a car and had no experience with truck driving. However, I learned how to drive a truck and had a few interesting experiences in the process.

One day, while returning to base at Fort Polk, Louisiana, I was leading a caravan of "duce-and-a-half" trucks when I topped a hill and saw a large herd of cattle in the valley below. At that moment, I happened to remember something I had heard that might give those cows a startle. That should be fun. As I headed down the steep grade, I turned the ignition off, left the truck in gear, and coasted. My speed picked up all the way to the bottom. When I reached the cattle herd, I turned the ignition on, and the audible response I got from the engine exhaust was many times louder than what I expected. It was huge! I was startled. The instantaneous backfire sounded like a bomb. Cows wildly raced in every direction with their tails up. The blast affected me too. I couldn't hear a thing after the reverberations died away. I thought I had burst my eardrums. After a few minutes, my hearing began to slowly return well enough to be aware of another unexpected noise. The muffler was split and almost blown apart. Now I had to listen to the rumbling roar of the truck engine the rest of the way back to base.

I just knew that I would be in big trouble with the Guard motor pool folks, but, to my surprise, that didn't happen. However, I guess the Army evened things up a couple of years later when they had Uncle Sam's letter delivered to me.

Shortly after arriving at Fort Bliss, I was doing calisthenics one day when I was approached by an officer in an impressive jacket decorated with stars and medals. My first thought was that whatever kind of trouble I was in must be pretty serious. I was thoroughly surprised when he asked me if I would be interested in playing baseball for the Fort Bliss Falcons. Boy, was I relieved! I must have jumped three feet in the air and couldn't say "Yes, Sir" fast enough. It was my great good fortune that this colonel had reviewed my papers and learned about my record in sports.

The Rifleman - Cotton Davidson

Baseball season was just getting started, and my schedule was adjusted so I could participate. In three or four days, I was playing baseball. Workouts were in the mornings and, when not on the baseball field, I managed gym workout cages. Things were looking up for me. I had been in the Army only a few days over eight weeks, and there was a good chance that might be all the time I would spend as a typical soldier.

In those early days at Fort Bliss, I had no way of guessing what might be in store for me in the next two years. Before I was inducted, I had no knowledge of what Army life would be like. Afterward, every day was a new experience for a while. Also, how the sports program would work was another large unknown. However, throughout the next two years, I was gratified to experience so many positive and satisfying opportunities presented to me. Baseball and football had everything to do with that. Successes on the field with my teammates sure brightened up our lives.

Without sports, military life would have been difficult for me. My teammates were great guys and a pleasure to play with. They were tough competitors, too. The military draft had acquired a large portion of the best baseball and football talent in the U.S. Most of them had extensive experience. Many of them had made impressive records and had received prestigious awards. Probably, eighty percent of them had four years of college ball. A few of them had played for one or two years on professional teams, like me. Playing with such high-quality teammates made our time in sports so much fun. I was exceedingly fortunate, and I kept thinking that somebody might catch up with me and put an end to that.

I can't overemphasize the extraordinary professionalism and talent of teams we faced in both baseball and football. Team rosters of the Army, Navy, Air Force and Marines, included surprisingly large numbers of players who were "top of the line." Every team had players like that. They came from colleges, the NFL, and the major leagues. Our Fort Bliss baseball and football teams routinely competed against the best athletes in the country. They included All-Americans, Heisman Trophy winners, MVPs, and All-Star honorees of all kinds. Associating with them was a privilege and an honor. They distinguished themselves not only on military sports fields but also later in life. After military service, most of those individuals continued in sports and had successful careers. Many of them became famous by setting remarkable sports records and making other exceptional achievements in the sports world. I played with, against, and crossed paths with so many of those people who continually made headlines for many years after Uncle Sam let us go.

Quality of life continued to improve for me throughout my early days at Fort Bliss. After I had been there a few weeks, Carolyn arrived, and we moved into a small apartment just across the road from the base and in the shadow of Franklin Mountain. She got a teaching job at a school a few blocks from our apartment. We settled into a pleasant routine of daily activities. I had sports to look forward to, and Carolyn was "entertained" by her school children. Also, both of us looked forward to her paydays. She made $300 per month, and that made it possible for us to afford our small apartment. Her salary was three times mine. That arrangement continued for about a year until our first child was born. Naturally, after Tommy came along, Carolyn's routine had a big change, but mine not so much. Also, we needed more room and moved to a small house in a nice neighborhood several miles from the base. Our expenses were up. We sure missed Carolyn's $300 per month, but I got a whopping $30 per month raise. With my raise and the savings from Carolyn's teaching stint, we were able to get by. Our new abode had an extra benefit for me. A dairy farm with 50 to 75 cows was right across the road. I sure liked seeing those animals every morning and evening. Living in El Paso continued to be pleasant and manageable for the rest of our time at Fort Bliss.

I had two great years of playing baseball and football for the Army. However, immediately after getting into the sports program, I was really bothered by the fact that I was having an easier time in the service than those soldiers with rigid daily routines. That thought plagued me for a while until I began to hear words of encouragement from lots of guys on the base. Many of those men had played some kind of sports at one time or another and had a big interest. After I had helped to win a few exciting games, I was often congratulated for providing much-appreciated entertainment. That sure made me feel better about what I was doing. Even though it was not readily apparent to me, perhaps, I was doing something worthwhile for my fellow servicemen.

Except for sports, entertainment on base was rather limited. Card and domino games were the most prevalent activities. However, we could stand only so much of that before getting bored. Whenever Carolyn and I felt the urge for something radically different, we would slip over to Juarez on Sunday evenings and watch bullfights. That was not Carolyn's favorite sport by any means but, she would reluctantly go with me. I always rooted for the bulls.

Jack Sanford was a star on our baseball team. He and I did the pitching. Jack was an exceptionally good pitcher. He could beat anybody. Similar to my circumstance, Jack played major league baseball for the Philadelphia Phillies when he was drafted into the Army. After his two-year enlistment was up, he went back to the Phillies in late 1956. For the next ten years, Jack had an outstanding record with major league teams. However, 1957 was his banner year. He was honored as the National League Rookie of the Year, as well as the National League strikeout leader. Also, he was selected for the All-Star team.

Jack was a very good friend. Carolyn and I spent many pleasant evenings with Jack and his wife, Pat, and we traveled to games together. I learned a lot from him. He was a master with all types of pitches. He was very good with sliders, and he tried to teach me that technique. However, I just couldn't get it down. Maybe, when I was a kid chunking rocks at squirrels, I should have worked on that.

Jack was an even-tempered guy most of the time. However, he did not tolerate being taken advantage of or being mistreated. Anyone, who rubbed Jack the wrong way, was quickly and effectively made aware that doing so was a mistake. Sometimes, the resulting confrontation was physical. I witnessed a demonstration of that one day when I happened upon Jack and our coach having a spirited consultation. Jack got fed up with rooming accommodations that our coach insisted on when we were on the road. Our coach was a fellow soldier and was not particularly well-liked by the team. His mannerism was abrasive and unsociable. Also, he apparently felt obligated to save money for the Army. Four of us slept in one room with two beds. Two grown men in one regular size bed was not a popular arrangement, to say the least.

One day, as we were preparing to board our bus back to Fort Bliss, I walked around the front of the bus and found that Jack had pinned the coach against the side of the bus. Obviously, Jack was very agitated about something. I didn't hear all of the conversations, but the "four-to-a-room" issue was definitely part of it. My first thought was that a court marshal sure was likely to be in store for Jack. This looked like a serious offense!

For several days back at Fort Bliss, I checked on Jack every day. Losing him would have been a serious blow to our team. Fortunately, nothing ever came of that "set-to" between Jack and the coach, and I sure was relieved. The only evidence that anything had happened was, we never slept four to a room again.

As a team, Jack sure was a good man to have on our side. We appreciated him, not only for his pitching skills but also for his attitude towards functioning as a cohesive unit where members looked out for each other. Another example of that happened when an opposing team's pitcher hit one of our batters. It might have been no more than a wild pitch, but Jack didn't think so. To him, the pitch looked intentional. Jack was on the mound when that pitcher came up to bat. We were not surprised when Jack's first pitch was a fastball that nailed that guy. In a rage, he threw off his batter's helmet and charged the mound. That was a mistake. Jack was not only an excellent pitcher; he was exceptionally capable of defending himself. His antagonist was on the ground before the guy knew what happened.

Our Fort Bliss Falcons team was outstanding. We had great talent. We could, just about, beat anybody. Both years of 1955 and 1956 were very good ones for us. Also, they were a lot better after we quit sleeping four to a room.

Jack and I helped win more than our share of games. However, one of my earlier pitching efforts wound up with a loss that was hard to forget. We were playing the Brooks Army Medical Center team in a tournament near San Antonio. Those guys were very good. They had several players who had played major league ball. Even so, we were in the lead, one to nothing, for the first half of the game. I was pitching, and the game really seemed to be going our way. I had only one more out to get when things began to unravel. The next three batters hit home runs. Unbelievable! After the third ball went over the fence, I took my time to settle down. As I was rearranging dirt on the mound with my foot and thinking about my next pitch, the third baseman trotted over and said, "Don't worry Cotton. You've got 'em right where you want 'em. That last ball barely cleared the fence." I could have clobbered him. We didn't recover from that trio of homers and lost the game. Perhaps, if I had learned to pitch sliders, there might not have been so many balls over the fence.

The memory of those three homers stayed sharply with me for a long time. Also, I never forgot the faces and names of the three batters who did that deed. When I was discharged from the Army and returned to the Colts in 1957, I was surprised to see one of those three guys in the locker room. I asked him if he remembered hitting my pitch over the fence. He said he did, but I am sure he didn't remember it as well as I did.

Between the end of baseball season and the beginning of football season, I had a few days when I wasn't busy full-time. I still worked in the gym but had time to look for other things to do. I became acquainted with a lieutenant in the military police. He was a friendly guy who had played college ball for Alabama. One day, he came by the gym for a short visit. He told me he was going into Juarez to get a soldier out of jail. That sounded like something a lot more exciting than tending to workout cages. I asked my sergeant if I could go, and he agreed.

Wayland Corgill

We found the jail in Juarez, and we found conditions there to be appalling. We were guided to a small enclosure that was about 20 X 30 feet. It was jamb packed with standing room only. At the doorway, the lieutenant loudly called, "Are there any American soldiers in here?" An excited voice immediately screamed from the far side of the enclosure. The soldier continued yelling as he elbowed his way through the crowd and finally got to us.

That poor guy was ecstatic in his joy to see us and the thought that his horrible confinement was at an end. However, that was not to be. He had tried to escape over the wall by standing on top of a commode. He not only failed in that attempt but broke the commode in the process. He was in big trouble. He would not be released until he paid for a new commode. He didn't have nearly enough money, and neither did the lieutenant and me. After the jailer had explained that to us, the soldier was devastated. He didn't "boo hoo," but big tears rolled down his cheeks.

I sure felt sorry for that victim of Mexican justice, but there was nothing we could do. The lieutenant said he would come back with money as soon as he could. We took off, and the captive mournfully watched until we were out of sight. I was really glad to be walking out of there, and I couldn't imagine what that fellow we left behind was thinking.

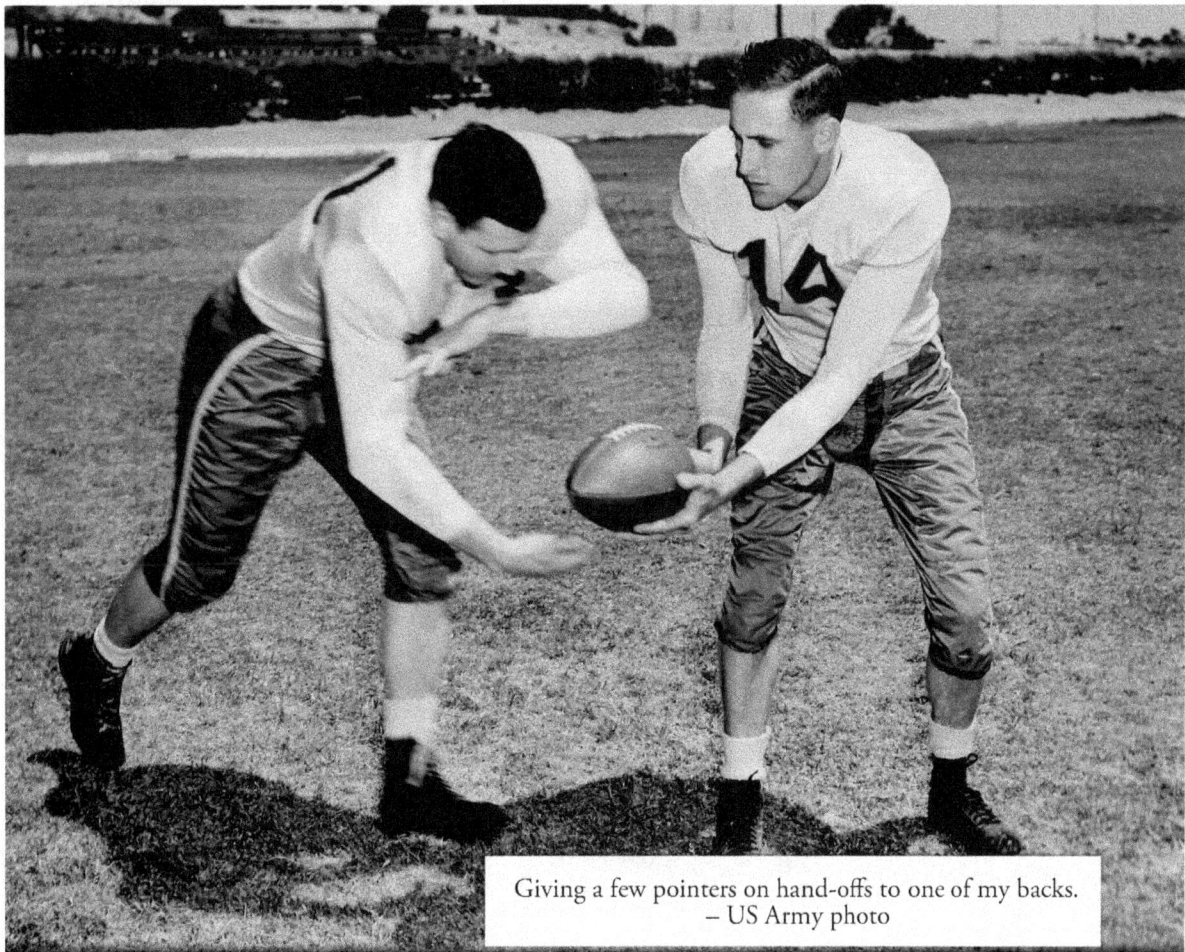

Giving a few pointers on hand-offs to one of my backs.
– US Army photo

The Rifleman - Cotton Davidson

When the 1955 football season started, I transitioned to that agenda. Team meetings were in the mornings, and practice was in the afternoons. My days were totally devoted to football. I was the starting quarterback for that season and also in 1956. During those two seasons, we faced really hard battles with most of the teams we played. Every team had at least a few outstandingly talented players on their roster. We played teams from coast to coast and beat most of them. By the end of 1956, we were exceedingly proud of our record. Luckily, I escaped injuries during both years, and they were extraordinarily successful and memorable for me.

Playing with that Fort Bliss team was a lot of fun. There was a lot of talent on the team. We needed to shore up a few areas, but we worked at it and steadily improved throughout the 1955 season. Our offensive line needed a fair amount of attention. I helped with that part of the coaching and noted rapid improvements. The dedication and commitment of team members were great, and we had an unbelievably successful year. We probably surprised everybody, even some of the teams we played.

One of the most memorable games in 1955, if not the most memorable, was when we played the Fort Sill, Oklahoma Cannoneers. They had a powerful team with four All Americans in their backfield. The three that I remember so well are; Leon Heath, Billy Vessels, and Buck McPhail. They were a powerhouse. They had played for the University of Oklahoma. All three of them had set national collegiate records and were instrumental in great years for the Sooners in the early 1950s, including a Sugar Bowl victory and a national title in 1950. Also, Billy Vessels had won the Heisman Trophy in 1952. I knew that we had our work cut out for us. Most people thought that Fort Bliss was very much the underdog.

For a number of reasons, I knew the Fort Sill game would be a major challenge. We had very good talent, but we were probably at a disadvantage in a few other areas. I was relatively new to the team, as was the coach. He had a few problems that affected the team. His coaching skills and knowledge of the game were not quite up to the level I had been used to. Also, he was not well-liked by the team. Therefore, we were a little deficient in the training and motivation of individual team members, as well as the execution of teamwork. I hoped that Fort Sill had similar problems.

I am in the middle with two of my Fort Bliss Falcons teammates
– US Army photo

Wayland Corgill

Our coach recognized that Fort Sill would be an extremely difficult test for us. Shortly before the game, he gave me, what he considered to be, a highly valuable personal incentive to "pull out all of the stops" and beat those celebrated guys. The coach had a beautiful, registered, Rhodesian Ridgeback dog. That dog was his pride and joy. He knew that I admired the dog too. He said, "Cotton if we win this game, I will give you one of her pups. I will probably have her bred next year."

To the delight of everybody on our side of the field, we beat Fort Sill. Probably, most people would have called it a big upset, but I didn't. I knew we had the talent and, that day, we did a better job than the Okies. Teamwork made the difference. Sometimes, teamwork can make magical things happen. Also, sometimes, a team can do the impossible if they believe they can. A coach, or somebody, has to be the instigator for the "believing" part. However, the promise of a Ridgeback pup didn't have anything to do with our win that day.

Regarding the Ridgeback pup, our coach didn't forget his promise. A couple of years after the Fort Sill game, I was surprised by his call one day. I was out of the military and back in Breckenridge, Texas. He said he had a beautiful little puppy that belonged to me and asked about when he could bring it by.

Fort Sill was just one of the tough games we played in 1955. We spent a week in southern California and played two very good teams out there. Those California teams seemed to have more than their share of "big-time" players. Our second game was with the San Diego Naval Base, and it was the toughest one. We had to "pull out all the stops" to win that one. Getting a win was great, but I remember the trip to San Diego for another reason too. We stayed two or three days in San Diego before game day. Most of my teammates were like me in that they had never been deep sea fishing. We decided to rectify that situation. Our coach didn't want to go. He said he was sure to get seasick. I told him that I would get a supply of seasick pills for him, and he would be fine. With that, he agreed to go. I got the pills and planned to hand them out to everybody as they boarded the boat the next morning.

The next day dawned perfectly clear and sunny with typical southern California weather. Our boat was calmly resting at its mooring with only a slight up-and-down and rocking movement from gentle swells. I stood on the dock by the boat and handed out pills to everybody as they came up. The coach ambled along the dock and stopped by the boat gangway where I was. He seemed to be having second thoughts about what he was going to do. I handed him a couple of pills. He didn't move but kept looking at the water and the slowly rolling boat. All at once, he lost his breakfast. It spewed all over everything in front of him within about five or six feet of where he stood. Luckily, his aim was away from me. None of us were in the projectile range, but he did christen a little bit of the boat. After he finished heaving for a few seconds, I was totally surprised by what he did next. He boarded the boat and headed for the restroom. We went fishing, and he didn't throw up again. Amazing! I guess he was empty and, maybe, the pills helped.

The coach's queasy stomach almost set off a few more sympathetic performances among bystanders waiting to get on the boat. However, nobody backed out, and we didn't lose a man at sea. Who would have thought that a fishing trip might be more hazardous than facing a bunch of formidable Navy guys on a football field?

On December 15, 1955, I received the All-Army Quarterback award from Major General Paul W. Rutledge, commanding general of Fort Bliss.– US Army photo

Wayland Corgill

Another memorable game in 1955 was with Sheppard Air Force Base in Wichita Falls. Again, I remember that game more for what happened after the game than what happened on the gridiron. Also, our coach was the reason for that. He was not a good coach, and guys that had played college and pro ball really got upset with him. Therefore, the coach became a target for pranks on several occasions.

Before driving back to Fort Bliss from Wichita Falls, we had a few spare days. For something to do, I suggested that the team go down to Possum Kingdom Lake, where Carolyn's parents had a lake house. We could have a day or two of fishing and take a dip in the lake to cool off once in a while. It was the middle of summer, and, of course, the Texas weather was hot. Everybody thought my idea was super, the coach included. The team was not too happy about the coach going, but we didn't have a choice.

We had a couple of great days on the lake and returned to Wichita Falls. That is when the more memorable part of the event started. The coach had driven his car to Wichita Falls, accompanied by his Rhodesian Ridgeback dog. He rarely went anywhere without that dog. While the coach was away from his car and saying goodbyes to his counterparts at the base, a couple of my teammates stuffed shrimp in the car's air vents. Not all of the team knew what was happening and one of the innocent ones was unlucky enough to ride back to El Paso with the coach. The weather was over 100^0F, and it was 550 miles to El Paso. The coach hadn't been on the road very long before the shrimp began to make their presence known. The further he drove, the more intense his comments became about that awful smell. His innocent passenger also helped with the complaints. By the time they reached Fort Bliss, they had ridden with windows down for most of the way. Sweating in the hot air whipping through the car was better than being cooped up with the rotten smell. Both coach and passenger couldn't get to the base fast enough.

Later, I had a chance to talk to the coach's passenger. I was quite amused by the story he told. The most humorous thing was the poor dog got the blame.

Most players behaved very well most of the time. Our games weren't much different from college ball. However, things boiled out of control one time when we played Fort Hood. Mother and Daddy had come over to see the game. I was behind the bench talking to them when a scuffle broke out between two players on the field. Within seconds, both teams were going at it with vigor. Officials were right in the middle of the mêlée and trying to break it up. They finally got the scuffling parties separated and began throwing players out on both sides. That happened toward the end of the game, and, luckily, we had enough players left to win. My teammates asked me why I didn't help them out, and I was glad I had the excuse of talking to Mother and Daddy.

Sometimes, spectators in the stands didn't behave as well as players on the field. The very first game I played for Fort Bliss was played there on base. Carolyn was in the stands. As we were warming up on the field, a man sitting in front of Carolyn made a comment about me that piqued her ire. He said, "Look at that guy, Cotton Davidson. He looks like he is too lazy to be a quarterback." Apparently, I wasn't moving around fast enough to suit him. Carolyn reached down to tap him on the shoulder and get his attention. She said, "Do you know Cotton?" That is all she said but the way she said it must have sent a strong message. The man never said anything else about me during the game. Also, I moved somewhat faster during the game, which we won, and I guess that satisfied him.

Carolyn remembered that first game for the "lazy" comment about me, but I remember it for another reason. An upper front tooth was knocked out. I was down on the ground and looked and looked for it but with no luck. I sure could have used a face-guard on my helmet.

Our 1955 football season was a satisfyingly successful one. We didn't lose more than a couple of games if that many. For the season, our Fort Bliss Falcons had the best win-loss record of any Army team.

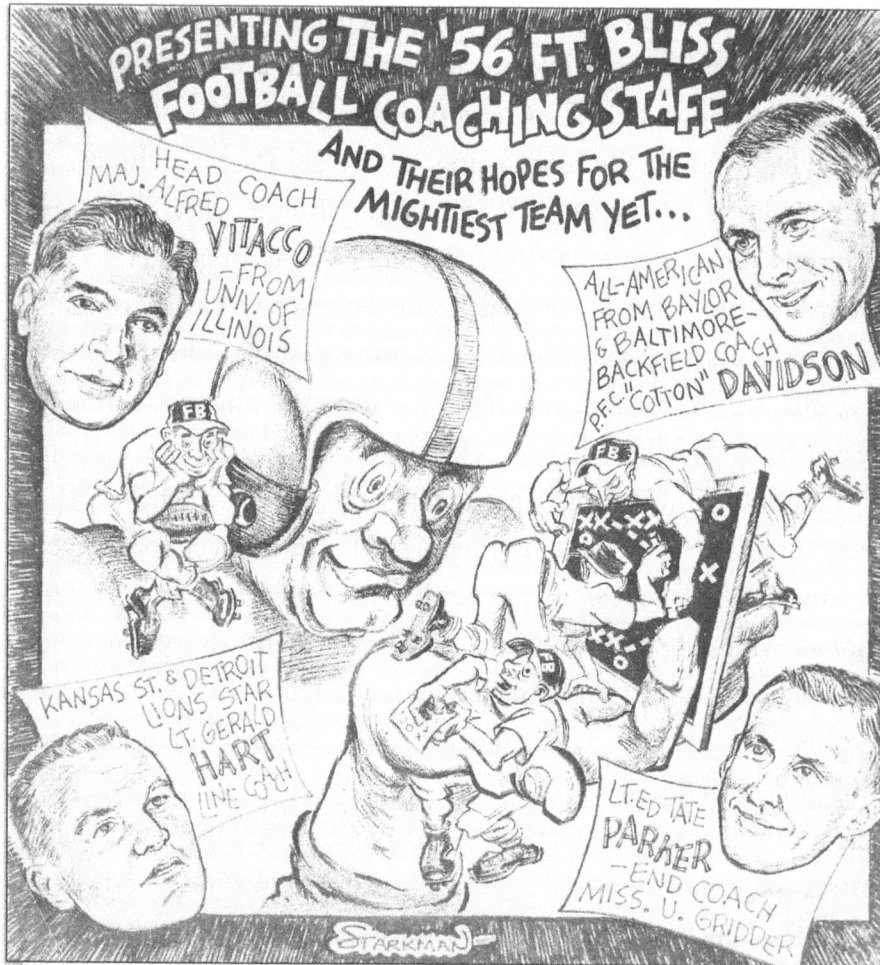

**Poster for the Fort Bliss Falcons 1956 football season
– courtesy of the Davidson family**

That accomplishment did not go unnoticed. Shortly after returning to base from our last game, I got a big, big surprise. I was informed that I had been selected as the All-Army Quarterback for 1955. It was an extraordinary award. That was beyond super. Quarterbacks of every Army team in the U.S.A. were in consideration for that honor. Every one of them was a first-class athlete.

The city of El Paso was exceedingly proud of being the home of the All-Army Quarterback. The newspaper made the award headline news. The city went "all-out" with a full evening of celebration. Downtown streets were blocked off to provide a spacious intersection in which to locate a stage for ceremonies. Food vendors were set up along streets and nearby parking lots. A live band provided entertainment, and dignitaries made speeches. Among the speakers were the Fort Bliss commanding general and El Paso mayor.

The "stage" was a flatbed wagon large enough to accommodate the speakers, other dignitaries, Carolyn, me, and a five-piece Country and Western band. In addition to musicians, the wagon had another occupant that was curious to me. It was a monkey. I didn't pay any attention to that primate until he sneaked around to where I stood and grabbed my leg. That rascal nearly put me in orbit. He wouldn't let go. I had the dickens of a time getting him loose. However, I got over that and, as a whole, affairs of the evening were extraordinary. Carolyn and I were just about overwhelmed by the outpouring of recognition and acclaim that was directed our way. It was a glorious evening to remember, among a gathering large enough to fill a stadium. I wondered if the man who made the "lazy" comment was in the crowd.

Wayland Corgill

After the 1955 football season ended, my life at Fort Bliss was soon headed for a big change. I was unaware that I had gained the attention of an influential officer on base. However, as baseball season was starting in early 1956, I became acutely aware of that officer. He was Colonel Pashiel, a bird colonel in command of the motor pool and, maybe, other departments too. He had exceptional clout on base and had a keen interest in sports. He loved football and focused on me to help make big changes in that program when the season started later in the year.

In the spring of 1956, Colonel Pashiel summoned me from baseball practice one day and made me a proposition I couldn't refuse. He said he wanted to make a few changes in the base sports organization, and he wanted me to help accomplish his agenda. He was not satisfied with the performance of the football coaching staff. That was where I would come in. In addition to being the starting quarterback, my duties would include taking charge of coaching. Additionally, I would work at improving team talent by reviewing personnel records in every department on base to search for potential new team members. Further, when not involved with sports activities, I would occupy an office space next to his office and assist him as needed. I was excited. Again, I couldn't say, "Yes, Sir," fast enough.

Occupying an office space next to the colonel's office had advantages and disadvantages. Frequently, a line of military personnel formed up in the hallway outside the Colonel's door. They patiently waited there until the colonel would see them. Many times, the line contained a few tough-looking sergeants who weren't very patient. Usually, the colonel was in no hurry to have his day disturbed by the requests or problems of the people outside his door. To delay giving audiences to those people, he would often call on me. He would summon me in a loud voice that I could hear through the wall. When I walked out into the hallway to enter the colonel's office, I would get some pretty glaring stares from the waiting lineup, particularly from the sergeants. The colonel never really needed anything, but he would keep me a little while on some insignificant task. I guess he was just taking time to get himself prepared for what was coming. I sure felt self-conscious when walking in front of those sergeants.

Colonel Pashiel was a good man to know. He was very friendly to me, and we spent a lot of time together. I had one more year to go in the Army, and I began to think a lot about what I was missing with the Colts. For the benefit of a career in the NFL, I really needed to get back there.

One day, I got my nerve up enough to ask Colonel Pashiel if he would approve my getting out of the service early. I had already done the research on formalities required for an "early-out" and had the necessary forms filled out. The colonel had the authority to grant my request. All I needed was his signature. However, that was not to be. His response was polite and friendly but not what I wanted to hear. He explained how he needed me in his plans for the sports program and couldn't let me go. He emphasized the importance of that program for boosting the morale of everybody on base. He was particularly detailed about his assessment of my importance to the objectives he had in mind. He was determined to have another record-setting, winning football team in 1956.

With that ruling, my pathway was clear for the next year. At the time, I was a little apprehensive about the colonel's expectations of me in his sports program, but those concerns quickly went away. When all was said and done, 1956 was another very good year for me and the Fort Bliss team. However, it was another year away from the NFL, and that had a lot of influence on how my career developed for the next several years out of the Army.

As 1956 progressed, I became more and more aware of just how influential Colonel Pashiel was. One day I was shocked to receive orders to report to the Enewetak Atoll in the North Pacific. I didn't know much about that place but knew it had been used for experimenting with exploding nuclear bombs. That seemed like a dangerous place to me. Also, the timing was awful because Carolyn was pregnant. In the worst way, I had no doubts about not wanting to go. I showed Colonel Pashiel my orders. He blurted out, "You've got to be kidding." He took my papers and picked up the phone. After a short conversation, he said, "You are not going anywhere."

My orders were canceled. I was elated, but that feeling was not shared by my sergeant in the unit where I was assigned. He was not happy at all. He didn't like me. I was assigned to his unit, but I was not doing anything for him. In effect, I was functioning as a member of Colonel Pashiel's department. My sergeant resented that. I wouldn't have been surprised to learn that he had volunteered me for Enewetak. However, I have to give my sergeant credit for offering me a few days to resettle Carolyn in Breckenridge and visit my family before leaving for Enewetak. After those orders were canceled, I doubt that he would have given me time off if I had a broken leg.

With the possibility out of the way for my being transferred to another post, 1956 proved to be a great year of baseball and football for me. In baseball, we continued to have lots of wins. Jack Sanford was just unbeatable. Generally, the teams we played were the same as the previous year. However, Jack and I had an additional treat one weekend. We pitched for the Alpine Cowboys, a Kokernot semi-professional team in Alpine, Texas.

The Kokernot family established a large ranch in the Alpine area in the late 1800s. Herbert Lee Kokernot, Jr., loved baseball. In 1947, he constructed a magnificent baseball stadium for his Alpine Cowboys. The stadium has been called "The Best Little Ballpark in Texas." Also, it has been referred to as the "Yankee Stadium of Texas."

Mr. Kokernot flew his private plane to El Paso to pick up Jack and me. In Alpine, we were treated like dignitaries, and we had a lot of fun on the baseball diamond. I was confident that Mr. Kokernot was pleased with our performance. The weekend was over too soon.

Carolyn drove down to watch us play and was fortunate to have arrived there in one piece. She had a harrowing experience on the way. She was driving our 1952 Pontiac that her parents had given her when she enrolled at Baylor. It was a brand new car at that time. She was zipping down the highway when the steering wheel came off in her hands! Without consciously thinking about it, her impulsive reaction was to try and put the steering wheel back in place. She was really lucky. It went back on the shaft, and the car stayed in its traffic lane. Amazing! Continuous down pressure was applied to the steering wheel for the rest of the trip. We drove the car back to El Paso just like Carolyn had finished driving to Alpine.

When football season started in 1956, I was a busy guy with my extra duties for coaching the team. Our previous coach with the Ridgeback dog was gone. Colonel Pashiel left the coaching entirely up to me. However, he stayed very much involved. He made sure we had things we needed and supervised our trips for games on the road. I sure appreciated his support.

Wayland Corgill

I always had the assistance of two or three teammates to help me out. One of those was Gerald E. Hart. I knew him very well since he had been on the team in 1955. Gerry had played football at West Point and Notre Dame. He was particularly effective with improving our offensive line. He was an enthusiastic young man and a valuable team member. From his stint in the Army, he had a storied career in the NFL as a player for the Detroit Lions and San Francisco 49ers, plus several years as a football official. He was another one of the many outstanding individuals that I was fortunate to associate with while in the Army.

Carroll Hardy was another player who I picked to help with coaching. He sure was a good kid and a top prospect for both baseball and football. He had been a star athlete for the University of Colorado in baseball, football, and track. He was the Hula Bowl MVP in 1955. Also, in 1955, he was drafted by the San Francisco 49ers but, after one year, he gave up football for baseball and went with the Cleveland Indians. Uncle Sam's draft caught him in 1956, and he wound up at Fort Bliss. He played a couple of games with our football team and, then, quit playing at the request of the Cleveland Indians. His love of sports and helping me coach was my good fortune.

After the Army, Carroll had a long and very successful career in sports. He is most noted for his unusual performances in baseball. He is the only person to ever pinch-hit for Ted Williams. That happened after Ted fouled a ball off of his foot and had to leave the game. Carroll was next at-bat and hit into a double play. He also hit his first major league home run when he was pinch-hitting for Roger Maris. That three-run homer won the game for Cleveland. After retiring from baseball, Carroll spent a couple of decades with the Denver Broncos and helped organize three teams that went to the Super Bowl. I like to think that, at least, some of his team-building capability came from his experience with helping me coach.

As with the baseball program, the football teams we played in 1956 were generally the same as those in the previous year. Again, our team was loaded with talent, and we were especially proud of our season win-loss record. However, we didn't win them all.

One memorable game that we lost was with the Fort Sill Cannoneers. We had soundly beaten them in 1955 when nobody thought we could. Apparently, those boys were still "smarting" from that loss. They were still a powerhouse and determined to "pull out all the stops" to avoid another embarrassment. It was a battle, and they prevailed.

An odd thing about that game was the game prize. It was a trophy titled "The Little Brown Dud." I was curious about the word, Dud. It didn't seem like a fitting word to use for a trophy. I knew what the word meant in Coryell County, but I had no idea what it meant to the Cannoneers. However, wondering about that was just a fleeting thought. At game time, I had more important things on my mind than the name of a mysterious trophy. Also, when the game was over, I was engrossed in matters other than thinking about a puzzling trophy. While I was with my team in the locker room, those Okies were proudly passing the "Dud" around and celebrating like they had won the Super Bowl. Clearly, it meant something special to them. To this day, I have no idea what that trophy was all about or why it had such a strange title.

Our last game of the 1956 season was a big one. It was the Army-Air Force Classic Penrose Bowl. This third annual event took place in Penrose Stadium at the Broadmore Resort near Colorado Springs,

Colorado. Our rival was a team from Hamilton Air Force Base in California. Going into the game, both teams had impressive season records but, our Fort Bliss Falcons appeared to have a slight edge. Our win-loss tally was 5-1-1 while Hamilton's was 5-3. Also, both teams had played three common opponents, and our Falcons had the better results in those contests. However, we didn't come out on top in this game, my last one in the Army. The Hamilton "flyboys" edged us in the final minutes of the game.

The Penrose Bowl was a celebrated affair in Colorado Springs. On Saturday morning, before the afternoon game, a huge parade made its way through downtown Colorado Springs. Army and Air Force units participated in the parade, as well as Bliss and Hamilton team members. The parade was led by a mounted color guard from Fort Carson. The December day was bitterly cold. The parade route was long. I certainly felt honored. However, the open-top car I rode in caused my thoughts to dwell more on the frigid football field than the bundled-up crowd lining the parade route. I sure was a long way from a shady spot on Coryell Creek with PaPa and his fishing pole.

At game time, the temperature had dropped a few more degrees. There was no snow, but it was icy cold. Carolyn was bundled up in the stands with all the clothes she had brought and could have used another layer. The weather affected both teams but, probably, was not an advantage for either one. The Hamilton boys were used to sunny California weather while we were acclimated to sunny El Paso. Both teams had the same challenge of keeping their hands warm enough so fingers would work and tolerating the stabbing sensations of heavy breathing of the cold, thin air.

The game was a battle all the way. Hamilton had plenty of first-class players to match our award-winning lineup. Dave Leggett was their quarterback. He was a standout for three years at Ohio State. He led them to an undefeated season in 1954 and on to a Rose Bowl victory over USC. He was the MVP of that game. He was drafted by the Chicago Cardinals in 1955, where he had a brief tenure before being drafted by another authority, Uncle Sam.

Another outstanding athlete on the Hamilton team was Earl Morrell. He was Dave Leggett's backup quarterback. Earl led the Michigan State Spartans to a record-winning season in 1955 and a victory over the UCLA Bruins in the 1956 Rose Bowl. He was drafted by the San Francisco 49ers in 1956 but, soon after that, he showed up at Hamilton Air Force Base. After military service, Earl had a storied career in professional football and became known as one of the greatest backup quarterbacks in NFL history. During the Baltimore Colts' 1968 season, he filled in for an injured Johnny Unitas and led the team to an NFL championship and on to Super Bowl III. In the Miami Dolphins' 1972 season, he filled in for Bob Griese and led the team to Super Bowl VII. Earl played for six pro teams in his NFL career and was a three-time Super Bowl champion. He also was voted the NFL's Most Valuable Player in 1968.

For coaching, I had my "top-notch" coaching staff of Gerry Hart and Carroll Hardy. Hamilton had a coach they were proud of, too. He was Ted Connolly. Ted was drafted by the San Francisco 49ers in 1954 but had his pro career interrupted by the military draft. In accordance with the 49ers' requirements, he didn't play for Hamilton, but he could coach. Ted earned All-Pro honors in his nine-year career in the NFL. As a right guard, he played with and blocked for many of the most famous names in pro football, including the legendary Jim Brown.

Wayland Corgill

With all the talent on the Hamilton team, we knew we had our work cut out for us. However, we were just as talented and were confident that we could win. Although that didn't happen, the game could have easily gone our way with a break or two in our favor. The weather was brutal, but that condition didn't decide the game. We fought until the last second, and at that point, I sure was glad to head for a warm locker room. My fingers felt like icicles. I also was very ready to get back to El Paso and hoped our plane wasn't frozen so we could fly. There had been talk about that possibility.

Fortunately, the plane was able to be flown, and I was glad to be on it. We left for a warmer climate early the next morning. As I watched Penrose Stadium diminish to a small spec in the distance, I kept thinking about the game and related events. What an experience that was! Also, I thought about Daddy, Mother, PaPa, Little Granny, and the folks in Pecan Grove. What would they think about me and what I was doing in a far-away place so different from where they were?

I finally got a stripe – photo courtesy of the Davidson family

The Rifleman - Cotton Davidson

We were in Colorado several days before game day. During that time, Carolyn had a much better arrangement than I did. Our Falcons' team was quartered at Fort Carson. Carolyn and her friend, Jan Hart, were ensconced in the beautiful Broadmoor resort. Their leisurely days allowed plenty of time for meandering through the Broadmoor's luxurious shops and elaborate surroundings. Parts of my days were spent in freezing weather on the practice field. However, on game day, Carolyn also got a taste of that raw weather. She was pretty graphic with her description of how uncomfortable it was in the stands. She needed a heavier coat. Also, long periods of immobility sure caused the cold to penetrate. Therefore, I didn't get very much sympathy from her when I told her about the conditions on the football field.

During evenings after practice, I also put in an appearance at the Broadmoor. It was a fantastic place with a large variety of entertainment venues. It even had an ice skating rink. That seemed unnecessary to me. A small, frozen lake nearby looked like a better place for ice skating. However, the inside rink provided a warmer place for skaters to practice their sport and the rink was well used. One day, against my better judgment, I was goaded by my teammates into trying my luck on the ice. I only agreed to do that if two people, who knew how to skate, would skate with me. I could hardly stand in one spot on those skates, much less move. I needed one person on each side to prop me up. As we built up speed across the rink, my two chaperones tried to abandon me. They had secretly concocted that plan, but it didn't work. I had such a firm grip on their shirts that the buttons went flying off, and they couldn't get away. All that cow milking I did for PaPa as a kid paid off with my vice-like grip. Thus, ended my ice skating lesson, and I think my helpers were glad.

A few weeks after the Penrose Bowl, my two years of Army service ended early in 1957. For the whole time, my rank of private remained the same as when I was inducted. Three or four days before I was discharged, out of the blue, Colonel Pashiel happened to notice my lowly rank. He was an extraordinarily observant officer but had overlooked that for a year. He asked, "Cotton, have you got a stripe?" When I said, "No, Sir," he said, "Well, you should have a stripe." By the time my discharge papers arrived, I was a private first class.

I had no plans to re-enlist in the Army, but I wondered if Colonel Pashiel might try to talk me into doing that. However, he didn't. I had a contract with the Colts and fully intended to be in their training camp when practice started in the summer. No doubt, the colonel understood that.

Colts to CFL to Baylor

I was discharged from the Army at Fort Bliss in February 1957. Although I was ready to go, saying goodbyes to my teammates, friends, and Colonel Pashiel was hard. Carolyn and I had developed many close relationships with those folks. We regretted severing ties that had matured in the past two years. However, we realized that this was an unavoidable part of our service experience. Continual changes were to be expected in the military. Our friends would be leaving the service sooner or later too. Even though we were moving on, we would do our best to stay in touch with them in the future.

How some relationships last is remarkable. Six decades after our last day at Fort Bliss, Carolyn and I are still in frequent contact with many of those friends. Also, I still hear from a few of those guys who stood with me on the field in that bitter-cold Penrose Bowl. Amazing!

Aside from missing friends at Fort Bliss, I had no regrets about vacating West Texas for familiar territory further east. Also, I was eager to get back to the Colts' training camp in the summer. While in the Army, someone with the Colts staff called me monthly, and I had kept up with their progress. I knew that major things had happened with their quarterback position. The Colts now had two first-rate quarterbacks: Johnny Unitas and George Shaw. Where would I fit in?

My leaving for the Army presented Weeb Ewbank with a big problem, and he quickly took action. He was not going to be caught short with the quarterback position. He acquired George Shaw in the first pick of the first round of the 1955 draft. George was an impressive athlete. He had led his Portland, Oregon, high school team to two state championships. He went on to the University of Oregon and made first-team All-American in both football and baseball.

With George Shaw, Weeb's quarterback position was secure for the 1955 season. However, disaster struck early in 1956. George broke his leg. Weeb wasted no time in finding a replacement. His selection was a slender young man who had had, off and on, shining performances during his four years at the University of Louisville. In 1955, after college, he had been drafted by the Pittsburgh Steelers. However, it didn't work out with the Steelers, and he was soon supporting himself as a construction worker and playing semi-professional ball on weekends for a team in Pittsburgh. That young man was Johnny Unitas. He was a "walk-on" in Weeb's 1956 training camp. Although an unlikely choice in some opinions, signing Johnny proved to be an exceptionally good decision. Johnny took over from George Shaw in the 1956 season. After a "rough" start in a couple of games, Johnny's performance remarkably improved. By the end of the season, he was setting records and making a name for himself.

I would be returning to the Colts with a lot of questions about my future with them. Unless something unforeseen happened, I expected that I would have little chance of playing in 1957.

Between February and the start of training camp in the summer of 1957, I was concerned with things other than football. Carolyn, Tommy, and I moved to Breckenridge, Texas, and bought a house there. We looked forward to getting back into civilian life. Her father had a plumbing business. I had an open offer to work for him. Even though I was not an experienced plumber, I was a good helper, and we stayed busy.

To stay in shape, I had an early morning and late afternoon workout routine. At one of my first workouts, I met a very interesting guy who was serious about staying in shape, too. He was Dean Smith, an award-winning sprinter. He had been a star athlete in track and football at the University of Texas. While there, he came within a tenth of a second of tying the world record in the 100-yard dash. Also, he and his relay team won gold medals in the 4 x 100-meter relay at the 1952 Helsinki Summer Olympics. Dean and I worked out together. Both of us would be going to pro football training camps in the summer. He would be joining the Los Angeles Rams.

Dean is a fine guy. He was born and raised in Breckenridge and lives in the area today. After an exciting, multi-faceted, award-winning career in rodeo events and movies as a cowboy and stuntman, he returned to his roots. He has a ranch on the northwest side of Possum Kingdom Lake. Once in a while, I still see Dean. Carolyn and I have a lake house on Possum Kingdom Lake. When we are at the lake or in Breckenridge, it is not uncommon for Dean and me to cross paths.

We only had a few months to get settled in Breckenridge before the Colts' training camp started. I went to Baltimore in July. Carolyn and Tommy joined me a couple of months later. It felt great to be back with the Colts. Reconnecting with former teammates was a pleasure. However, team personnel had undergone numerous changes in my two-year absence. In many ways, this was a different team as compared to the one I left in 1955. Under Coach Ewbank's supervision during the past three seasons, the Colts had become a considerably strengthened team.

There were many new guys to get to know, including Johnny Unitas. Soon, he and I got to know each other very well. However, that didn't happen on the football field or at social gatherings. Johnny was a quiet, private person. We never talked much during the day and we didn't socialize as families. Although

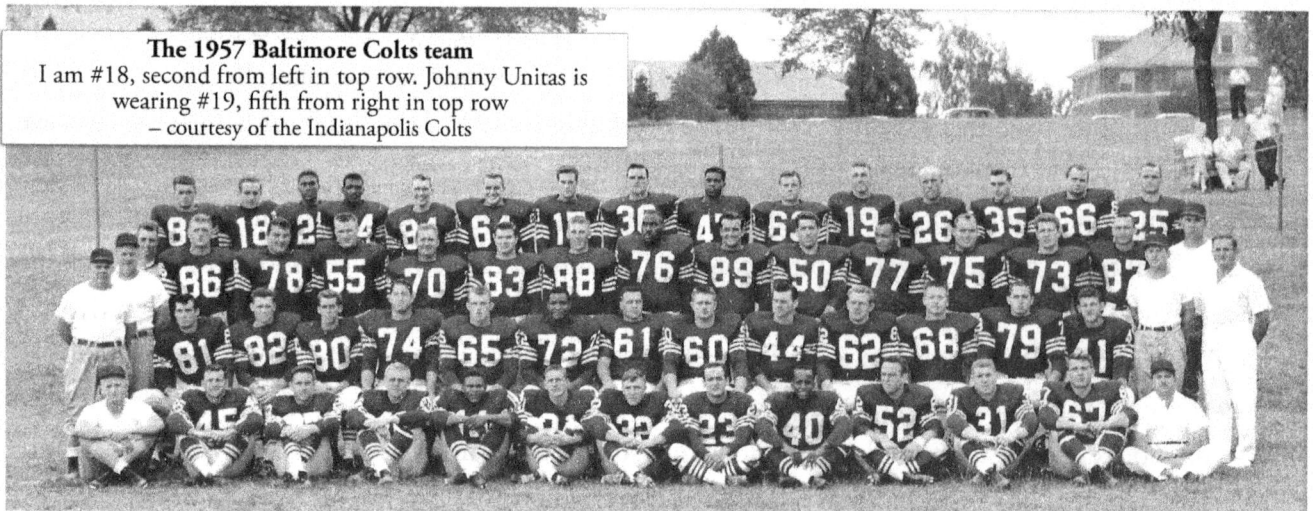

The 1957 Baltimore Colts team
I am #18, second from left in top row. Johnny Unitas is
wearing #19, fifth from right in top row
– courtesy of the Indianapolis Colts

we spent a lot of time together during the 1957 and 1958 training camps and the 1957 regular season, our talking time was at days' end. We always roomed together. I don't know whose idea that was, but it was good for both of us. That is where Johnny and I got to know each other.

Johnny was friendly and a gentleman. Our personalities fit together well, and we "hit it off," essentially, from the first day we met. I enjoyed his company. Throughout our time with the Colts, there was never a cross word between us. Also, both of us were one-hundred percent team players. We never had a problem with working together. In fact, we supported each other. It was his second year with the Colts, and he was unquestionably the starting quarterback. Even at this stage, I knew that Johnny was as good as any quarterback I had seen and was not surprised by his great accomplishments in later years. I had often wondered about how things might have turned out if I had been the Colts' starting quarterback when Johnny joined the team. In that case, I expect that I would have played a little harder to keep my job.

During those evenings of bunking together, Johnny and I quickly became comfortable with being around each other. Both of us were not overly-talkative, but Johnny had me beat on that score. He didn't talk much at all. On the field and in the locker room, he never participated in idle conversation. He was always a serious man of few words. However, before drifting off to sleep in our bunks, we always had a

Me (#18) and Johnny Unitas (#19) in 1957
– courtesy of the Indianapolis Colts

conversation about one thing or another. He would talk about any subject I mentioned, but he rarely ever started a conversation. If there was to be one, I realized that I would have to start it. It became kind of an unspoken understanding that that was my job.

There were plenty of things to talk about that were of interest to both of us, and I didn't hold back. Johnny was relatively new to the Colts and the NFL, and so was I. Also, I had come back to a very different team than the one I left in 1955. There were many things to learn about the team and what we were doing. We helped each other. As our mutual trust and friendship grew, so did our curiosity about each other. Often, non-sports-related topics entered our conversations. Each of us had an interest in learning about the others' life before winding up in Baltimore. We exchanged a lot of information on that subject. However, we never talked about intimate personal issues or very personal family matters. Without exception, conversations were always interesting, respectful, reasonable, and understood to be strictly confidential. I couldn't have asked for a better guy to be around, on and off of the field.

When I got to our room after a long day on the practice field, my head was often full of thoughts and questions about what I had experienced during the day. That time in the room was a good time to think about them and review them with Johnny. If there was a play that I was confused about, we would discuss it. More often, we talked about the good plays and what made them work. We didn't always talk about football but, when we did, it was helpful to both of us. No doubt, his mind was full of football thoughts too. Johnny was an excellent counterpoint in those discussions. The word "sharp" is a good one to describe his understanding of the game and his mastery of handling the offense.

Football was about the only thing that Johnny and I had in common. He was from the big city, and I was from the country. Neither of us knew anything about the other's way of life while growing up. They

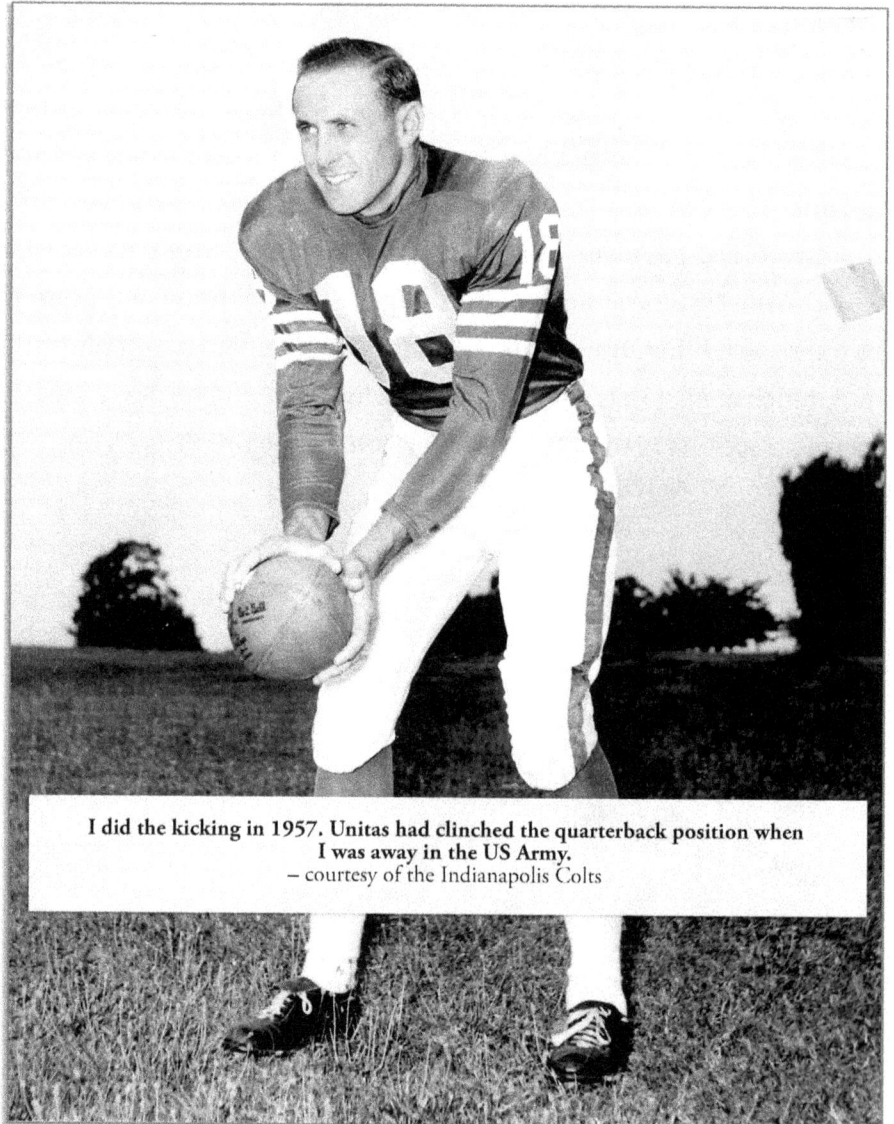

I did the kicking in 1957. Unitas had clinched the quarterback position when I was away in the US Army.
– courtesy of the Indianapolis Colts

were so different. Our nighttime conversations often drifted to talking about those times. He was full of questions about my life on a Texas ranch, and I wondered what life was like in a Pennsylvania steel mill town. Those were always interesting and pleasant conversations, and they helped us drift off to sleep by clearing our minds of football for a little while.

Big city life was not appealing to me, but Johnny thought ranch life would be something he would like to experience. I told him that was easy to fix. All he had to do was to come to Texas in the off-season, and I would take care of it. He planned to do that but, unfortunately, it never happened because our careers went separate ways in 1958 and we lost touch with each other.

In addition to talking about football and things back home, there were plenty of conversations on the "lighter side." One subject that came up quite often was jersey #19. The discussion was always good-natured banter. I was always kidding about that, but Johnny, in accordance with his nature, was always serious. I had worn #19 at Baylor and also as a Colt in 1954. Now, Johnny had my number, and I was given #18. I would rib him about having my number. I would say, "Your conscience should hurt you, at least a little bit, for taking my jersey while I was away protecting you and this country, and you had good times with football." His reply was always something like, "You can have it back." In answer to that, I would grin and needle him with, "I don't want it back. I just want you to realize what you have done to a guy who was risking life and limb to take care of this nation while you were living the good life." That kind of back-and-forth banter would go on until one or the other of us would give up and say good night. Without question, if I had really wanted #19, Johnny would have given it to me.

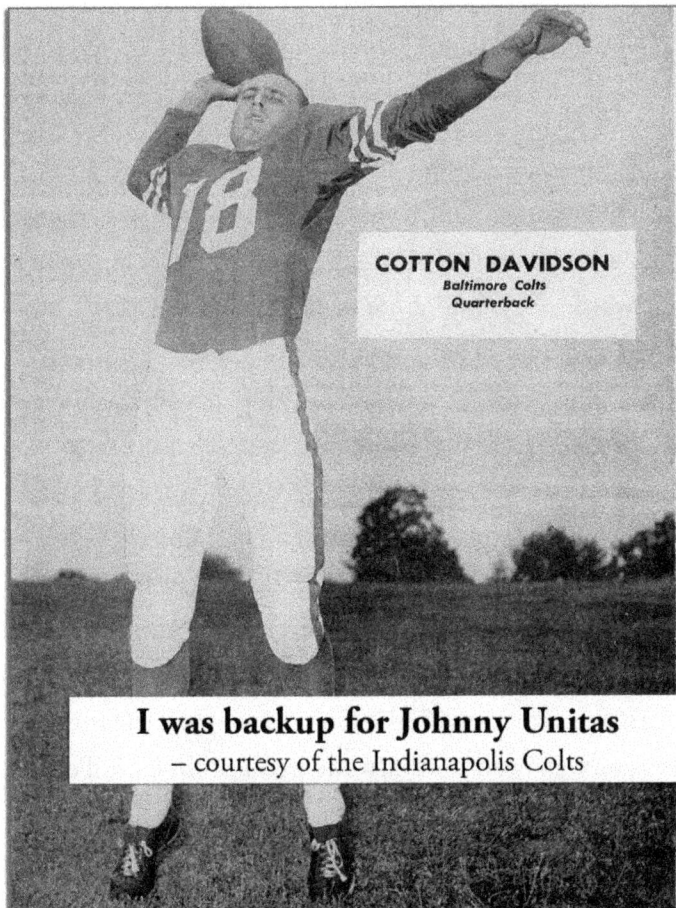

COTTON DAVIDSON
Baltimore Colts
Quarterback

I was backup for Johnny Unitas
– courtesy of the Indianapolis Colts

Johnny not only got my number, but he also inherited my whole wardrobe. I heard that was an economic decision by team management. When Johnny joined the Colts as a backup quarterback in 1956, George Shaw securely held that position as a starter. It remained to be seen how the newcomer would work out. After all, he had been tried once in the pros by the Steelers and didn't make the cut. Johnny and I were almost identical in size. We were 6 ft., 1in., tall and almost the same weight. Therefore, management thought, why spend money on another set of uniforms? Mine were still in good shape after only one year of use, and they fit Johnny perfectly. That is how I lost my #19. The decision was not Johnny's, but I wouldn't let him off the hook by letting him know I believed that.

The Rifleman - Cotton Davidson

Johnny was an interesting young man. He stood out in a crowd, off of the field as well as on the field. For example, at that time, he didn't wear high tops, and his socks were attention-getters with their vivid colors and wild patterns. Another attention-getter was his old car. It was well worn out and had to be carefully driven. The tires were also well worn, but they looked like new because Johnny had made them into whitewalls by adding separate white trims that fit under the wheel rims. It should be noted that none of us made much money in those days. I was no better off than Johnny and understood why frugal measures were often needed. Both of us had families to support, and we couldn't afford very many frills. Johnny's socks might have been a little excessive in some opinions, but not mine. I got a kick out of teasing him about those socks.

Johnny stood out in other ways too. He was a highly respected, even-tempered gentleman. He got along with everyone. The whole team liked him. He and I fit together, as well as any two quarterbacks ever did, and I couldn't have asked for a better guy to play with.

Regrettably, I never saw Johnny again after I left the Colts for the CFL in 1958. Years later, a few times, when I was back in Texas, someone who had seen Johnny would tell me that he had asked about me. Back in the 1960s and 1970s, staying in touch was not so easy. Both Johnny and I had very little spare time to think about anything but taking care of our profession and family. I could never forget him, though. He was a rare individual and a good friend.

Although I spent a lot of time on the bench during games in 1957, I really enjoyed reconnecting with teammates from 1954 and getting to know the new guys. Coach Ewbank had been very busy while I was away in the Army. He had acquired a large number of impressive players, and the team had markedly improved each year on both offense and defense. Those outstanding athletes produced a good year for the Colts in 1957 but, in 1958, they broke all records. Every position on that team was filled by an outstandingly talented player. Suiting up with them was an exciting experience.

In addition to Johnny, members of the 1957 backfield were very impressive. Those who were new to me included Alan Ameche, Lenny Moore, Jim Parker, and Raymond Berry. Another new member, who was not new to me, was my Baylor Bears college teammate, L.G. Dupree. Seeing his familiar face helped me get over missing my old friend, Dan Edwards, who had gone to the CFL. Only one member of that starting backfield had been with the Colts in 1954, and that was Jim Mutscheller.

Fullback Alan Ameche was a Heisman Trophy winner and NFL Rookie of the Year in 1955. He had six record-setting years with the Colts and was inducted into the College Football Hall of Fame. He scored the winning touchdown in the 1958 NFL Championship game.

Halfback Lenny Moore was with the Colts for twelve seasons. He was named NFL Rookie of the Year in 1956 and was a seven-time Pro Bowler. He was inducted into the Pro Football Hall of Fame in 1975.

Left tackle Jim Parker was another rare talent that fit well into Coach Ewbank's game plans with Unitas and the passing game. Parker was not only big, with his quickness and strength, but he provided outstanding protection for Unitas. Early in his eleven-year career with the Colts, he earned the reputation of being the premier pass blocker in the game. Parker was inducted into the Pro Football Hall of Fame in 1973 and the College Football Hall of Fame in 1974.

Halfback L.G. Dupre was an award-winning and record-setting football player at Baylor, where he was one of the "Fearsome Foursome" that included Jerry Coody, Allen Jones, and me. L.G. was nicknamed

"Long Gone" because of his superior rushing performance. He played five seasons with the Colts and two seasons with the Dallas Cowboys. L.G. was awarded membership in the Baylor Athletic Hall of Fame.

Split end Raymond Berry was a skinny kid who was thought to have a questionable future in the NFL when he showed up in the 1955 Colts training camp. However, after thirteen seasons with the Colts and two seasons with the Dallas Cowboys, there was no question about his being one of the greatest receivers in NFL history. He was Unitas' favorite target. Their teamwork was a dominant factor in winning the 1958 NFL Championship game. Raymond had a long, exceptionally successful career in coaching pro football after playing his last game with the Cowboys. He was inducted in the Pro Football Hall of Fame in 1973.

Raymond was one of the most dedicated, detailed, hard-working people I have ever known. He was consistently that way in whatever he did, both on and off the field. On the field, every move he made was unbelievably precise. While Unitas and I worked out with him, I was always impressed with his incredible accuracy. When starting a particular route, his "plant foot" would be within an inch of the same spot, every time. He would run a particular route exactly the same way. A quarterback always knew where Raymond would be on the called route. Also, he had phenomenal hands for catching a ball. Unitas and I would take turns in staying with him on a route and bump him when he was going for the ball. He caught every ball that had even the slightest chance of being caught. Also, he never dropped a ball. A couple of times, Coach Ewbank told me I was throwing the ball too hard, and I should slack off to help Raymond catch it. Raymond heard what was said at one of those "coaching sessions." Afterward, he eased up to me and let me know that we were doing just fine, no changes needed. He caught them all, whether they were low, high, fast, or an outstretched arm's length.

It was uncanny how precise Raymond's perceptions were of positions, locations, and dimensions. Before one game in California, he walked onto the field and immediately said it was not regulation size. He insisted on the field being measured, and sure enough, it was too narrow. Nobody else noticed, but that was Raymond.

Raymond Berry was one-of-a-kind, and it made him a super success. When I left the Colts in 1958, I didn't expect to ever be on the same field with him again. However, the next year, unforeseen events conspired to bring us together once more.

Jim Mutscheller was the tight end on the opposite side of the field from Raymond Berry. Jim excelled in football at Notre Dame and was a member of their 1949 national championship team. He had an award-winning nine seasons with the Colts and, in 1957, was the NFL leader in receiving touchdowns.

Since 1954, Weeb had also been busy with improving the Colts' defensive talent. Many of those players are still talked about today. Among them were Big Daddy Lipscomb, Art Donovan, Gino Marchetti, Don Joyce, and Don Shinnick. Defensive talent just about overshadowed offensive talent.

Right defensive tackle Eugene Allen "Big Daddy" Lipscomb was not only "big," but he was fast and agile. According to Coach Ewbank, Lipscomb was one of the best tacklers there ever was. During his five seasons with the Colts, he was instrumental in helping 1958 and 1959 be such great years. "Big Daddy" was a "gentle giant." He often asked an opposing player if they were alright when picking them up after knocking them down.

The Rifleman - Cotton Davidson

Left defensive tackle Art "Artie" Donovan had such a remarkable nine-season performance with the Colts that his #70 jersey was later retired. He was a key factor in the Colts' win over the New York Giants in the 1958 championship game dubbed as "The Greatest Game Ever Played." As with so many others on that Colts' team, his list of honors and awards is long and was capped by being inducted into the Pro Football Hall of Fame in 1968. He was the first Colts team member to be so honored.

Art was a "character" in every sense of the word and kept us laughing. It was almost impossible to top the stories he told. However, I did that one time. When we were showering one day, he noticed a depression in my chest where my sternum bent down for some reason. It had been that way since birth. Artie said, "What's that hole in your chest?" I replied, "When I was little, a Brahma bull stuck his horn in my chest, carried me across the field, and threw me against the wall." Artie quietly thought about that for a minute and had no reply. That was most unusual for him. I am pretty sure he believed me. I never told him anything different.

Left defensive end Gino Marchetti had thirteen preeminent seasons with the Colts, where he was noted for his fierce pass rushing. He was voted "the greatest defensive end in pro football history" by the Pro Football Hall of Fame in 1972 when he was inducted into that elite organization. Also, Sid Gillman, the Los Angeles Rams head coach, credited Gino as the greatest player in football.

Right defensive end Don Joyce was another strong, tough member of one of the foremost defenses in the NFL during the 1950s and 1960s. His seven-year presence with the Colts was much appreciated by the offense. Raymond Berry gave Don and his defensive teammates a lot of credit for the Colts' successes in those years.

Middle linebacker Don Shinnick was with the Colts all of his thirteen-year pro football careers. Opposing team quarterbacks were wise to keep track of Don's location during pass plays. He had 37 career interceptions. That is still a record today for a linebacker.

When I arrived at training camp in 1957, I noted that one of our starting defensive backs in 1954 was missing. That was Don Shula. He had gone to the Washington Redskins. I didn't think too much about that at the time but, several years later, he was involved in events that were very interesting to me. In 1963, the Colts fired Coach Ewbank and replaced him with Don Shula, my old teammate.

As the 1957 season progressed, it rapidly became apparent to me that my chances for playing as a quarterback would be slim to none. Unitas had that position well in hand, and George Shaw was his backup. George's leg had healed, and he was back to one-hundred percent. Throughout the season, Johnny kept on improving and setting records. He led the Colts to their first winning record in franchise history. Also, he finished first in the NFL, not only in passing yards but in touchdown passes too. At the end of the season, the Newspaper Enterprise Association honored him with the Jim Thorpe Trophy as the NFL's Most Valuable Player. Johnny was on his way to greatness.

The 1957 season was a dull one for me. Besides punting, I didn't play much. For that reason, I have difficulty remembering very much detail about any of the games we played. Actually, when the 1957 season was over, I was eager to get back to Texas. I needed to involve myself in something besides football for a while and do some thinking about the future. I had a lot to think about. Carolyn had a lot to think about too. We were expecting an addition to the family in the coming year. Carolyn, Tommy, and I wasted no time packing up and heading back to Breckenridge. We intended to resume our normal routines there, and I would work for her father.

I was back in Baltimore when the Colts' training camp started in 1958. However, I didn't stay long. Johnny Unitas and George Shaw were there, and I could see that the coming season would probably be like the last one: I wouldn't play much. Training camp had only been in session for a couple of weeks when I had a talk with Coach Ewbank. I told him that I wanted to leave and explained why. I wanted to find a place where I could be the starting quarterback. He understood and asked me where I wanted to go. I told him that I would like to try the Canadian Football League (CFL).

I had been made aware of the CFL in my last year at Baylor. Coaches from the Calgary Stampeders had visited Baylor and approached me about playing for them. They had seen me play and were very convincing with their presentation about Canadian football. The CFL had strong teams and, the more I learned about them, the more interested I became. I believed the CFL might be a pretty good place to go. However, at that time, Canada seemed like it was just too far away for me. Now, four years later, I had a different view of Canadian football prospects.

Weeb didn't try to hold me back. He was an honorable gentleman. He said that he didn't want to let me go but he knew, and I knew, that Johnny would be the starting quarterback and would generally play every down of every game.

I parted company with the Colts right away and went to the Calgary Stampeders. After that, Weeb and I rarely crossed paths, and we didn't stay in touch. However, we always had a friendly relationship. Later, I was told some of the good things he had said about me, and I really appreciated that. I even read somewhere that he said I was one of the best boys he ever coached and that I was all heart but couldn't beat out Johnny Unitas. A lot had happened to both Weeb and me in the four years since I had first talked to him at Baylor. I had covered a lot of ground, and now I was moving on again.

Going to the CFL turned out to be a big, big mistake. I should have stayed with the Colts the rest of the 1958 season. That season was phenomenal for Johnny Unitas and the Colts. If I had stayed, I would have been part of a championship team for the ages. The Colts won the Western Conference title and went on to play for the NFL Championship. That championship game, with the New York Giants, has been praised as "The Greatest Game Ever Played." The Colts won in sudden death overtime with a score of 23 – 17. It was the first overtime game in NFL history. The game was nationally televised by NBC and did wonders for dramatically increasing the popularity of professional football. Being part of that historical event would have been a great experience to remember, even if I only did the punting. Instead of being in Baltimore, I was in Calgary, and that experience was memorable for reasons not so good.

Staying with the Colts would have avoided a debilitating injury in Canada that was a major setback in my career. Also, I might have been in a better position to have a chance at being starting quarterback with another NFL team. Those thoughts have crossed my mind many times. However, at the time I left the Colts, I wasn't thinking about what their season might bring. I was concerned with my immediate future. I was determined to find a team where I would be the starting quarterback.

The Rifleman - Cotton Davidson

I contacted the Calgary Stampeders, and they were definitely interested in me. They needed a quarterback who could improve their passing game. Maybe, we would be a good match. In no time, we reached an agreement, and I was bound for Canada. The Calgary Stampeders was a talented team. Also, the other Canadian teams had experienced players, many of whom came from the U.S. More than half of the Stampeders' players were from the U.S. It was a good group. I got my #19 back and had no misgivings about the big move I had made.

A couple of weeks after I got to Calgary, Carolyn arrived with our two young ones, Tommy and Kelly Ann. It was a bit of an arduous journey for her. Her flight was from Denver, Colorado. The trip took twelve hours which was a long time of traveling with small children. There were no disposable diapers in those days. However, she arrived in good spirits and ready to meet the challenge of transplanting a family of Texans into a foreign country.

Both Carolyn and I found quite a few unexpected and surprising conditions in Calgary. It certainly wasn't like Gatesville. I had no way of knowing what to expect and hadn't seriously thought about it. I doubt that Carolyn had considered that either. We had more pressing things on our minds before making the jump to Canada. However, once there, our first look at the city left a strong impression that we had definitely taken a small step back in time. It wasn't exactly a "frontier days" town, but it wasn't what would be thought of as a modern city, either. Carolyn was somewhat taken aback by her first observations. There was not one paved road in town. Most dwellings appeared to be a little primitive as compared to those in Gatesville or Breckenridge. Sizeable grocery stores and shops didn't exist. Many items readily available in the U. S. were nowhere to be found in Calgary. That did make taking care of two small children a little more difficult.

Even though living accommodations were slightly "Spartan," as compared to what we were used to in the lower forty-eight, we found a very nice apartment and settled in. Getting accustomed to the inconveniences of limited stores and shops, plus dealing with limited availabilities and absence of products and materials, was more of a problem. I was reminded of my younger days and how the Davidson clan got by in Pecan Grove when frugality was the order of the day. Back then, we did without a lot of things. PaPa even saved his chew of tobacco and let it dry for use in his pipe. However, Carolyn and I came to terms with the conditions we faced and planned for a long term in Calgary.

The countryside around Calgary was beautiful, and the people were exceptionally friendly. They loved football and welcomed another addition to the team. Football and the Calgary Stampede Rodeo were the main sources of entertainment in the area. Sightseeing and hunting, particularly goose hunting, were great outlets, but football was especially popular and enjoyed wide support from the community. We quickly made friends with many Canadians, as well as several Americans who were there in the oil business. Those folks from the lower forty-eight states were exceptional in helping us get adjusted to our new environment and included us in their social circles. Even though the city was somewhat rustic, we found a lot to like about Calgary. From our first days there, Carolyn and I loved the area.

Interestingly, 36 years later, Carolyn and I went back to Calgary with Forrest Gregg when I was helping him coach the CFL Shreveport Pirates in 1994. The Pirates was one of four teams that the CFL

Wayland Corgill

was starting in the U.S., and the Pro Football Hall of Famer Forrest Gregg was the Pirates' head coach. That was my second intimate experience with the CFL. When we arrived in Calgary, I was surprised to find a large, modern city that was totally different from the way it was in 1958. The most noticeable changes were the streets and buildings. All streets were lighted and paved, and attractive, multi-story buildings dominated the skyline.

Back in 1958, I arrived at the Stampeders' training camp a couple of weeks before the season started. I didn't know anything about their offense and didn't know any of the players. That made for a difficult start. I expected to have a lot to learn, but there was much more to that than I had imagined. Canadian football offense formations and rules were so different from those I knew in the U.S.

Me in 1959 – a great year as a Baylor football coach
– courtesy of The Texas Collection, Baylor University

For example, before the ball was snapped, player movements were allowed on both offense and defense that would have caused penalties in the U.S. There was so much to learn. The coaches were good, and a couple of them were from the U.S. That helped because they understood my situation and worked with me to get me up to speed as quickly as possible. Training camp went well, but there is only so much that can be done in a couple of weeks. However, when the season started, I felt that I knew enough to lead the team.

Even though I was still learning the game according to CFL rules, our season started great, and I effectively handled the offense. Our passing game was acceptable and, generally, better than the teams we played. Our first four games were almost blowouts. We beat the British Columbia Lions 42-0. The Edmonton Eskimos fell by a score of 35-7. The British Columbia Lions had improved a little bit by our second contest, but we beat them again, 34-13. The Winnipeg Blue Bombers gave us a pretty good workout, but they lost with a score of 11-3.

That game with the Winnipeg Blue Bombers was my last one in the CFL. It was a disaster for me. While throwing a pass, I got a hit that tore up my shoulder. I immediately knew it was a very bad injury. I didn't need a doctor to tell me that. The pain was almost mind-numbing, but it didn't blank out the realization that my playing days for the Stampeders were over. Later, as other thoughts occurred to me, I figured that my career in football might be over as well. However, right then, I couldn't concentrate on anything besides getting help for the terrible pain in my shoulder and a right arm that wouldn't move.

The Stampeders' medical staff and trainers did what they could for me, but it wasn't much more than pain control. After a few days of therapy, it was time for a decision. There was nothing to do but pack up and go home. Calgary was a long way from Texas, and I was anxious to get started as soon as possible. Before I left, a trainer worked with me to give me guidance on exercise and weight lifting regimens. After that, the cord was cut between the CFL Stampeders and me. I had no support from the CFL after I left Canada. Years later, I learned that I qualified for a few benefits but, prior to leaving, that was never mentioned. My future was in my hands. I had no idea about how effective the prescribed rehabilitation training program would be, but I was going to give it my best.

That shoulder injury was a severe blow to my football career. As with the letter from Uncle Sam in 1955, the injury caused another huge change in the direction of my life. Everything would be influenced by the injury for a while, and again, I would be venturing into unknown territory with many questions. What would I do now? If not for the injury, I would probably have stayed in Canada for several years. I was really beginning to get a feel for the offense, and I was confident that I could be the Stampeders' number one quarterback.

After getting back to Breckenridge, I had many other things on my mind besides how the Calgary Stampeders were doing. I had to find a job, and Carolyn and I had two children to take care of. However, at the end of the season, I checked on my Canadian friends and found that the Stampeders' season wasn't very good after I left. They played twelve more games and won two, tied one, and lost nine. They finished fourth out of five teams in the Western Division. The team that finished in the first place was the Winnipeg Blue Bombers. They won the title by a wide margin. They only had three losses. That was extra interesting to me because I had a hand in giving the Blue Bombers their first loss. We beat them in the game where my shoulder was injured.

Perhaps, in a roundabout way, due to my injury, I had a hand in helping the Blue Bombers have a winning season. During games back in the 1950s, players were permitted to use a few practices that are unacceptable today. Back then, quarterbacks were fair game for being hit as hard as possible. The objective was to eliminate the key opposing player and, thereby, greatly improve the chances of winning. That technique worked very well for the Winnipeg Blue Bombers. With me out for the rest of the season, the Stampeders' passing game was not very impressive.

For the rest of 1958, I worked for Carolyn's father and judiciously stayed with the training program for my shoulder. Improvements came slowly, but I could tell that the exercises and weight lifting were helping. That was encouraging, and I stayed with it.

By early 1959, my shoulder was healing well, and exercise routines were steadily improving my strength and mobility. I began to feel more optimistic about the possibility of playing again. I had more good news when, out of the blue, I got a call from John Bridgers, the new head football coach at Baylor. It was his first year there. I knew John from my time with the Colts in 1957, where he was on the coaching

Wayland Corgill

staff. At that time, he was an assistant to Coach Weeb Ewbank. Now at Baylor, he needed help with offensive coaching. His objective was to install the Colts offense that relied heavily on a passing game. He had seen me practice with Johnny Unitas and knew of my experience in the Army and, previously, at Baylor. He was aware of successes I had had with the passing game and was hopeful that I could do the job of teaching others.

John had no knowledge of my coaching experience and capabilities. He didn't know that I had, in effect, been the coach and recruiter for the Fort Bliss Falcons in 1956. I knew I could do what he wanted. So, without reservation, we sold our house in Breckenridge and bought another one in Waco. I thought there was a very good chance that I had a shot at a long-term coaching position at Baylor. Little did Carolyn and I know that Waco would be another relatively short stay. A year later, we would be selling the Waco house and moving to Dallas.

That year at Baylor was great for me. It felt good just to be back on the campus. Every day, I would see old friends and would have reminders of the pleasant times I had there as a student and football player. Five short years had put me on the other side of the ball, and I was now in the business of teaching instead of learning. Teaching would include a lot of ball throwing, and I believed that I would be ready to do the job when training camp started. My shoulder would have had approximately nine months of healing and exercising by that time. It was feeling better every day, and already, I was throwing the ball fairly well and without pain. I didn't doubt that I would be ready.

Baylor's football coaching staff in 1959. Front (L-R): Chuck Purvis, Head Coach John Bridgers, M. A. Smith; Back (L-R): me, Charley Driver, Walt Hackett, Hayden Fry, Tom Pruett
– courtesy of The Texas Collection, Baylor University

The Rifleman - Cotton Davidson

Coach Bridgers had assembled a first-class coaching staff. He was a very good coach too. Also, he was easy to get along with, as was everyone on the staff. I knew about half of them from my days at Baylor or in the pros. One was my teammate from 1950, Hayden Fry. I was very pleased to work with him again. It would be his first year in a long career of coaching football in a half dozen universities. The whole staff worked well together, and that sure helped make the 1959 season enjoyable.

We had a great group of young guys on the team. I loved working with them. I spent a lot of time with quarterbacks and, particularly, the receivers. By the time training camp started, my shoulder was in good shape, and I could throw the ball almost as hard as I could before the injury. We had eight receivers, and I threw balls to them every day. During warm-up, I would have receivers running routes, and I would throw each one approximately thirty balls. I threw every type of pass that a receiver might have to catch in a game, particularly those over their shoulders. Those young men were easy to coach and very receptive to the training. In two or three weeks, I could see big improvements. I was very happy with how quickly they came around. They made my job easy.

Throwing thirty passes to each of eight receivers a day is a lot of throwing. Before long, my arm was in better shape than when I was playing. By the end of the year, I could throw every ball I expected my receivers to catch. Usually, I didn't throw the ball as hard as I did back then but, once in a while, I would do that. When working with quarterbacks, I, occasionally, would put them on drills to throw at top speed. Receivers needed practice for those throws too.

We had very good quarterbacks. They were talented athletes and great to work with. They were quick learners. After two or three weeks, as with our receivers, I could see major improvements in their performance. Coach Bridgers and I conferred on pass plays that I thought we could handle, and he trusted me to do what was needed to make them work. To win games, he understood very well that we had to have an effective passing offense coordinated with a strong running game. A good running game sure helps the passing game. The coaching staff understood that, and we worked well together for that objective. For me, being back with Baylor's football team as a coach was a pleasure, and I looked forward to each day.

Soon after our training camp started, I had an extraordinary bonus when Raymond Berry took the time to come down from Baltimore and work with me. With Raymond, we were tremendously effective in showing our young charges how the passing game should be done. Raymond was the best.

When Raymond told me he was coming, I had a huddle with the team to let them know about the rare experience they would be in for. I told them how unbelievably dedicated he was and how he was a stickler for details and thoroughness. That was the way he was with everything, even paperwork.

Raymond is one of the most interesting and talented people I know. He left nothing to chance. He made a special map for his trip from Baltimore to Waco. To define the route, he cut strips from state maps and taped them end-to-end into one long map. That specialized map stayed in full view at all times while on the road. He was not going to get lost. Also, he took every precaution to avoid delays due to car problems. He made a visual inspection of that car before starting each leg of his journey. Tires got a lot of attention. Checking air pressures was high on his agenda. No doubt, Raymond's methods contributed heavily to his phenomenal success in football. No one even hinted that he should change anything. His consistent, spectacular performance on the football field was an example to be studied and copied, if possible.

I sure was glad to see my old friend in Waco, and we had a lot of fun with the Baylor team. I'll bet every one of those guys has a vivid memory of playing with one of the greatest football players of all time.

Baylor's win-loss record of 4-6 for the 1959 season was certainly not as good as I had hoped. Although consistency in the execution of our passing game evolved more slowly than I expected, that was not the reason for most of those losses. The overriding problem was fumbles and penalties. They plagued us throughout the season and made a huge difference in game outcomes. Also, the protection of our quarterback could have been much better. If not for those handicaps, we would easily have won at least three more games.

Even though I thought there was room for improvement with our passing game in the 1959 season, without question, we had come a long way. One measure of that was a comparison to SMU who had set passing records with Don Meredith as quarterback for the Ponies. For the season, Baylor ranked second to SMU in yards passing. I was very proud of our guys.

Coach Bridgers was head coach at Baylor for ten years. He quickly turned Baylor's football fortunes around. In the next four years, he led the Bears to three bowl games and won two of them. The 1963 season was a record-breaker with outstanding performances by All-Americans: quarterback Don Trull and wide receiver Lawrence Elkins. Installing the Colts' wide-open passing game made a big contribution to Coach Bridgers' success.

By the end of 1959, I had convinced John Bridgers and the Baylor coaching staff that I could do the coaching job they wanted. I had also reminded myself of how I liked coaching and working with young athletes. We sure had a good group of kids. There was no question in my mind about coaching and recruiting being "my cup of tea." However, the possibility for that career move would have to wait a few years. Toward the end of 1959, pro football prospects entered my life again. Big changes were coming in the world of football with the startup of a brand new league, the American Football League (AFL). Quarterbacks for the AFL were in demand.

The 1960 Dallas Texans
Front Row: 14 Hunter Enis, 18 Don Flynn, 19 Cotton Davidson, 21 Dave Webster, 22 Johnny Bookman, 28 Abner Haynes, 30 Jack Spikes
Second Row: 32 Bo Dickinson, 33 Curley Johnson, 35 Smokey Stover, 36 Clem Daniels, 42 Johnny Robinson, 44 Jimmy Harris, 48 Duane Wood, 50 Jim Barton
Third Row: 54 Ted Greene, 55 Tom Dimmick, 56 Walt Corey, 60 Al Reynolds, 62 Sid Fournet, 63 Marvin Terrell, 64 Billy Krisher, 66 Dick Frey
Fourth Row: 69 Sherrill Headrick, 70 Jack Stone, 71 Ray Collins, 72 Paul Rochester, 74 Jerry Cornelison, 76 Walter Napier, 79 Charley Diamond
Fifth Row: 80 Max Boydston, 85 Ed Bernet, 86 Paul Miller, 87 Mel Branch, 88 Chris Burford
– courtesy of the Kansas City Chiefs

The 1960 Dallas Texans Offensive Starting Lineup

Front Row: 80 Max Boydston, 74 Jerry Cornelison, 64 Billy Krisher, 50 Jim Barton, 62 Sid Fournet, 79 Charley Diamond, 88 Chris Burford
Back Row: 42 Johnny Robinson, 30 Jack Spikes, 19 Cotton Davidson, 28 Abner Haynes – courtesy of the Kansas City chiefs

Dallas Texans

The American Football League (AFL) was founded on August 14, 1959. It was the creation of Lamar Hunt, the owner of one of eight teams that would make up the new league in the 1960 season. Lamar's team was the Dallas Texans. The AFL had two divisions, Eastern and Western. Teams in the Eastern Division were the Houston Oilers, New York Titans, Buffalo Bills, and Boston Patriots. Teams in the Western Division were the Dallas Texans, Los Angeles Chargers, Oakland Raiders, and Denver Broncos.

Lamar was only 27 years old when he undertook the formation of the AFL. However, his business insight far exceeded what might be expected of someone twice his age. Also, he was a gentleman and as fine a person as I ever dealt with.

Lamar knew what he was doing, although many people in the sports world thought differently. Conversations over coffee often opined that Lamar might lose over a million dollars the first year and, perhaps, more in later years. Lamar's father, H.L. Hunt, had an interesting reply to that opinion. He said, "Well, if it turns out that way, Lamar can probably last at least fifty years."

The Texans needed a quarterback, and I was Lamar's first choice. In the fall of 1959, he approached me with a proposal. We had a lot to discuss. I knew absolutely nothing about the AFL. Other topics included the condition of my shoulder and my commitment to the Baylor coaching staff. Throughout the rest of the year, Lamar called me almost every other day and visited me at Baylor a few times. Clearly, he was confident of being successful and impressed me with his knowledge of football and plans for the new league. Lamar was insistent that I should be the quarterback to help get his Texans started.

A deciding factor in my prospects for joining the Texans depended on the condition of my shoulder. It had steadily improved with the exercise program I had been following. By the fall of 1959, I began to believe that my chances for playing again were very good. My shoulder was feeling good, and I was having no problem with throwing the ball. Lamar and I agreed that a final decision would be delayed until the end of the year and, unless something unexpected happened, I would seriously consider his offer.

When John Bridgers asked me to help him coach at Baylor, we had a gentlemen's agreement and a handshake. There was no contract and no commitment for my staying a length of time beyond that required to install the Colts offense. When the 1959 football season was over, I had completed my assignment and was free to leave. Before Lamar Hunt entered the picture, I had thoughts of staying longer on the Baylor coaching staff. I really liked coaching. However, I was only 28 years old and loved playing. I was certain that my shoulder would not hold me back, and I knew that I would like to have

The 1961 Dallas Texans

Front Row: 15 Randy Duncan, 18 Don Flynn, 19 Cotton Davidson, 21 Dave Webster, 26 Frank Jackson, 28 Abner Haynes

Second Row: 30 Jack Spikes, 32 Jack Johnson, 35 Smokey Stover, 42 Johnny Robinson, 44 Edward Kelley, 45 Dave Grayson, 48 Duane Wood

Third Row: 54 Ted Greene, 55 E.J. Holub, 60 Al Reynolds, 62 Sid Fournet, 63 Marvin Terrell, 64 Billy Drisher, 65 Jon Gillam, 69 Luther Jeralds

Fourth Row: 71 Ray Collins, 72 Paul Rochester, 74 Jerry Cornelison, 75 Jerry Mays, 76 Walter Napier, 77 Jim Tyrer, 79 Charley Diamond

Fifth Row: 80 Tony Romeo, 86 Paul Miller, 87 Mel Branch, 88 Chris Burford

- courtesy of the Kansas City Chiefs

another shot at the excitement of being in the game. I couldn't turn down a fair offer for a chance with the AFL. That is what I indicated to Lamar, and needless to say, he was happy about that.

After Baylor's last game of the season, I met with Lamar in Dallas to discuss details of his offer and review his plans for organizing a new team in a conference that was in the process of being created. I thought that was a very complicated and ambitious goal. I wanted to learn as much as I could and be as certain as possible that I was doing the right thing before giving up my ties with Baylor. I was interested in Lamar's coaching arrangements, and he introduced me to his head coach, Hank Stram. Hank and I had never met. I didn't know anything about him, and I don't think he knew much, if anything, about me. Our conversation was pleasant but formal. He struck me as being a serious, reserved gentleman and very business-like. He didn't seem to be concerned about my capabilities or experience, and he didn't inquire about personal interests. By the end of our short conversation, I hadn't learned much about him. However, I had heard enough to make me feel that I could work with him. After Hank left the meeting, Lamar and I agreed on a contract, and I signed it. I didn't see or talk to Coach Stram until I reported to training camp a few months later.

Wayland Corgill

Getting back into the pros would be another, in a growing list, of unexpected, bold steps in my football career. This move presented a whole new set of things to consider. Also, I wondered what PaPa would have had to say about this latest turn of events. No doubt, he would have reminded me of the importance of common sense in whatever advice he offered.

Carolyn and I had planned for a possible longer-term of coaching at Baylor than one year. That is why we bought a house in Waco. With a move to the AFL, we were faced with a decision for housing in Dallas. Based on our experience with moves since I got out of college, I was somewhat sure that we shouldn't sell out in Waco and buy in Dallas. We had made six big moves in the last six years. Probably, the smart thing to do would be to rent a house in Dallas and "test the water" in the AFL for at least a couple of years before considering more permanent accommodations. PaPa would probably agree with that approach. We would stay settled in Waco until the Texans' 1960 training camp started. Until then, we would have plenty of time for proper farewells to all of our great friends at Baylor.

The 1961 Dallas Texans Offensive Starting Lineup

Front Row: 81 Max Boydston, 74 Jerry Cornelison, 64 Billy Krisher, 65 Jon Gilliam, 60 Al Reynolds, 77 Jim Tyrer, 88 Chris Burford

Second Row: 42 Johnny Robinson, 32 Jack Johnson, 19 Cotton Davidson, 28 Abner Haynes
- courtesy of the Kansas City Chiefs

Between the signing of a contract and reporting to training camp, my only contact with the Texans had been with Lamar. Our conversations were limited to personal matters, and I had no idea how the team was shaping up. That caused me to wonder if I might be in for interesting times with helping to start a brand new organization. Hopefully, I would know some of the team members. When I arrived at training camp, I found that I didn't know anyone except Coach Stram. Most of my teammates had the same problem. Out of 42 guys on the roster, I was the only one from Baylor. We had a big job ahead of us to learn all we could about each other as soon as possible. I had no idea about the capabilities of anyone. However, I soon realized that either Lamar or Coach Stram, or both, had recruited a remarkably talented group of athletes. Most of them were experienced players from NFL teams. In succeeding years, many of them achieved exceptional records. A couple of them were even inducted into the Pro Football Hall of Fame. Abner Haynes, Chris Burford, Jack Spikes, Johnny Robinson, Billy Krisner, Mel Branch, and Sherrill Headrick were just a few of that powerful group. It didn't take long for me to believe that we could win with those guys.

From the first day at camp, getting to know Coach Stram was the first order of business, as well as getting to know my teammates. As I expected from my first impressions during our short meeting in Dallas, he always conducted himself as a gentleman. In addition, I quickly learned that he insisted on proper conduct and was the "definition" of a disciplinarian. He had to have everything precise and perfect. Coach Tom Landry could have learned from him in that department. Locker room meetings were conducted in strict order with no "fooling around." Those meetings were commonly referred to as "Hank's Sunday School Classes."

In addition to gentlemanly behavior, Hank also had a few rules for how the team should look in public off of the field. When traveling, the whole team dressed alike. We would wear black pants, white shirts, black ties, and red jackets emblazoned with the Texans' crest. Needless to say, we stood out and, sometimes, the attention we got was not what we expected. At a hotel in New York, one lady said to me, "Would you take my bags to the car?"

Coach Hank Stram insisted that the Texans looked sharp when travelling. I am on the ramp, fifth from the bottom. – courtesy of the Kansas City Chiefs

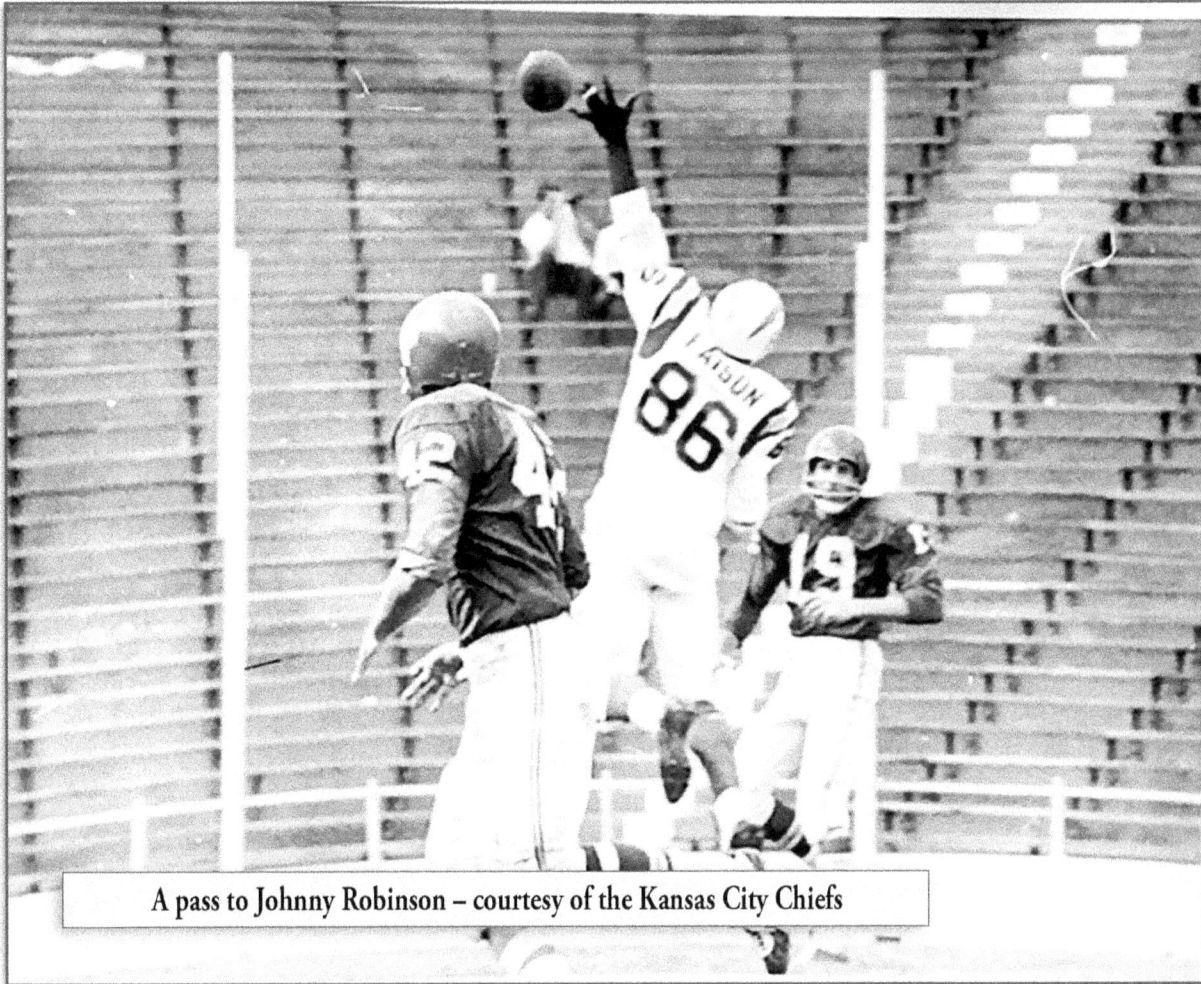

A pass to Johnny Robinson – courtesy of the Kansas City Chiefs

The training camp was in Roswell, New Mexico. Even though I didn't see, or otherwise encounter, any unidentified foreign objects (UFOs), I found Roswell to be a very interesting place. The training camp location at a local college was great. The dorm rooms were very comfortable, but the best feature was the large training field. It was large enough to have three fields, side by side. We would practice on one field for two or three days and then move to another field. The field we had vacated would be watered and cared for until we circulated back a few days later. That way, we were always playing on good grass and ground that was not as hard as concrete. That sure was a lot easier on bodies that got slammed to the ground. Our practice field at Baltimore was always as hard as a rock at the end of training camp each year.

As practice got underway, I became concerned about a few unexpected issues that quickly became apparent. Most important to me was that we didn't have, and wouldn't have, an offensive coordinator. How would we get around that? How would the game be managed, and who would determine the plays? Another important item was the need to include a significant passing game in our game plans. My experience had been that a winning team had to have a strong passing game. Hank didn't seem to share my opinion on that. He had come right out of a college coaching position, and his notions about a passing game were quite different from customary practices in the pros. He was more attuned to running plays than passing plays. It was looking like I might have a bigger job than I expected.

Abner Haynes breaks clean for a TD against the Denver Broncos – courtesy of the Kansas City Chiefs

Several precedents evolved in that first training camp, and they carried over into standard practice during season play. It was effectively left up to me to be the dominant organizer of plays and the creator of our playbook. Also, I had a lot of freedom in deciding game plans. While playing, I essentially managed the offense from the quarterback position and, in the process, I coordinated with the coaching staff as best I could. That was a complicated situation for me, but we made it work. My previous coaching experience in the Army and at Baylor sure came in handy.

During practice, I worked with receivers just like I had done at Baylor the previous year. They were great guys and continued to improve throughout the year. Our passing game developed well. To prepare for games, I would watch opposing team game films during the week and devise game plans. I kept game plans as simple as possible with only a handful of plays that I thought would work against the particular team we would be playing. Those were the plays we practiced. During games, I didn't call all the plays, but a lot was left up to me in deciding what to do.

My experience with the Texans was quite different from previous teams I had played with. The players were as good as any I had ever played with, but coaching techniques were new to me. Hank's reserved personality and coaching methodology left so much up to me. He didn't talk to me during games, and he rarely talked to me at other times. We never coordinated on game plans. Often, I wondered if I was doing what he wanted. However, we had a respectful relationship with never a cross word. Hank was also relatively quiet in the locker room with few pep talks before a game. If we were losing at halftime, he would try to fire up the team, and occasionally, he would have a few words to say after a game. That first training camp in Roswell set a lot of precedents for the rest of my time with the Texans.

Another precedent that was established at the Roswell training camp was related to how Coach Stram expected the team to act in public. Our interaction with town folks was pleasant and uneventful. There were no problems, and Hank's rules helped ensure things stayed that way when we were "off the reservation." He was particularly concerned about any of his guys consorting with local members of the opposite sex.

DALLAS TEXANS vs. LOS ANGELES CHARGERS
Memorial Coliseum, Los Angeles, California
Saturday nite, September 10, 1960

INDIVIDUAL STATISTICS (CONTINUED)

PASSING

CHARGERS	PA	PC	PI	YDS.	TD	LONG
KEMP	41	24	0	275	2	36
LOWE	1	1	0	24	0	24
	42	25	0	299	2	36

TEXANS	PA	PC	PI	YDS	TD	LONG
DAVIDSON	40	22	1	230	2	21
HAYNES	1	0	0	0	0	0
	41	22	1	230	2	21

PUNTING

CHARGERS	NO.	YDS.	AVE.
MAGUIRE	4	160	40.00

TEXANS	NO.	YDS.	AVE.
DAVIDSON	5	237	47.50

PASS RECEIVERS

CHARGERS	NO.	YDS.	TD	LONG
LOWE	3	14	0	6
WOMBLE	7	92	0	26
CLARK	3	42	0	36
FERGUSON	3	8	0	4
ANDERSON	5	103	1	46
FLOWERS	2	25	0	20
KOCOUREK	1	12	0	12
WALLER	1	3	1	3
	25	299	1	46

TEXANS	NO.	YDS.	TD	LONG
ROBINSON	5	52	0	21
BOYDSTON	3	45	0	17
HAYNES	7	62	1	17
BURFORD	3	31	1	12
SPIKES	1	21	0	21
BRYANT	1	9	0	9
SWINK	2	10	0	9
	22	230	2	21

PUNT RETURNS

TEXANS	NO.	YDS.	AVE.	TD
ROBINSON	1	2	2.00	0

CHARGERS	NO.	YDS.	AVE.	TD
HARRIS	2	7	3.50	0
SEARS	1	0	0.00	0
	3	7	2.33	0

KICKOFF RETURNS

CHARGERS	NO.	YDS.	AVE.	TD
LOWE	2	36	18.00	0
SEARS	1	24	24.00	0
	3	60	20.00	0

INTERCEPTION RETURNS

CHARGERS	NO.	YDS.	TD
SEARS	1	26	0

TEXANS	NO.	YDS.	TD
NONE			

TEXANS	NO.	YDS.	AVE.	TD
ROBINSON	1	8	8.00	0
HAYNES	2	45	22.50	0
	3	53	17.66	0

Stats for the very first game played by the Texans. It was against the Los Angeles Chargers on Sept. 10, 1960. I was disappointed with the narrow loss of 20 to 21 – courtesy of the Kansas City Chiefs

A ticket stub from our fourth game of the 1960 season. It was another narrow loss of 35 to 37 – courtesy of the Kansas City Chiefs

Consequences for that behavior were emphatically laid out in his first message during the first day in camp. For anyone caught in a compromising circumstance, Hank would call the person's hometown newspaper and then call his wife. Hank was serious; no question.

There was no "fooling around" in Roswell. However, I had dinner with an attractive young woman one night, and early in the evening, I began to worry about Hank's rules. I had not advised him on what I was doing.

My host for that evening was my first cousin who lived in Roswell. She invited me to dinner, and I readily accepted. We made arrangements for her to pick me up after practice and, for the rest of the day, I looked forward to having a nice evening and a home-cooked meal. I was still thinking about that when I got in her car and forgot to say anything to Coach Stram about where I was going or who I was going with. Later, when I remembered the coach's impassioned words, I thought it might be advisable to track him down when I got back to camp. When my cousin dropped me back there, I found Coach Stram straight away and informed him that I had stayed true to his rules. Nobody was fooling around.

When the Roswell training camp was over, Carolyn and I began making plans for moving to Dallas. We renewed our decision to rent and not buy. Another requirement was to find a place large enough for our growing family. Tommy and Kelly Ann would soon have another sibling. We lived in a Dallas apartment for a couple of months before locating a house that would fit our needs. That house was within a couple of blocks of the Texans' practice field that was on the east side of University Park and near Central Expressway (Highway 75). We quickly settled into our new surroundings and our new network of coaches and teammates. So far, our move to the Dallas Texans suited us just fine.

The Texans' 1960 season was a good one, and we played well. We steadily improved as the season progressed. I enjoyed playing with those guys. We had very good receivers, and they performed well as we included more and more pass-plays in our game plan. That definitely helped win games. However, pass plays also have inherent amounts of risk. An often-quoted proverb highlights the bad things that can happen when a ball is intercepted. The first time the Texans ever played the Houston Oilers was on October 16, 1960. During that game, I had an interception by a young linebacker, Albert Witcher, whom I had just coached at Baylor the previous year. Albert was a tough competitor and surprised me by beating my intended target and making a very difficult catch. My first thought was that I had coached Albert too well. After the game, I told him I had thrown him the ball because I liked him. Of course, he knew better. We lost that game, but I don't think the interception was the reason. It didn't help, though. Our win-loss record for the season was 8 to 6, and we finished second in the Western Division. Only Sid Gillman's Los Angeles Chargers had a better record.

Lamar and his staff had proved that they were exceedingly capable of recognizing talent. Equally important, they had the skills and financial means to acquire a significant share of that talent. Lamar knew what was needed and how to get it done. As the inaugural year of the AFL progressed under his leadership, it increasingly looked like this new organization would be unquestionably successful. Attendance at games was good, and the quality of play was exciting. Developments in the AFL were making sports news headlines, and football players were taking note. About three-fourths of players in the 1960 draft went to the AFL. That result was not by design or intent on the part of the AFL. Lamar was confident that the sports world was large enough to accommodate both the NFL and AFL. For example, he had no opposition to another new team forming in Dallas in 1960; the NFL Dallas Cowboys. He considered that there were plenty of quality players to share, and Dallas was big enough for both teams.

Lamar had plenty of money to comfortably keep the Texans going without jeopardizing his financial well-being. I had no idea about his worth but, according to his father, it must have been very substantial. However, a person would never know that by judging from the way Lamar lived and conducted himself in public. He was not extravagant. From outward appearances, a stranger would likely guess him to be an ordinary businessman living from paycheck to paycheck. For example, he and his family lived in a modest-sized, relatively plain house, and he drove a 1948 Oldsmobile. He was an unusual man in many

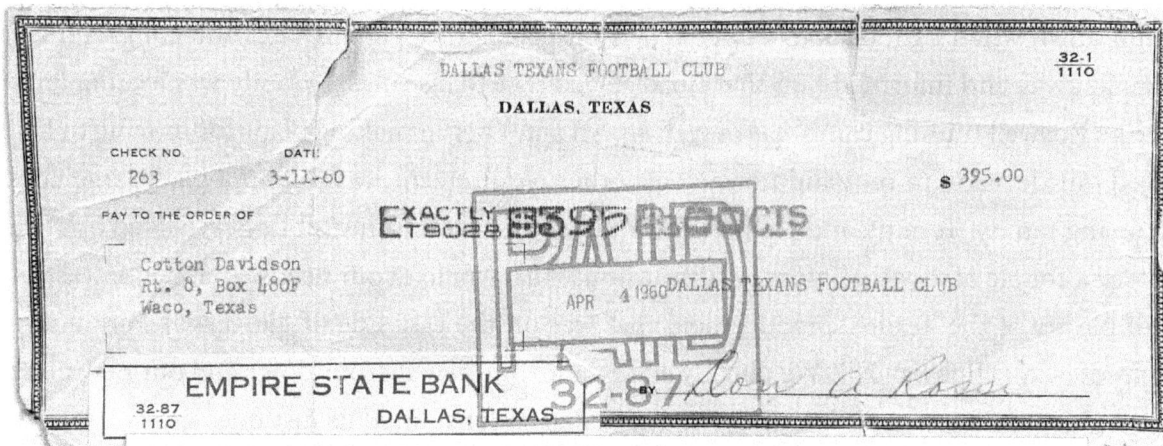

DALLAS TEXANS FOOTBALL CLUB

DALLAS, TEXAS

32-1
1110

CHECK NO. 263   DATE 3-11-60

PAY TO THE ORDER OF

Cotton Davidson
Rt. 8, Box 480F
Waco, Texas

$ 395.00

EMPIRE STATE BANK
32-87
1110
DALLAS, TEXAS

**My first paycheck from the Texans - $395.00
– courtesy of the Kansas City Chiefs**

ways and an admirable example of honesty, integrity, and fairness with everyone around him. Those characteristics made him an extraordinary individual without any consideration for his wealth.

Halfway through the 1960 season, Lamar and his wife invited the Texans' quarterbacks and wives to their home for dinner. The meal was spaghetti and meatballs. It was a "no-frills" dinner. We dined on card tables, and the table settings were plain and functional. The food was plentiful and very good, but that was not what made the evening unforgettably pleasant. Lamar and his wife were such gracious and interesting hosts. The conversation was great, and we felt right at home. Carolyn thoroughly enjoyed the evening, and she was made especially comfortable because the birth of our third child was expected any day.

The next day was memorable for Carolyn too. Before sunrise the next morning, November 4, we were in a hospital maternity ward and were soon introduced to our third child, Tracy. Later that morning, Lamar came to the hospital. Carolyn remembers that visit very well. He told her that he wouldn't invite her for spaghetti and meatballs again. Clearly, Italian food had dramatic after-effects. Other types of food would be on the menu.

Not long after the exciting event of Tracy's birth, another notable event happened. This one was totally unexpected. Dallas area sportswriters had plenty of things to write about with two brand new football teams in town: the Texans and the Cowboys. Everything that involved both the Texans and the Cowboys always evolved into a big contest. It was sportswriters' heaven, and they looked for ways to promote encounters. Writers and sports announcers teamed up to stage, of all things, a cow milking contest. It was Dairy Week in Dallas. Competition would be between the Texans, Cowboys, and three or four of the guys who had cooked up the bizarre affair. I would represent the Texans, and Jerry Tubbs would represent the Cowboys.

Those media folks had publicized the event as if it was a playoff game. On the day of the contest, a huge Holstein cow was trucked to our practice field, and a crowd gathered. There were lots of ballyhooing, and a few contestants did a fair amount of bragging about their milking prowess. Jerry Tubbs was a big linebacker from Breckenridge, Texas, who had set records in high school and at the University of Oklahoma. On this day of competition for a trophy, he appeared to be the picture of confidence with the prospect of also adding that one to his collection. There was no question about his being a force to be reckoned with on the football field, but I questioned his skills with a milk cow. I doubted that he had ever had the in-depth, quality training I got as a kid when I was paid a "copper" for every cow I milked for my PaPa. Surely, I had an edge, and my competitors just might be in for a surprise.

There was only one rule for the contestants, and that was to get as much milk in a bucket as possible in one minute. That big cow had a bag that probably held five gallons of milk. Therefore, the order of the "milkers" wouldn't matter. I expected that most of my competitors wouldn't get more than a pint of milk in their bucket in one minute. However, I volunteered to go last, so no one could complain that I had an advantage. Not to be outdone, Jerry also volunteered to go next to last.

The milking performance of all of the writers and announcers was nothing to write home about. A couple of them barely wet the bottom of the bucket. Luckily, the cow was good-natured and paid no attention to their inexperienced handling of the source of the milk. Jerry's turn finally came, and he did an acceptable job. In fact, it was the best, so far. When I sat down, everybody was out of the contest except Jerry. Tension built. I particularly had his undivided attention but only for about 30 seconds. He could see the trophy slipping away after that. When the minute was up, I had blown them all away, and I still have the trophy to prove it. That was one time the Texans beat the Cowboys.

After the milking contest, our 1960 season soon ended without too much excitement, except for winning our last three games by landslides. Two of those wins were especially satisfying. They were with the Oilers and Patriots, who had beaten us earlier in the season.

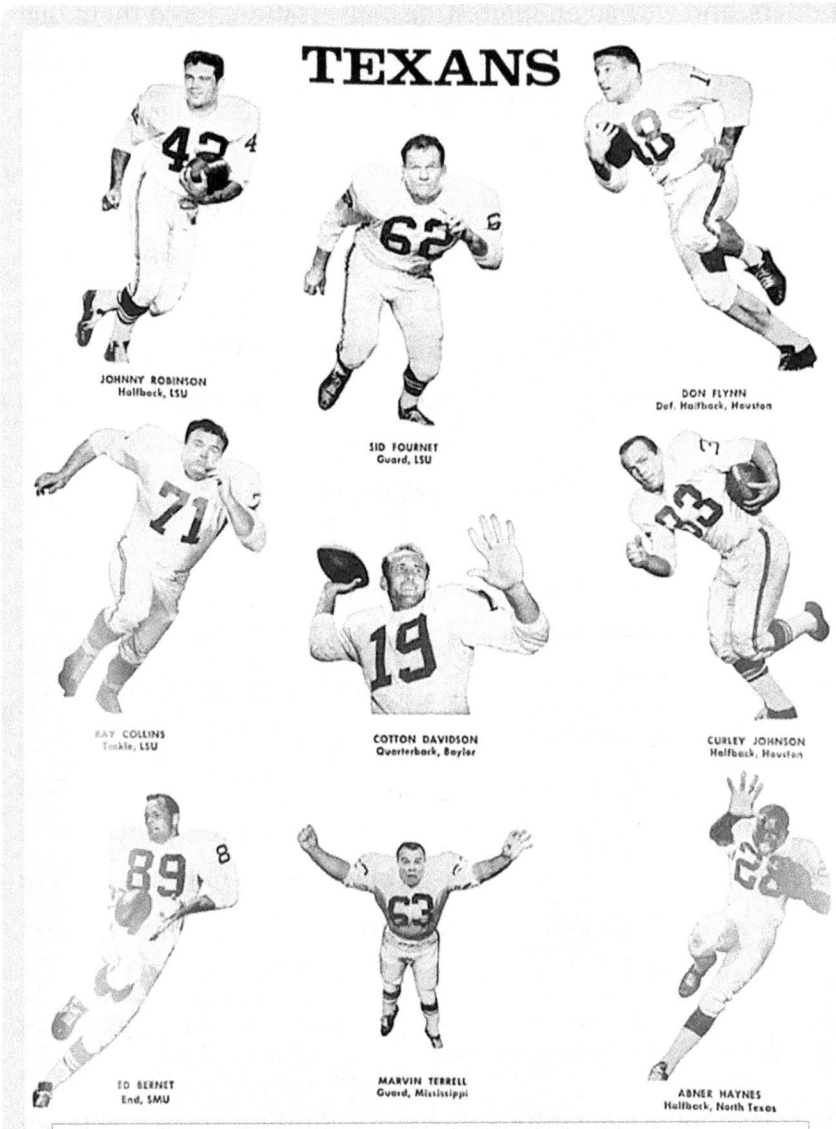

TEXANS

JOHNNY ROBINSON
Halfback, LSU

SID FOURNET
Guard, LSU

DON FLYNN
Def. Halfback, Houston

KAY COLLINS
Tackle, LSU

COTTON DAVIDSON
Quarterback, Baylor

CURLEY JOHNSON
Halfback, Houston

ED BERNET
End, SMU

MARVIN TERRELL
Guard, Mississippi

ABNER HAYNES
Halfback, North Texas

The Texans program cover for the Dec. 4, 1960 game against the Houston Oilers. That was a resounding win of 24-0 – courtesy of the Kansas City Chiefs

The Rifleman - Cotton Davidson

I hadn't been in Dallas very long before another extracurricular opportunity was presented to me. The Lee Riders jeans company had a big presence in Texas and the Bealls store chain handled them. The Lee Riders company engaged me to represent their jeans. I traveled all over Texas as their representative. I even went to Louisiana a few times. My job was to sign cards that the Lee Riders company had made with my picture on one side and an advertisement of their jeans on the other side. I also signed football cards that folks brought with them. My appearance at a Bealls store was advertised well in advance, and fifty or more people usually showed up to get my autograph. That was a really fun job. However, when I left Texas in 1962, that was almost the end of my being a representative for Lee Riders. Their popularity hadn't spread widely in California and, after making a small number of engagements, I discontinued helping Lee Riders sell jeans. However, I continued to enjoy all the Lee Rider jeans I could wear for several years after that.

I became acquainted with a few professional rodeo cowboys through the Lee Riders connection. In 1961, the National Finals Rodeo competitions were held in Dallas at the fairgrounds. I went out there to get a few tickets for three or four of my teammates and, also, my brother, Hy, and a couple of his friends. While out there, I met a couple of bull riders, and we had an interesting conversation. I told them that I wouldn't get on one of those bulls at any price. They laughed and surprised me with their opinions of football. They said that no amount of money could get them to line up on a football field against giants who would pound them into the turf. I didn't expect that.

The 1961 season was a "roller coaster" of wins and losses, and our record was not quite as good as the previous year. However, it was an interesting year with uniquely memorable events. One of those events occurred on November 3 during a game with the Boston Patriots on their home turf. The Patriots won that game but only because of an unorthodox play by a rogue participant who was not suited up on the Patriots bench. That game provided "fodder" for years of conversations and is still puzzled over by a few "old-timers."

The questionable play that gave the game to the Patriots happened in the final seconds of the game. We were down with a score of 21 to 28. We had the ball, and our chances for a touchdown were very good. I threw a long pass to our star wide receiver, Chris Burford. He caught it at the goal line, where he was tackled and fell into the end zone. We were confident that we had scored. Also, people in the stands thought we had made a touchdown. They began to flood onto the field. That is when things started "going off the rails" because the officials ruled that Chris didn't cross the goal line.

The field we were playing on was small. It had sideline and end zone spaces about like a high school field. Attendance was not large, approximately 25,000, but within a matter of minutes, people were standing all over our playing space. The sidelines and end zone were solid with fans. Officials went to work trying to clear spectators off of the field, but that was slow going. After several minutes, the best they could do was to push the crowd back behind the end zone.

Finally, the ball was placed on the one-yard line, and we were able to get set for one last play. Chris ran a quick post to the inside, and I threw him the ball. As soon as the ball was snapped, I saw a guy in a trench coat sprint out of the crowd behind the end zone. He took off like a middle linebacker who had been in the huddle and knew where the ball was going. The ball was almost on the tips of Chris' fingers for a sure catch when the trench-coat guy lunged in front of Chris and deflected the ball. Sprinting back into the crowd and out of the end zone, that "12th member of the Patriots' team" disappeared in a split second. Few people realized what had taken place since it happened so quickly, with views obstructed by the crowd. However, I saw it clearly. Apparently, the officials did not. They ruled that Chris had dropped the ball, and the game was over. I couldn't believe it!

I went over to Coach Stram and said, "We need to protest this." He was reluctant to do that. As was the case for so many other people, Coach Stram was unsure of what had happened. Therefore, he trusted the officials, and we added another mark in the loss column.

For a long time after that Patriots game, I had numerous conversations with people who doubted my version of how the game ended. One of the more prominent doubters was John Madden. I was playing for the Oakland Raiders in 1967 when John was hired by Al Davis as a linebacker coach. For reasons unknown to me, John had an interest in that bizarre sequence of events involving the mystery man in the overcoat. John and I had several conversations about that play, and he never believed my version of what happened. I left the Raiders at the end of 1968. For several years, I didn't have another conversation with John about the "Patriot's 12th man" in an overcoat, but the controversy continued. After Madden left the Raiders in 1978, he soon became one of the CBS network's top football broadcasters. In that capacity, more than once, he mentioned the crazy ending of that Texan-Patriot game back in 1961 and how the final play of the game was still disputed by some people, namely me. However, after a few years, I was vindicated when a video surfaced that corroborated my story. The controversy was finally settled. One question was never resolved, who was that "masked man" who charged out of the crowd and deflected the ball?

When the 1961 AFL Western Division season wound down, Sid Gillman's Chargers had the best record. The Texans came in second. Our record was not as good as the Chargers but it was much better than our other competitors: the Denver Broncos and the Oakland Raiders. All four teams in the Western Division had extraordinary, outstanding players on defense, as well as offense. Also, the four Eastern Division teams had similar players. In its two-year life, the AFL had managed to sign a very large complement of top-of-the-line players. The Texans certainly had their share of those. The AFL was off to a very good start, and the future looked bright. With that in mind, organizers of the AFL planned one more event after the season ended. Talents of selected players from both divisions were put on display for one more game: an All-Star game.

The first AFL All-Star game was played at Balboa Stadium in San Diego, CA, on January 7, 1962. It was the East against the West. The West roster included 10 players from the Dallas Texans, 12 from the Los Angeles Chargers, 5 from the Denver Broncos, and 2 from the Oakland Raiders. The East roster included 12 from the Houston Oilers, 7 from the Boston Patriots, 6 from the Buffalo Bills, and 4 from the NY Titans. The head coach for the East was Lou Rymkus of the Oilers. Sid Gillman was the head coach for the West. Also, Al Davis was helping on Sid's side of the field and that had implications for me the very next year.

The Rifleman - Cotton Davidson

I was in the group of players selected from the Texans. My teammates who were also selected from the Texans were: E.J. Holub at center and linebacker, Abner Haynes at running back, Chris Burford at split end, Bill Krisher at offensive guard, Jon Gilliam at linebacker, Sherrill Headrick at linebacker, Mel Branch at defensive end, Paul Rochester at defensive tackle, and David Webster at defensive back. Those were great guys, and they proved that during the game.

The 1961 season, Texans All-Stars of the first AFL All-Star Game
Back Row: David Webster, Cotton Davidson, Abner Haynes
Front Row: E.J. Holub, Mel Branch, Bill Krisher, Jon Gilliam, Sherrill Headrick, Paul Rochester, Chris Burford – courtesy of the AFL Hall of Fame

The East did all of the scorings in the first quarter, which ended with a score of 5-0. In the second quarter, I replaced Jack Kemp of the Chargers at the quarterback position, and things began to turn around for us. In our first possession, I hit Donnie Stone of the Broncos with a long pass that he took for a touchdown. The East came back with a touchdown, and the score was 12-7. On our next possession, Abner Haynes ran for a touchdown and, just before the half ended, I hit the Charger's Dave Kocourek for another score. With a half-time score of 21-12, we went to the locker room in high spirits.

The West didn't let up on scoring in the second half. In the third quarter, Abner Haynes returned a punt for 66 yards and a touchdown, and I completed a pass to the Charger's Don Norton for another score. Oilers' George Blanda replied with a touchdown pass to Boston's Gino Cappelletti and the third period ended with a score of 35-19. In the fourth quarter, the East made only one touchdown with a two-point conversion. However, we continued our aggressive play with a touchdown from an interception and field goals to end the game with a winning score of 47 to 27.

I had had a very good day on the field, and it was made even better when I heard the news about the Most Valuable Player (MVP) selection. It was me. The Commissioner of the AFL, Mr. Joe Foss, presented a beautiful trophy to me, and I was truly honored. However, while cameras were clicking, I thought about the rest of the guys on my team. As any quarterback will tell you, every one of those guys is extremely important to the man behind the center. They make a huge difference to the ball handler in so many ways, such as:

how hard and how often he is hit, how good his passing stats are, and how often he gets a chance to handle the ball. My teammates were stars. Most of them went on from this game to have very distinguished careers in the pros. They won all manner of awards, set astounding records, and their names constantly made headlines in the sports world. Many of them played in numerous all-star games, pro-bowls, and super-bowls. After they retired from football, most of

In the locker room after the first AFL All-Star game on Jan. 7, 1962, Coach Sid Gillman presented me with the AFL All-Star MVP trophy and shakes Abner Haynes' hand. In 1960, Abner was AFL Rookie of the Year and AFL MVP – courtesy of the AFL Hall of Fame

them were inducted into athlete halls of fame all the way from high school to the Pro Football Hall of Fame. I think of those guys when I look at that MVP trophy.

My third (1962) season with the Texans didn't last very long. Len Dawson joined the team, and I was traded to the Oakland Raiders. Ironically, that happened right after the Texans played the Raiders in Lithonia, Georgia, on August 4, 1962. That was our first preseason game and the last game where I was the starting quarterback for the Texans. By the way, we easily beat the Raiders 13 to 3 in that game. The Raiders did not have a good team. It was the worst one in the AFL.

Immediately after I found out that I was to be traded, Lamar Hunt paid me a visit at home. He explained things and apologized for having to make the trade. He completely understood how it would "upset my apple cart" but was positive that I could make a big difference in the Raiders' performance. They needed help, and Lamar was doing his best to make sure the AFL survived and prospered. For that to happen, all of the teams had to be strong, and Oakland must improve.

I listened to Lamar and, when he finished, I didn't mince words when I told him my opinion. I said, "I am not going! There is nothing in California that has an attraction for me. I have just seen the quality and condition of the Raiders' team, and I really don't think I can effectively work with that group. I will go back to Waco, or somewhere in Texas, and make a living doing something other than playing pro ball."

Lamar wouldn't give up on getting me to California. A few days after he talked to me about the trade, Al Davis called. It wasn't much of a guess about who instigated that call. I had known Al since 1954 when he assisted Sid Gillman with coaching the College All-Star Football Classic game in Chicago. Al had coached me then and again, just eight months earlier, on January 7, 1962, the AFL All-Star Game. He was Sid's assistant in both games and concentrated on working with quarterbacks. Al and I spent a lot of time together, and we got along very well. He had excellent knowledge of football, and we agreed on virtually everything.

I was puzzled about Al's call. As far as I knew, he had nothing to do with the Raiders. He was still an assistant coach on Sid Gillman's staff for the Chargers. Perhaps, Lamar thought someone in California might be able to convince me to take this giant step. Lamar knew that I liked and respected Al. Maybe Al could change my mind.

Lamar's approach for getting me to the Raiders worked. Al was convincing. After numerous phone conversations with him, I finally told Al that I would pack my bags and be out there. Carolyn and I would give it a try for the 1962 season. It would be another venture into a world of unknowns: new teammates, new coaches, new territory, etc. I was getting used to that. My time with the Texans had exposed me to a wide variety of new things. However, it had been a good experience, and I would have done it over if I had had a second chance. They were a great bunch of guys. By staying in the AFL, I would probably see some of them again on the field, and Coach Stram too. As it turned out, I did see many of my old teammates, and some of them joined me in Oakland. However, I rarely crossed paths with Hank.

August was almost over. Season games would start soon. We needed to move fast and get settled as soon as possible. I left right away. Carolyn and our three children followed a little later. I was glad that we hadn't bought a house in Dallas.

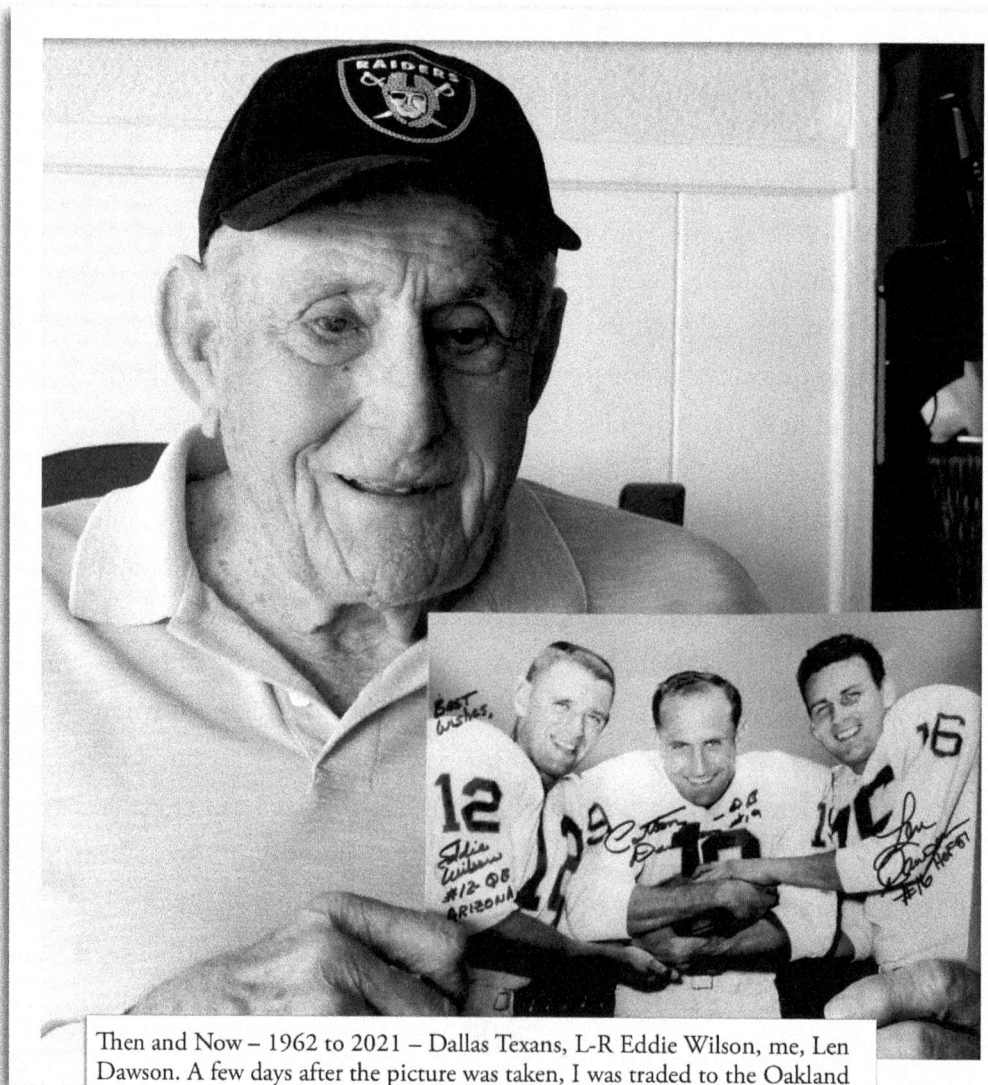

Then and Now – 1962 to 2021 – Dallas Texans, L-R Eddie Wilson, me, Len Dawson. A few days after the picture was taken, I was traded to the Oakland Raiders – courtesy of the Davidson family

Oakland Raiders

In 1961, the Oakland Raiders were hardly a team. They won only two games. In 1962, I would be part of that team, and I didn't expect any miraculous turnarounds. Playing for the Raiders was not likely to be one of my better experiences. However, I had committed to go out there and try to make a difference. Maybe I could. At least, Lamar Hunt and Al Davis thought so. After a short two years with the Texans, I was moving again. This would be my seventh major move in the eight years since leaving Baylor in 1954.

By 1962, most of the eight teams in the AFL had either made significant improvements in their capabilities and performance or had maintained their standings during the two years since the AFL began. Only Oakland was noticeably struggling. Oakland was on the bottom of the list in 1961, and improvements didn't seem likely. Before heading west, I knew relatively little about the capabilities of the Raiders organization. I had a lot of questions, and it certainly remained to be seen whether or not I could effectively help improve their standings. We would be facing teams that were getting very serious about winning games.

When I arrived in Oakland in mid-September 1962, the AFL season had already started, and the Raiders had lost their first game on September 9. I would be their quarterback in their second game on September 23. Ironically, that game was with the Dallas Texans. Therefore, I had been in Oakland only for a week before traveling back to Dallas. This time, I was on the Raiders' side of the field in the Cotton Bowl. Facing friends and former Texan teammates was an almost surreal situation for me. One month earlier, on August 4, I had been the quarterback for the Texans playing the Raiders in a pre-season game. Now, I was the quarterback for

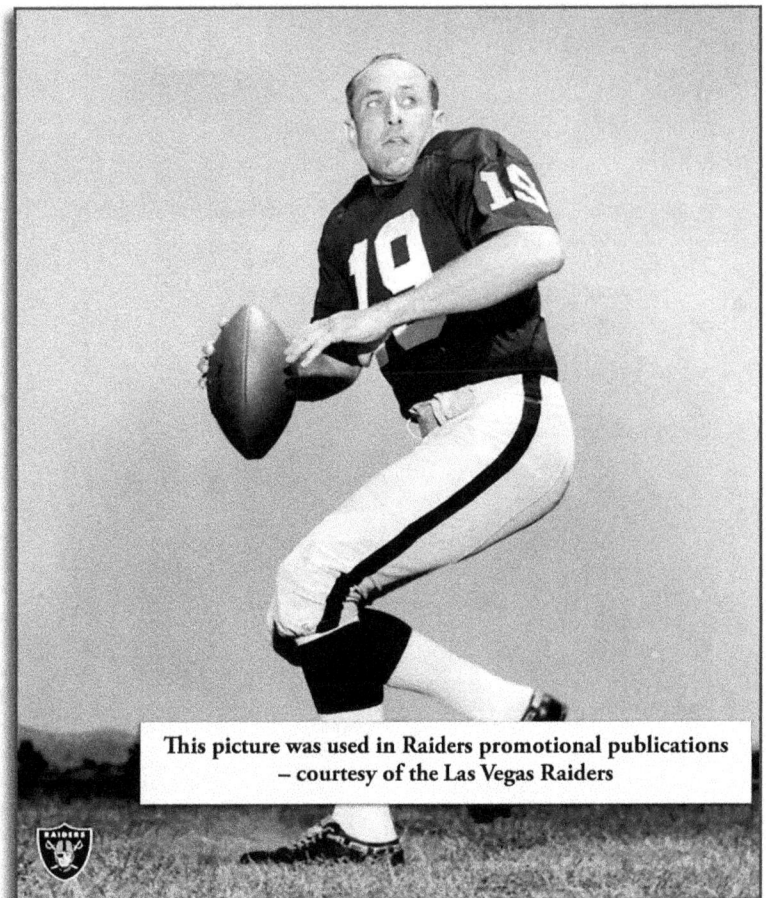

This picture was used in Raiders promotional publications – courtesy of the Las Vegas Raiders

Cotton Davidson

Baylor Bears
Selected in the First Round of the 1954 Draft by the Colts
111 games, 770 completions, 1752 passes, 43.9 11760 yds, 73 TDs,
129 rushes, 533 yds, 11 Tds
280 Punts, 38.1 yard average
Baltimore Colts, Dallas Texans, Oakland Raiders
Pro Bowl: 1961, 63

SUPER BOWL II

COTTON DAVIDSON
QUARTERBACK
DALLAS TEXANS

COTTON
DAVIDSON
QUARTERBACK · DALLAS TEXANS

COTTON DAVIDSON
QUARTERBACK

COTTON DAVIDSON
OAKLAND RAIDERS QUARTERBACK

DALLAS TEXANS
FOOTBALL CLUB
1961
DALLAS
TEXANS

REVITALIZES RAIDERS – By Alan Maver

AT THIS LATE STAGE OF THE CAMPAIGN, FOOTBALL'S ALSO-RANS CAN'T BE BLAMED FOR INDULGING IN "WHAT MIGHT HAVE BEEN" FANTASIES. ESPECIALLY THE AFL'S OAKLAND RAIDERS, WHO WERE 0-5 WHILE THIS VET WAS SEEING LIMITED ACTION.

BUT WHEN COTTON DAVIDSON WAS SWITCHED TO A FULL-TIME QUARTERBACK, HE EQUALED HIS ONE-SEASON HIGH BY TOSSING 17 TD PASSES IN HIS NEXT 6 GAMES. AS THE RAIDERS FINALLY GOT IN THE WINNING COLUMN, GOING 3-2-1.

THIS 33-YEAR-OLD IS ALSO THE TEAM'S 3RD LEADING RUSHER AGAIN- PICKED UP 156 YARDS ON HIS FIRST 27 CARRIES.

COTTON DAVIDSON
QUARTERBACK
OAKLAND RAIDERS

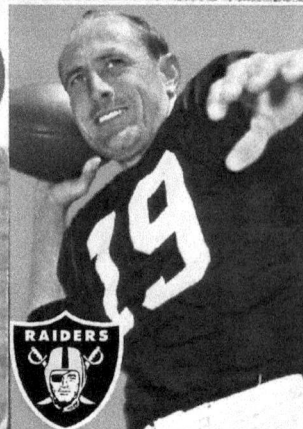

RAIDERS

RAIDERS

My history on a poster
– courtesy of the Davidson family

the Raiders playing the Texans. In August, I was on the winning side of the contest. In September, I was on the losing side. Neither contest was a close match. The Raiders were soundly beaten both times.

Playing the Texans in my first game as a Raider was an unexpected turn of events. After arriving in Oakland, there were a million things to do, and one short week was hardly enough time to prepare for playing with a brand new team. I had no time to think about how it would be to go against my friends and former teammates. However, as game time approached, I began to wonder how it would feel to line up against those familiar faces. What would they think? Would they think, as I did, that my presence on the other side of the ball was a little strange?

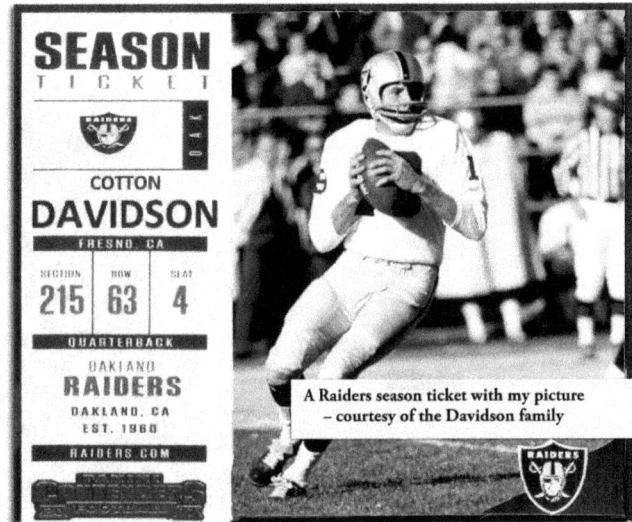

A Raiders season ticket with my picture – courtesy of the Davidson family

Even though the Texans showed no mercy regarding their scoring of 26-16, I got a little special treatment from their defensive guys. The hits I got were not nearly as hard as they could have been. Also, I was often given a hand-up. E.J. Holub laid me down a time or two and, then, grabbed my shoulder pads and picked me up. E.J. is one of the most interesting characters that ever played football. He not only made a name for himself with his superior athletic achievements but also with his outgoing personality. When he would pick me up, he would also dust me off to add to the show. That first game, wearing number 19 for the Raiders, is one I won't forget.

Our Raiders 1962 season was really bad. We won one game out of fourteen. The Raiders organization had so many problems. They ranged from a poor place to play to ineffective coaching. There was considerable talent with the team members, but they were not well-led. Coaching and leadership deficiencies were just too prevalent, which had a tremendous impact on our performance throughout the season.

Most high schools had a better football field than the Raiders. Our home turf was Frank Youell Field in Oakland. It only would seat approximately 20,000, and the surface was rough. We played on that field for four years until the Oakland-Alameda County Coliseum was built in 1966. Moving to that stadium was like moving from a log cabin to a palace.

Inadequate and inefficient coaching was a big problem. Also, as players, we were continually dealing with new coaches because of frequent turnovers in the staff. It seemed that there was little interest in really getting serious about preparing the team to win. No one was "building a fire" under either the coaches or team members. Perhaps, there was a lack of knowledge on the coaches' part too. There were no organized lessons and drills for teaching players how to set up, adjust and react to changing situations that might be encountered in a game. There were no blocking schemes being taught, and of course, it followed that there were no organized workouts for such. Before the 1962 season was half over, I quit counting all the times I was sacked.

1967 RAIDERS 1967

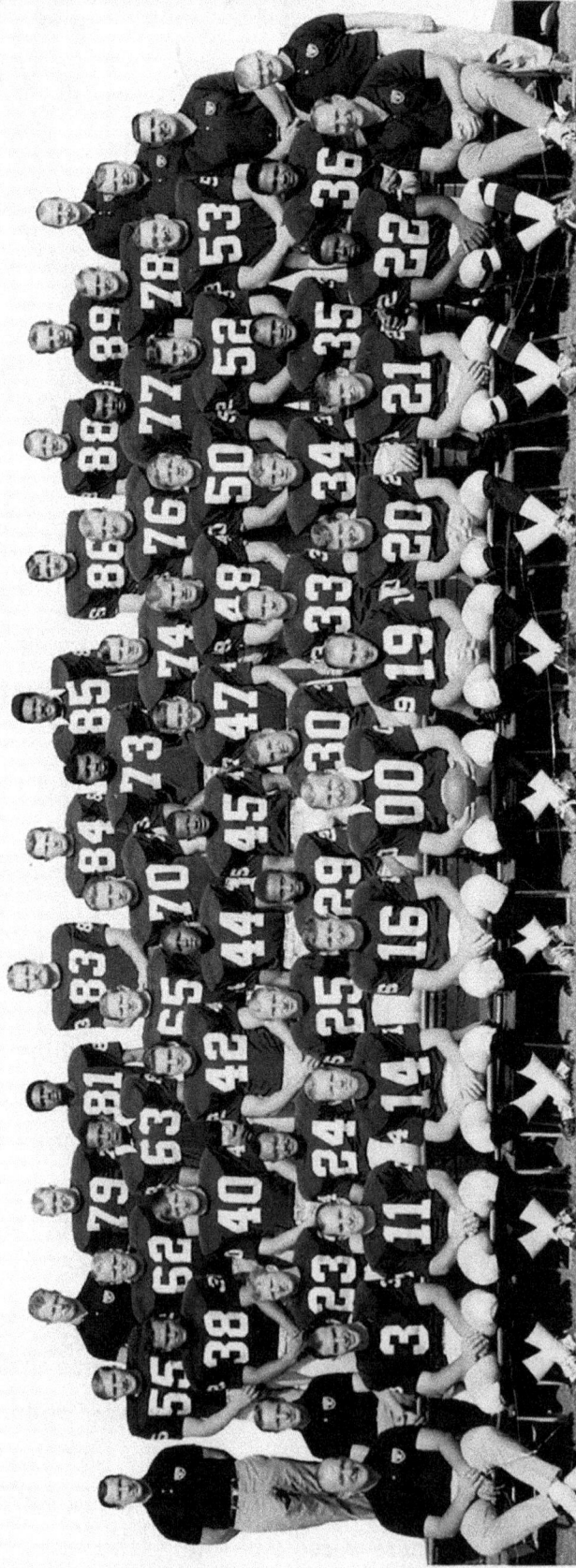

The 1967 Oakland Raiders. The team that went to Super Bowl II. I am # 19 in the first row
— courtesy of the Las Vegas Raiders

Front Row: Head Coach Rauch, Lamonica, Eischeid, Egloff, Blanda, Jim Otto, C. Davidson, Powers, Bird, Todd, Assistant Coach Spencer.

Second Row: Assistant Coach Polonchek, Sherman, Brown, Biletnikoff, Williams, Hagberg, Cannon, Gus Otto, Dixon, Daniels, Equipment Manager Romanski.

Third Row: Banks, Banaszak, Laskey, Johns, Grayson, McCloughan, Budness, Benson, Williamson, Birdwell, Assistant Coach Dahms.

Fourth Row: Assistant Coach Sumner, Conners, Kruse, Upshaw, Hawkins, Harvey, Sligh, Keating, Svihus, Lassister, Archer, Assistant Coach Madden.

Fifth Row: Assistant Coach Marinovich, Schuh, Wells, Ben Davidson, Ken Herock, Oats, Fairband, Kocourek, Miller, Trainer Anderson.

Wayland Corgill

Again, I was back in a situation where I had very little contact with coaches and, most of the time, calling plays was left up to me. That was okay with me, but I had very little help on game plans or advice during a game. I never had meetings with coaches before or after a game. That certainly was a handicap that put a large amount of extra work on a quarterback. I often remembered how much better it was at Baylor and the Colts where I always had close coordination with coaches and spent extra time with them on game plans and reviews after a game. That type of relationship goes a long way in helping to win games. It just didn't exist in Oakland.

After we had lost about six games in a row, the coaches tried a new approach in game planning. They started adding new plays to our playbook. They thought that might solve the problem. However, at that time, plays already in our playbook had not been coached well enough to be effectively executed. Success with implementing new plays was much worse. Locker room and practice sessions immediately got complicated and unmanageable. Confusion and misdirection were rampant with the attempt to incorporate numerous, poorly coached new plays. That idea was soon scrapped. We muddled through the rest of the year without any more changes that significantly improved things.

During all of the 1962 season, I worked on trying to turn things around but without much success. I felt like I was climbing a mountain. The guys on the team were not the problem. They did as good as they could without adequate coaching and team-building influence from the coaching staff. Several of them developed into very good ball players in the next few years. However, in 1962, we were far from functioning as a well-coordinated team. We had to deal with a debilitating lack of adequate training, guidance, and supervision in the locker room and on the practice field. Leadership was lacking to promote "can do" attitudes and extraordinary performances. Those conditions remained throughout the whole season. I didn't have much to work with. It was hard for me to feel good about most anything we did. It was a tall mountain and the whole season was very frustrating.

Probably nobody expected it to happen, but we won our last game of the season. We soundly beat the Boston Patriots 20-0. I sure was glad to finish that last game. It felt good to finally win a game but, I had made up my mind, it would be my last one as a Raider, win or lose. It had been a disappointing year. Carolyn, Tommy, Kelly,

I looked a little bit serious in this photograph – courtesy of the Las Vegas Raiders

The Rifleman - Cotton Davidson

Tracy, and I would be heading back to Texas as quickly as we could load up our belongings. It was December 16 and, if we hurried, we could be home for Christmas. That thought was a very happy one for all of us.

On my last trip to the Raiders' locker room, I shook everyone's hand and told them I would see them on TV, and that was it. I would not be back. I got in my car and waved goodbye with absolutely no thoughts of ever returning.

We had kept our rent house in Dallas. When I left for California in September, Carolyn stayed behind in Dallas until I could arrange for a move. After a few weeks with the Raiders, I had had enough time to evaluate my prospects for a future there, and it didn't look encouraging. Therefore, we decided to keep the house in Dallas after Carolyn and the kids came to Oakland. As the season progressed, I resolved that 1962 would be my last year with the Raiders. I was glad we had kept that house in Dallas. Moving back would be easy.

Our 1962 move to California with three children and going through the hassles of finding places to live had not been the easiest of ventures for Carolyn. She never complained, though. We had moved so many times since college and, with a growing family, the moves were a little more difficult each time. When I had committed to play for the Raiders, Tommy was entering the first grade. That was a complicating factor. Also, we had lived in a few marginally habitable places, to say the least. Carolyn didn't complain about that either. However, leaving Carolyn and the kids in Texas while I was in California was not an option. My first commitment was to family, and we would all head west, or we would all stay in Texas. So, my agreement to join the Raiders was with Carolyn's agreement to move. When that time came, she started making preparations without so much as a look backwards. Her attitude was that she had done this before, and she would do it again. It was part of our life. That move to California was in August. Five months later, we were moving again back where we had come from. It was my great good fortune to have Carolyn for a partner.

It was good to be back in Texas. Throughout the Christmas and New Year holiday season, the Raiders and California were far from my thoughts. That was a closed chapter of my life, I thought. However, in late January, I got a call from California. It was Al Davis. I was on guard, and, for a good reason. He wanted me to go back to the Raiders. That was a proposition I was not prepared to contemplate. I had just come from a whole season of grueling experiences with the Raiders, and I didn't think I could tolerate a repeat.

Al's message was about the same as it had been a few months earlier when he convinced me to go to Oakland. However, now, there was one very significant difference in the deal. Al was leaving Sid Gillman and the Chargers and would be the Raiders' head coach. As I thought about that, I wondered if Al had been planning his move to Oakland when he had talked me into going out there the first time. I never asked him that question.

I believed that having Al coach the Raiders would make a monumental difference in that team. I had had considerable experience with him, and there was no doubt in my mind that he was one of the best coaches in the pros. He was a particularly good offensive coach and a great quarterback coach. I liked him, and we saw things the same way. If we had taken tests on how to handle game situations, we probably would have had identical answers to every question. However, I was not interested in going back to the Raiders. I knew they would have a long way to go before they were a serious contender for successful seasons and championship games. How long that would take was a big question. Al would surely be able to turn the Raiders performance around, but I didn't want to struggle on the bottom for another year or two before things started looking up. Nope, I wasn't going.

Very plainly, I told Al that I would not go back. I also detailed my reasons for declining. There wasn't much about the Raiders that I could get excited about. The situation there was about as bad as it could be and certainly no fun for a quarterback. On top of that, there was not much about California as a place to live that excited me. I just couldn't see myself committing to fighting another frustrating, hopeless set of conditions where the outcome was almost guaranteed to be a miserable failure.

Al would not give up. That first call in January was not the last one. Al had his plans well thought out for shaping things up. He reviewed them with me in detail. I had a lot of confidence in Al's capabilities, but I didn't believe he could turn things around quickly enough to interest me. That is what I told Al, and he assured me the Raiders would not have another year like 1962. He finally wore me down. With reservations, I agreed to show up for training camp. Of course, that was after Carolyn, and I had thoroughly talked about the prospects of going back. I was confident in her total support and commitment. We were optimistic that California would be better the second time around, and happily, it was. The football part of our experience was incredibly better. As it turned out, Al had not made empty promises. From his first day in Oakland, the Raiders were put on an accelerated path to becoming a markedly different team.

If I had not gone back to California, what would I have done? Very soon, I would have had career-changing decisions to make. The prospect of leaving pro-football brought up a host of uncertainties about my future. I had been seriously thinking about that ever since saying goodbye to my Raider teammates a month earlier. Going back to the Raiders, just put those decisions off for a little longer. Sooner or later, I would need a plan for life after football. My immediate plan would have included moving to Gatesville and helping Daddy on his Coryell Creek ranch. He always needed help. However, that was only a stop-gap measure. I needed a different long-term plan, and now was a good time to get started.

I knew that I wanted to live in the Gatesville area and wanted my own ranch or a business. During those last days of 1962 and the early days of 1963, the unsettling events in my football career started my pursuit of establishing a permanent presence in Coryell County. Before 1964 ended, I had bought ranch land in the county, a gas and oil business in Gatesville, and a house in town. The next time I left the Raiders, I wouldn't be wondering what I would be doing to make a living.

Moving to Oakland in 1963 was much easier than it was in 1962. We had plenty of time to plan and make a move without rushing. I went out in June for the training camp, and Carolyn followed in August. We were familiar with the area and found a livable place that was convenient to an acceptable school for Tommy. We also developed a valuable connection with my first cousin in Fresno. She and her husband, Mary Inez and Ted Williams, were the best people and seemed to make it their mission to make our lives easier. They were particularly helpful to Carolyn. We lost count of all odds and ends of little things we hadn't moved, but they supplied. Some items were donated, and some were borrowed. Even kitchenware "migrated" from Fresno to our house in Oakland. For the next six years, we spent each Thanksgiving with Mary Inez and Ted. They were kinfolks, and we were proud of them.

We rented a house in Castro Valley, and Tommy had yet, another adjustment to an unfamiliar school. He would be in the second grade, and, already, he was an experienced young man in trying out different schools in Texas and California. This situation would not end in 1963. We would have five more years in California before returning to Texas for good. However, Tommy endured like a trooper and, perhaps, his variety of school experiences had unexpected educational benefits. At least, they didn't impair his ability to earn a couple of doctorate degrees and achieve extraordinary successes in the medical field later in life.

Interestingly, the house we rented was owned by an NFL player named John Crow. However, he was not the John David Crow who had won the Heisman Trophy in 1957 as a halfback for Texas A&M. The house was comfortable enough and furnished with a few "extras." With three young ones, Carolyn welcomed the clothes washer and dryer. Even an ironing board was provided. That was a major step up from several of our prior houses and apartments. However, the best feature of our new location was the good people in our neighborhood. A French couple lived next door, and they were the best of neighbors. They had a large vegetable garden and were very generous in sharing fresh vegetables.

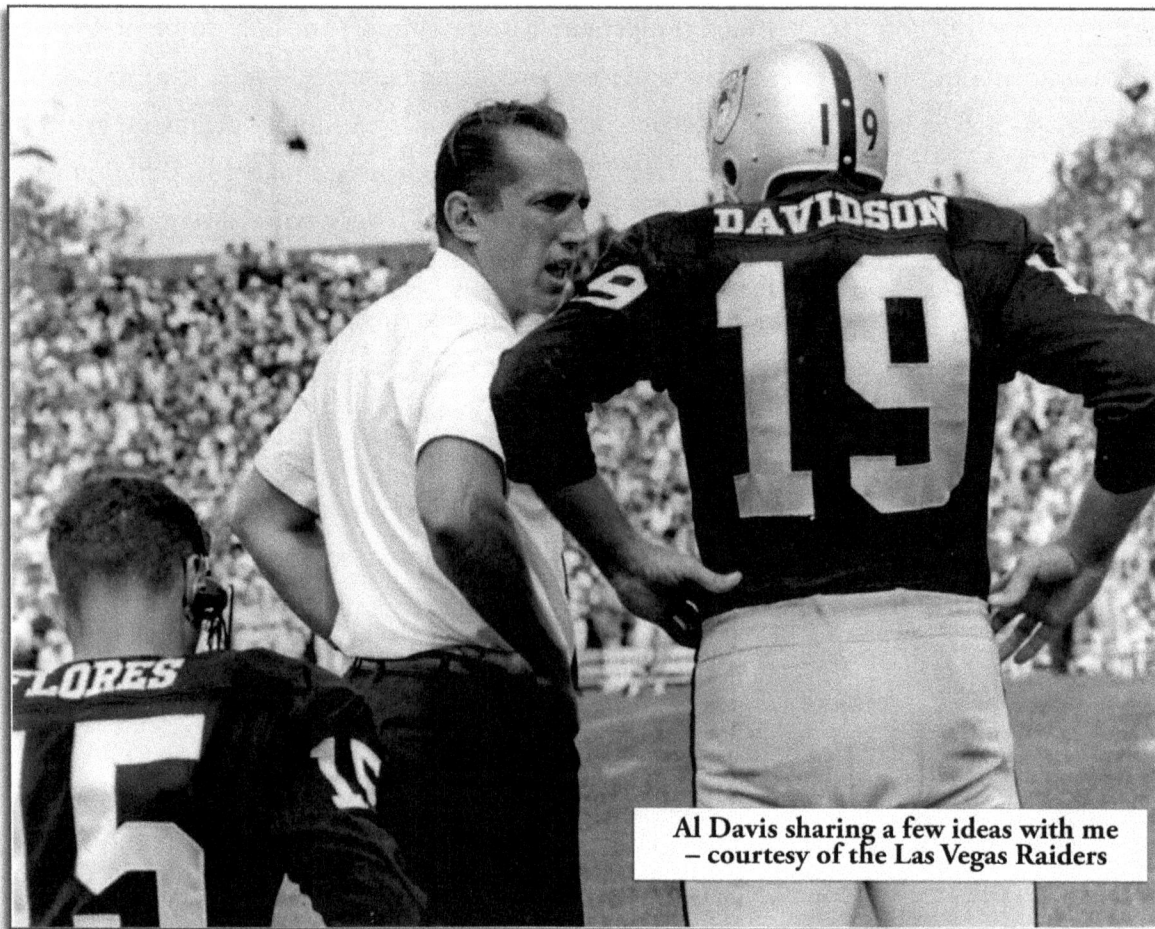

Al Davis sharing a few ideas with me – courtesy of the Las Vegas Raiders

A few Raiders teammates also lived in the area. A couple of them paid us a visit as trick-or-treaters when Halloween rolled around. That night, during a barrage of pounding on the door, I opened it to find two, six-foot, sheet-covered ghosts with their big fists stuck out and declaring, "Beer, we want beer." I had no beer, and, for a moment, I figured that I might be in just a little bit of hot water. However, I quickly recognized them as Raider defensive linemen. To my relief, they were easily convinced to come inside for a visit and accept a Coke. They were the most interesting trick-or-treaters we had that year. Living in Castro Valley turned out to be one of our better moves.

I saw lots of changes in the training camp. It was completely different with Al Davis in charge. No doubt, he implemented a lot of Sid Gillman's philosophy and techniques. Also critically important, he brought in quality coaches. With the exception of perhaps one man, the coaching staff was all new. This was certainly not the same Raiders organization that I had left a few months earlier. Attitudes on the field and in the locker room had made major turns for the better. Everybody seemed to get together and decide that we wanted to win. I was amazed at the improvements. They were showing everywhere. Al had "hit the ground running" before I got there. Maybe we were going to surprise a few people this season.

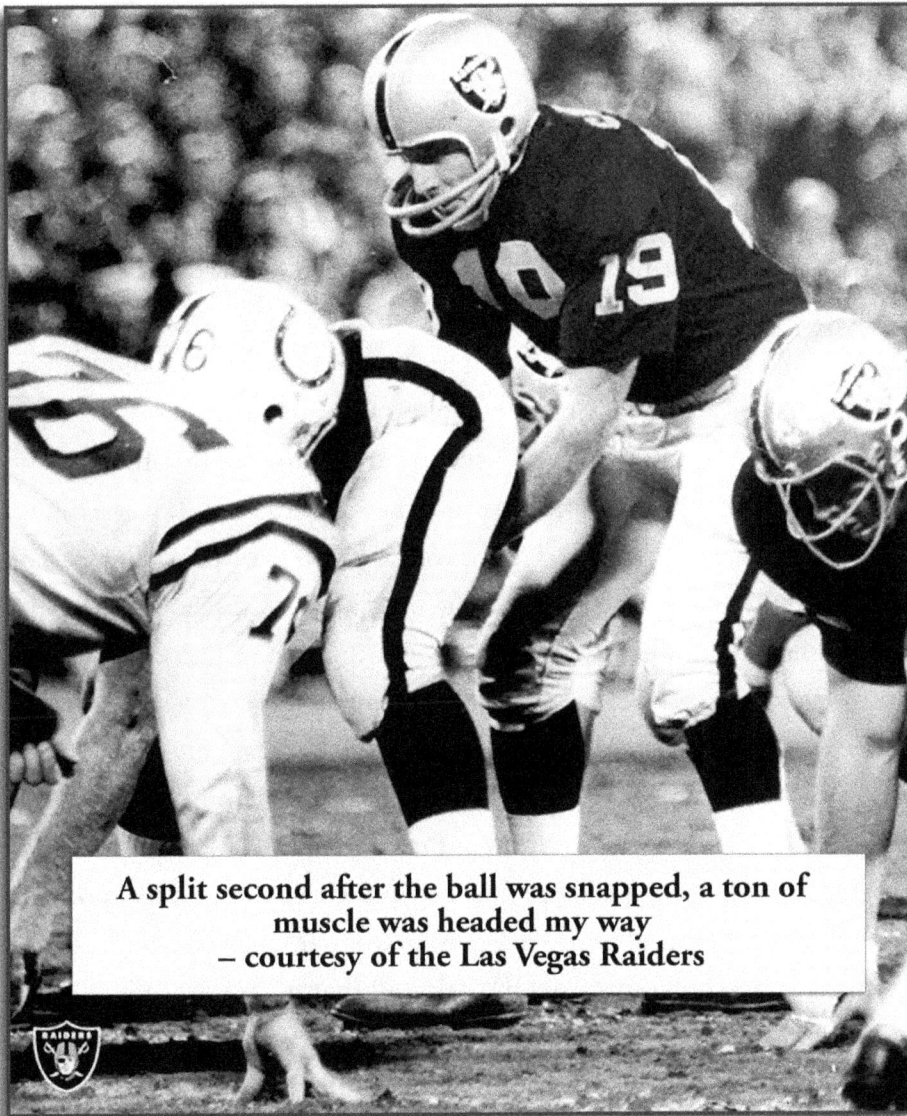

A split second after the ball was snapped, a ton of muscle was headed my way
– courtesy of the Las Vegas Raiders

Al Davis' attitude and coaching methods were exceptionally effective. He was a very good communicator, a good judge of talent, a team builder, and he understood the game. Equally important were his enthusiasm and fierce desire to win. He didn't holler at players, but those characteristics were unmistakably and consistently transferred to others by his attitude and demeanor. Probably, he thought about football every minute he was awake and, maybe, he dreamed about it too. He came to the Raiders with a conviction to put the team on a winning path. He even had "Win Baby Win" stitched on the side of our caps. That attitude rubbed off on everyone.

The Rifleman - Cotton Davidson

Our 1963 season was, in fact, totally different from the previous year. Our first game was a good example of that. That game was with the Houston Oilers in Houston. We won handily with a score of 24-13. In each of the past three years, the Oilers had the best record in the AFL Eastern Division. I think they were very surprised when we beat them and Raiders' fans were probably surprised too. It felt good. Our next game was with the Buffalo Bills, and we won again. The Bills had beaten us twice the previous year. They were not the best of teams, but our win with a score of 35-17 was gratifying. Things were really looking up for us. Folks in Oakland began to take notice.

Our next four games were a different story than the first two. We lost all four of those games. Our opponents were with Eastern Division teams. The Boston Patriots beat us twice, once in Oakland and once in Boston. The New York Jets beat us on their home turf as did the Buffalo Bills. Losing to the Bills was just a little disconcerting after having beaten them earlier in game number two.

After those four losses, we had an eight-game winning streak and ended the season with a win-loss record of 10 to 4. We beat the mighty Houston Oilers twice. Also, we beat the powerful Chargers twice and the talented Kansas City Chiefs (previously Dallas Texans) twice. The Chargers and Chiefs had dominated the AFL Western Division in previous years. Clearly, the Raiders were threatening to change that situation. Other teams were beginning to take serious notice.

Those games with the Chiefs always had a special interest for me. My former teammates were not as soft on me as they were in the first game that I played them in 1962. However, a few of them still gave me a little special treatment. My former training camp roommate, E.J. Holub, noticeably slacked off with the hardness of his hits. Four or five other guys, who I used to hunt and fish with, did the same.

One of the most interesting and satisfying games for me was our win over the Chargers in Oakland on December 8. At halftime, the Chargers were ahead. Tom Flores had started the game, and I came in after halftime. In the fourth quarter, I hit Art Powell with passes for two touchdowns; I rushed for one touchdown, and Alan Miller rushed for another. The Chargers were somewhat stunned. It was a damp, chilly day. One of the Charger coaches was wearing three or four layers of jackets or heavy shirts. The frigid breeze off of the bay in December could be rather bone-chilling for a coach on the sidelines. When we started scoring points late in the game, their coaches came alive. Until then, the Chargers had been calmly confident of a win. The coach wearing those layers of clothing became particularly agitated. Every time we made a touchdown, he would rip off a layer. We made 31 points in that last quarter, and the Charger coach was down to his shirt sleeves when the game ended with a 41 – 27 win for the Raiders.

As the season progressed, we made more and more headlines in the sports world. Also, the Raiders' popularity in Oakland surged. Enthusiastic, cheering Oakland fans began turning out in large numbers for home games. The crowd even got a little wild sometimes. We began to wonder when the stands in our little Frank Youell Field would be filled to overflowing. I couldn't help but marvel at how different this season was, and I knew what had made the difference. It was the presence of our new head coach, Al Davis.

Al Davis was a "complete" coach. He was a motivator and understood football. He was also practical. We didn't employ a large number of plays that first year, but we sure learned how to execute the ones we had. Al was always looking for ways to win and getting everyone on the same page with a less complicated

Wayland Corgill

playbook that improved consistency and reduced mistakes. He also promoted team spirit, improved teamwork with his interest in what team members might contribute, and he listened.

I particularly liked Al's methods for handling quarterbacks. He had confidence in me. Usually, I called most, if not all, plays during games. However, game plans and plays had been reviewed with Al many times before setting foot on the field. Occasionally, Al would signal a play to me, but I always had the option to change it in response to last-second defensive changes. We spent lots of time together. During practice, he often walked beside me coming off of the field and asked what I thought about something we had put in. In those conversations, he often asked what I thought he should do about particular situations. During games, we also had similar interchanges. He was great with asking insightful questions and understanding what I saw on the field. We met every Sunday and Monday night to review game films and prepare for the next game. Once in a while, he would come by my room at other times when he needed another opinion on a particular subject. He was always thinking about football. We had very few disagreements, and even those didn't amount to anything. I had had enough experience with Al before going to Oakland to give me a feeling that we would get along well, and that is the way it was. We didn't socialize, but we didn't need to. We were busy doing what we loved: football and winning. He knew that a quarterback is a key guy for winning, and he sure put a lot of emphasis on making that position successful. I think many quarterbacks would like to have been handled the way Al handled me.

Al had transformed the entire Raiders' environment. Also, he continued to make improvements in each succeeding year. Effects of Al's management and coaching talents clearly showed up in our win-loss record, and the 1963 season was one I really felt good about.

I had the utmost confidence in Al's capability to coach and manage a winning football team. Other than bringing in new coaching staff, he had made few changes in the talent that existed in Raiders' team members when he took control. He had brought in four or five players but, other than that, he worked with the team that was there when he arrived. Tom Flores and I shared the quarterback position as we had in 1962. Tom had been with the Raiders since the team was organized in 1960. Under Al's guidance, the Raiders quickly began to function as a team, and individual players were soon performing up to their potential.

In addition to our remarkable winning record in the 1963 season, several players won AFL All-Star awards for the very first time as a Raider. Those players included running back Clem Daniels; wide receiver Art Powell; offensive lineman Wayne Hawkins; defensive lineman Dave Costa; and linebacker Archie Matsos. Several other players also won awards. Defensive back Tommy Morrow was selected to the First Team All-AFL. Defensive back Fred Williamson received his third AFL All-Star award as a Raider. Those players also won many other awards in 1963 and succeeding years. For example, in 1963, Clem Daniels was the AFL MVP, and The Sporting News named him as the AFL Player of the Year. His powerful running garnered him the distinction of being the AFL All-Time Leading Rusher, and he was selected to the All-Time All-AFL Team.

Center Jim Otto, was an especially outstanding player in his 15-year career as a Raider. In 1963, he received his third AFL All-Star award. After 1963, Jim continued winning awards for eleven more seasons.

The Rifleman - Cotton Davidson

As a Raider, he was a nine-time AFL All-Star, ten-time First Team All-AFL, AFL All-Time Team selection, and was inducted into the Pro Football Hall of Fame. Jim loved football. He wouldn't have his picture taken without a football in his hands.

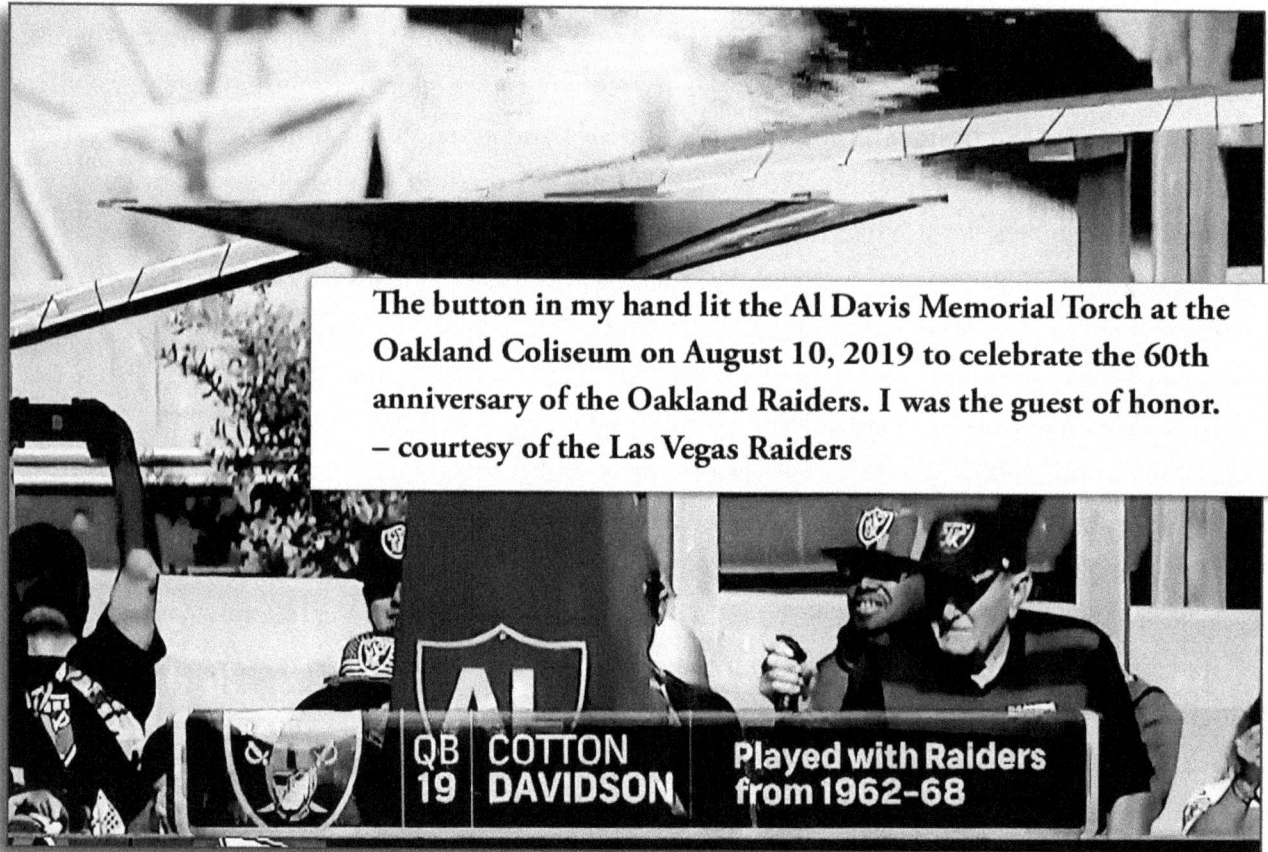

The button in my hand lit the Al Davis Memorial Torch at the Oakland Coliseum on August 10, 2019 to celebrate the 60th anniversary of the Oakland Raiders. I was the guest of honor. – courtesy of the Las Vegas Raiders

QB 19 COTTON DAVIDSON — Played with Raiders from 1962-68

Those Raider backs and receivers were as good as any in the league. Of our three receivers, Art Powell was my favorite target. He was big, fast, and had exceptional capability with the use of his body and hands for catching a ball. He was one of the players that Al acquired in 1963. Art played for us four seasons. Clem Daniels was another outstanding Raider. He was a powerful halfback. Clem and I played for the Dallas Texans in 1960. In 1961, Clem joined the Raiders, and I sure was glad to see him there in 1962 and again in 1963. Having him in the backfield always gave me a feeling of confidence when we had to have yardage on the ground.

The comparison of the Raiders' performance in 1962 and 1963 couldn't have been more different. We won only one game in 1962. In 1963, we came close to winning the Western Division Championship. That was won by the Chargers, who we had beaten twice during the regular season. The Chargers ended the season with an 11 to 3 win-loss record, one game better than the Raiders. For the Raiders to have had such a remarkably successful 1963 season, with virtually the same team from 1962, was a strong indication that Al knew what he was doing. It also proved that players had not been the problem in the bleak 1962 season. It was altogether fitting that Al was named the AFL's 1963 "Coach of the Year."

Our banner season was rewarded by a large presence in the East-West AFL All-Star game that was played at Balboa Stadium in San Diego on January 19, 1964. I was on the West's roster, along with seven of my team-mates. Five Raiders played on offense, and three Raiders played on defense. With me on offense were Jim Otto, Clem Daniels, Art Powell, and Wayne Hawkins. On defense were Archie Matsos, Dave Costa, and Fred Williamson.

My signature is on the torch – courtesy of the Las Vegas Raiders

This was the third AFL All-Star game. The first two All-Star games had been won by the West. The East appeared to be determined to prevent the West from winning another one. They led throughout the entire game until the final seconds. A couple of minutes after the fourth quarter started, I was sent in as quarterback. The score was 24-17 in favor of the East. We quickly executed a drive into East territory but had to settle for a field goal, making the score 24-20. From that point, neither team was able to score until the game was almost over. It was beginning to look like the game would end with a win for the East. However, as the game clock was inching toward the last minute, we got the ball. We put together a drive that got us near enough to the East's end of the field to give us a chance for a touchdown. Things were looking up for us, but we had to do something fast. With 43 seconds left in the game, I hit Art Powell with a 25-yard pass for a touchdown. Art was at the back of the end zone. It was not an easy catch, but big Art did what he excelled at doing. He caught a ball that many other receivers would miss. It was a diving catch that beat the defenders crowding around him. The game ended with a score of 27-24, and the West had won its third AFL All-Star game. I sure was glad that Art, my favorite target, was on the field.

All of our Raiders' players performed exceptionally well, and Archie Matsos was named the Defensive MVP. Keith Lincoln of the San Diego Chargers was the Offensive MVP. Beginning with the second AFL All-Star game, two MVPs were selected. One for offense and one for defense. In the first AFL All-Star game played on January 7, 1962, there was only one MVP, and I was fortunate to have been selected for that honor. I knew how Archie Matsos must have felt.

With the All-Star game over, Carolyn and I would set about gathering up our belongings and moving the family back to Texas. We would be there for a few months until the 1964 football season started. We had had an unbelievably good year with football, and that sure helped ease the thought of moving back to California in the summer for training camp. Perhaps 1964 would be another successful year. I had a completely different opinion of the Raiders than I had had the previous year. I really felt good about the season we had just completed. However, at this point, I had a six-month activity scheduled ahead of me that was very different from football. I had a business to manage and work to do.

We had kept the rental house in Dallas and, therefore, had a place to move to. We stayed there until May 1964, when we bought a house in Gatesville. Gatesville was where we really needed to be. I had recently bought a gas and oil company business there, and I also had purchased ranchland near town. I would be plenty busy when I was not playing football.

My ranch was composed of three pieces of land in the South Mountain area, a few miles east of Gatesville. Those three places totaled approximately 1,000 acres. I had cows plus sheep and goats in those places, and naturally, they required constant attention. However, I was only in Gatesville half of the time. Being a part-time rancher and oil company manager was tricky business for me. Taking care of those investments was certainly more than a part-time, one-man job. Fortunately, when I was away during the football season, I had expert, reliable, trustworthy help from family and employees. However, until training camp started in the summer, I was committed to doing part of the work.

My brother, Hy, looked after one of my three places east of town. Also, I couldn't have done without Daddy's help. He kept a check on another one of those places, the Painter place. The third place was the Parker place. It had close supervision by Mr. and Mrs. Bus and Dean Barton, who lived there. They were exceedingly reliable and resourceful. I rarely ever got a call from them about something they couldn't handle. Dean Barton was amazing with her capabilities in handling ranching duties.

My gas and oil company was part of the Sinclair Oil Corporation. I named it the Cotton Davidson Oil Company. Company assets included a service station on Main Street in Gatesville and bulk storage of oil, gas, and diesel for delivery to independent gas stations, plus farmers and ranchers. A tanker truck for delivering fuel was part of the company's assets. I owned that company until I went back to coaching at Baylor in 1972.

After we moved into our Gatesville house, my gas and oil business and ranch were only a few minutes away. In some respects, they were too convenient because I often put in very long days doing work that was not necessarily what one would expect a pro quarterback would do. Football was not an easy job but, operating that oil company business was not very easy either. However, the frustration level was a lot less than with a few of my recent football experiences.

That oil company and ranch kept me, and the men who worked for me, plenty busy. In the 1960s, a service station was a lot more than a gas station. Service included washing windshields plus checking engine oil and tire pressures. I got pretty good at pumping gas, fixing flats, changing oil, and washing windshields. I also became familiar with all the back roads in Coryell County while delivering gas and diesel to farmers and ranchers. In a way, those deliveries were the most interesting thing I did because of the people I met and got to know. I really liked that part of the business. Also, it was certainly better than fixing flats.

Luckily, I was able to keep good employees. Ex-military men were the best. Two retired Army sergeants worked there as long as I owned the company. They were the most reliable, trustworthy guys imaginable. I was lucky to have them. They took care of things. Also, I had a very reliable and capable secretary, Mrs. Louise Matthews. All of those people were a pleasure to work with, but I couldn't have done without Hy and Daddy. From 1964 until 1969, when I was away during football season, I didn't worry about management matters in Gatesville. Hy and Daddy took care of things.

For the next four years, until I left the Raiders at the end of 1968, my time away from football was spent in Gatesville. Life there each year was a repeat of 1964. From Christmas until training camp started, I did my share of tending to the gas and oil business. Those were interesting times around the gas stations. Over the years, memorable people were always dropping by. One of those was my Raider teammate, Ben Davidson. He paid us several visits over the years. Ben joined the Raiders in 1964. As far as I know, we were not related, but having the same last name might have prompted him to venture so far away from his California home to see how other Davidson's lived. Ben was a physically imposing figure. At 6 ft. 8 in. tall and 275 pounds, he sure stood out in a crowd. His big handlebar mustache didn't contribute to his obscurity, either. When he first came to the Raiders, he also had a thick beard. Al Davis didn't particularly care for that, so he and Ben compromised on a mustache. On one of Ben's visits, he spent some time with me at my downtown gas station at the junction of Business Hwy. 36 and Hwy. 84. While I was pumping gas, he stood between two gas pumps with his outstretched arms resting on top of the pumps. I was concerned about a possible wreck in front of the station because, as cars merged from Hwy. 36 onto Hwy. 84 lanes, drivers had their attention focused on the giant who made gas pumps look small.

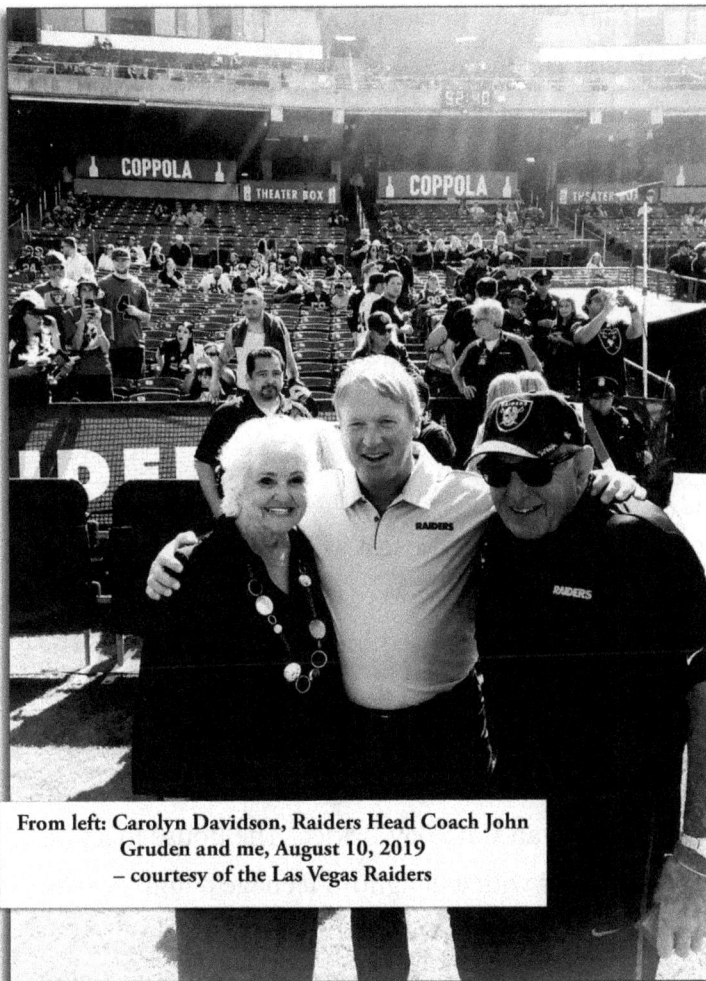

From left: Carolyn Davidson, Raiders Head Coach John Gruden and me, August 10, 2019
– courtesy of the Las Vegas Raiders

Ben was a lot of fun and was always welcomed by Carolyn and me. He was the most likable, good-humored man. However, he was an awesome force on the football field as a defensive end. He earned a reputation of being a tough, gutsy, physical player who caused every opposing team to take special precautions when facing him. His name became widely known throughout the U.S. after the Raiders-Jets game in Oakland on December 17, 1967. In that game, he was credited with breaking Joe Namath's jaw. Controversy surrounded that call since Ike Lassiter thought he did the damage in an earlier play. However, the tremendous hit on Joe by Ben sent Joe's helmet flying, and the resulting photographs were dramatic. Even if that hit didn't break Joe's jaw, Ben got the credit. In 1970, Ben made headlines again during a Raiders-Chiefs game when he "speared" Chiefs' quarterback, Len Dawson. That incident eventually led to a new NFL rule protecting a downed ball-carrier. Although

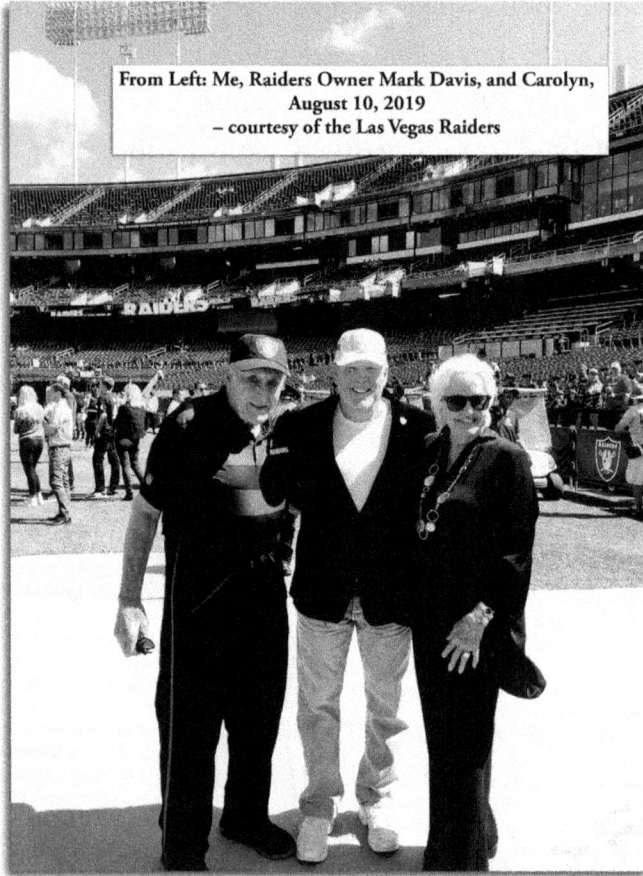

From Left: Me, Raiders Owner Mark Davis, and Carolyn,
August 10, 2019
– courtesy of the Las Vegas Raiders

the official name of that rule is not the "Davidson Rule," it is commonly referred to by that name. Ben Davidson was a good man to have on your side of the field.

One year, Ben stopped by Gatesville with his traveling partner, Tom Keating. Tom was a defensive tackle for the Raiders. They were riding Yamaha motorcycles. Ben and Tom were promoting the Yamaha brand. They rode motorcycles all over the U.S. and even rode down to the Panama Canal. Carolyn and I had a delightful evening with Ben and Tom and put them up for the night. After breakfast, the cyclists prepared to resume their journey but didn't leave without a bit of fanfare. They persisted in convincing us to let them take our girls, Kelly and Tracy, to school. Of course, the girls were excited about that. I wasn't so sure. However, as the motorcycles roared through town, each one had a little girl holding onto a guy that dwarfed her. They never forgot that escort to school.

The year 1964 was a good one for the Davidson family. Our fourth child, Tyree Francis Davidson, was born on the first day of July. However, 1964 was not necessarily good for the Raiders. The Raiders' season won-loss-tie record was 5-7-2.

Carolyn and I waited until August before heading back to California with four small passengers in the car. Back and forth moves between Texas and California were getting to be just a little more complicated with each addition to the family. However, Carolyn never complained. We were fortunate to rent a house in Piedmont, near the Berkley campus. The Berkley football field was used for Raiders' practices. The house was owned by Chris Burford, my friend, and teammate when I played for the Dallas Texans. He was my favorite target as a wide receiver in those days. Chris was a California boy, but he spent his eight years in the pros with the Dallas Texans/Kansas City Chiefs. The house was in a great location. From the deck, we had good views of the Golden Gate Bridge, Alcatraz, and the Bay Bridge. The house location was also great for another reason. We had a very good neighbor with a delightful teenage daughter who was a terrific babysitter. Carolyn surely welcomed her help many times with our four young children.

In the 1960s, Berkley was a hotbed of activity with demonstrations and protests. That activity quickly attracted the attention of a few of my Raider teammates. Ben Davidson and several of his buddies couldn't pass up the opportunity to have some fun and get involved. Whether or not they agreed with the protesters' viewpoints might have been a question, but that never interfered with those rugged linemen opposing whatever a demonstration was about. They would walk over to the campus and join the march. However, they would march right through the crowd, in the opposite direction of the demonstrators. As far as I know, their disruption of the marchers never caused any problems. Still, I imagine the size of those big guys was the major deterrent of fisticuffs. What rational person would want to try tackling a 6-ft 8-in guy who looked like Paul Bunyan?

Oakland's 1964 season was totally different from the previous year. Instead of almost having a clean sweep like 1963, we struggled to win five games. Our first win didn't happen until the seventh game of the season when we beat the Denver Broncos. That win wasn't much consolation because Denver was not really a contender and was also having a terrible year. We still had the same talented players, but the game results sure were different. I think our opponents might have been somewhat caught off-guard in 1963 and redoubled their efforts to not let that happen again in 1964.

For me, one of the more memorable things that happened in the Raiders 1964 season was the arrival of Billy Cannon. Billy came with a very enviable record as a halfback and

Me and one of my Raiders teammates, a young giant named Ben Davidson (no relation) who visited me in Gatesville – courtesy of The Gatesville Messenger

BEARDED AND BIG, PRO STAR BEN DAVIDSON VISITS HERE

return specialist. At Louisiana State University (LSU), he twice received unanimous All-American honors and helped LSU win a national championship in 1958. The next year, he received the Heisman Trophy and made a punt return against Ole Miss that football fans are still talking about. That return covered 89 yards. After breaking seven tackles while making his way through a crowded field, Billy outran his pursuers in a 60-yard dash to the end zone. It was a game-winning touchdown for LSU. Billy was a remarkable athlete who excelled in whatever position he played. We certainly were glad that Al Davis did whatever it took to get Billy on our roster.

A couple of days after Al got Billy, I got a late-night visit. Al knocked on my door shortly before midnight and roused me from a deep sleep. I couldn't imagine what would be so important that couldn't wait until morning, and I told him that. Also, I reminded him that tomorrow would be a long day on the practice field, and I sure needed to sleep. He paid no attention. He had other things on his mind. He asked me what I thought about Billy and how he would fit into our team. I told Al that I thought Billy would make a great tight end. With his size, he could block, and his speed and ball-handling capabilities were exceptional. I thought Billy would be more effective there than as a halfback or fullback. Apparently, Al agreed because Billy was an outstanding Raiders' tight end for the next six years.

The Rifleman - Cotton Davidson

Billy Cannon and his wife, Dot, were great people. They became very good friends with Carolyn and me. Our children were about the same ages as Billy and Dot's three girls and one boy. Our families "hit it off" from the start. We spent a lot of time together. Picnics and bar-b-ques were a couple of our favorite activities, combined with occasional trips to the mountains. Also, Billy and I attended horse races now and then. He really liked horse racing, and he had an unusual technique for picking horses to bet on. He always bet on the gray ones. When I inquired about that method, he said, "I can easily see them and keep up with them around the track. They stand out from the brown ones." I don't recall if that method worked very well, but I don't remember any big winnings.

Dot and Carolyn always sat together at games. Neither Carolyn nor Dot would hold back when being confronted with an unreasonable or unfair situation. Dot came to my defense in a big way during one of my games. I had just thrown an interception and a fan, directly below Dot, hollered, "Get that quarterback out of there!" Dot politely leaned over and tapped the man on the shoulder. He looked up to find a very serious lady who was about to give him some advice. Dot said, "Mister, you don't know sheep shit from shoe polish about that quarterback." The man was quiet for the rest of the game. Carolyn and Dot certainly were good fans to have on the Raiders' side.

The Raiders' 1965 and 1966 seasons were mediocre, with identical win-loss records of 8-5-1. Both years, we finished in second place in the AFL Western Division but won no awards. However, 1966 was a year of welcomed change in one way. We had a big improvement for a place to play home games. On September 18, 1966, we played our first game in the brand new Oakland-Alameda County Coliseum. That huge stadium was a major step up from where we started at Frank Youell Field. Playing there was a pleasure, but we lost that game to the Kansas City Chiefs, 32-10. Our only touchdown was made on my pass to Clem Daniels.

The 1967 season was entirely different from the two previous years for both Oakland and me, especially for me. It was a phenomenally good year for the team and a time of catastrophic injury for me. The Raiders winning streak started early in the season. From game one to game 14, our win record was almost perfect. The only loss was to the New York Jets in game four. Championship wins followed, and that led to Super Bowl II. My debilitating season started early too. I was out for the whole year.

On the practice field during training camp in September, my shoulder was almost irreparably destroyed while throwing a pass. As I turned to throw the ball with my arm cocked in an upright position, one of our defensive linemen charged at me. Just as my hand started forward, the lineman raised his hand to block the pass. He missed the ball but hooked my arm with his arm as he flew by. The result was almost like a violent, split-second, arm-wrestling contest, and I lost big time! His momentum twisted my arm backwards and far behind me. Talk about hurt! Instantaneously, I knew that this was the most serious injury I had ever had. My arm was useless. I couldn't move it, and the pain was excruciating.

That hit was, potentially, career-ending or worse. The damage to my shoulder was severe, but I didn't know just how bad it was for almost six weeks. During that time, I lived with constant pain and a useless arm. I couldn't put a shirt on without Carolyn's help. As it turned out several months later, I was extremely fortunate to eventually regain the use of my arm and only missed one season.

Wayland Corgill

As I limped off of the practice field that day, my mind was almost blanked out by the searing, stabbing sensations shooting all over my torso. I was almost beyond the capability to reason, but I knew there was no one close by, except our trainer, who might be able to help. Maybe, he knew what to do? Our trainer, George Anderson, was a great guy. I had confidence that if a trainer anywhere could do something for me, it would be George. George's tools for helping with my injury were nowhere adequate, but he did what he could. Ice packs helped a little bit, and the mind-numbing pain subsided somewhat. As I quit thinking about the pain so much, I began to contemplate the seriousness of this injury. A million thoughts raced through my mind while I sat there with George. What might my chances be for getting over this injury? What should I do next? How might my future be affected? Chances were that the rest of my career would involve something besides football. Could I recover enough to take care of my ranch near Gatesville? Would my arm be mobile enough to cast a fishing line into Coryell Creek once in a while at places where PaPa used to go? One thing was for sure; I was facing a long list of unknowns.

George realized that I needed help far beyond what he could provide. In a few days, I consulted an orthopedic surgeon in San Francisco. After X-rays and examinations, his recommendations were no better than George's. I was not satisfied. I knew this injury would require more than ice packs or heating pads. There was no question in my mind that something was seriously torn up in my shoulder. I was determined to get another opinion as soon as possible. In the meantime, I would keep my useless arm in a sling, endure the pain and depend on Carolyn to be my other arm.

On October 7, the Raiders played the Jets in New York. I went with the team and consulted another orthopedic surgeon while in New York. His recommendations weren't much better than what I had gotten from the doctor in San Francisco. I would keep on looking.

Back in Oakland, Al Davis told me about an orthopedic surgeon and his friend, Doctor Levinthal, in Los Angeles. Al said he had a lot of faith in him. The doctor had an excellent reputation and had put more football players back in the game than any other orthopedic surgeon in California. I was overjoyed with that information and the thought that I might, possibly, find the right doctor to help solve my problem. Making an appointment to see this doctor as soon as possible was my number one priority.

Tolerating a useless right arm and painful shoulder for more than a month had been an agonizing trial in many ways. Not only was I an invalid when it came to performing normal functions, like dressing myself, but I had too much time to think about "what if" situations. What if I couldn't find a doctor who could fix my shoulder? What if I couldn't get full use of my arm again? What if I couldn't play football again? Those thoughts, and many others, were unavoidable. However, I also had other thoughts that weren't worrisome. Those were reflections on life back home and the folks in Pecan Grove. I remembered Daddy and his long, debilitating recovery from back surgery. I remembered PaPa's constantly positive, cheerful attitude and his friendly advice about common sense. Those people were great examples of being strong and enduring adversity. Thoughts of them were always comforting and reassuring. I would endure, but I needed expert attention as quickly as I could get it.

On my first visit to Dr. Levinthal, I learned that he had an interesting variety of patients. Football players weren't his only clients, by any means. As I sat in his waiting room, I recognized a couple of movie stars. That happened every time I visited Dr. Levinthal. It seemed odd, but it was somewhat reassuring. I reasoned that if Dr. Levinthal had a good reputation with those famous people, surely, he must be good at what he did. Hopefully, I had finally found the "right" doctor for my problem. I learned, later, that he was "the doctor" for many movie stars; particularly, stuntmen. I was in fine company every time I visited him.

I was not with Dr. Levinthal very long before getting a feeling of confidence that I had found the doctor I had been seeking. Even before being X-rayed, he seemed to have a good idea about what the damage to my shoulder looked like. Also, I was reassured by his positive presentation of options for corrective surgery. No doubt, this man knew what he was talking about. To demonstrate his explanation of remedies, he opened a drawer and pulled out a set of bones that would be involved in the surgery. I was surprised. I wondered whose grave had been robbed. I asked him where he got those bones. He said they weren't really bones; they were plastic models. When I remarked that somebody did a good job of making fake bones, he agreed and said they came from a little town in Texas named Gatesville. He had been getting those "bones" for the last eight or nine years. Before then, real bones had been very, very hard to come by. He said those Gatesville bones had been super beneficial for his practice, and he appreciated that they didn't stink.

Wow, I almost couldn't believe what I was hearing! Gatesville was making plastic bones for a renowned surgeon in Los Angeles! My hometown of Gatesville was 1,500 miles away. Didn't anyone in Los Angeles make plastic bones? For a few minutes, I forgot about my shoulder, and our conversation was about bones made in Gatesville. Dr. Levinthal told me that the small company, Medical Plastics Laboratory, was the only place in the U.S.A. that could supply the plastic bones. Amazing! Who would have imagined that such a thing could be? I had no idea that Gatesville had such ingenious people, who had done what no one in the U.S., or maybe the world, could do or had done. I was fascinated with the thought that people I knew, went to school with, and went to church with, were capable of such a phenomenal accomplishment. Dr. Levinthal remembered the names of two doctors who were involved in the business. They were Elworth and Wendell Lowrey. I was surprised again. They were my doctors. I would make it a point to find out more about that business when I got back to Gatesville.

When we resumed discussing my shoulder, Dr. Levinthal used the Gatesville bones to explain his estimation of what the surgery would entail. Of course, he wouldn't know exactly how extensive the surgery would be until he exposed the damage and evaluated it. However, the reconstructive process would surely involve drilling holes in bones to permit the reattachment of muscles and ligaments. Once that was done, the healing process would take a few months, after which an exercise regimen would begin. The Gatesville bones sure came in handy for my understanding of what needed to be done. I was ready to get started as soon as possible.

The surgery was done during my next visit with Dr. Levinthal in late October. I left his office with a cast that covered my shoulder and extended down to my elbow. I also wore a sling fitted for my right hand. It was awkward, but I didn't mind. The surgery went well, Dr. Levinthal was optimistic, and, hopefully, I was on the road to recovery. Maybe, I could start exercising in early 1968.

Wayland Corgill

I stayed in Oakland the rest of the season. While I was not having such a good time, the Raiders were having a great time. The 1967 season was their best one yet. After winning thirteen of fourteen games, they won the AFL Western Division Championship and went on to beat the Oilers 40-7 for the AFL Championship. That win qualified them to play the Green Bay Packers in Super Bowl II. Losing to the Packers, 14-33, spoiled an almost perfect season. However, it was, nonetheless, an exciting season and a banner year for Raider fans. We were drawing huge crowds as compared to the small ones at Frank Youell Field in the early 1960s.

There were several reasons for the Raiders' remarkable success in 1967, but chief among them was Al Davis' keen judgment of player capabilities and skillful maneuvering to acquire quality players. The 1967 Raiders team was loaded with players, who just continued winning awards throughout their careers, and a large number of them are now enshrined in the Pro Football Hall of Fame. He was particularly proficient in quarterback considerations.

Me and my teammate, Daryle Lamonica, more than a few years after our playing days – photo by Carolyn Davidson

Earlier that year, he surprised many people by trading Tom Flores and Art Powell to the Buffalo Bills for Daryle Lamonica. Daryle fit well in the Raiders' organization and made very big contributions to the team's progression to Super Bowl II.

Daryle was an exceptional athlete and a great young man. He was a four-sport standout athlete in high school in Clovis, California, and a three-season starting quarterback for the University of Notre Dame. He and I roomed together and, from the start, we got along with never a conflict. He would quiz me every night about certain situations, and I did my best to advise him. In 1968, when my shoulder healed enough to shoot a gun and cast a fishing line, we also hunted and fished together at every opportunity. His being a "California boy" certainly was an advantage in locating places for those outings. Hunting and fishing trips with Daryle were some of my best times in California.

As the Raiders advanced in their award-winning 1967 season, I couldn't play, but I did what I could with moral support. It was a pretty dull time for me. The cast stayed on my shoulder for about a month. After it was removed, I kept my arm in a sling for a few more weeks. I was still nursing that arm in January when I went with the team to the Orange Bowl in Florida for Super Bowl II.

The Rifleman - Cotton Davidson

During Super Bowl II, I was the Raiders' "spy in the sky." I sat in the press box and communicated with coaches on the sidelines. Throughout the game, I was kept busy with looking for weaknesses in the Packers' formations and making suggestions for how to exploit them. We needed every advantage we could find. Unfortunately for us, there just weren't many weaknesses to find. The Packers were an extremely talented and well-coached team.

Carolyn flew over from Texas and sat in a choice seat on the 50-yard line. It was an exciting time and, at the same time, a little bit depressing for me. I was very glad to do my part, but I would much rather have been suited up and on the field. I knew that events like Super Bowls don't come along very often in a lifetime. It was a day never to be forgotten. Also, it would have been a perfect culmination of a season for the record books if the score had ended differently than 33-14 in favor of the Packers.

Leaving Florida after the game, Carolyn and I returned to Gatesville. After a short few days there, I flew back to Los Angeles to see Dr. Levinthal. At this point, I thought my shoulder had healed enough to allow a rehabilitation program to begin. I expected the doctor to evaluate my condition and advise me on details for a rehab process. That he did, and I was surprised by some of his recommendations. He was very satisfied with the healing condition and agreed that exercise routines could start. His instructions were very thorough as related to timing, techniques, intensity, and equipment to use. He said that I should not lift weights but work out by punching a boxer's speed bag instead. He explained that the bag must be mounted, so the bottom of the bag was level with the top of my head. Then, using proper punching techniques, all muscles in my shoulder joint would be exercised. Lifting weights would use only a few of those muscles. To keep a speed bag going at a rapid-fire rate using one arm/fist, a punch through the bag is followed by a back-handed through-punch as the fist returns to the starting position for another through punch. Such action with the arm flexes all the muscles in a shoulder joint. To keep the bag going requires extremely precise timing and coordination; the faster the punching, the more rigorous the timing and coordination. Dr. Levinthal was confident my shoulder had a chance of, possibly, coming back to full strength if I tried to wear out a speed bag. As I left Dr. Levinthal, I had an intense feeling of optimism about recovery. I found a sporting goods store, and a speed bag accompanied me on my flight back to Dallas.

Punching a speed bag is no easy trick. I finally mastered the technique, but that took a while. Our house on Park Street in Gatesville had a separate garage building. I mounted the speed bag in the garage and was soon rattling the walls. My workouts included punching that bag for at least 30 minutes, twice a day. Neighbors never complained, but they might have thought about it a few times. The more I punched that bag, the better my shoulder felt. The good doctor knew what he was talking about. Before long, I tried gently throwing a football. Tommy helped me with that. We started with short, easy passes in the backyard. Soon, we were practicing on the Gatesville high school football field. By May, I could throw the ball pretty hard and far. Tommy was still my practice partner, but we also picked up a few more boys. By the end of the month, every time Tommy and I went to the football field, we would have a half-dozen, or more, boys running routes for me.

Wayland Corgill

My shoulder was coming along great. I felt no pain in any of my activities except one. I was leading a horse for Daddy one day, and the horse jerked his head when he was spooked by something. I was holding the reins in my right hand, and of course, my arm was jerked a little too hard. I saw stars for a few moments and thought seriously about giving that mare a good whack. However, my arm stopped hurting after a few minutes, and I gave the horse a reprieve. After that, I used my left hand to hold the reins.

I was back in Oakland when the Raiders' training camp started in 1968. I thought I was put together and, during my last visit with Dr. Levinthal, he cleared me to play. By the time the season started, I had at least 90 to 95 percent of my throwing capability back. I might have lost a little speed, but it wasn't noticeable. However, I didn't play much. Daryle Lamonica had had that great 1967 season, and his performance was the same in 1968. That young man had a great arm and tremendous talent to go with it. With him at the quarterback position, Oakland finished the season with a 12-2 record and won the AFL Western Division Championship. The Raiders lost to the Jets in the AFL Championship game with a score of 23-27 but could have won that one too, with a little bit of luck. Oakland had beaten the Jets in regular-season play.

For me, the year was not very exciting, as related to football. However, it was very good for other things. Daryle loved hunting and fishing as much as I did. We did a lot of that together. Many places in Northern California are like a sportsman's paradise. We didn't have to go very far from Oakland to find choice places to hunt and fish. We hunted deer, ducks, geese, and pheasants. Shooting a gun didn't hurt my shoulder, but I still had a pad on the stock of my 12-gauge shotgun to soften its kick. In between hunts, excellent fishing areas were close by in the bays and estuaries. We brought home wide varieties of fish and game that certainly were different from those that PaPa and I collected along Coryell Creek when I was a kid. Back in those days, squirrels and perch were about all we brought home from those trips. However, my hunting and fishing excursions with PaPa were just as much fun as those with Daryle.

When I joined the Raiders in 1962, their record for winning was not good, and their fan base was small. As our record improved in succeeding years, so did our media coverage and fan base. By 1968, we were enjoying large crowds at games and attracting attention from so many different directions. Also, we had acquired many new friends on our way to the Super Bowl. Some of those friends owned, or had access to, a large number of those sportsman's paradises that Daryl and I frequented.

We really appreciated one gentleman who had duck blinds located in the bay estuaries just north of Oakland. He let Daryle and me have a key to one of his boats and welcomed us to use it any time to access fishing areas and duck blinds. Duck and goose hunting in that area was unbelievably great. Those blinds were in the flyways, and during hunting season, birds by the thousands crowded the skies. Canadian geese were awesome with their enormous wingspan and powerful maneuvering in flight. Those blinds were conveniently close enough to Oakland for us to reach them by daylight. We could hunt for a couple of hours and be back in Oakland in time for practice. There were so many places to hunt ducks. Sometimes, we were close to channels where large ships came in. Occasionally, we would be invited to join other duck and goose hunters on outings that included food and accommodations.

The Rifleman - Cotton Davidson

Those were such enjoyable affairs. Clearly, successes of the Raiders' organization in recent years had garnered not only trophies but other benefits as well. Those "other benefits" went a long way in helping 1968 to be less of a dull year for me.

In Coryell County, there was not one wild pheasant. However, about two hours east of San Francisco, pheasants were plentiful on a ranch owned by a couple of bankers. They invited Daryle and me to hunt there as often as we liked. Those trips were great fun, and we easily got our limit every time we hunted. Pheasants are so quick that they really test a hunter's reflexes and dexterity. Bagging a limit also gave my shoulder a workout. Although I could have done without it, I kept the pad on my shotgun just to avoid chances of disturbing what Dr. Levinthal and his speed bag regimen had put back together. They had done a remarkable job, and I never had a problem when shooting a gun.

Some of the best deer hunting I have ever done also was in California. Another friend, up north in the Santa Rosa area, had a ranch where Daryle and I hunted. That rancher also loaned us a key to his place so we could hunt on our own schedule. On one trip, I bagged two bucks. We also hunted deer in Daryle's home territory, near Fresno. My son, Tommy, killed his first deer there.

As 1968 wore on, those hunting trips surely helped keep my interest up while in California. I had made up my mind that this would be my last year to be away from Texas. Tommy was never in the same school twice during our seven years with the Raiders. I was committed to relocating to Gatesville before he entered high school, and that would be happening in one more year. I wanted Tommy to have his high school years in one school so he would have a chance to develop his skills in sports if he chose to do so. It was time for me to move on.

Our Raiders' last regular-season game was with the Chargers in San Diego on December 15. We didn't expect to win that game. The Chargers had beaten us earlier in the season, and the odds were that they would do it again. Our plan was to head for Texas after the game. Therefore, Carolyn and Dot Cannon packed our cars with all our belongings for moving back to Texas and drove to San Diego. We were wrong about the game. We won with a score of 34-27. That required a change of plans and a delayed trip home for Billy and me. My last year with the Raiders would be extended by at least a week, but not for Carolyn. She and Dot went on to Texas with their eight small passengers and left Billy and me to fend for ourselves.

Carolyn and Dot didn't know that they would be driving to Texas without their husbands. We surprised them with that bit of news when meeting them after the game. They had not gone to the game. Back in those days, each player was offered only two tickets for family members. Carolyn and Dot each had four children. In their case, having only four tickets for ten people was problematic. Therefore, in deference to the desires of eight small children, they declined game tickets and went to the San Diego Zoo instead. It was a very good thing that Carolyn and Dot were always up to whatever situation came their way in the world of pro football. Without so much as a grumble, they accepted their fate and headed for Texas. They had been looking forward to this day and being home soon. It was a welcomed point in time, even if the trip was to be made without a driving partner. Unless we won the next game, chances were good that I could be home for Christmas.

Wayland Corgill

Our next game would be the Western Division Playoff against the Kansas City Chiefs in the Oakland-Alameda County Coliseum on December 22. The Chiefs were the second team that had beaten us earlier in the season, and they were expected to beat us again. However, that didn't happen. We won again, big time, with a score of 41-6. Unbelievable! The year 1968 was turning out to be successful beyond everyone's expectations. It was rather uncanny that the only two games we had lost during the regular season were to the Chargers and Chiefs, and now we had beaten both of them. That was something I had not planned on. Christmas was not going to find me at home in Texas.

Our next contest would be a big one for the AFL Championship. Our opponent would be the New York Jets. It would be played at Shea Stadium in New York on December 29. We had handily beaten the Jets earlier in the season and felt good about our chances of doing it again. That earlier game got almost unprecedented national attention for at least a couple

In my home with a rare unblemished Raiders helmet – courtesy of the Davidson family

of reasons besides ending with an unexpected 43-32 upset for Joe Namath and the Jets. The Jets led throughout the game until the final minute. In the fourth quarter, Oakland made three touchdowns, two of which were made in that last minute. The game was televised, but the viewing audience didn't see how it ended. That was a big, big problem! The game ran long and, through a communication error, the television network cut away to begin a film, Heidi, as scheduled. When the broadcast of the game had ended, the Jets were ahead. When the game ended, the Raiders were ahead. The only people who knew that were in the stands and on the field. Fans watching television didn't learn about the totally unexpected outcome until much later, and they didn't appreciate that. That game will probably always be remembered as the Heidi Game.

Winning the last two games with the Chargers and Chiefs had given our confidence a tremendous boost. As we prepared for going against the Jets, I wondered what they were thinking and how the Heidi Game had affected their resolve to win. No doubt, they would be "charged up," and the game would be a battle. The Jets were always a tough team to beat, but the rivalry between the Jets and Raiders made for a really tough game. Also, Joe Namath was having a great year, and the Jets would have home-field advantage. Surely, the Heidi Game was still a "thorn in their side."

As expected, the 1968 AFL Championship Game was a hard-fought contest. The Jets prevailed with a score of 27-23. Neither team "ran away" with the game. The outcome was uncertain until time expired in the 4th quarter. Neither Daryl Lamonica nor Joe Namath had one of their better days with a passing game. It was just a very tough game, but it was a very important one for Joe and the Jets. It propelled them to Super Bowl III, where they pulled out a win that no one thought was possible. They went into the game as almost a three-touchdown underdog and won with a score of 16-7. By beating the heavily favored Baltimore Colts and my old friend, Johnny Unitas, they effectively notified the football world that the AFL was just as good as the NFL.

After that AFL Championship Game, my pro-football playing days ended. The days of the AFL were almost over too. Next year, 1969, would be the AFL's last season. Early in 1970, the AFL merged with the NFL, and all of their teams were organized into two conferences, the American Football Conference and the National Football Conference. I had been with the AFL as a player from its beginning in 1960 and for nine of its ten years of existence. What an unusual, interesting, educational, challenging, and gratifying experience, different in so many ways from life along Coryell Creek in Coryell County. Also, my experience in the pros was made all the more rewarding by the dozens and dozens of fine people I found everywhere. I might not see many of those folks again for a long time, but they certainly wouldn't be forgotten.

Finally, I was on my way to Texas and glad to be going home. I was also eager to re-establish relationships with family, friends, and all the fine folks in Coryell County. I would settle in Gatesville, and I had no plans of ever leaving again

Baylor Football Coach

As I left New York and headed for Texas after the AFL Championship game with the Jets, I had time to think about the consequences of my decision to leave the pros. There was a lot to think about! For almost two decades, football had been my life from the time I enrolled at Baylor on a football scholarship. From now on, my life certainly would be different. Hopefully, I wouldn't miss playing football too much. I didn't think I would. I was 37 years old, and my body was hinting that it was time for a change. I was reasonably confident I could make the adjustment, but I also wondered how easy or difficult that would be. How many unknowns would I encounter? How long would it take?

This new phase in my career would involve taking care of my oil company and ranch. I wouldn't have time hanging heavy on my hands. I would have plenty to do from the time I arrived home. No doubt, long days of working with my businesses would leave little time for thinking about the way of life I was leaving. While pondering those issues, I had no thoughts of ever being actively involved with football programs in the future. However, three short years later, a conversation with Coach Grant Teaff caused most of my plans to take a different direction. I was back in Baylor football.

Retiring from football at the end of the 1968 season generally fit into my long-term plans. With the ranch and oil and gas retail and distribution company I had bought in 1964, I expected to be able to support my family and accomplish a key element of my long-term plans. That objective was to have our kids settled in a place where they could grow up with no more moves. There was no better place for that than Gatesville, my hometown. I had resolved to be settled there before Tommy entered high school in 1971. Until now, he had attended a different school every year. I was determined that he, Kelly, Tracy, and Ty should have a chance to play sports and mature in one location. My shoulder injury in 1967 just reinforced that objective. Making a living from raising livestock and operating the oil and gas company wouldn't be easy, but I was confident that I had adequately set myself up to accomplish my goals.

Those three years of 1969, 1970, and 1971 were busy. They were also great years. Workdays were long, but they didn't get in the way of so many pleasant reconnections and associations with family and friends and being close to our children's daily activities. Also, it was satisfying to renew close ties to our church and make long-term plans for participation in church activities. Church had always played an important role in our lives from the long-ago time when we attended services in the little Pecan Grove Baptist Church on Coryell Creek. We quickly settled into life in Gatesville. Gradually, thoughts of football popped up less and less and, when the time came along for training camp, I sure was glad I was not going.

Baylor's football coaching staff in 1972. Top (L-R): Duke Christian, Bill Lane, Skip Cox, Cotton Davidson, Billy Mills, Bill Hicks; Bottom (L-R) Wade Turner, John O'Hara, Head Coach Grant Teaff, Corky Nelson, Joe Broeken
– courtesy of The Texas Collection, Baylor University

Gatesville was and still is a great place to raise kids. Its small-town character and variety of sports activities available throughout the year were a huge benefit for us. Our children ranged in ages of 4 to 13. The older two were beginning to think about expanding their horizons, especially Tommy, our teenager. They needed things to do and places to roam. Gatesville and Coryell County "filled the bill" for that. Our kids played football, basketball, baseball, and volleyball. Our backyard became a baseball field. When Ty got old enough to play baseball, I squeezed in a baseball diamond behind the house. Needless to say, our yard was a popular place for neighborhood kids. We followed our kids to all their games. We even did that in later years when I was coaching at Baylor. However, on Baylor game days, it was only Carolyn who attended our kids' games. Whenever my schedule permitted, I would accompany Carolyn because Coach Teaff was so gracious about letting me off. He understood the importance of sports' positive influences on children and supported us. Gatesville was working out fine for us. We certainly didn't miss moving back and forth to California.

During the five years leading up to 1969, my oil company and ranch had been well taken care of when I was away with football. Daddy and Hy saw to that. I can't say enough good things about my family. Their extraordinary support went a long way in helping to make it possible for me to play football. I could not have held onto my ranch and oil company without them. Bus and Dean were very reliable help with my ranch too. However, there was no one more responsible than my gas station employees, Bob and Louise Matthews, Fred Williams, and Gene Dyer. All of those folks had done a great job of taking care of business while I was away with football. Now, it was my turn to shoulder some of the load, and there was plenty to do. Daddy and Hy had helped me so much in the past, and now, I would be in a position to help them too. That is the way it was for many years. All three of us helped each other. It felt great to be back with family, and the feeling was mutual. They seemed to think it was time for me to get on the other side of the ball, and they helped me do it.

The ranch didn't require nearly as much attention as the oil company. The Barton's virtually took care of managing everything on the place where they lived. Also, they had a tremendously talented helper, a border collie named Sidewinder. That dog came with the Parker place when I bought it. He stayed in the barn. Bus and Dean fed him. If that dog could have talked, I believe we could have had an intelligent conversation. He had no problem understanding me. He was better at herding sheep and goats than a half-dozen men would have been. My other two places were near the Parker place, and I could easily check on all three of them every two or three days. I had sheep and goats on the Parker place and cows on the other two. Daddy helped me with those places too. He was a trapper and, with his help, I didn't have many livestock losses from coyotes and other predators. However, I did lose about twenty sheep to the weather one year when we had a late freeze right after shearing time. I really liked ranch work and loved the land. Dealing with adverse weather conditions and wild animals was just part of the job.

Assets of my Cotton Davidson Oil Company included a gas station (service station) in downtown Gatesville on the north side of the intersection of State Business Highway 36 and U.S. Highway 84. That location was my headquarters. Other structures at that site included a separate office building and storage shed. Three aboveground storage tanks for regular and ethyl gasoline and diesel were located at the back of the lot. As a distributor for the Sinclair Oil Corporation, I also had a tanker truck for fuel delivery to farmers, ranchers, and a half-dozen independent gas stations. Two of those independent gas stations were in downtown Gatesville. One was located where POCO Auto & Tire is now, and the other was on the parking lot just east of the National United Bank. Other gas stations were located from South Mountain to Turnersville.

My gas station was a busy place. In addition to pumping gasoline, we sold and mounted tires, fixed flats, changed engine oil, and washed cars. Our tire supplier was Powell Auto Supply on the courthouse square. Those were the days when gas stations were called service stations. Customers didn't get out of their cars while we provided the service. We even washed windshields and checked the engine oil. If asked, we would also check tire pressures.

For changing oil and washing cars, the service station had two enclosed bays: one for oil changes and one for car washing. A half-wall separated the two bays. Tommy turned 13 in 1969 and was a big help with car washing. I am sure the job was a little tedious at times. Being a resourceful young teenager, he livened things up by starting water fights with whoever was changing oil on the other side of the half-wall. One day, he tired of water fights and tried a new method for avoiding boredom. He set off several cherry bombs in the car wash bay. All of the windows in both bays were blown out. Luckily, he wasn't hurt, but his ears rang for a while. Also, it gave the rest of us at the gas station a pretty healthy jolt out of our routines. Understandably, an explosion of any kind in a gas station will set every nerve in a person's body on edge within a split second. For a minute or two, we didn't know whether or not we were headed for obliteration. That was just a little bit more excitement than Tommy had bargained for. There was no more boredom that day. When things quieted down, I told Tommy, "We don't do things that way," and he meekly went back to washing cars. The water fights never stopped, but it was the end of the cherry bombs.

So many people would ask me, "Why are you pumping gas?" Well, that was part of the job of operating my gas and oil company. However, pumping gas was not all that I did. Actually, I only pumped gas whenever I wasn't making deliveries to other gas stations and farmers and ranchers. I liked that part of the business much better. Daddy knew just about everybody in the county, and he was very good at getting customers for me. Also, I knew a lot of people, and my reputation didn't hurt. I probably supplied fuel to half of the farmers and ranchers in Coryell County. Business was good, and I liked meeting people. They were always interesting to talk to and were always glad to see me. We kept the neighborhood news circulating.

Two full-time employees operated the gas station, and occasionally, I had three. They were all retired Army sergeants, and they were great. They worked like they owned the business. One of them, Bob Matthews, was exceptionally important to me because his wife, Louise, was my secretary. She was a jewel. I depended on her for so much, and she never let me down. She was a lifesaver. Days were usually long for me but, no doubt, they would have been much longer without Louise. I would close the station at 8:00 p.m., do a little bit of office work, and be home before 9:00 p.m. Without Louise, I am sure I wouldn't have had such a leisurely schedule.

Life back in Gatesville quickly settled into being everything that Carolyn and I had envisioned. It was so satisfying to be around Davidson family members and old friends. It was comforting to be able to commit to church activities and community affairs without the interruptions of being away for football season. However, the best benefit of all was having our kids settled in a place where they could grow and prosper without moving again. Gatesville was and is a great community, and its school system, including its sports programs, is outstanding as well. Carolyn and I were confident we could make our life just what we had planned. We would have to work long hours, and our income might be stretched a little bit in the beginning, but we were so glad to be where we were.

The longer we lived in our house on Park Street, the smaller it seemed to be. In 1970, I began to look for a piece of land near town where I could build a house. I talked to my high school football coach, Lloyd Mitchell, about that. I thought he might know of a suitable property. Coach Mitchell had meant everything to me in high school, and he was still one of my all-time favorite people. He was a great, all-purpose coach, and we were as close as a father and son. Also, he was my Sunday school teacher, and I saw him often. He had a large piece of land on top of a small mountain near the eastern edge of town. His residence was there, along with a couple of large sheet metal buildings that housed his massive collections of cowboy equipment and antiques. Once in a while, we would have Sunday school class around a campfire at his place. At those campfire classes, the view of the countryside was inspiring. It was unobstructed for at least fifteen miles distance in a range from southwest to northwest. The whole city of Gatesville was included in that expanse. The courthouse shone like a jewel in the middle of it.

I began to think that I sure would like to be on that mountain with Coach Mitchell as my neighbor. I mentioned that to him one day and asked him about selling me enough land to build a house. He was noncommittal. For a couple of months, I would occasionally bring that subject up with him but got nowhere. Then, one day in church, as we sat next to each other in Sunday school class, to my surprise, he slapped me on the leg and asked, "When are you going to start building? After a few moments of being speechless, I said, "Well, I think I need to get some ink on a piece of paper for land first." Needless-to-say, after that, my mind was not on what was being talked about in Sunday school class.

A couple of weeks after that conversation in the church, I did get some ink on a deed for a few acres of Coach Mitchell's mountain top. After he said it was mine, I could have hugged his neck. The financial part of the bargain was the most unusual deal I was ever involved in. When we got around to talking about the price for my parcel, Coach Mitchell said, "I know how much Carolyn loves those live oak trees. I will sell it by the tree." I was to count the trees and, then, he would tell me the price.

That piece of land was a choice spot. From my front porch, I have the same view that we used to have from Coach Mitchell's campfire Sunday school classes. We built our house in 1971, and we are still there.

While working at my gas station one day in January 1972, Baylor football coach, Bill Scoggins, stopped by. I had known Bill for several years, although we had not worked or played together. He lived near San Angelo, west of Gatesville, and passed through Gatesville on his trips between home and Baylor. Whenever he could, he would stop by my gas station. Bill was a likable, down-to-earth, West Texas native. We had a lot in common, and we always had a pleasant visit.

This time, Bill was full of news about big changes being made in the Baylor football coaching staff. A new head coach, Grant Teaff, had been hired, and Bill was certain that Coach Teaff meant business about putting Baylor on a path to winning seasons. It had been a long time since Baylor had had one of those. In the past five seasons, Baylor had only won seven (7) games. Something had to give, and Coach Teaff needed help to make it happen. He was already working on that by changing staff and hunting for the best available coaches. Bill was excited about an idea he had for me. It was about something entirely different from pumping gas. Coach Teaff needed a coach for quarterbacks and receivers. I think my name had been mentioned in that regard by the Baylor Athletic Director, Jack Patterson. Jack was an old friend from the time I was a freshman at Baylor in 1949. He was a basketball coach then. Bill's idea was that coaching quarterbacks and receivers was an ideal job for me.

Wow! Bill's suggestion caught me totally off guard. How could I seriously think about doing something like that? How would such a move impact my long-term plans and family life? I was settled with my family into pleasant routines of living and working and being happy in the process. Did I want to disrupt all of that? How much disruption would there be? For so many years, until the last three, I had to move my family every year when football season rolled around. I didn't want to do that anymore. Staying in one place was such a relief. One thing was for sure: I would not move from Gatesville. I had already turned down an offer to coach at Rice University because I would have to move to Houston. If I could stay in Gatesville and drive back and forth to Baylor, I might be interested. I would see what Carolyn had to say.

Without question, the thought of coaching at Baylor was much more than a passing interest to me. Actually, I believe I was more homesick for football than I had realized. During the last three years, I had put out of my mind any thoughts of seriously returning to football. I had done a little scouting for the Raiders but, other than that, the only contact I had had with the pros were previous teammates' visits. Bill's conversation stirred so many thoughts and memories of why I loved the game. Also, I always loved coaching. Working with young athletes and helping them improve their skills and be successful was one of the most rewarding jobs I could imagine. Seeing them develop into young men and use the things they learned in football to advance in their careers was even more gratifying. I had had experience with that when I spent the whole year of 1959 on Baylor's football coaching staff with Head Coach John Bridgers. However, at this point in my life, I had four children, who would soon be grown, and they needed the same "coaching." That had to be considered in the balancing act of satisfying the needs of both family and work. Other factors required attention too. I was aware that I might not be able to keep my oil company business and, also, coach at Baylor. I could keep my ranch, but I would probably have to depend more on Daddy and Hy to help with that. Presently, they were just too busy to help with my oil company. No doubt, there were several more issues that hadn't occurred to me yet; hopefully, not too many. It would be such a big career move! I had a lot to think about and critical decisions to make if I joined Coach Teaff's staff.

When Bill Scoggins went on his way, he left me with a head full of new thoughts. I couldn't concentrate on pumping gas or doing anything else at the service station. All I could think about was what Bill and I had discussed and the possibility of getting back into football. I told my employees I would be gone for a little while and headed home. Carolyn and I had a lot to talk about.

I was a little uncertain about Carolyn's views on the prospects of coaching at Baylor, but I really shouldn't have been surprised by what she had to say. She was one-hundred percent supportive of the idea. She was certain that I would be happier coaching at Baylor than I was operating my oil and gas business. However, she had one non-negotiable provision. She would not move from Gatesville. If I could do the job by commuting from Gatesville, she was all for it. We agreed on that point. I would not move either. If that requirement could be satisfied, coaching might even have significant advantages, in addition to job satisfaction. Financial prospects might be better, particularly, if we could hang onto our oil and gas business. Another benefit would be college educations at Baylor for our four children. We had a few years before dealing with that, but coaching at Baylor surely would be an advantage when our kids became college age. We even thought coaching might require fewer hours away from home. However, that was before I knew how much recruiting time would play into the job.

Carolyn and I looked at a possible, major career change from every direction we could imagine. After that, I called Coach Teaff and told him I would like to come over and talk to him. That visit changed my life for the next 21 years.

On my way to Waco, I happened to think about my PaPa and what he might think about how things were turning out for me. He passed away in 1956, and a lot of water had gone under the bridge and down Coryell Creek since then. However, his memory was as fresh as when we used to sit on the creek bank and sing to the fish. PaPa didn't know anything about football, but he knew a lot about life. His advice was very good. Almost all of his life was spent in Coryell County, and his travels didn't go far beyond the county line. What would he have thought about the life I chose, which had taken me all over the U.S.A.? What would he think about the move I was making now? PaPa was a broad-minded man. Also, he was reliable and resourceful. He took care of his responsibilities in the best way he knew how when options and opportunities were extremely limited. He never had the remotest chance of doing things similar to what I had done. If he had, I believe he would have taken advantage of opportunities that came along, provided that they passed his test of "common sense." I never forgot his advice: to be sure to take a couple of courses in "common sense" when I went off to Baylor as a teenager. In that same conversation, he also told me, "Make something out of yourself." I believed he would be in my corner now as I was heading back to Baylor. However, without a doubt, I knew what his advice would be for any deal I agreed to.

I didn't know Coach Teaff, but I was very favorably impressed after we talked for a few minutes. He had an extraordinary friendly personality and an exceptional talent for speaking and expressing himself. He made me think everything would be okay, and I easily got a feeling that I could work with him. After only a few minutes, we got down to business and put things together rather quickly. I found out what he was looking for and what he wanted. In effect, we talked about installing the Colts passing offense again, as I had done in 1959. He wanted Baylor to have a passing game that would rival any team in the Southwest Conference. He needed a coach that could make that happen and handle the kicking game too. I knew I could do the job if I could get talented kids to train.

I think Coach Teaff knew enough of my background to have confidence in my ability to do what he wanted. Our meeting was relatively short, and I went back to Gatesville to tell Carolyn the job was mine if I wanted it. We would not have to move from Gatesville. Carolyn was agreeable.

The way this coaching opportunity came about was great for me. If it had been any other school except Baylor, I would have had a tough time accepting. I could coach at Baylor and take care of my ranch. Whether I could keep my oil company business was questionable at this point, but at least I knew I could keep my ranch. That was most important. In time, I was confident I could work out how to handle my personal business. At this time, I was looking forward to showing up in the Baylor locker room. I really liked coaching. It didn't eat me alive. Within a week, I started my new coaching career.

Spring training had started, and my first concern was getting familiar with the players and assessing their capabilities. At that time, Baylor had a terrible record, about as bad as it had ever been. With that in mind, I expected I wouldn't find much talent on the roster. If I didn't have much to work with, Baylor might be headed for another miserable year. That worry began to fade after a few days. One big reason for optimism was the starting quarterback, Neal Jeffrey. First impressions of Neal didn't work in his favor because of his stuttering, but right away, I could tell he had plenty of talent with a football. I could win with him. I wondered what previous coaches had done with that talent? Other team members were similar to Neal. They were talented but, apparently, not coached very well. That was encouraging. The more I learned about the team, the more I believed we could have a winning season in 1972.

Spring training is a very important element in making a winning football team. Things get put together in spring training. During that time, players are taught physical parts of the game. That goes a long way in helping them avoid injuries, protect themselves and be effective on the field. Even a simple thing like a player's stance requires careful training.

As the days went by, I became more and more encouraged about the talent of the "kids" I was working with. They were all fine young men and eager to learn and perform. Neal Jeffrey and I "hit it off" from the very beginning. I knew his father, James Jeffrey, who was an All-Conference running back on the Baylor football team in 1949 and 1950 when I was there. Neal had what it took to do a great job for us. His stuttering was not a problem. He rarely ever stuttered when he and I talked. More importantly, it never bothered him when barking orders over the center. Also, he had confidence in himself, his delivery was good, and he was up and off with a quick 1-2-3 plant and throw. He consistently performed up to expectations for the next three years, and sometimes, he was brilliant. Perhaps, his father had something to do with that.

The talent I found in all areas was encouraging. We had several pretty sharp kids, football-wise, but had not been taught a very good "brand" of football. After working with them for only a little while, they became excited about what we were teaching. In practice, they were learning so many things they had not previously seen. Each workout showed them that they were getting better. Even kids on the sidelines got excited about what they saw happening on the field. The whole team began to get the idea that they had to work hard and we would get somewhere. Their confidence grew. They got those attitudes from the coaches. Coaches make the difference. Coach Teaff had done a good job of assembling a staff of coaches who made that happen.

The offensive line had respectable talent. Receivers responded well to my coaching techniques and, one of them, Charles Dancer, made remarkable improvements in a short time. He really worked hard and was a top receiver in his senior year. The guys on the defensive side of the ball were impressive too. One defensive lineman, Roger Goree, got my attention because of his size. He was fairly small but powerful, and man could he play. In one of our games, he blocked two field goals, and that won the game for us. Other examples of kids doing extraordinary things were showing up right along. The more I worked with those young men, the more I began to believe we could put up a winning season.

As far as I know, I was the only football coach at Baylor who had played in the pros. During that time, I had learned from many of the best coaches in the business. From Weeb Ewbank in 1954 to Al Davis in 1969 and other coaches in between, I had learned so much from what each one had to offer. That experience could help me do a better job of preparing the quarterbacks and receivers. I believed they had the potential to be a threat to any team we might play. I spent lots of time on the chalkboard with quarterbacks and lots of time on the field with receivers.

My coaching philosophy was to keep things as simple as possible. That applied to both the passing game and the running game. The powerhouse Green Bay Packers under Coach Vince Lombardi were very successful with making that approach work. About eighty percent of the time, they based their running game on two basic plays: sweep and cutback. They would run them, run them, and run them until they could do them perfectly every time. Ideally, plays must become second nature when working out or in games.

I wanted quarterbacks to be aware of any formation they might see on the field (blitzes, in particular) and teach them how to respond. That learning process involves evaluating every formation imaginable on the chalkboard and then setting up those formations on the field. That method, along with continual repeat, repeat, repeat, and practice, practice, practice, produces good results. Having quarterbacks draw up plays on the chalkboard is a good learning tool too. Training them to levels where they are not surprised by any set formation or formation change that might be encountered during a play sure helps win games. However, getting to that level requires training that is understandable and not confusing. Accomplishing that starts with the effective use of classrooms and chalkboards.

The classroom was the place to simplify situations and explain actions in ways that everybody would understand and know what to do on the field. It was my job to "un-complicate the complicated" in the classroom and on the field and use repetition until actions and reactions become second nature. I wanted young charges to be successful, and I would do whatever I could to make that happen. I think the beginnings of those ideas were "coached" in me by my high school coach, Lloyd Mitchell. They were based on a desire to bring out the best in a person if that person worked hard, listened to me, and tried to do what I said. If so, I would try to teach them everything I knew.

That rationale grew as I moved through college and the pros. It was especially practiced between Johnny Unitas and me. Johnny had the same set of values I did about helping others. We were about as close as any two quarterbacks in the league. We "hit it off" from the beginning and maintained an excellent relationship. We continually helped each other. Now, at Baylor, practicing those principles was an integral, full-time part of my job. I had always had good luck with finding people who would listen to me and appreciate what I was telling them when they learned that it worked. Surely, I would have the same experience with the Baylor football team.

There is more to coaching than most people know. The way I look at it, coaching responsibility goes beyond the football field. Football is one thing; life is another. However, the two are mixed. Many of the kids I worked with didn't have much of a home life, and I felt responsible for setting a good example for them. I wanted them to be like me. If they didn't have a strong "father figure" in their life, I would try to help fill the void. If I could influence a kid to be a better person, that was my reward. I had to practice the golden rule of treating them as I would like to be treated. If they got good vibes from me and we got things going in the right direction, we were going to be good. I never hollered at a kid, and I didn't like coaches who did. There is always more than one way to do things, and I could usually get the results I was looking for without being critical. Respect is a good word, and mutual respect between coaches and players goes a long, long way in fostering good attitudes and promoting effective teamwork. Teamwork is another important word. Teaching teamwork is another essential coaching responsibility that is best taught by example.

Of course, a receiver is supposed to catch passes; ideally, any kind of pass. To do that, he has to practice, practice, practice, too. Each of my receivers had to catch at least thirty passes from me every day of training. My objective was for them to be proficient in catching any type of pass in a game. I threw them all kinds, and I didn't slack up on how hard I threw. They had to handle passes: over their shoulders, behind their back, in their face, near the ground, almost out of their reach, and through the arms of a defender fighting for the ball. I wanted them to see that ball coming from every direction. I made sure that every receiver wouldn't be faced with trying to catch a pass that he hadn't caught a thousand times in practice. I wouldn't ask any player to do something in a ball game that he hadn't done over and over in practice.

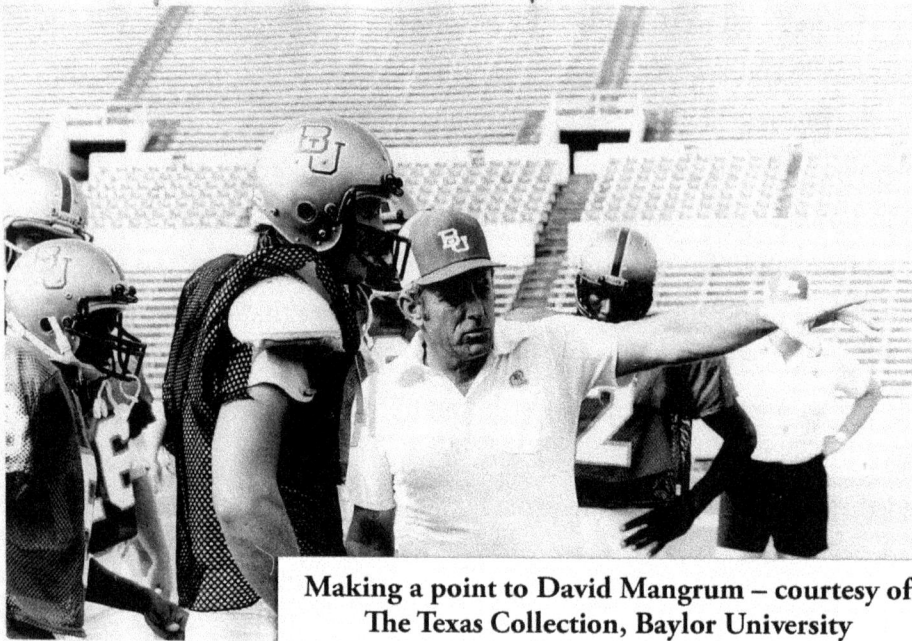

Making a point to David Mangrum – courtesy of The Texas Collection, Baylor University

Part of catching a ball is a mental exercise. A catch and fumble are just terrible. I would tell them what my old friend, Raymond Berry, had to say about that. His guiding principle was: "catch – tuck – explode." That was followed by more advice: "Concentrate on only one thing at a time, or you will mess up. Don't look for a place to run when you are trying to catch a ball."

Those were pretty strenuous workouts for receivers and me when I was training six or seven receivers. However, Dr. Levinthal in California had done a good job of putting my shoulder back together, and I never had a problem with throwing more than two hundred passes at a time.

Quarterback ball-handling skills are improved by proper instruction and drills, of course, but arm strength and stamina are important too. I don't believe I could have had better advice than Dr. Levinthal's after he operated on my shoulder. He told me to get a boxing speed bag and work out with that. After mastering the technique of striking that speed bag and routinely exercising with it, I regained virtually all of my arm and shoulder strength and mobility. With that in mind, I installed five speed bags in our gym and started a new exercise program for our quarterbacks. I wanted them to get in shape to really put some zip on the ball.

Spring training went well, and players got excited about drills that they had never done. We worked hard on the field and off the field. We paid attention to all elements of the game and watched films to evaluate performance. We concentrated on avoiding penalties. They can be "killers." I could see very positive changes in a week's time. Seeing kids come around the way they did, made me feel great.

Under Coach Teaff's leadership, our coaching staff rapidly improved. He did an excellent job of getting good, seasoned head coaches from high schools. He paid particular attention to offensive line coaches and managed to recruit good ones. A good offensive line coach is hard to find. That is just about the toughest position to coach. An offensive line coach has to teach five players to recognize all types of blocking for run plays and pass plays. Blocking for those plays is completely different. The success of the offensive line was extremely important to me and whoever the quarterback was. Without a well-functioning offensive line, a quarterback doesn't have much of a chance to do his job. I wanted to congratulate the offensive line guys every time they got a block. If they did a good job, I did a good job. Generally, we always had offensive line coaches I could easily work with, and I made sure they were my best friends. Bill Young was one of those. Their interests were the same as mine; protect the quarterback and win games.

An offensive line's effectiveness depends on both player capability and coaching. During that first year at Baylor, I spent a lot of time in coordination with offensive line coaches and the players. We had a lot of work to do to develop techniques the offensive line should use. We had good success, and the results began to show up with wins early in the season. Coaching made the difference.

From the earliest days of Coach Teaff's time at Baylor, his coaching staff jelled into an organization that demonstrated exceptional teamwork. He was a family man and made a family of his staff. He could make you feel right at home. We all got along and had many pleasant social gatherings outside of football. That comradery and cooperation sure paid off for me during games when I was in the observation tower and talking to the offensive coordinator to advise of situations on the field and send down plays. Offensive coordinators and I always had very good relationships and worked together for both of our benefit. The excellent teamwork and attitudes in Coach Teaff's coaching staff made for a pleasant place to work.

During games, I was always in an observation tower. I would study the opposing team's play and communicate with our offensive coordinator. We were in constant conversation. By the end of the first quarter, I had usually picked up on a few things that would help our game plan. I had always called every play I ran throughout my college and pro career. With that experience, I could easily send down plays that would take advantage of an opponent's weaknesses. Offensive coordinators and I always maintained good working relationships, and that helped win games.

As the 1972 spring semester ended and Baylor's locker room became silent, the next phase of my job soon started: recruiting! Recruiting is a big part of coaching, but it was not my favorite activity. You never know what you might run into on the other side of a door when you call on a prospective recruit. Most of the time, there was no problem, but, occasionally, it was a difficult situation. Misunderstandings created by other schools' coaches complicated matters. Sometimes, those coaches stretched the facts and left a family believing things that wouldn't happen. However, dealing with whatever adversity might be encountered was just a part of recruiting. The job had to be done. If you don't recruit good players, you don't win games. That's the bread and butter of a football team. I recruited all quarterbacks and receivers. If needed, I would recruit for other positions too. There were plenty of pleasant experiences of talking to potential recruits and their families. Still, I was on the road and away from home a lot for the entire summer. That part, I didn't like. I would leave home Monday morning and be gone most of the week. My area for recruiting stretched from Waco to the Rio Grande Valley, including Austin, San Antonio, and Houston. Normally, I didn't go to the North Texas area or into Oklahoma. Getting a kid out of there was really tough. Universities in Oklahoma recruited very aggressively there.

That first year of recruiting was a little rough due to Baylor's poor record of not winning games for the previous several years. Winning ballgames sure helps recruit. Everybody wants to play on a winning team. It's hard to get quality players unless you have a good record. Recruiting at least one good quarterback every year is a must. Without a good backup quarterback, one lick on the starting quarterback and the season is headed down the tubes. You never know when an injury might happen. We really had to work at having good backup players. We had to be thinking about that all the time. Recruiting two good quarterbacks every year is advisable. With three quality quarterbacks on the roster, one can be red-shirted while the other two can play. Without a good record to talk about, I had my work cut out for me that first year. I relied heavily on explaining the big moves Baylor had made in its coaching staff and my honest opinions about the excellent prospects of Baylor strongly coming out of their long-time slump. I had good luck with that approach. People believed me.

Recruiting is a time-consuming job that requires a lot of preparation. There is more to it than just visiting with a kid and his parents. In addition to parents, other people get involved, including the head coach, assistant coach, and teachers. Before talking to a young man, I would have reviewed his record, seen him play, and talked to his high school coach. A visit came next in order to make a judgment of the young man. The work done prior to a visit was easy and interesting but time-consuming. I liked watching a kid play, but that tied up a lot of my Fridays. Also, I enjoyed talking to coaches. I made an effort to get to know coaches, and I never had one of them mislead me. Sometimes, the tricky part of recruiting was the visit to a home. Usually, families would really get involved. I never had trouble with talking to a kid or his parents. But occasionally, competing with other recruiters became an issue that required a dose of ethical diplomacy. However, I was usually successful and didn't lose very many kids that I really wanted. If I could get "Mama" on my side, I had a strong advantage. Baylor had a lot to offer, but no doubt my reputation as a quarterback in the pros helped too. Most kids knew my background. I was somewhat surprised that so many people knew something about that.

Often, visits turned into much more than a discussion of the football aspect of attending Baylor. I was always careful to clearly represent what we were looking for in a football player. That was easily understood. However, there was often a lack of understanding about what a scholarship was all about and what Baylor had to offer. Those topics usually required a lot of attention to make sure there were no surprises later on.

Maintaining credibility by being consistent was essential. I treated every kid the same way and told each one the same thing. Once in a while, I would compete with a recruiter from another school who didn't operate that way. He might stretch his "story" to the point of bordering on being illegal. However, that usually didn't work in his favor. I never had a problem with someone thinking I misrepresented the facts. When a kid's parents would tell me about another recruiter's offer that sounded a little too good to be true, I would say, "Tell him to put that in writing." Most moms and dads could see through those empty offers easily. However, again, most people were aware of me and my record and trusted what I told them.

Baylor could offer much better personal attention and less crowding than larger schools, and that could translate into better education. Regular classes at Baylor would have 20 to 30 students, while classes at the University of Texas could be more than twice as large. That was a big selling point, particularly with a young man's parents. If his mother was convinced, that was almost a deal clincher.

Coach Teaff was a very good recruiter. He would usually go with each recruiter once or twice so a kid and his family would know him. He tried to make it into the home of every player. When I wound up with six or seven players I wanted, he would accompany me to visit each one and his family. He did an excellent job of presenting Baylor's advantages and comparing them to other schools. Several times, Coach Teaff's presence made the difference on signing day when a kid we wanted was sought after by another school. Sometimes, the competition was fierce, and it wasn't all "fun and roses." Lots of times, kids, or their families, wouldn't have their minds made up before signing day. In those cases, two coaches from different schools in the same room sometimes caused situations to evolve that were a little less than dignified. However, in every one of those cases involving Coach Teaff and me, there was no question about who the master statesman was in the room and who was, unquestionably, most convincing. I don't remember ever losing one of those contests.

Potential recruits were invited to visit Baylor. When they showed up, we took good care of them. If they came on a Friday, we would put them up in a dorm, and they would go home on Sunday. One of our players would show them around and introduce them to coaches and teachers. We would make sure they had a good weekend experience. I would also encourage potential recruits to come to see us play.

Over the years, I had quite a few memorable experiences with recruiting; most of them were good, and a few were disappointing. I lost one West Texas quarterback because his girlfriend went to Texas Tech, and therefore he did too. I lost another one to Texas A&M because his sister was going there. Recruiting a kid from a TAMU family was a challenge. However, I did recruit one young man, Keith Jones, whose father was a TAMU alumnus. I visited him after two or three other recruiters had been to see him. After we had talked for a while, Keith's daddy said, "You made a promise of a scholarship, and I'll make you a promise. Keith will come to Baylor." Remarkable!

Regarding quarterbacks, recruiting two of equal-high quality at the same time was a rare accomplishment, indeed. However, I was that lucky as the 1980s began. Actually, they were one year apart, but they played together for three years and excelled in that position past the middle of the decade. The first was Tom Muecke in 1982 and Cody Carlson in 1983. I wished I could have split them up, but it sure was good to have two talented quarterbacks when injuries happened. Cody and Tom had a special, heartwarming relationship of helping each other, which sure helped win games.

There were so many other success stories with recruiting, too many to name. I found talented players in so many places, even Gatesville. One of those was Ricky Thompson, who made a sensational catch and run for one of the touchdowns that helped win the "Miracle on the Brazos" game against the University of Texas in 1974. Another outstanding receiver, who came from Gatesville a year later, was Tommy Davidson. I didn't have too much trouble recruiting that young man. I had thrown passes to him from the time he was old enough to catch a ball.

In this book, I wish I could acknowledge and compliment each of those fine young men I recruited or, at least, mention their names. Since I can't do that, each and every one should know my appreciation for his contributions during my time as a Baylor coach and also know he is not forgotten.

Soon after I started coaching at Baylor, I realized I couldn't hold onto my oil and gas business. I had almost no time to spend with it, and Daddy and Hy had very little spare time. Hy was now a county commissioner, plus being a rancher. Daddy looked after his own ranch. However, Daddy could help look after my ranch, and that would help me keep it. That was my main concern. I had to sell my oil and gas company.

Me and some of my offensive starters for the great teams of 1983-1986. Quarterbacks are Cody Carlson #14 and Tom Muecke #7 – courtesy of the Davidson family

Selling that business was not a problem at all. When I bought it in 1964, it was a Sinclair dealership. In 1972, it became an ARCO dealership. ARCO had bought Sinclair in 1969. As a dealer with ties to a major oil company, my company had no problem getting products. Independent gas stations got their oil and gas from dealers and, occasionally, had difficulties with running out of gas. Therefore, a few of the larger independent companies had considerable interest in buying my business. One of those "independents" was a man in Waco who owned gas stations that I had supplied. We quickly made a deal, and I was out of the gas and oil business.

Late the next year, the Arab oil embargo started an oil crisis that grew into a giant "headache" all across the U.S.A. I was glad I had sold my company when I did; lucky again.

When the 1972 football season started, we were ready.

Our first game was on the Georgia Bulldog's home turf. Georgia was a powerhouse. We didn't win, but we "played the devil out of them." The final score of 14-24 was a respectable one, and I was proud of our team. Georgia knew they had faced a serious opponent. Our Bears were a much different team than they were the previous year.

Our next game was at Missouri. The odds were probably in Missouri's favor, but we shut them out, 27-0. With that win, we tied Baylor's record of wins in the previous year of 1971. Baylor had only one win that year.

We had our next win when the Miami, Florida, team came to Baylor. Miami was probably favored but could only score three points. The score was 10-3. Our defense played well in that game.

We finally had another loss when we went up against the Razorbacks in Arkansas territory. We lost with a score of 20-31, but the game was closer than the score indicates. Probably, no more than two other teams played Arkansas better than we did.

Wayland Corgill

We had a tough opponent north of the Red River for our next game too. Oklahoma State was always a powerhouse and often beat the other Oklahoma powerhouse, Oklahoma University. We lost that one too. Not much will take the place of winning, but the 7-20 score was one I was proud of. Those Okies never had a chance to slack up.

We finally got another win when Texas A&M met us in Baylor stadium. Normally, if a team beat A&M, they did a good job. The game was close, but we were satisfied with the 15-13 score. Texas A&M was always an interesting opponent. Sometimes, they tried to win the game before they got on the field. For example, they had been known to add excitement to a contest by harassing the other team's mascot.

Another win was added to our scorecard when we traveled to Fort Worth and played TCU. We beat them handily, 42-9. We had now racked up a total of four wins. That equaled the total number of wins Baylor had in all of the previous three years.

After TCU, we had a "dry spell" for wins in the next three games. We lost, 3-17, to No. 9 ranked Texas. We played them hard, and they certainly didn't run away with the game. The next game was with Texas Tech, and it was a close one, 7-13. The next loss was to SMU, 7-12. All three of those opponents were quality teams. We played them well and, with a little luck, the score could have turned out in our favor.

Our last game of the season was with Rice. That was always a hard-fought contest, and we won it with a score of 28-14. Ending the season with a win sure felt good.

Baylor football, under the new leadership of Coach Teaff and his staff, had made attention-getting improvements and successes in 1972. Our overall win-loss record of 5-6 and our Southwest Conference win-loss record of 3-4 needed to be improved, for sure. Still, those records were certainly better than they had been in several years. Attitudes were changing in a positive direction on campus, off-campus, and with alumni and fans. What was happening with the attitudes of team members was particularly important to me. Those guys were getting excited about playing. They believed they could win. I was going to help them.

I put a lot of miles on cars that first year and the miles just kept racking up for the next 20 years. Luckily, I drove cars furnished by car dealers, and Baylor reimbursed gasoline expenses. From my house to Baylor was 40 miles. Morning and evening traffic was usually light, and the trip took less than an hour. I didn't mind the driving, but there was always one difficulty in the morning and one in the evening, too. On the east-west road to Waco, the sun was right in my eyes, going and coming. We weren't moving from Gatesville, so I kept a ball cap pulled low over my eyes and tolerated the minor nuisance.

Between daily trips to Baylor during the school year and traveling for recruitment, I spent a lot of time on the road. Sometimes, I didn't watch my speed close enough, and I collected more than a few traffic tickets; probably, more than two dozen. I didn't pay very many of those because I had a guy in Waco who would "fix" them. However, my friend in Waco couldn't help me with one traffic ticket I got in Midway, Texas. That was the worst place for a ticket. I had neglected to pay the ticket, and I got a sharp reminder at a very inopportune time. During a pre-game meal before playing The University of Texas, a trainer came up to me and said, "Somebody wants to talk to you." That guy was a policeman from Midway. He said I needed to get out of there right then and take care of a ticket. I said I couldn't do that because we had a game to play. He said, "I'll have you arrested on the field. I said, "I'll be there." I guess he relented because no one escorted me out of the game.

The Rifleman - Cotton Davidson

The ups-and-downs of football caught Baylor at the bottom of Southwest Conference rankings in 1973. From a respectably successful first year under new coaching leadership, the second year was a major disappointment. Our overall win-loss record was 2-9, and our Southwest Conference record was 0-7. Several key players had graduated, but we still had a good team. We practiced and played hard but lost too many close games by a touchdown or less. Perhaps, the teams we had surprised and beaten the previous year had made up their minds to not let that happen again. However, we kept our spirits up and prepared for next year. We had seasoned players, who would still be on the team, and we had recruited good players who we had worked with for a season. Next year would be better.

Next year was better, a lot better! In the ups-and-downs-cycle of football, Baylor wound up on the very top, number one in the Southwest Conference. Our win-loss record was 8-4 overall and 6-1 in the Southwest Conference. The only conference loss was to Texas A&M at a homecoming game, of all things. That was disappointing. However, it was a record-setting, triumphant year with plenty of things to get excited about throughout the season.

Our season started by playing the No. 1 Oklahoma Sooners in Oklahoma. Over 62,000 fans attended. Based on our terrible record the previous season, oddsmakers had Baylor figured so far in the hole that it was a wonder anybody showed up. Oklahoma had trounced us the previous year. However, fans got their money's worth that September 1974 when Baylor fought the mighty Sooners to a relatively close loss of 11-28. Our next game was against Missouri. It was a loss too, but a close loss of 21-28. People in the college sports world were beginning to take notice of Baylor. After Missouri, the wins started again. We had three in a row. Sportswriters started wondering what had happened at Baylor. Then came the disappointing loss to Texas A&M. After that game, five commanding wins followed, and we won the Southwest Conference Championship for the first time in 50 years. That put us in the Cotton Bowl Classic against No. 7 Penn State. Playing in the Cotton Bowl was another first for Baylor. Unfortunately, we didn't win that one.

In a game that no one at Baylor will ever forget, we beat No. 12 Texas in Waco on November 9, 1974. That game was dubbed the "Miracle on the Brazos." It was a game for the record books. Undoubtedly, at halftime, no one thought Baylor could possibly win, except guys in the Baylor locker room. The team left the field at halftime with a score of 24-7 in Texas' favor.

The last time Baylor had bested Texas was 18 years earlier. This game was looking like it would surely be a continuation of that losing streak. Empty seats were beginning to show in the stands. Fans were probably thinking, why watch another blowout? With over 43,000 people in attendance, the parking lot was full. The idea was to leave now and avoid heavy traffic later.

In the locker room, I told the quarterbacks and receivers, "We have 30 more minutes of playing time, and you will regret it the rest of your life if we don't come out on top. You can do it." Coach Teaff was particularly effective with encouragement. Positive vibes filled the room. Quarterback Neal Jeffrey was a "picture" of confidence, and it spread. The whole team came out of the locker room with their chests sticking out a little bit. When the second half started, those guys were ready.

Wayland Corgill

Early in the third quarter, Baylor got off to an explosive start with a touchdown. Near the end of the third quarter, another touchdown was made on a beautifully executed 58-yard slant and run-pass play from Neal Jeffery to wide receiver Ricky Thompson. The score was now 24-21, and Baylor's momentum was going strong. People in the stands were getting excited. Apparently, folks who had left had their radios on and were getting excited too. I was in the scouting booth and could see cars coming back into the parking lot. I called down to Coach Teaff to let him know cars were streaming back. Many didn't bother to park in designated slots. They left their car at the nearest open space and rushed into the stadium to see if what they had heard on the radio was really happening.

Early in the fourth quarter, our Bears capitalized on a Texas fumble and added another touchdown. A little later, Bubba Hicks kicked two field goals. That was the end of the scoring. Unbelievable to many, Texas was shut out in the second half. The final score was 34-24, the greatest comeback in Baylor's history. Baylor and Waco celebrated for days. Sportswriters chronicled it a lot longer.

Everybody played well in that game. Quarterbacks were on target, and receivers looked like pros. However, they will be the first to acknowledge that football is a team sport, and their "looking good" depends on the whole team "looking good." We executed our offense as good as we could operate it that day and got critical big plays going for us. Our defense was great too. We made very few mistakes in the second half. Everybody did his job. Texas couldn't beat us man for man. It was a 100 percent effort. My chest was sticking out a little bit too.

Many of our players received awards and honors for their outstanding performance in 1974. Offensive lineman Aubrey Shultz and linebacker Derrell Luce were named to the All-American team. Also, Aubrey and Derrell, along with quarterback Neal Jeffrey, running back Steve Beaird, and defensive back Ron Burns, were consensus all-conference selections. Jeffrey also won the SWC Sportsmanship Award. Beaird also was named the Southwest Conference Most Valuable Player by the Houston Post. He was Baylor's first 1,000-yard rusher. Wingback Phillip Kent, offensive linemen Mike Hughes, Gary Gregory, Rell Tipton, and defensive backs Ken Quesenberry and Tommy Turnipseede were named to at least one all-conference team.

Coach Teaff received major honors too. He was voted National Football Coach of the Year by the American Football Coaches Association. In addition, he was selected as The Eddie Robinson Coach of the Year and Southwest Conference Coach of the Year.

Football seasons like the great one Baylor had in 1974 don't come around too often for most schools. So many things have to be just right. Our 1975 season was not even close to being as good as the previous year. We only won two conference games and lost five. Our overall record was 3-6-2. I felt like we were much better than the record showed. We were playing well and scored a lot. We had a good start with a win against Mississippi and respectable ties against Auburn and Michigan. We missed a field goal that would have won the Auburn game for us. A close loss to South Carolina followed. However, things started falling apart with a big loss to Arkansas. The next six conference games were a little better, but not by much. We won two and lost four. Two of the four losses were very close. Winning them surely would have improved how we felt about our 1975 season. However, there was not a quitter in the locker room, and we were resolved to be a championship contender next year. That didn't happen "next year," but it did five years later when Baylor came roaring back.

The Rifleman - Cotton Davidson

A year like we had in 1975 presents a challenge to both coaches and team members. Although many of our starting players from 1974 had returned, five of the most outstanding offensive and defensive players had graduated. Neal Jeffrey was one of those. However, Mark Jackson had replaced him and was doing a good job. Other replacements were quality players too. But new players are not always able to step in and do everything the seasoned players had done. In addition, every player is different, and approaches for dealing with each one might take a while to figure out. Coaches must have confidence in themselves and continually evaluate the effectiveness of their techniques. What worked with last year's team might not work with this year's team, even though the players are just as good. That puts a sizable load on coaches, who must adjust to the situation and, often, go back to the basics.

Following such a successful season as 1974, attitudes and team spirit easily slump when wins are few and far between. What can be done to maintain "can-do attitudes" and motivate players to work hard and do their best? That is not an easy job. Of course, coaches' attitudes and actions play a key role in influencing how the team thinks and performs, but team members are an important part of that process too. I always thought that it was important to keep reminding everybody that we were a team. Regarding attitudes and motivation, coaches can't "fix" everything, and neither can the players. However, together, it can be done. I considered that my job included getting the team to understand those things. I worked at getting experienced players to help teach younger ones coming up. Senior players could often motivate the younger ones as good or better than coaches. Operating that way on the field and in the locker room seemed to pick up everyone's interest and dedication. Positive attitudes are essential for playing well. If managed well, players' roles in maintaining positive attitudes and keeping spirits up in a losing season can be a big, big resource to tap. The momentum that rolls from players, who believe in themselves, is a powerful force and critical for winning. Coach Teaff and his coaching staff were very good at fostering that approach, and positive results were plainly evident. Also, Coach Teaff was exceptional at saying the right things at the right time and building players' confidence.

When our 1975 losing streak started with game number four, each loss caused me to contemplate more and more about what to do differently. Surprisingly, I began to look forward to that 40-mile commute to and from Baylor. It became an important part of my day and worth putting up with the sun in my eyes. Those two hours on the road were valuable thinking time. On the way home, I would review things that happened in practice. By the time I got back to Baylor the next morning, I often had a problem figured out or something different to try. There are so many things for a coach to think about. Quiet time in my car was valuable for doing that. I would recall experiences from my time in the pros that might work for us. From fifteen years of playing and learning from many of the best coaches in the business, I would, occasionally, come up with something we could use. I was always searching, not necessarily for big things, but more often for smaller things that would give us an advantage.

My primary coaching responsibilities were focused on quarterbacks, receivers, and kickers. In the pros, I was coached by several of the best coaches in the business, including Weeb Ewbank, Hank Stram, and Al Davis. I knew how to teach quarterbacks what they needed to know, how to prepare for a game, and how to communicate with them so they could understand what they saw on the field. Baylor emphasized the passing game. I had drilled with the passing game since high school and continuously improved those skills in the pros, particularly under Al Davis. Al was a master as a coach, and the passing game was his specialty. That was a remarkable accomplishment since he didn't play football in college or the pros. Coaching football came naturally to him but, surely, he learned a lot from the years he spent with Sid Gillman. I had played with, and learned from, award-winning receivers, such as Raymond Berry. Coaching receivers to levels where they didn't drop, or fumble passes was not a problem. However, I felt responsible for more than quarterbacks, receivers, and kickers. I wanted the team to be successful. I wanted us to win. I would help in any way I could, and quiet time on the road between Gatesville and Waco was put to good use.

Playing in the pros was a good attitude-building experience. Positive attitudes paid off, and quitters didn't last very long. However, I didn't really learn that in the pros. I grew up among people in Pecan Grove and along Coryell Creek who lived that way all of their lives. Outstanding examples were all around me. Daddy spent three months in a body cast during the summer of 1940. He lay, immobile, on his back, without even a fan to stir the air. Mother worked day and night to keep things together. Neither one complained. PaPa, Little Granny, and our neighbors pitched in and took care of situations that overwhelmed Mother. It was an orderly team effort with plenty of civility, respect, and appreciation all around. Daddy would not think of giving up. He was going to get well. With his positive attitude, he toughed it out and recovered.

At Baylor, when I walked into the locker room or onto the football field, I made sure I had a positive attitude and never used a negative approach. I expect those traits might rub off on others around us more than we realize, and they could make a difference.

I remember having only one notable difficulty with a Baylor player. It didn't amount to very much, and it was resolved before the day was over. During practice, the young man was somewhat rude to me. I told him I wouldn't work with him unless his attitude improved, and he must go practice with another group. On his way over there, he walked by Coach Teaff, who noticed the unhappy look on the young man's face and asked me about it a little later. I told Coach Teaff what had happened, and that was the end of it until I went to the locker room after practice. There, I found three offensive linemen surrounding the young man, and I heard one of them say, "You don't talk to Coach Davidson that way." I caught the young man as he was leaving the locker room and apologized to him. He apologized to me too. He and I got along fine the rest of the time he was at Baylor. Again, respect is a very good word to remember.

I had a new wide receiver to coach in 1975, Tommy Davidson. Actually, I had been, sort of, coaching him since he was eight years old. In the beginning, it was not really coaching; just throwing a football back and forth. That started in California in 1964. I was playing for the Raiders. We had rented a house in Piedmont (near Berkley) from Chris Burford, my friend, and teammate from the Dallas Texans' days. That house had plenty of yard space, and a quiet side street, for throwing a ball. I didn't have to throw many balls to Tommy before I recognized that he had a natural talent for catching them. As years went by, and we continued to "play catch," I tested him with every kind of pass a receiver should catch. He caught them all; any way I threw them. He had a great pair of hands.

The Rifleman - Cotton Davidson

Tommy loved sports, all kinds. In Gatesville High School, he played football, basketball, baseball and participated in track and even pole vaulting. He was a good athlete. On the football team, he was a wide receiver. He wasn't the fastest guy on the field, but he was smart, and he could get open. More importantly, he never missed catching many balls. Now, in 1975, I had him to coach, along with a couple of top-notch wide receivers: Alcy Jackson and Ricky Thompson. Ricky was another Gatesville star athlete, who I had recruited a couple of years earlier. We would see how Tommy stacked up against them.

"Stacking up" was not a problem for Tommy. In 1976, Ricky Thompson had joined the pros, and Tommy had his chance to show what he could do. The whole season was so much better for Baylor than 1975. It was a good season for Tommy too. One game really stood out for him. On September 18, we played Auburn in Alabama. Late in the fourth quarter, we were down seven points, with a score of 7-14. However, we were on Auburn's 10-yard line with a good chance to score. After a couple of plays that didn't get the job done, Tommy was sent to the right and, when the ball was snapped, he headed for the right-hand corner of the end zone. He caught the pass, and that put us a point behind Auburn. On the next play, Tommy went to the left, and what happened there was a mirror image of what had happened on the previous play. Tommy caught the ball in the end zone, giving us a two-point conversion and a one-point, 15-14 victory.

The third and last year at Baylor for Tommy was 1977. That year was not quite as good for Baylor as 1976, but Tommy continued to perform well. He was still the guy to go to. I don't remember stressing Raymond Berry's principle of "catch – tuck – explode" to Tommy. However, that's the way he did it. Perhaps, that way of thinking was picked up, somehow, during all the ball throwing and catching we did in earlier years. That "catching" earned Tommy a letter in football for three years.

Tommy was not the only young athlete in the Davidson family. He had two younger sisters, Kelly and Tracy, and a younger brother, Ty, who were excellent athletes too. They loved competing in sports.

Kelly and Tracy excelled in basketball and track events. Kelly graduated from Gatesville High School in 1976, and Tracy followed in 1979. During high school, they were key members of basketball and track teams that participated in district and state competitions. Kelly and Tracy have numerous awards and honors from their high school days.

Kelly was outstanding in track events such as short distance races, mile relay races, hurdles, and long jump. She even threw the discus while nursing a hamstring injury. Kelly and her track team went to state in the mile relay competition. In 1976, she was on the basketball team that went to state and, unfortunately, lost to Midway.

Tracy excelled in track competitions too. She was fast and led the track team in sprints and relays. Also, for two years, she won district competitions in hurdles. Basketball honors included selections to the All-District Team and All-State 2nd Team.

Bill Bradley was the high school track coach for both Kelly and Tracy. He has a clear memory of how they performed under his tutelage. At the mention of their names, he readily affirms that both girls were "top drawer" athletes, students, and teens who were a pleasure to know. They were key players wherever he put them, and they often made the difference in winning. Also, he fondly recalls their healthy sense of humor that occasionally bordered on being mischievous. One of his favorite (perhaps favorite) recollections is of a prank played on him by Tracy at a track meet in Keller, Texas, on the first day of April. As Tracy crossed the finish line in a sprint relay, she grabbed her leg and hobbled a few steps before falling to the ground, where she started rolling around and groaning. Coach Bill was in the stands with the other coaches. The stands were separated from the track by a five-foot-tall chain-link fence. The sight of his star athlete in that condition triggered an instantaneous reaction. He bounded out of the stands, scaled the fence, and was bending over Tracy in a few "heartbeats." In the middle of a stream of questions about where and how bad the injury was, Tracy looked up and said, "April Fool, Coach." Bill is reluctant to say what his first thought was but, in a split second, the following emotion was unbelievably intense relief that Tracy was okay.

My youngest child, Ty, was the last athlete that Carolyn and I could provide to Gatesville's sports programs. He played football, basketball and participated in track events, especially the high jump. Ty had what it took to effectively handle a football and manage a game. He put those skills to work as the quarterback on the varsity team. He was just as capable as a receiver too.

From high school to Baylor in 1983, Ty was a football team "walk-on" as quarterback. That year was one of the best years for quarterbacks in Baylor's history. We had two of the best, Tom Muecke and Cody Carlson. Tom was having his second year as a starter in 1983, and Cody was having his first. Behind them, getting a chance to play was remote. However, Ty stayed with the program. He went to the Bluebonnet Bowl in 1983 when, interestingly, Jimmy Johnson and Thurman Thomas were suited up for Oklahoma State. Unfortunately, that game was a close loss for Baylor. In 1985, Baylor played LSU in the Liberty Bowl and handily beat them 21-7. Baylor football provided Ty with lots of memorable times and friends who still stay in touch.

Baylor bounced back with a moderate winning season in 1976. Our new players had matured pretty fast. Unfortunately, we slipped back into a losing status in 1977, but not as bad as in 1975. We had another very rough year in 1978, but again we scored lots of points, and five of our losses were by a touchdown or less. With confidence that we could turn that situation around, we continued to work hard at recruiting quality players and making a viable contender of the team we had. The importance of successful recruitment of talented athletes cannot be overstated. Those efforts began to pay off in 1979 and, then, paid off big-time in 1980. All of those years were busy times for me. I sure spent lots of time on the road and lots of time pursuing the best high school football talent available.

Of the five seasons between our great year of 1974 and the next great year of 1980, 1979 was the best, by far. It was a very good year. We finished with a conference win-loss record of 5-3 and an overall record of 8-4. Our hard work was paying dividends, but so was our recruiting work. Our running game had markedly improved with the addition of a young man from Waco, Walter Abercrombie, and another, from far West Texas, Dennis Gentry. They were already setting records in 1979, and that was only their second year. Walter went on to set records and receive honors for the next two years to become Baylor's all-time leading rusher. We all felt really good about the 1979 season that was capped off by a 24-18 win over Clemson in the Peach Bowl. We did a good job in that game.

The Rifleman - Cotton Davidson

Even though 1977 was not a good year for Baylor's football record, it was a memorable year for me. I always enjoyed coaching and looked forward to coming to Baylor every day. We had a roster of great players, and I liked working with them. Watching the first-year guys develop was both interesting and rewarding as coaching efforts began to take effect. I was interested in the whole team, not just the offensive players that I coached. In 1977, two new guys, who really caught my attention, were running back Dennis Gentry and linebacker Mike Singletary. They were standouts for their hard work and dedication. Another first-year player, who caught my attention for a long, long time, was quarterback Greg Wood. I had recruited Greg in Jackson, Mississippi. At that time, I had no idea I was recruiting a future son-in-law. My daughter, Kelly, was a Baylor student during the years that Greg was there. Between football activities and the inevitability of seeing each other frequently on the Baylor campus, they managed to become acquainted enough to figure out a permanent arrangement after they graduated in 1980. That was a memorable year for them, and Baylor too, in more ways than one.

Baylor's 1980 season was one that "makes a coach's day" and provides memories of success that keep the coach coming back during lean times. We only lost two games. One loss was to San Jose State in a non-conference game. We should have won that one. The other loss was to Alabama in the Cotton Bowl. Alabama was just too good. All of our wins were decisive, with half of them big wins; not even close. Baylor was on top of the world again with another Southwest Conference Championship.

That 1980 team was well balanced, but it had a historically powerful group of running backs. Walter Abercrombie rushed for well over 1,000 yards. Dennis Gentry rushed for almost 1,000 yards. Alfred Anderson, in his first year and playing behind Walter and Dennis, rushed for almost 300 yards. At the quarterback position, Baylor was so fortunate to have another member of the Jeffrey family, Jay Jeffrey, Neal's younger brother. When Jay took to the field in spring training, he hit the ground running and the rest of his year was great. It was a great year for coaches too. I was proud of those exceptional young men.

After the great 1980 season, the next two years were anything but great, as far as win-loss records are concerned. Each year, we scored a lot of points but lost three or four close games that we should have won. Sometimes, that is just the way it goes, and when it does, a coach might be tempted to re-evaluate his whole approach to coaching. However, I always thought that when a coach and team got a winning system together, they should stick with at least 50 percent of that system in every game and adjust the rest only as necessary for the particular team being played. Changing the whole game plan should be avoided. Just change small parts to take advantage of the opposing team's vulnerabilities. Large changes are guaranteed to be confusing. The offensive lineup on the field will be at least 75 percent the same in every game, and they should execute the system they know best. Keeping things simple usually pays off. If I put in over three pass patterns, I put in too many.

Those years of 1981 and 1982 were trying years. As the 1982 season unfolded with more losses than wins, I sure was unhappy with the way things were turning out. Looking back at that time, I hope I thought about quitting. I guess it was just another one of those losing years that defies plainly identifying reasons. Coaching was not the reason. In his first year at Baylor, Coach Teaff assembled a remarkably talented coaching staff and maintained that high-quality standard throughout the next 21 years. He was exceptionally capable of finding and keeping the best coaches. Players were not the reason either. We had a talented team but, since Jay Jeffrey, Walter Abercrombie and Dennis Gentry had graduated, we had new guys in key positions. Even so, we had three close losses by a touchdown or less, and winning those would have turned a disappointing year into a great year.

I was in my twelfth year of Baylor coaching in 1983, and our performance that year made me glad I didn't quit the previous year. It wasn't a huge year for wins, but we outranked all Southwest Conference teams except Texas and SMU. Also, we played Oklahoma State very hard in the Bluebonnet Bowl. However, throughout the year, the team was such a pleasure to work with. Baylor was fortunate that we had recruited two exceptionally talented quarterbacks, Cody Carlson, and Tom Muecke. To have both of them on the team at the same time gave us an advantage that rarely comes along. In addition to being strong in the quarterback position, we had receivers Bruce Davis, Gerald McNeil, and Bobby Joe Conrad. They were a big threat for every team we played. Bruce and Gerald were super fast. They ran two legs on Baylor's sprint relay team for track coach Clyde Hart. If we couldn't win with those young men, we might as well pack up and go home. With the quarterbacks and receivers I coached that year, I could stay at home and win. They were as good as anyone could want. They were fast learners and hard workers too. I couldn't ask for any better.

The 1983 team was outstanding in many ways. The offensive line was very good with award-winning players like Mark Adickes. You can't win without some "studs" on the team, and we had recruited our share. Getting so much attention from our outstanding years of 1974 and 1980 was certainly helping in the recruiting department. With those young men, good coaching to give them a system they could win with was all they needed to take it from there and win. With that group of guys, it would be my fault if they didn't win.

The 1984 season turned out to be "so-so," but the 1985 and 1986 seasons were great. They were made even better by beating Rice each year and beating Texas in 1986. Our win-loss records were the same for both years, 6-2 in the Southwest Conference and 9-3 overall. We played a bowl game each year. In 1985, we beat LSU 21-7 in the Liberty Bowl and, in 1986, we beat Colorado 21-9 in the Bluebonnet Bowl. The powerful quarterback team of Cody Carlson and Tom Muecke ended in 1985 when Tom graduated and went to Canada to play football. However, Cody didn't miss a beat in 1986 and had a great year. I was glad I was there to be a part of it.

In 1987, we started the year with a new quarterback, Brad Goebel. When I recruited Brad, I was confident he could step in and do the job, and he did. We didn't have a very good year, but we started with several new players, and it would take time to get better. We knew how to get better. We just needed to work hard on those things. One bright spot in 1987 was beating Rice. Beating Rice had been a personal objective for me ever since 1954 when I was the starting quarterback for Baylor. We had a great season going that year, until the very last game when Rice beat us. I felt responsible. By winning that game, we would have knocked Rice out of a Southwest Conference co-championship. Also, we would have had the best record in the Southwest Conference and would have shared championship honors with Texas. That was my senior year, and I sure wanted to end up with a championship.

The Rifleman - Cotton Davidson

The next two seasons, 1988 and 1989, were about the same as 1987, but we did beat Texas twice and Rice once. Since 1972, we had come a long way in our ability to beat Texas. We were doing that fairly often. Our 3-6 loss to Rice was disappointing, and it was a game we should have won. That would have made me happy. The 1990 season was much better than the previous three years, but it didn't get us to a bowl game. However, we did beat Rice, and that was satisfying. We had trounced Arkansas 34-3 the previous week, and that got us all "tuned up" to go at Rice.

Our fortunes began to turn to the better in 1991 and 1992. In both years, Baylor was ranked second in the Southwest Conference, behind Texas A&M. Notably, in each year, we lost to Rice, and the loss in each game was by three points. Painful! However, we did beat Texas both years. Also, we played in a bowl game each year. We lost to Indiana in the 1991 Tucson Copper Bowl, and we beat Arizona in the 1992 El Paso Sun Bowl. That Sun Bowl game was my last game to coach for Baylor. It was so good to go out with a win.

Going into the Sun Bowl game, I knew it would be my last game. Baylor had decided it was time for coaching changes. After the Sun Bowl, Coach Teaff and most of his staff didn't have a job. I had no idea how that affected each of my fellow coaches. Not having a job might have been an economic difficulty for some, but I didn't hear about anyone contesting Baylor for a settlement. If we had had multi-million dollar contracts, those feelings might have been different. However, at least in my case, what I was getting paid was closer to a million with all the zeros cut off. Years before, I had prepared for making a living after football, and my future was pretty well set. I had my ranch, and it would be a full-time job. That was a big advantage for me. I just went home whistling and looking forward to working my ranch.

Daddy and Hy had helped so much when I needed it. Age was creeping up on both of them a little bit, and now was a good time for me to give my full attention to ranching. I was sure that Carolyn would like for me to be closer to home every day too.

Those 21 years of coaching at Baylor were a great time for me in so many ways. That period was a continuation of a long and extraordinarily good relationship with a first-class school. I wouldn't replace my Baylor experience for anything. We were a good fit. Baylor had been so good to me from the time I went there with a football scholarship in 1949. I graduated with a good education and a great head start in professional football. In addition, my Baylor experience connected me with scores of the best people whom I am privileged to have as friends. So many of those are the fine young men I coached. Seeing them develop and mature into admirable individuals was a reward beyond compare.

Coaching at Baylor reconnected me with so many friends from my younger days too. Every Baylor football game was sure to attract guys I had played with in college and also the pros. I always looked forward to visiting with them at every opportunity, whether on or off-campus. Relationships with old friends were renewed and strengthened to levels that have kept us in touch with each other for almost thirty years since that Sun Bowl game. Many of those guys live in the Waco area, and I see them regularly at Baylor sports functions. Others, who live further away, are seen less often but, never-the-less, we stay in touch. I am extremely fortunate to have so many really good buddies who would be there when needed. For that, I credit Baylor and my experiences there, including coaching.

Wayland Corgill

Chances to renew old friendships were absolutely a major, satisfying bonus that came with coaching. Also, there were a few other benefits as well. I had not even thought about those possibilities when Coach Teaff hired me. Among my most rewarding experiences were the frequent occasions of spending time with one of my best friends, Gale Galloway. He and I played for Baylor in the 1950s. He was a couple of years ahead of me, but we were on the same field many times. Gale played at center and linebacker and was the team co-captain. He was a heck of a ball player. We were on the team that played Georgia Tech in one of the most exciting Orange Bowl contests on New Year's Day of 1952. That was Gale's last game for Baylor. After college, he became a heck of a successful businessman in the oil industry too. Gale had a ranch in South Texas, near Pearsall. There were lots of big deer down there, and I had several outstanding deer hunting trips, courtesy of Gale. He is a great friend, and we see each other often.

Baylor and I parted ways on the best of terms after the final play of the Sun Bowl game that day. From there, Carolyn and I had a great couple of days in Ruidoso, New Mexico, and then headed back to Gatesville. I never considered seeking a coaching job at another school after Baylor. Baylor was "my school" and couldn't be replaced by any other. For me, at this time, all I could think about was saddling up and giving my ranch a close inspection. However, before another year had passed, totally unexpected prospects for football coaching came calling again.

Old coaches at a gathering after a spring game. I am sitting between Wade Turner on my right and Coach Grant Teaff on my left. My son, Tommy, is behind my right shoulder
– photo by Wayne Dunlap

The Comeback
'70s & '80s

My two decades of coaching at Baylor were filled with satisfying experiences of helping young men develop to their potential and win on the football field. Many times, their victories were against almost impossible odds. Their performance turned Baylor's football fortunes around and wrote their names in halls of honor. They made me proud. They also made countless memories for me that are priceless in my books. Actually, I could fill several books with what I think of those young men and what they did on the gridiron. I was privileged to have been a part of their success stories.

I am also fortunate to have made scores of friends in those comeback years of the 1970s and 1980s. Numerous reconnections were made with former teammates, and so many new friendships were formed. Among those new friendships is a long list of players that I coached. Not surprisingly, their views on what was happening in Baylor's football program at that time are often different from mine. While working on this book, three of those friends expressed an interest in making a contribution with their thoughts on those exciting years of the '70s and '80s. Two of them were teammates of mine in the '50s, and the third was Baylor's quarterback in one of the greatest games Baylor ever played. The perspective of that guy-behind-the-center helps round out a brief look back at those comeback years. I welcomed their input, and I am pleased to include them in this chapter. My two teammates are Gale Galloway and James Ray Smith. The quarterback is Neal Jeffrey, the master of Baylor's "Miracle on the Brazos" win against Texas in 1974.

Gale was a couple of years ahead of me at Baylor. He graduated in 1952, and I graduated in 1954. The 1951 football season was Gale's last one at Baylor and my first one on the varsity team. That powerful team had ranked second in the Southwest Conference for three years and the 1951 season was one for Baylor's record books. In fact, our 1951 team ended the season ranked higher nationally than any other Baylor team. That record lasted for over 50 years. It climaxed in a thrilling Orange Bowl contest with Georgia Tech. By most accounts, Baylor outplayed Georgia Tech but Tech's field goal in the final minutes put them ahead by three points. The game ended with a 17 to 14 score. Gale was a key player as the center, linebacker, and team co-captain in one of the most exciting Orange Bowl games to that date. The packed stadium had a great afternoon to remember. So did Gale. He was named to Baylor's 1950 All-Decade Team as a first-team linebacker along with Mike Singletary.

Wayland Corgill

Ever since those early days at Baylor, Gale has been a staunch supporter of the university that he has loved from his first days there. After graduating, he excelled in the business world, and his successes took him all over the world. However, his personal interests never diminished his enthusiastic ties to Baylor and Baylor football. He has been passionate about Baylor football from the '50s when he was wearing green and gold. During my 21 years of coaching, I sure saw him a lot. I doubt that he missed many games unless he was outside of the U.S. Throughout all those years, he has been an extraordinary, good friend. We have covered a lot of ground together and are still on the ball.

James Ray and I were starters for Baylor for three years before graduating in 1954. He was a star on the offensive line. He was and still is big, strong, and quick. Also, he was often the fastest man on the field. However, by now, that part of his talents may have slipped a little bit. As quarterback, I sure felt better every time that 6 ft. 3 in., 240-pound weapon lined up with me. I will be the first to tell anyone how important a good offensive line is for winning games and saving the quarterback a lot of headaches. James Ray's college football honors included two-time All-Southwest Conference selection and two-time All-American. Numerous honors continued during his seven seasons with the Cleveland Browns and two seasons with the Dallas Cowboys.

James Ray is a native Texan and has been a businessman in Dallas for many years. That location was convenient for him to keep up with Baylor football and to attend games. I saw him a lot during my coaching years. We have continued to see each other often. We have been in the same boat many times on fishing trips to local lakes and the Gulf Coast. He is a great fishing partner. If you want a full stringer of fish, James Ray is your man. He can catch more fish than anyone I know. Part of his technique is to talk to the fish. That definitely works better than the singing that I did for PaPa back in those days on Coryell Creek. There is no one better than my friend James Ray to have in your boat, particularly if the motor quits and you have to paddle for shore.

Neal Jeffrey was an outstanding contributor to Baylor's football program. He was the starting quarterback in 1972 when I arrived as coach. That was his first year to start. He played really well that year and did a good job with the passing game. He improved each year, and in 1974, he was instrumental in a team performance that is still talked about today. Baylor was the Southwest Conference champion for the first time in 50 years, and we beat Texas for the first time in 17 years. That Texas game was not just a victory, but it was a second-half, come-from-behind masterpiece of professional performance that not one person in the stands expected or probably thought possible. However, Neal and his teammates believed/knew they could do it. That made the difference. Those events were just two of the many exciting exhibitions that wowed Baylor crowds in 1974. Neal was always in the thick of it.

Helping to coach that 1974 team, and every team had many rewards. Chief among them were the many bonds that developed between the players and me. They were all great guys and made our time together a pleasure. My connection with Neal was one of the best. I couldn't have asked for a better young man to work with. Actually, I could say that about all of those I coached. Each and every one of them was equally important. However, during a game, the one on the field deserved my undivided attention. Neal learned quickly, his athletic skills were great, and he was a team player. However, equally important was his attitude. It was as good as it gets, and happily, it still is. Neal is a fine Christian example of manhood and a credit to Baylor. I have been proud to know Neal and stay in touch with him for all these many years.

The following is what Gale, James Ray, and Neal had to say about the comeback years.

Gale Galloway

Nineteen-seventy-two was a year of big changes for Baylor football, particularly in the coaching staff. Grant Teaff became the head coach. Since he had no experience in the big leagues, he realized the importance of acquiring that capability in his assistants. The best thing he did was to hire a rancher from neighboring Coryell County to round out his staff. This was no ordinary cowboy. He happened to be one of the most talented quarterbacks that had ever played in the NFL and AFL to that date and, in my opinion, for all time. He knew football and the passing game like few others in the sport. On top of that, although he was 40 years old, he could still play like a 20-year-old and accurately throw a football like a rocket. He was called, The Rifleman. That was Cotton Davidson, #19. For the next 21 years, his contributions were instrumental in helping to turn Baylor's football fortunes around and keep Baylor's teams as a threat to everyone they played. Equally important were the positive influences he had on everyone around him. He is a team player and conducted himself that way as a coach. He freely did his part and more.

Cotton brought an explosive offensive scheme to Baylor that he had experienced as quarterback for the Baltimore Colts, the Army, the Dallas Texans, and the Oakland Raiders. He not only knew what to do but also was an aggressive competitor with exceptionally effective teaching techniques. His patient and thorough explanations and demonstrations on the practice field rapidly paid off in helping to put games in the win column. Also important, in the process, he helped develop all-star quarterbacks and receivers, one after another. He had a keen personal interest in the young men he coached and an exceptional desire to help them be the best they could be and win. Without question, those young players knew that and responded well. Notably, Cotton's desire to help others succeed and win is as strong today as it was back then.

Since graduating in 1952, I have kept a very close relationship with Baylor. Throughout those years, I have been afforded numerous opportunities to demonstrate my esteem and appreciation for that great university. I was honored to have served on the Board of Regents and function as Board Chair. That association permitted a more intimate focus of my interests in academic affairs and sports programs. Naturally, Baylor Football has been a passion for me since the days when I was a Bear team member. Close ties to Baylor and often being on the Baylor campus were satisfying rewards. Winning football seasons, record GPA's and record graduate rates were even better.

Wayland Corgill

In the 1970s, we had a couple of great seasons and numerous exciting games. However, the 1980s were much better. The decade started off with an excellent 1980 season that was loaded with great games and finished with a Southwest Conference championship and a Cotton Bowl bid. That was the last conference championship for Baylor, but it wasn't the last of the winning seasons filled with exciting victories against teams that no one thought Baylor could beat; that is, no one but Baylor coaches and players. Baylor continued to surprise every team in the Southwest Conference. Game after game, Baylor turned in performances that made Baylor fans proud. Baylor played four bowl games and, several times finished the season near the top of the Southwest Conference. Every year was memorable in some way, and notably, most every game was exciting, win or lose.

Throughout the '70s and '80s, every team that played Baylor knew they had a fight on their hands and were likely to get beat. Cotton's calling plays had made a huge difference in Baylor's ability to win. Interestingly, that was affirmed by Darrell Royal, the renowned University of Texas coach. He and I got to know each other and became friends after I moved to Austin. Naturally, when we got together, football was a frequent topic of conversation. For most of the '70s and '80s, Darrell thought that Baylor had the best offense in the Southwest Conference. He said, "Baylor was dangerously effective in the opponent's red zone. Every time that Baylor got into Texas' red zone, I would tell my guys in the press box to watch what Cotton did. If the head coach put on the headphones, the play probably would be three downs and a cloud of dust. But if Cotton continued to call them, we never knew what would happen, and a touchdown was very likely."

That was one example of what Cotton did for Baylor football. He was so modest that very few people knew that he was the most knowledgeable coach on the staff and a very outstanding recruiter. He brought a wealth of knowledge from his experience in the pros. However, that is not all he brought. I don't know of anyone with a more admirable attitude than Cotton Davidson. In my books, he is one of the finest Christian gentlemen to ever walk this earth and the most loyal friend a man could ever have crossing his path.

James Ray Smith

Back in the '50s, it felt really good to play on Baylor's winning football teams with Cotton calling the plays. The '60s and early '70s were completely different stories. Baylor football was in a terrible slump during that time, and that is a big understatement. That was so disappointing for me. In the five years from 1967 to 1971, Baylor had won a total of four conference games and six games overall. In two of those years, no conference games were won, and in 1969 not one game was won. A change was desperately needed and, fortunately, a very good one was made in 1972. That year, a whole new face was put on the coaching staff with Grant Teaff as head coach, plus a man who had quarterbacked Baylor's winning teams back in the '50s, Cotton Davidson.

With the new coaching staff, changes started happening relatively fast. Baylor began to win games. The first two seasons were better than previous years but not impressive. However, in the third season, Baylor was ranked #1 in the Southwest Conference for the first time in 50 years. That 1974 season was a phenomenal one for Baylor in many ways. Baylor fans were given something to be excited about in every game, and a climax was reached when Baylor beat Texas in a home game that was dubbed, The Miracle on the Brazos. That win, and the way it happened, surprised everyone in the state except Baylor. It was a great, great year that was capped-off with a Cotton Bowl bid. That was Baylor's first bowl game in many years. Notably, most of the players on that Cotton Bowl team were at Baylor when Cotton and Grant showed up. The talent was there; it just needed direction. That says a lot about the importance of effective coaching.

A major part of Baylor's successes depended on Cotton's general understanding of football and, particularly, his knowledge of the passing game. No doubt, he understood that part of football as well as anyone in the pros. He had effectively practiced it there for more than a decade. However, knowing how to do something and teaching others how to do it are two different things. Cotton excelled in teaching others what he knew. Ask any of the quarterbacks and receivers he coached, what they think of him, and their replies will all be very similar. They will say that Cotton was a master at coaching, an excellent example of proper conduct, and a mentor on and off of the field.

My son played for Baylor in the late 1970s and, naturally, I had an extra, up-close, and personal interest in the program during those years. I didn't miss any games. The games were exciting, but following Cotton and seeing how he handled those young men added a large measure of interest for me.

Most kids, who play college football, have dreams of going on to the pros. They expect that they will have better chances for doing that if they play for a school that wins and has coaches that can prepare them for the pros. Quarterbacks and receivers pay particular attention to those factors when choosing a school. They know that at least half of the plays in the pros rely on a passing game. Probably, every high school quarterback in Texas was well aware of Cotton's record in the pros and his moniker as, The Rifleman. No doubt that was considered by every quarterback and receiver who decided to come to Baylor. Throughout the comeback years, Baylor's winning record and coaching staff reputation were major advantages in recruiting talented players, many of whom did go on to the pros.

The young men under Cotton's care got a lot more than an education in football. A surprisingly large number of those guys came from family situations that often were somewhat less than desirable. Many had grown up without the influence of a supportive father figure. They needed guidance for improving acceptable conduct as a team player and a human being. Cotton put a tremendous effort into making up for that deficiency. He was the example that anyone would be grateful for their young man to follow. That was Cotton's practice on and off of the field. When he closed his office door and headed home in the evenings, his concern and care for those guys went with him. They knew that, and I am sure it was a significant factor in motivating players to be the best they could be.

Between 1972 and 1992, Cotton put a huge amount of effort into helping turn Baylor's football fortunes around and keeping them that way. I know he was gratified by the resulting remarkable successes for his esteemed Baylor that had given him an invaluable start in life. During those 21 years, Baylor had an overall winning record and played in eight bowl games. Some years were loaded with phenomenal successes, particularly in the '80s. Several of those games were unbelievable, come-from-behind wins against teams that no one but Baylor thought they could beat. Baylor had returned to the winners' circle and was a recognized threat to every team in the Southwest Conference. I knew what had made the difference. It was the coaching, and a big part of that was Cotton and his pro-offense passing game.

Those were days and games to remember. As a Baylor teammate and friend of Cotton, I looked forward to every one of those games in the '70s and '80s. With Cotton involved, I knew that anything could happen and, win or lose, it would be exciting. It felt good to be in the Baylor stands.

Neal Jeffrey

I was fortunate to be the quarterback in Baylor's memorialized win against #12 ranked Texas on Nov. 9, 1974. We beat a team that no one thought we could, and we did it in a manner that kept fans and our Texas opponents wondering what had happened throughout the second half. From a 24 to 7 deficit at halftime, the game ended with a 34 to 24 win. It was a home game, and Waco went wild. That was the "Miracle on the Brazos" game, and it gave sports writers something to write about for a long time. Also, it served notice to the Southwest Conference that Baylor was serious about being a winner and knew how to do it.

The groundwork for that November victory started a couple of years earlier when Baylor acquired a new football coaching staff with men of remarkable character, two of whom were very important to me: Head Coach Grant Teaff and Quarterback/Wide Receiver Coach Cotton Davidson. Both men were gentlemen in every respect. They knew the game and were supportive, encouraging motivators and positive thinkers. They were what Baylor needed to win.

What Cotton brought to the program was invaluable. He was a legend. He had made his mark on the biggest football stage of all; the pros. No doubt, every football player in the U.S. was well aware of Cotton's accomplishments and knew him as, The Rifleman, for his strong arm. I could hardly believe that he was going to be one of our coaches. Having a guy like that was indescribable. That was 1972 and my first year as Baylor's starting quarterback. During the next three years, I got an in-depth exposure to Cotton's monumental storehouse of football knowledge. However, even better, he was a treasure to work with. We sure were lucky to have him.

Importantly for me as a quarterback, the characters, personalities, and actions of Coach Davidson and Coach Teaff were always so supportive. Even when we were losing, they believed in us and never gave up with their guidance for chances to win. Also, they listened and took players' ideas and concerns to heart.

Our 1972 season was so much better than the previous year when Baylor had only won one game. We had three conference wins and five wins overall. Our 1973 season started with high hopes for improving that record. However, that was not to be. We had a tough year without a conference win and only two wins overall. Notably, and in my everlasting appreciation, those coaches never gave up on us or stopped believing in us.

The next year, 1974, expectations for Baylor football were probably not very high by everyone except the coaches and players. Losing the first two games, even though they were close losses, didn't help matters. Again, Cotton and Grant were never discouraged and never stopped believing in us. They made

The Rifleman - Cotton Davidson

us believe that we could have a winning season too. Coaches' leadership, positive attitudes, teamwork, and hard work got the job done. The season ended with a Baylor Southwest Conference championship title for the first time in 50 years.

The most talked-about game of the year was our stunning win against Texas. That unforgettable game shocked everyone in the Southwest Conference. However, it was just one of so many well-played and hard-played games on our schedule. How we beat Texas is a prime example of Cotton's performance in every game. He made the difference.

Cotton stayed in the press box during games and helped call plays from there. That is where he was in the Texas game when halftime found us in a 24 to 7 hole. In his usual custom, Cotton hurried down to the field at halftime and walked beside me to the locker room. On the way, he was excited about things we had done well and full of encouragement. Also, he asked me what I thought, and he listened. He was not fazed or upset in the least. We had moved the ball well and passed for 260 yards. We just didn't score. He would have a new plan for the second half. Cotton was the personification of confidence, and it made me feel like I could do anything with him in my corner.

As we gathered in the locker room, there was not a dejected look on the face of any team member. Cotton and Grant were upbeat. Amazingly, they never stopped believing in us. Cotton started explaining his plans for a major change. No doubt, he just knew what to do in any situation we were in. If I saw a blitz coming from the outside linebacker, I would signal our wingback, Phillip Kent, to run a short, "hot route" on the outside and hit him with a pass. That change worked great. Throughout the second half, Texas never stopped that little down-and-out route. They never figured it out. That change by Cotton opened the game up for us and made big plays possible. Our 34 to 24 victory gave Waco something to remember for a long time, and for me, it provided a priceless permanent memory of a magical day with one of the greatest men I know, Cotton Davidson.

Baylor had great quarterbacks throughout the '70s and '80s, and they learned so much from Cotton. In addition to teaching me and those young men about football, he also taught us how to be leaders, champions, and good men. Remarkably, he did that in a way that made each and every one of us feel like he was Cotton's favorite. Just ask any one of them, and he will say, "I was Cotton's favorite."

Back to the Ranch

aking up in the morning with nothing on my mind except what I needed to do on my ranch that day was a great feeling. However, for quite a while, my first thoughts included Baylor too. Needless to say, after spending twenty-one years of dedication to Baylor's football program, it was impossible for me to not think about what would be happening at Baylor on that particular day. Eventually, ranch responsibilities took control, and thoughts of Baylor cropped up less and less – but never forgotten. Ranch work was the best occupation I could have wanted at that juncture in my life. I loved it and the freedom it gave me to interact with family, friends, and community.

The day after Carolyn and I arrived home from Ruidoso, I went right to work and spent a long day on my ranch. I enjoyed it so much. The weather was close to freezing that first week of January, but I didn't mind. Tolerating all kinds of weather was just part of ranching. Actually, for me, working in weather extremes of winter and summer added to the attraction of being outdoors. However, the incomparable weather attractions were in springtime and the fall. Working outside, with winter fading and being replaced by a "new world" turning green under spring rains, is an experience that makes a person feel alive and appreciate this beautiful place we inhabit. Also, as days began to cool in the fall, enjoying relief from broiling summer temperatures, bundling up for the first "norther," and getting ready for

I swapped a football helmet for a straw hat
– courtesy of The Texas Collection, Baylor University

winter were rare experiences that never got old for me. I always enjoyed those changes in the seasons so much. There is just something about being outside in all kinds of weather conditions that made me eager to head for my ranch early every morning. During my years in California, where there are no seasons, I sure missed Texas weather.

For months, I didn't want to do anything but be out there on my ranch every day, all day, in every kind of weather. Even if I didn't have much to do, I liked riding around in the pasture to inspect every feature of the ranch and, in the process, check on livestock, water in the tanks and fences. Fences always needed repairs.

**I loved working with the livestock
– courtesy of The Texas Collection, Baylor University**

I didn't have to check on livestock every day, but I liked to do that anyway. Cattle didn't require very much attention except for feeding during winter months and when they were calving in the spring. Also, when it was time to sell those calves later in the year, separating calves from their mamas was a little bit of a chore. Calves never liked that. My sheep and goats required more attention. They needed an annual "drenching" to control internal parasites. Also, sheep and goats, especially newborns, were easy prey for predators. Daddy was a trapper and a big help with keeping my losses under control.

There was a good market for wool and goat hair in San Saba and Goldthwaite. Sheep were sheared once a year and goats twice a year. Daddy and I were on the schedule of a Mexican crew that had done our shearing for years. Five men in that crew could shear so fast that I could hardly keep up with what I had to do. I picked up the wool or hair and stuffed it into five-foot-tall sacks. Then, I would climb into the sack and tromp it down. We all got a good workout on shearing day. However, those Mexicans had the most difficult job. Bending over a sheep or goat for hours at a time is back-breaking work.

While coaching at Baylor, I had managed to take care of those ranching duties, but I sure stayed busy all the time. If I really got in a bind, Daddy and Hy would help me out, but that didn't happen very often. Now, I could handle the work at a much more leisurely pace, and it was pure enjoyment. Also, I was at home a lot more, and that was great. I sure felt fortunate that I had set myself up for this way of life so many years ago.

I hadn't been back to full-time ranching but a few months when I did get into a bind. It happened while Carolyn and I were visiting our daughter and her husband, Kelly and Greg Wood, in Jackson, Mississippi. Greg and I were playing golf when he noticed that I was not walking normally. Greg is an orthopedic surgeon. I recruited him from Jackson as a quarterback for Baylor in 1976. Of course, at that time, I had no idea he would be my son-in-law one day. That day on the golf course, I was very glad I had started a long-term relationship when I convinced him to come to Baylor. Greg took me to his medical office and checked me out. He found that I needed back surgery and referred me to his medical partner for further analysis. Three of my vertebrae were way out of place. The remedy included repositioning those vertebrae and screwing them in place.

Greg's partner performed the surgery perfectly, and I have never had back trouble since I walked out of the doctor's office. However, for a few weeks after the operation, I was gussied up in a girdle-type brace. I couldn't travel, so I was a guest of Greg and Kelly during that time. I couldn't do much more than sit on the back porch and throw rocks at squirrels. That sure reminded me of my squirrel hunting days with PaPa on Coryell Creek.

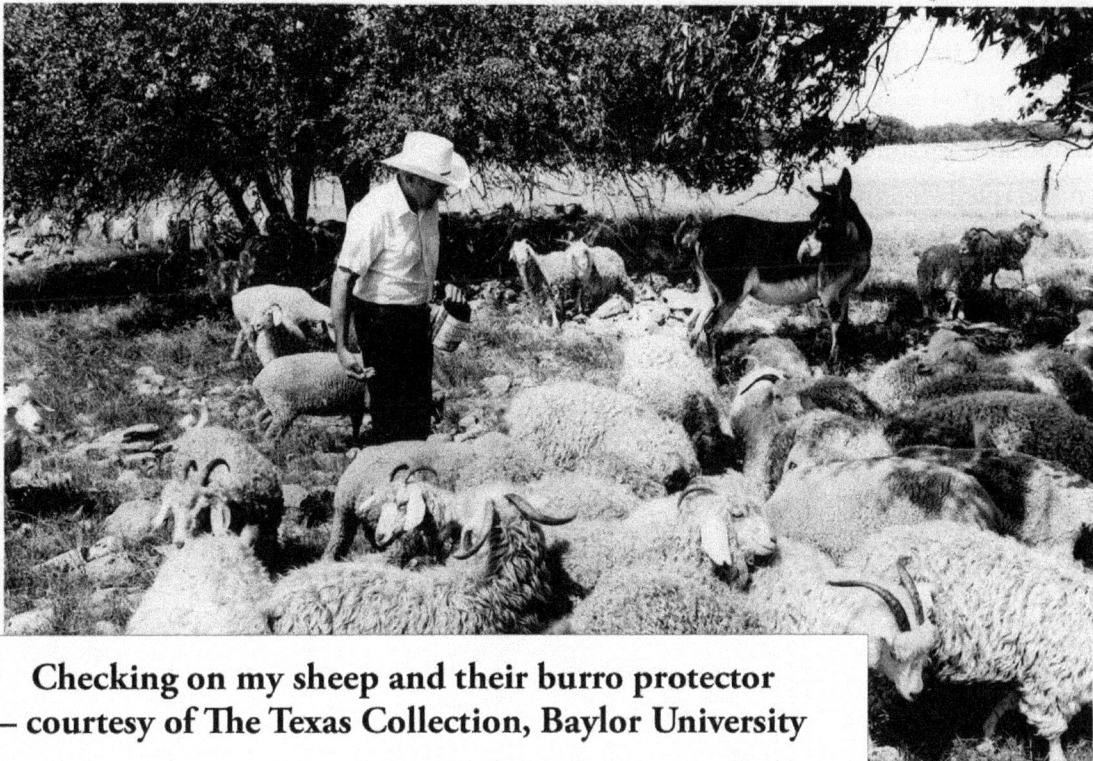

Checking on my sheep and their burro protector
– courtesy of The Texas Collection, Baylor University

The Rifleman - Cotton Davidson

While I was harassing the squirrel population in Mississippi, Daddy and Hy were looking after my ranch. Luckily, my misfortune happened at a time of year when livestock needed relatively little attention, so Daddy and Hy weren't overburdened. By the time I got back to Gatesville, I was able to pick up from them and carry on with no problems. For the rest of 1993 and the first half of 1994, I was just a rancher. However, another unexpected change was on the horizon, and it involved football again.

I thought the December 31, 1992, Sun Bowl game was my last one to be involved in. As far as football was concerned, I thought my involvement would be little more than watching Gatesville play on Friday nights and, occasionally, Baylor on Saturdays. I was wrong about that.

In mid-1994, an old friend and fellow Texan, Forrest Greg, called me with a proposal. Forrest had taken a position as head coach of the Canadian Football League (CFL), Shreveport Pirates, and he needed an offensive coordinator.

Forrest was a pro football "stud" who wound up in the Pro Football Hall of Fame. He was an offensive tackle on the Green Bay Packers record-setting teams in the late 1950s and through the 1960s. During that time, he won All-NFL honors eight years in a row and played in nine Pro Bowls. Vince Lombardi said Forrest was the finest player he ever coached. After Forrest's playing days were over, he had a couple of decades of coaching in the pros and for his alma mater, SMU. That brought him to the CFL and Shreveport, Louisiana.

In 1994, the CFL established four teams in the United States. They were the Shreveport Pirates, San Antonio Texans, Sacramento Gold Miners, and Baltimore Stallions. It was a short-lived experiment. After two years, all four teams were taken out. There was no more CFL in the US. That was surprising to me. Even though the league wasn't put together very well, there was considerable interest by the public. In Shreveport, those Cajuns really liked the CFL brand of football, and attendance at our games was good.

Forrest is a good man and easy to get along with. No one could keep from liking him. Also, he is a convincing "salesman." He got my attention enough for me to take up the subject with Carolyn. She agreed to try another adventure. She and Forrest's wife, Barbara, were friends, and that probably helped make the decision. Within a couple of weeks, we were in a rented apartment in Shreveport.

When I arrived in Shreveport, spring training was near the end. I got there with a big, big disadvantage. I didn't know any of the team members, and I knew very little about CFL-style football. I had a lot to learn and a lot of work to do. The team was receptive to me but, by not knowing their system, it took me two or three games before I felt like I was ready to call plays. There are not many similarities between CFL and NFL football other than the type of ball they play with. To describe all of the differences in rules for playing and coaching would almost take a book. For example, before the ball was snapped, offensive players could move any way they wanted, as long as they didn't cross the line of scrimmage. It was hard for me to adjust after I had lived my life under different rules.

Even though I was working with such different rules, I was able to help players in a number of ways. I concentrated on quarterbacks and receivers. As I did at Baylor, I threw twenty or thirty passes to each receiver during each practice session and drilled them on Raymond Berry's principle of "catch–tuck–explode." Also, I taught quarterbacks a few things they didn't know, including basic forms for improving football throwing skills. Team-play steadily improved as the season progressed, and I felt like I was helping the team more in each game. However, coaching under those CFL rules was never a comfortable situation.

The most troublesome events during my time with the Shreveport Pirates happened while getting through Canadian customs for games up there. Canadian customs inspections were unbelievably unreasonable. Carolyn and I would have to unpack every single item we were carrying with us for their scrutiny. The process took forever and, then, we had to repack. Also, our papers were inspected and re-inspected. That caused more lengthy delays. The problem was the same, going into or out of Canada. That alone was enough to make me want to give up and go back to Texas. Those trips to Canada were ridiculously difficult.

I now had time to spend with my great neighbor and friend, Coach Lloyd Mitchell, my high school coach. We are checking his vast collection of spurs – courtesy of The Texas Collection, Baylor University

One season with the Shreveport Pirates was enough for me. Looking back, it was a mistake to take the job. If I had it to do over, I wouldn't do it. However, I really liked living in Shreveport. That was a pleasant experience. The problem was just too many frustrations with an unfamiliar style of football as well as the hassles of playing in Canada. The money wasn't all that great either. Immediately after our last game, Carolyn and I were on the road back to Gatesville. My ranch never looked so good. It was a good time to return. Daddy and Hy had been looking after my livestock and, now, I needed to be back there for winter feeding.

Getting back into ranch life was a much-welcomed change. I didn't want to do anything else. It was great. I had about 400 sheep, 400 to 500 goats, and 60 to 70 head of cattle, but I could still take care of the ranch and spare enough time for duties at home, including leisure activities. Carolyn and I had time for getting out of town once in a while. Also, if anyone found me working at the ranch and asked me to go fishing or hunting, chances were that I could immediately drop whatever I was doing and grab my rifle or fishing gear.

The Rifleman - Cotton Davidson

I had time to help friends and neighbors too. Two of my cousins had about 100 head of cattle on Fort Hood, where they were free to roam in approximately 300 square miles of open land. Taking care of cattle on Fort Hood was almost like it was in the old days of open ranges. Three or four times a year, those cattle needed to be penned up for doctoring, branding, or separating the young ones for selling. During those times, I became a cowboy again when I helped with the roundup. The work was done with horses. We would drive the cattle to a large, makeshift pen made by stretching barbed wire around a group of trees. Once the cattle were penned, separating them was done by the old-fashioned method of roping. Head and heel team-roping was required to get a cow on the ground for doctoring or branding. Two men had to skillfully work closely together for the team-roping part. That was a challenge, but it was fun too.

I always loved roping. If I could have made a living with roping, I might have followed that instead of football. When I started college at Baylor in 1949, I took my lariat with me. Whenever I had time, I would practice roping in the athlete's dorm and, in good weather, on the lawn. My makeshift calf was a couple of chairs turned over and lined up in an open space. The back of the front chair was the "calf's head." One of my

The First Board of Directors
Coryell County Sheriffs Posse

Members of the first board of directors for the Coryell County Sheriff's Posse
Front (L-R): J.K. Hamilton, Coach Lloyd Mitchell, Bailey McCalister, Bernice Chambers; **Back** (L-R): me, Billy Ben Woodson, Ollie Bynum, Windy Cummings, Jack Painter, Knox Lovejoy
– courtesy of the Davidson Family

teammates, Jimmy Davenport, took a big interest in learning how to rope. Jimmy was a West Texas guy, but he had never roped a calf. After he had roped chairs for a couple of weeks, I took him home with me one weekend to rope a real calf.

I often roped calves with my friend, Jack Fry, who had a roping arena near Gatesville. Early Saturday morning, Jimmy and I met Jack at the arena. Jimmy was excited. He was anxious to get on a horse and get started. However, Jack and I wouldn't let him do that until we showed him how things were done and gave him plenty of instructions. Finally, we let him give it a try. Jimmy's "try" didn't last very long and left me with a memory that I could do without.

Jimmy mounted up and backed his horse into the chute. We had a lively calf in the pen. When we turned it loose, the race was on. Jimmy did a great job of roping the calf but, in the blink of an eye, things came unwound in a hurry. When Jimmy started his dismount to grab the calf, both the horse and calf were still running, and the lariat had slack. He was partially out of the saddle when his leg got tangled in the lariat. A split second later, the calf hit the end of the lariat, and Jimmy was jerked to the ground near the horse's front hooves. He still held the horse's reins tightly in his left hand, and that caused the horse to rear on his hind legs. With the rearing and Jimmy pulling on the reins, the horse lost his balance and fell on top of Jimmy. Unbelievable! Horrible! My first thought was, "What am I going to tell Jimmy's folks?" There was no doubt in my mind that this accident was about as bad as it could be.

Jack reacted instantly and ran across the arena with an opened knife in his hand. He cut the lariat and helped the horse get up. There was no blood, but Jimmy didn't move for a few seconds. I was afraid he would never move again. Also, I was afraid to move him. There was no telling how many broken bones he had. However, to my intense, everlasting, total relief, he slowly sat up and reached out his hand for a boost to his feet. Again, unbelievable! He was not hurt at all! Thankful is a word that doesn't come close to describing how I felt at that moment.

Needless to say, roping lessons were over for that day. Also, I think they were permanently over for Jimmy.

That was a terrible experience, but it didn't stop my roping. During the summer of my second year at Baylor, I entered rodeo calf roping competitions in a couple of towns near Waco. At one rodeo, I won a small amount of prize money. It was hardly enough to mention but, as I soon found out, it was a problem for a guy going to Baylor on a football scholarship. There was an important distinction between being an amateur and a professional, and prize money had a lot to do with that. I didn't know that when I was "rodeoing," but Coach George Sauer educated me when I got back to Baylor. He said that I would be advised to hang up my spurs and lariat. That was the end of prize money. However, I still roped chairs and, every chance I got, Jack Fry and I roped the real thing.

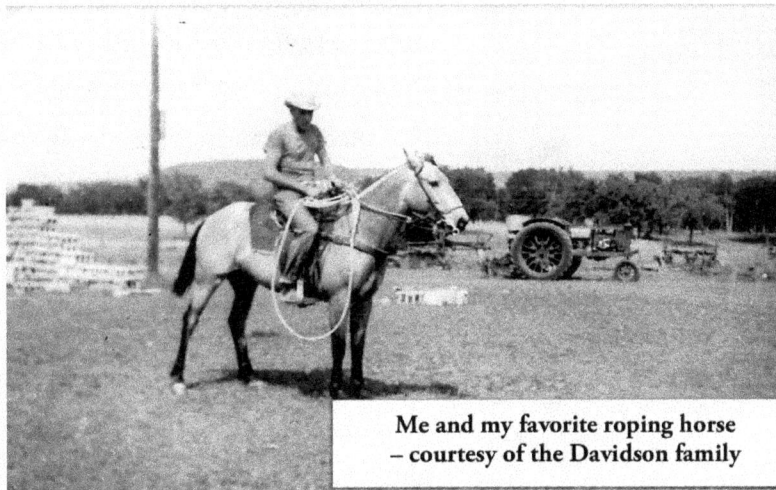

Me and my favorite roping horse – courtesy of the Davidson family

After a couple of years of doing nothing but ranch work, football "re-entered the picture" in a small way. Gatesville high school football coaches asked me to help with their summer training camps. They proposed that I work with the kids every other day for two or three weeks and concentrate on throwing, catching, running with the ball, and tackling. That was a "tall order" that would put me in just about every coaching area. At first, I was apprehensive about doing any of that. The last thing I wanted was to get crossways with coaches. I made sure the coaches understood my concerns. If I told the kids something the coaches didn't want, the coaches had to speak up. They said I should not worry about that, and that's the way it worked out. My son, Tommy, and I helped with the football team for about three years and never had a problem with coaches or players.

The Rifleman - Cotton Davidson

Tommy was living in Gatesville, and he often showed up at the football field with me. We showed them by example how quarterbacks and receivers should work together and concentrated on individual instruction too. So many little things make a big difference. Kids are not born with all good habits. They have to learn. Most of the kids had a pretty good feel for throwing and catching, but all of them had something to learn. If Tommy and I had worked with those kids three or four years earlier, getting them to do things properly would have been much easier. Breaking habits usually takes a long time.

Those training sessions gave Tommy and me a workout. He still had Raymond Berry's receiving techniques "down pat," and my arm was still working fine. However, I noticed that I was slowing down a little bit. After throwing passes for an hour at a time, most of the kids wanted to keep going, but I was ready to quit. Probably, we were doing enough because we got good results. After eight or ten workouts, I could see that improvements in receiving really came around with fewer and fewer fumbles. Fumbles are so frustrating.

My ranch had been in the family since the 1860's and, before that the Indians roamed there. They left many artifacts – courtesy of The Texas Collection, Baylor University

Tommy and I finally gave up working with the high school football team and went back to our normal routines. For a few years after that, Carolyn and I became settled into a peaceful lifestyle with our interactions with family, church, and community. There were no unusual events interrupting ranch work. That was a real pleasure in the quiet little town of Gatesville. I became a member of the school board and helped with other community activities where I could. There were always community projects that needed assistance. One very important project that I was glad to be a part of was getting a new hospital built. With my ranch and involvement in community affairs, time was never heavy on my hands. We stayed busy and relatively close to home. There were no more long-term commitments, such as coaching jobs or working away from home. Our longest trips were made to visit family members a state or two away or to New Mexico and Colorado to escape summertime heat for a few days. Shorter excursions were to places like Possum Kingdom Lake, where we had a lake house, or to the Gulf Coast for a fishing trip. This suited Carolyn, who had had plenty of traveling all over the United States and Canada during my football-playing days. As for football, we became spectators as we watched our grandchildren grow up and participate. Also, Baylor was only 40 miles away and, with our strong ties to that institution, we were usually there on game day.

In the fall of 2004, a major addition to our community took place with the founding of the Boys & Girls Club of Gatesville. The importance of this organization for children cannot be overstated. The club developed into one of the most notable improvements the Gatesville

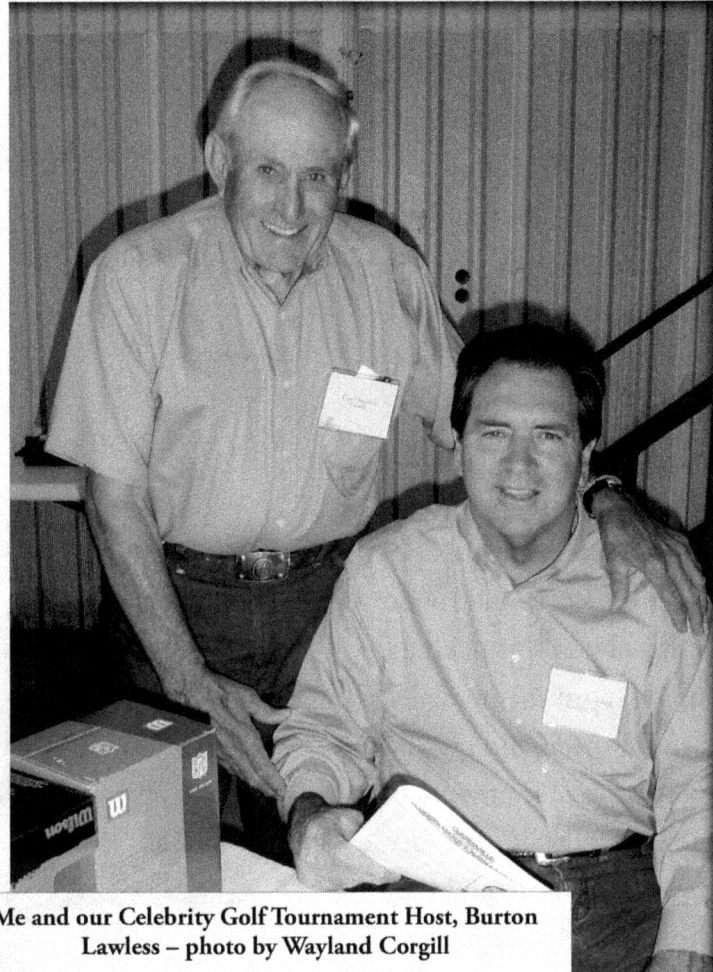

Me and our Celebrity Golf Tournament Host, Burton Lawless – photo by Wayland Corgill

community has ever had. However, the club's beginning was tenuous at best. There was absolutely no problem with the quality of care and supervision provided for kids. The managing staff's professionalism, talent, experience, and concern for children were second to none. Problems were elsewhere: namely, money. Adequate finances were a huge problem for the first half-dozen years. During that time, the club just barely hung on and struggled to pay its bills. It would not have survived without help from other Boys & Girls Clubs in neighboring cities, numerous fundraising activities by our club throughout the year, and generous financial assistance from board members and local citizens. The club did survive and grow, though, and is now a shining example of what a community can do to dramatically improve the lives of young children. I am honored to have been part of the club from its inception, and I am so proud of its success. It is one of the best things that ever happened to Gatesville.

In those early days of the club, when operating funds were so slim, we continually wracked our brains for how to raise money. I had an idea, and football entered the picture again.

I had played in fundraising golf tournaments for other worthy causes. I thought, "Why not organize a golf tournament in Gatesville?" We had a good golf course, and I knew a lot of guys from my many years in the football world. They all played golf, well enough, at least. We could invite a couple dozen of them to come to Gatesville and play in a Celebrity Golf Tournament. They would be the celebrities, and local citizens would pay to play a round of golf with them. Also, we would organize a dinner and auction on Friday evening before the tournament on Saturday. For the auction, we would round up donated items of all kinds, including sports memorabilia. Hopefully, the auction would bring in a sizeable amount of money. I proposed that idea to the club's board, and they enthusiastically approved. That was in early 2006, and a few months of high activity followed for planning, organizing, and making necessary arrangements.

My first objective was to coordinate with the young lady and board member who headed up the club's fundraising activities.

GATESVILLE CELEBRITY GOLF TOURNAMENT of 2006

BENEFITING the BOYS & GIRLS CLUB of GATESVILLE

I helped organize golf tournaments to raise funds for the Gatesville Boys & Girls Club. Those were great events with my football friends – photo by Julie Hudson

We got together and scoped out our plans. She would take care of written communications, advertisements, notices, brochures, arranging for golf carts, arrangements for the dinner and auction, and on and on. I would take care of commitments for attendance by football colleagues, reservation of the golf course, arrangements for complementary hotel rooms, collection of donated items for the auction, and on and on.

Needless to say, my fundraising partner and I had taken on a very big obligation. For about four or five months, we almost had a full-time job with getting everything done and in place. However, by tournament time, we were ready.

Wayland Corgill

For the dinner and auction, an auditorium had been reserved, and a caterer was set up. The evening began with a "meet and greet" of the celebrities who autographed Gatesville Celebrity Golf Tournament brochures. We had a good "turn out" from the Gatesville community, and several soldiers from Fort Hood attended, including the Commanding General. My Pro-Football Hall of Fame friend, Burton Lawless, served as our celebrity host.

Celebrities of the 2008 Gatesville Celebrity Golf Tournament
From left to right: Jerry Hopkins, Brad Goebel, Albert Witcher, Ken Jolley, Ira Terrell, James Ray Smith, Burton Lawless, Jerry Overton, Jerry Norton, Alfred Anderson, Bobby Joe Conrad, Dave Parks, Mike Connelly, me – photo by Wayland Corgill

He, and all the other celebrities, served up an evening that I will never forget. It was great to "rub elbows" with all those guys again. I had played with a few of them and coached the rest. We had shared so many gridiron and locker room experiences and left a lot of sweat in both places. One evening was not enough time for even beginning to "catch up" with each of those old friends.

My golf cart is full of happy kids, 2010
– photo by Julie Hudson

After the meal, an auctioneer began his part of the program. I had collected a pickup-load of sports items donated from football, baseball, and basketball teams, and by individual players too. The large variety of articles included many very collectible items, such as a football autographed by Roger Staubach, a baseball autographed by Nolan Ryan, and a baseball cap autographed by Sammy Baugh. The auctioneer did a great job, and the bidding was lively. Actually, the bidding often became rowdy when my old friend, teammate, and roommate, E.J. Holub, jumped into the competition. That was fun for a while until I noticed that he was using Carolyn's bid card to do his bidding. That began to concern me just a little bit because he was doing an awful lot of bidding and didn't hesitate to raise and raise.

The whole evening was delightful. For me, the best part was having so many of my old friends together in one place for the first time in years. It was just great to see each and every one of them. Also, it was a good evening for fundraising. We didn't make as much money as I had hoped, but it was a lot more than we had that morning. Perhaps, E.J. was trying to help increase our collections with his wild bidding, but I doubt it. He was known to occasionally give me a hard time. When the accounts were settled that evening, I was relieved that he hadn't put me in the hole too bad.

The tournament began early the next morning. It was not the smoothest shotgun start I had imagined. My football friends were full of energy and eager to get going. Before I could get the teams lined out, golf carts were zipping here and there around the club house, and what had been a neat lineup of golf carts was no more. However, I got that situation resolved after a few minutes, and we managed an orderly start.

It was a great day and a lot of fun. A lot of tall tales were swapped, and old memories renewed. One celebrity played with each team of Gatesville guys. E.J. Holub showed up, but I don't think his knees allowed him to hit many balls. After 20 knee surgeries during his career, he would say they looked like he had been in a knife fight with a midget. No doubt, his team was glad to have him, though for entertainment. Everyone enjoyed being there; me most of all.

That tournament was such a great success that we had one the next year, and the next, until the last one in 2010. I really enjoyed those tournaments and, especially, with the guys that came.

I have stayed closely associated with the Gatesville Boys & Girls Club. As the club has grown, their needs have grown. More space was needed as more kids joined. Also, additional employees were required. Perhaps surprising for many people, a relatively large number of the kids who joined were from families struggling to provide for them. Therefore, the club continually needed more resources to help in those situations. There have always been needs that I could help with, and fortunately, I have been able to occasionally contribute to solutions and make a difference. To see how that difference readily shows up in the conduct and attitudes of the young children makes it all worthwhile.

As events of 2012 unfolded, an old friend's last wishes presented me with additional possibilities for helping to sustain the Gatesville Boys & Girls Club. My friend, Joe Hanna, was a fellow rancher. His first name was Marshall, but probably most people didn't know that. Joe's love of ranch life began in his teenage years. Shortly after World War II, he bought a beautiful, large ranch along the Cowhouse Creek, southwest of Gatesville. He was still ranching there when he passed away in the fall of 2011.

In our younger days, my brother Hy and I had roped many a cow and calf with Joe. He and I even roped a few calves a couple of days after Carolyn and I were married in 1954. We were married in Breckenridge, Texas, and spent our honeymoon at Carolyn's father's lake-house on Possum Kingdom Lake. The day after our wedding, Joe came over from Gatesville and stayed with us at the lakehouse. He happily bunked on the screened-in porch and, during the day, he livened up the process of getting to know each other better. The Breckenridge rodeo was in full swing, and on the weekend, all three of us went "rodeoing." Joe and I entered the tie-down calf roping and cow milking contests while Carolyn watched from the stands. I don't remember winning any prize money, but Joe didn't come for that. He was a good friend who would do anything for his friends, and in a roundabout way, he did Carolyn a unique favor too. She has a honeymoon memory that few, if any, young brides ever came close to experiencing. We still talk about that.

Wayland Corgill

Joe was one of the best-known and most respected men in Coryell County for his strength of character, dedication to "practicing what he preached," hard work, and generosity to charitable causes. There was never a question about where Joe stood, and no one who met him would ever forget him.

Joe never married. Probably, spending those days with Carolyn and me at Possum Kingdom Lake in 1954 was as close as Joe ever got to anything like having a honeymoon of his own. When he died, he had no heirs. Joe was a very successful rancher and left a sizeable estate. All of his assets, including his JH Ranch on the Cowhouse Creek, were put in the M.J. Hanna Trust. Joe was proud of that ranch and laid out rules for its operation and the handling of proceeds from the trust. Those arrangements were directed by Joe before he died. He did an excellent job of putting his affairs in order. He even selected the board of directors to manage

Baylor Sports Network presents
LUNCH WITH A LEGEND
HOSTED BY JOHN MORRIS
"Voice of the Bears"

Featuring
COTTON DAVIDSON

Notice of Lunch with a Legend function held for me at Baylor on August 9, 2018
– courtesy of the Davidson family

the trust. Those named to the board were: David Barnard, Monte Comer, Will Coward, David Mayhew, Cullen Smith, and me. One of Joe's last requests was for me to be president of the board.

Joe had always been generous with giving scholarships to Gatesville High School students who wanted to study agriculture-related courses in college. The M.J. Hanna Trust has continued that practice and gives more than a dozen scholarships each year. Also, Joe supported the Boys & Girls Club, and the M.J. Hanna Trust continues that practice today. When the growing club needed a gym, the trust made significant financial contributions. To provide a safe place for teenagers, the club needed a separate building. Again the trust's generous contribution helped make that possible too.

At the Lunch with a Legend, I was interviewed by John Morris, "Voice of the Bears" – photo by Wayne Dunlap

The JH Ranch is one of the most beautiful and productive pieces of ranch property in Coryell County. The Cowhouse Creek, which winds through the ranch, adds rare, scenic, archaeological, and geological features with its wide limestone bottom that is laden with dinosaur tracks. The ranch is a great place for kids, young and old, to visit. Baylor science lectures have even been conducted on the steep banks of the Cowhouse.

Clearly, Joe Hanna held the Gatesville community in the highest regard. His legacy is proof of that. He won't be forgotten in Coryell County.

The Rifleman - Cotton Davidson

Except for a short stint with the CFL, ranching has been my only occupation since leaving Baylor in 1992. Even so, interactions with people and events related to Baylor and football have continued to be ever-present and important in my life. I could never forget all the friends I made through Baylor and football, and I am appreciative that they haven't forgotten me either. For example, in the last couple of years, I have been remembered at a Baylor Sports Network luncheon, "Lunch With A Legend," and also at an Oakland Raiders season-opening football game. I was the guest of honor on both occasions, and I really felt honored to be there.

The "Lunch With A Legend" program was organized by the Baylor Sports Network and held on August 9, 2018, in the Texas Sports Hall of Fame building on the Baylor campus. It was hosted by John Morris. I was interviewed "front and center" in a large room full of people with whom I had crossed paths during my long career in Baylor sports. Coach Teaff and a quorum of quarterbacks and receivers I had coached over the years were in attendance. Also, a sizeable group of my Gatesville friends and neighbors were there, as well as friends from neighboring cities. Visiting with all those folks was just great. The quarterbacks and receivers were particularly entertaining. Their memories were very good, perhaps, too good. Also, they tried to put me on the spot and get me to name my favorite of the group. They weren't successful with that attempt. They are all my favorites. After they had a little fun with me, each one said some of the nicest things to me. I am so glad there is a video recording of those festivities.

Such complimentary affairs, as the "Lunch With A Legend," don't come around too often, and just a year later, I was surprised with a similarly unexpected honor by The Oakland Raiders. On August 10, 2019, the Oakland Raiders celebrated their 60th Anniversary at a pre-season game with the Los Angeles Rams in the Oakland Coliseum. Two people, Al Davis and I were honored at that game. Many more ex-Raiders were there, and we were all recognized. However, I had an "edge" on all of them. I was told that I had the distinction of being the oldest-living Raider. Ceremonies began when I was honored to light the Al Davis Memorial Torch. As the evening progressed, so many memories were revived of those long-ago days when I was on this very field as a Raiders' quarterback. In 1966, I took the first snap in the first game to be played in the brand new Oakland Coliseum. Now, I was high above the field and standing next to a huge torch with my signature inscribed on its pedestal along with those of a hundred other torch lighters. The evening was great, and the Raiders treated my family and me like royalty. I am not expecting any more evenings like that one.

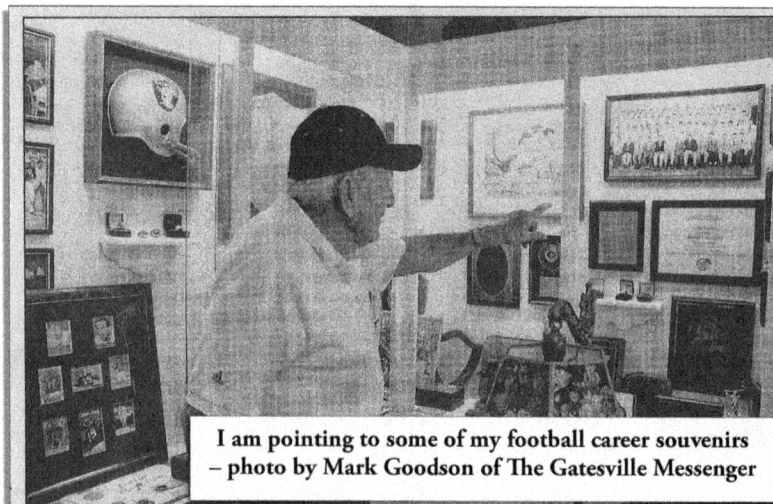

I am pointing to some of my football career souvenirs
– photo by Mark Goodson of The Gatesville Messenger

Photo by Mark Goodson

Coryell roots

Cotton Davidson points out some of his favorite memorabilia during a recent visit with the legendary quarterback from Gatesville. The 87-year-old was born in Coryell County. He had a distinguished football career as both a player and coach that has taken him to a lot of places, but he likes "Texas the best."

Wayland Corgill

I was inducted into the Texas High School Football Hall of Fame in 1999 – courtesy of The Gatesville Messenger

Hall of Famer

Gatesville's Cotton Davidson is shown minutes after he was presented his plaque that inducted him into the Texas High School Football Hall of Fame. The ceremony was held Saturday night in the Ferrell Center in Waco and Davidson was one of nine persons inducted into the hall.

A career in both football and ranching worked out well for me. I loved both and was successful in both at the appropriate times in my life. Football is a younger man's occupation. Ranching fit the bill for me later in life. "Fortunate" is not a strong enough word to describe how important those circumstances were for me.

I still have the ranch that my great-grandfather, James Madison Davidson, established in the 1850s and was passed down through the next generation to Daddy. My story began on that ranch, and it has continued to be a huge part of my life. Just setting foot on it revives memories and emotions like nowhere else. Five generations of Davidson family history is connected to that stretch of land along Coryell Creek in the Pecan Grove Community. Through the hard work of so many Davidsons who lived there, that ranch provided their livelihood through early times, hard times, war years, lean times, and lots of good times. It never made anyone rich, but it made the difference in "getting by." Also, family, plus the rural community of neighbors, provided a support group that taught priceless life values for young adults leaving Pecan Grove to seek their fortune outside of Coryell County. I am so glad the Davidson Ranch on Coryell Creek is still intact. When I stand with my back against James Coryell's blazed live oak tree in the Davidson Cemetery and look across the Coryell Creek valley to the rim of low mountains in the east, I have a clear view of all the places, so many of my ancestors spent their lives. Memories of Daddy, Mother, Hy, Anita, Sandra, PaPa, Little Granny, and so many other relatives and neighbors are triggered by every feature in the landscape.

I was one of the first Davidson's to leave and, even though I would not change my life outside of Coryell County, I am glad to be back.

Carolyn and I holding twin additions to the growing Davidson family, 2018 – courtesy of the Davidson family

Epilogue

Carolyn and I still live in the house we built in 1971 on land sold to me "per tree" instead of "per acre" by Coach Lloyd Mitchell. He sure was a great guy for me. There are a lot of priceless memories in this house. We have glass display cases in one room showing trophies, awards, pictures, and memorabilia of all kinds, collected during my years associated with football. They are important, and I am very proud of them. However, another room has a different kind of display. We have a shelf in our breakfast room lined with a growing number of pictures of family: kids, grandkids, and great-grandkids. I am more proud of what's on that shelf than anything else in our house. I pass by and inspect that lineup every time I enter and leave the house.

Athletics were a big part of my life since I was 12 or 13 years old. High school football earned a Baylor scholarship for me. Baylor football got me into the pros. Army football provided additional recognition in the sports world. After Army service, more pro football eventually led back to Baylor and a long tenure of coaching football. That was made possible through Carolyn's steady support. I love the game. More importantly, it helped me take care of my family and furnished me with more great friends than a man could ask for. I have kept them all, and we stay in touch.

In addition to football, I have been incredibly fortunate to be able to follow my other passion, ranching. I didn't realize it at the time but growing up on Daddy's Coryell Creek ranch molded my desire to never get too far away from that way of life. Back then, there was a "double helping" of family and neighbors helping each other and, in general, just being neighborly and taking time to enjoy life. No one had a lot of money, but it was a good way to live. For me, ranching activities have gone a long way in partially replicating that way of life. Ranching has kept me in touch with so many people in

Gatesville and all over Coryell County. Another big plus is being able to walk along Coryell Creek and shoot a squirrel where PaPa and I hunted. Those were good days.

Although football and ranching were important to me, family is much more important. God gave me a family that has yet to be a problem family, and I am so thankful for that. Our four children grew up to be respectable, honorable people. They established successful careers, married great partners, and are raising great children. I couldn't ask for more. Although state lines separate some of us, we get together often, and that is a big, big importance. Usually, they can't all be with Carolyn and me on Thanksgiving Day and Christmas Day, so everyone gathers at our house a few days before Christmas. That occasion is a three-day, combined celebration of Thanksgiving, Christmas, and my birthday. We call it "Thankmas." My birthday is celebrated on a Wednesday. Thanksgiving is observed on Thursday. Friday is reserved for celebrating Christmas. Part of that tradition is a bonfire and wiener roast in the yard near the spot where Coach Mitchell used to have a campfire for his Sunday school classes. There is nothing better than having our family together. Seeing all the young ones makes it all worthwhile.

Our 2019 "Thankmas" was not a traditional one. The overriding emphasis was on the commemoration of our oldest child, Dr. Tommy Davidson. Regrettably, Tommy was not with us. Tragically, on October 11, 2019, that fine young man had a fatal traffic accident on a rain-slick highway. Our family sustained an irreplaceable loss. He will be sorely missed by so many others in Gatesville, Coryell County, and at Baylor too. However, Tommy's legacy of an honorable, respectable family man and a splendid reputation are rewarding accomplishments to celebrate. There are no better people than his wife, Nina; three children, Dr. Casey Davidson and wife, Ericka, Claire Bostic and husband, Gable, and Will Davidson and fiancé, Jasmine Martin; and three grandchildren, Kate, Lily, and Collins Davidson. Carolyn and I are so thankful they are part of our family. We will carry on and celebrate Tommy's admirable life during "Thankmas" each year.

Mine has been a great life with so much to be thankful for.

Appendix 1

Notes from Colleagues

My Note:

Writing this book has been an exceptionally pleasant trip down a memory lane that has spanned nine decades. Of particular importance in this trip are memories of the remarkably fine people I connected with, from the very beginning and all along the way. There are so many of those folks, more than I can count. They are intricately intertwined with my story, and therefore, I am honored to include remarks from a few of those people. This book is not big enough to include all of them. The following is a token attempt to recognize typical expressions of so many friends who, I trust, know the feelings are mutual.

Mark Adickes, MD

Baylor offensive lineman; Graduated 1983

Cotton Davidson

I don't have many mentors in my life. It turns out I'm just downright too "nitpicky." It's not enough that someone has intelligence, wisdom & experience. What I look for in a mentor includes the following: 1) a person of faith 2) someone who participated in team sports 3) someone who is exceptional in their chosen field 4) someone who treats others as they wish to be treated 5) a humble man 6) a good husband 7) a faithful husband 8) a good father 9) and, finally, someone who just generally carries themselves in a manner that I admire. Whew! A long list, I know. But all of that said, I consider Cotton Davidson to be one of my mentors. He is one of the kindest people I have ever met and excelled as a football player and a coach, all while being an exemplary husband, father and human being.

I met Cotton in the fall of 1978, about halfway through my senior season at Killeen High School. He came to recruit me for the Baylor University football team. As he approached, I thought to myself, "Well, here is a friendly-looking coach." He was balding and slightly slouched but with surprisingly broad, square shoulders. When he shook my hand, I thought he would crush it to dust. He had powerful, weathered hands. He informed me he was from Baylor, and I let him know straight away that I had narrowed my choices down to two schools. He smiled and said, "Nice to meet ya. Let me know if you change your mind. I think you'd fit in well at Baylor." I had made up my mind that I wanted to go to school in the Southwest Conference, and the school had to show interest from the beginning. Only Rice and Texas Tech fell into that category. When I called Cotton to let him know I wanted to open up my recruiting further, he quickly said, "Well, let's get you up here for a visit then!" He never made me feel awkward for rebuffing him initially.

As I had an injury redshirt, I spent five years with Cotton Davidson and always knew him to be the most thoughtful coach. He mentored guys all over the team, not just those in his position of specialty. I was lucky enough to go to his ranch in Gatesville, where he taught me to haul hay and castrate sheep. I saw how he treated his wife and his children, and his neighbors. His humility was remarkable, given his time as an NFL player, a successful Baylor coach, and an owner and manager of a successful ranch. I could tell that he genuinely didn't feel like he was anything special. He just told me that he thanked God for his many blessings. Cotton Davidson is a blessing to me and remains a mentor. He gave me a template by which I could pattern my life. I will be forever grateful and strive daily to live up to his standard.

Alfred Anderson

Baylor running back No. 46; Graduated 1984; Minnesota Vikings (1984-1991)

Coach Davidson and I met before I ever stepped foot onto the Baylor campus. In fact, we both still get a kick out of the story of how I learned to drive my first car that I purchased from his daughter. It was the spring of 1980. As a recent graduate of Richfield High School, I was desperately in search of my first "ride." One day, around noon, Coach Davidson came up to the First National Bank, where I was working at the time, and gave me a five-minute 101 course on how to drive a stick shift. I had never driven a stick shift in my life, but he had complete confidence that I could learn within that short timeframe. He told me repeatedly to push the clutch down whenever I turned the key on, and the car would start. He may or may not have told me to slowly take my foot off of the clutch every time I took off. Nonetheless, he ended up leaving the car with me. I had another four hours to work while trying to remember everything he had told me about driving a stick shift. At 4 p.m., I was so excited to be leaving, getting into my car, and driving home. I opened the car door; put the key in the ignition, and my car wouldn't say anything. So, I got out of the car and raised the hood to see why my car wouldn't start. Determined, I got back in the car, put the key in the ignition, and silence. Nothing! Then, it dawned on me that I needed to push the clutch in. So I did, and Walla! It started right up. As I kept stripping the gears, it probably took me about five minutes to move the car from that spot. Finally, I found myself cruising on the highway. I cruised on Waco Drive until I reached a red stoplight on a hill. Whoa! I had the hardest time with making that car move because it kept rolling backwards. So, I started praying and asking God to get me home safely because Coach Davidson didn't mention anything about how to operate a stick shift when it stopped on a hill. Through trial and error, I learned that you had to take your foot off of the clutch slowly and press harder on the gas. And, Praise God, I made it home. I continued to practice daily with the help of my big brother and mastered driving the best "ride" ever – the Pontiac Astre.

I was so blessed to have Coach Davidson as my Quarterback and Receiver Coach at Baylor University. He impacted so many lives. The love and compassion he had for his players were immeasurable, and you couldn't help but love this awesome guy who was also a great coach and a pretty good golfer. There's a saying, "You don't know someone unless you spend time with them." I am so grateful for the quality time that I spent with Coach Davidson.

Cody Carlson

Baylor quarterback No. 14, Graduated 1987, Houston Oilers (Commander Cody) 1988-1994

In the summer of 1982, I walked the sidewalk outside of my childhood home with my parents. My car was packed, and I was almost ready to leave San Antonio, Texas, for Waco and Baylor University. I had one last question for my dad, "Are you sure I can compete at the college level?" He assured me that I could, and more importantly that I would have the chance to learn a lot from the process. I am sure he gave me a few more instructions and inquired as to whether I had a toothbrush, but I really don't remember. I do remember his parting comment, "Pay attention to what Cotton Davidson tells you."

What I learned along the way was that it wasn't only what Cotton Davidson said that mattered; it was also what he did. It was who he was. He was arguably the best professional quarterback to come out of Baylor (but you would never hear that from him). He was arguably the most creative offensive coach in college football at that time. He was absolutely a man that every single person and player could trust. It had occurred to me over the years that it was this that led to my committing to Baylor and sticking with my commitment when Tom Muecke, the probable best quarterback in the state, also committed to Baylor. It was also why I didn't lose hope as injuries and losses became a frustration.

In my first collegiate year, I was a suitemate with Tom, against whom I would compete for the starting job for 3 years. Our room assignments were not a mistake but, instead, wisely arranged to the benefit of the team. It encouraged friendship and healthy competition, so there was no divisive rivalry. The coaching staff probably knew, long before Tom and I did, that the depth of our relationship was key to the team succeeding. In all of the hours we spent with Cotton, a favorite between us was never revealed, not even when one of us played well, and the other one didn't.

The very first game Tom and I played in together was against highly favored Brigham Young. They were quarterbacked by Steve Young and had a prolific offense. Our team was going into the battle with two quarterbacks, neither one who had proven a thing at the college level. In the lead-up to the game, we were both so nervous and so inexperienced that we couldn't talk much. And, when it was decided that the quarterbacks would bring plays in from the sidelines as we alternated each play, we might have only thought about how tiring that would be. But, the advantage was that we would be given clear instructions communicated from Cotton through the headset to Coach Teaff, who was on the sideline. It was a genius plan, and it worked to near perfection as we pulled off a victory in our first game as a quarterback duo. It was the first of several big wins we would share. And sharing the accolades was somehow fine with us. That was the effect that friendship had on us. It was also what Cotton wanted from us, so it was what we did.

Over the years, people have asked about the difficulty of sharing duties. I am sure there were days when Tom and I let our minds wander to being the "man", but what I recall was looking forward to practice each day because it was a chance to improve, to play a fun game, to be around good people. It was a chance to learn from Cotton about being a leader of the team, about being a man, a good man. When Tom passed away, I thought about how similar Tom and Cotton were. They competed hard, but they were always fair and kind. Win or lose, each day was a great day when we were together.

Carroll Dawson

Baylor Basketball All-Southwest Conference honors 1960; Army Tank Commander; Baylor men's basketball head coach (1973-1977); Houston Rockets assistant coach 1979; Rockets general manager (1996-2007)

Cotton Davidson is one of my most favorite people in the whole world, along with his wife, Carolyn, who I have known for many years. I am so glad that he is writing about his experiences, and I appreciate the chance to make a small contribution.

I first met Cotton (Coach Davidson) in July of 1960 in a Baylor gym. I had graduated from Baylor in the spring. Cotton had come back to Baylor in 1959 to join Coach John Bridger's football coaching staff. Although I didn't know Cotton, I had kept up with his career from the early 1950s as a Baylor quarterback and on to the pros with the Baltimore Colts.

We were both working out in the gym that hot July day. He was practicing with a football, and I was practicing with a basketball. I had joined the Army and would soon be leaving for Ft. Jackson, South Carolina. My intent was to stay in shape to play on the Fourth Army basketball team when I got to Ft. Knox after basic training. Coach Davidson was working out to also stay in shape, but not for coaching. He had bigger plans.

One day, as I looked toward the back of the freshman gym, I saw Coach Davidson throwing a ball against the wall. He had about four footballs lined up on the floor. He would drop back and throw a football to the other end of the gym. After I quit working out, I went down and asked Coach Davidson, "What's up?" He said, "Well, this guy in Dallas is starting a new football league, and he asked me to go up there and try out." The guy was Lamar Hunt, who had formed the AFL at the time. I didn't even know what it was until Cotton told me about it.

In the gym a few days later, I told him that I could catch a football if he wanted to throw me some passes. He said, "Okay." We went to the big gym, and he would tell me the routes to run. I thought I could catch a football, but I had never had a ball come at me like he threw. I couldn't close my hands fast enough when we first started. The ball would hit my hands and bounce off. So, I practiced with closing my hands early, and I got to where I could catch it. He would get me to run different patterns, and we would do this every day. It was a lot of fun for me. I had never seen anybody who could throw a football like this man could. It would come at me so hard that I really had to concentrate on making a catch. That ball was like a bullet.

In the fall of 1958, the number one TV show was, *The Rifleman*, with Chuck Conners as Lucas McCain. One of my basketball teammates was married and had a house and TV. Our whole team would go over to his house on Saturday night and sit on the floor to watch The Rifleman. We just loved that show. Because of the way Coach Davidson threw the football so hard at me, one day I said, "You know, you remind me of the Rifleman." I started calling Cotton that and it kind of stuck through all these years. However, I did that because of how hard and how accurately he threw it.

After the Army, I served as the Baylor men's basketball head coach for a few years and then joined the Houston Rockets coaching staff. In those days, we would play the Lakers and Clippers twice but never played both of them on the same trip. Therefore, we had four trips to California each year. We always stayed in a Marina Del Rey hotel. For food, we would walk down along the ocean inlet boardwalk to Edie's Diner. Big, beautiful houses lined the inlet. While looking at the houses one day, I saw the owner of the Oakland Raiders, Al Davis, lying out in the backyard. He was sunning. I wanted to say something, but I just waved. He waved back. He was very friendly. That whole year went by, and we came back. When walking down to Edie's Diner one day, I saw Al again. He was lying out there in the sun in his backyard. I said, "Coach, Coach Davidson said to tell you hello." Well, Holy Cow! He jumped up off of that cot and came running up to the fence and said, "Do you know Cotton Davidson?" I said, "Yes, sir. I coached with him at Baylor." He said, "Oh, that is the finest man! Tell me, what's he doing?" Al had a million questions. From then on, every time we would go out there and play, he would run down and ask how Cotton was doing. Al was the biggest fan.

Cotton could really throw a baseball too. I think he and Bob Feller could throw the first 100 mph pitch. Cotton's was never tested, but I had talked to people when he played in the old leagues in Texas. They say he threw the hardest, fastest ball that anybody had ever seen. They were guessing, but they were thinking it was around 100 mph. This was back in the day when nobody could do that but Bob Feller.

Cotton and I both coached at Baylor in the 1970s and shared so many good times, both in and out of sports venues. It has been a great relationship with Cotton and Carolyn and, I still see them all the time. They are two of the best people you would ever want to meet.

There is no one more humble than Cotton, The Rifleman. He is a "one-of-a-kind athlete" but even a better man.

Gale Galloway

Baylor center and linebacker No. 50; Graduated 1952; Co-captain of Baylor Bears Orange Bowl team Jan 1, 1952; Air Force officer in Korean War; Baylor Regent (1990-1998); Chairman of Baylor Board of Regents (1994-1995); Industry Leader of Fortune 500 companies; Gale and Connie Galloway, recipients of Baylor Founders Medal

I was recently asked by a national publication to "name somebody 50 years or older who is making a big difference by giving their time, talent, and skills to enrich the lives of others and who is growing older with dignity."

As soon as I read that request, one name flashed in my 90-year-old mind; COTTON DAVIDSON – "The Rifleman." Most people referred to Cotton as "The Rifleman" because of his great ability to throw a bullet, speed-line-drive football.

I knew him also as one of the finest rifle shots that ever set foot on my game/cattle Buck Creek Ranch in Frio County, Texas. We had hunters come from all over the U.S. and elsewhere, who were great shots, but none were better than Cotton. At 150 yards, he could flip a running wild boar hog with one shot.

Everyone on the ranch fell in love with Cotton. My farmers and all the ranch hands kept asking me, "When is that Mr. Davidson coming back to see us?"

Cotton is one of those special people who has left his "mark on the land" wherever he has been. I know my life has been greatly enriched for having known him, and – Hey – it's not over yet. We're just now starting the fourth quarter!

I am a United States Air Force veteran and, should we ever go back to war, I want Cotton Davidson as my wingman – or I'll be proud to be his!

Francis "Cotton" Davidson is the most ethical man I have ever known!! If I would compliment Cotton for his ethical conduct, I am confident he would either just smile a little smile or say, "No big deal – because that's the way you're supposed to live your life."

Dennis Gentry

Baylor running back No. 29; Graduated 1982; Chicago Bears (1982-1992)

Cotton Davidson was not only a great coach; he was a tremendous leader, father figure, and teacher of the game. One of the best things I learned from Coach Davidson was his demand for excellence, payment of attention to details, and giving 100 percent effort in every play. He wanted me to execute each play as if it was my last one. Coach Davidson played in the NFL, and he coached me as if I were already in the NFL. He knew what it took to advance to the NFL.

When NFL coaches and scouts came to Baylor to evaluate Walter Abercrombie, Coach Davidson told those coaches and scouts, "Don't forget about Dennis Gentry. Gentry plays much bigger than you would think by judging from his natural, physical size." Additionally, Coach Davidson told those NFL guys, "You can get three positions out of Gentry. He is a running back, slot receiver, and kick return specialist. Also, he can run a hole in the wind."

Coming out of high school at 155 lbs, Baylor was the only school that offered me a full scholarship. No NCAA Division II or III institutions or junior colleges offered me a scholarship. I am so glad I had the opportunity to attend Baylor and be coached by Cotton Davidson.

Thanks ……. you are the GREATEST!!

Brad Goebel

Baylor quarterback No. 8; Graduated 1991; Freshman consensus All-SWC QB in 1987; NFL 1991-1996

Without a doubt, Cotton Davidson was the reason that I decided to accept a football scholarship to Baylor University in 1986. From the moment he walked in and sat down with my parents and me in our house outside of Cuero, Texas, I knew I wanted to play football for this man. He was a friendly, down-home, humble gentleman who could be trusted and knew football, having played quarterback in the NFL. He and Carolyn treated me like I was a part of their family. We spent many Sunday afternoons out at Cotton's ranch in Gatesville. Whether it was fishing, bird hunting, or eating some of Carolyn's homemade chicken fried steak and mashed potatoes, I enjoyed them immensely.

One story that I heard about Cotton involved his early recruiting of me. The story goes that I was playing a high school football playoff game in Austin at Memorial Stadium, located off of Interstate 35. As it happened, Coach Davidson, Coach James, and Skip Cox were heading down to a South Texas ranch to hunt that weekend. As they were driving through Austin, Cotton mentioned that he wanted them to pull off of the highway and park on a high point in the parking lot at Memorial Stadium. Soon after they stopped, Cotton pulled his binoculars from his hunting bag and used them to watch the pre-game warm-up for our game that night. After about five minutes, Cotton yelled out, "Yep, that's my guy. We need to sign him."

Cotton's approach to teaching me the position of quarterback focused on being able to read the defense and, particularly, one side of the field. He would teach us to key the safeties. We would know which side of the field to focus on once we saw the rotation of the safety. Then, we would have a progression of receivers to throw to whoever was open. This was so valuable to me once I landed in the NFL and had the opportunity to play in a few games as a rookie. I knew that I had a great teacher in Cotton when several pro coaches commented on how knowledgeable I was at such a young age in reading defenses.

I'll always remember my years at Baylor University as some of the best in my career. Cotton Davidson was, without a doubt, the reason for that.

Jay Jeffrey

Baylor quarterback; Graduated 1982; led Baylor to Southwest Conference championship in 1980; Named first-team All-SWC and the league's Newcomer of the Year in 1980; Inductee into the Baylor Athletic Hall of Fame

Cotton Davidson was a legend by the time I got to Baylor. He was a great Baylor quarterback that was an All-Pro for the hated Oakland Raiders (I grew up in Overland Park, Kansas, and was a diehard Chiefs fan). He was friends with my father and had coached both my quarterback brothers, Neal and John, at Baylor. I transferred to Baylor from Missouri University after the football season of 1978. I sat out the 1979 season as NCAA transfer rules dictated.

From the first day I arrived on the Baylor campus, Coach Cotton Davidson was gracious, concise, and a very clear thinker who understood everything there was to know about the passing game. He taught me many things, including how to think on my feet. However, the greatest lesson he taught me was to understand what I was seeing on the football field.

"What did you see?" was the question that Cotton would ask me after every play that we discussed. When I would come to the sideline after an interception or a failed pass attempt, Cotton would ask me that simple question, "What did you see?" Sometimes, I would tell him what I had done, and he would respond by saying, "Jay, I just suffered through what you did. I want to understand what you saw or what you think you saw, so we can understand why you did what you did."

It was through these eyes that Cotton taught me to understand what was really happening on the field. That is when the game started to slow down. Cotton did not need to create a new play. He would just tell me over the headset, "look at the backside post" or "tell radar to fake a post and run a seam, and throw it early." Blitzes were never a problem because I understood the game and knew what the defense was doing and why.

Cotton understood the difficulty of being a quarterback playing at the highest level of collegiate football. He knew the game moved fast and that, sometimes, a quarterback doesn't see the play develop, he loses his read, or, for whatever reason, he simply gets lost. Cotton drilled it in my head by constantly saying, "Whenever you get lost, don't worry about it. You know where your outlets are. Just go to them early and, sometimes, good things happen." Well, that advice paid off big-time when we were playing SMU in 1980. Early in the second half, we were down 21-0 but we came back to win the game, 32-28. Our come-back started when we called a pass route. I dropped back to pass and ended up hitting my outlet receiver, Walter Abercrombie, in the flat for a huge gain. After we scored, Cotton asked me what he always did, "Jay, great decision to hit Walter in the flat; what did you see?" Well, I hesitated and did not really answer the question when Cotton said, "You got lost, didn't you?" Well, yes, I did get lost. That is what I love about Cotton Davidson. He helped me find my way as a quarterback and as a man.

Neal Jeffrey

Baylor quarterback; Graduated 1975; Two-time All-Southwest Conference (SWC) quarterback; In 1974, led Baylor to first defeat of University of Texas in 17 years; Also in 1974, led Baylor to the first SWC Championship in 50 years; Inductee into the Baylor Athletic Hall of Fame; Presently, Associate Pastor of Prestonwood Baptist Church in Plano, Texas

Coach Davidson – you are the Very Best! You are, and always have been, one of my all-time Heroes. I knew who you were long before you were my quarterback coach at Baylor. Starting with your days as a great quarterback at Baylor, I had followed your career to the Dallas Texans and Oakland Raiders. I had your football card, and I also had a little picture of you in an Oakland Raider uniform. They were a real inspiration for me as well as your legend as "The Rifleman" because of the incredible way you threw the football. I wanted to follow in your footsteps as a Baylor quarterback and also an NFL quarterback. I loved Baylor because I was raised as a Baylor fan by my father, who played football at Baylor from 1947 to 1950. He also told me about you since you were both playing at Baylor in 1949 and 1950.

In 1972, my dream of being a Baylor quarterback was beginning. I had a shot at being Baylor's starting quarterback that year. In the spring, I heard that Coach Teaff had hired Cotton Davidson to be our quarterback coach, and I was thrilled. We were all excited. This great college and professional quarterback, the legendary "Rifleman," was going to be our quarterback coach! Awesome!

Playing for Coach Davidson was a priceless experience. His talents as a teacher and leader were incredible. He knew the position because he had played it so well throughout his career. He coached and taught us well. Also, he was an inspiration in so many ways. He always believed in us and impressed upon us to believe we could do better. He was always patient but expected the very best from us. He loved watching us succeed, and we always wanted to make him proud. He would come running down the stands from the press box at halftime and walk us off of the field. In the locker room, he was a master at making halftime adjustments in positive, encouraging ways. He had our complete confidence because he knew what he was talking about and was so effective in teaching us how to do what he had done. He was so much fun to play for. Every quarterback, who played for him, thought that they were his favorite (though I really think that it was me).

The biggest mistake of my life, at one of the biggest moments of my career, happened during the final seconds of the 1973 homecoming game with TCU. We had had a great comeback with three quick touchdowns and drove down for the winning touchdown. With the ball on the TCU four-yard line and needing one yard for a first, I forgot what down it was. With no timeouts left, only a few seconds on the game clock, and thinking it was third down, I threw the ball out of bounds. A major blunder! Yet, the way Coach Davidson responded to me was incredible, always affirming. He still believed in me and still said, "You are the guy." He helped me through a difficult week and guided my comeback from a tough situation. I will never forget his strength and faith in me during one of my lowest moments ever.

From a losing year in 1973, we went to a magical, winning season in 1974. We won the Southwest Conference championship for the first time in 50 years and played one of Baylor's all-time greatest games, called "The Miracle on the Brazos." That game was with the University of Texas. We were down 24-7 at halftime. Coach Davidson's confidence and the adjustments he made for us in the locker room made all the difference in the second half. We scored 27 unanswered points and beat UT for the first time in 17 years.

No question, Coach Davidson made me a better quarterback, but more importantly, he made me a better man. He remains, to this day, as one of my all-time heroes. He had a powerful impact on my life, as I know he did for all those who played for him.

Keith T. Jones

Baylor Graduate 1979, Football Letterman 1977, 1978

I Recruited Cotton.

I first met Cotton Davidson the summer before my senior year in high school. I was working for KWTX as a roving reporter for Johnny Watkins' television show, Ten Acres. One afternoon, while at the studio, I shared with Mr. Frank Fallon, the sports director, that I really wanted to play football for Baylor. Mr. Fallon recommended that I go by Baylor Stadium and talk to Cotton, who recruited in Central Texas.

That afternoon, I went to Baylor Stadium and met Cotton for the first time. We talked for more than an hour and, immediately, I felt that Cotton cared about me and wanted the best for me. I even shared with Cotton that I had always struggled academically, and he encouraged me to stay in touch and to set a classroom goal of making an 85 in all my courses. I left our meeting with a clear academic goal and an intense desire to have the best senior year possible on the football field.

From that day on, I recruited Cotton.

He had asked me to stay in touch, and I did. I called him periodically, and we eventually arranged for him to visit my parents and me in Mart. My mother fixed lunch, and Cotton came to our house. Of course, my parents loved him.

One Sunday evening, soon after the end of our football season, we received a phone call from Cotton. I remember it like it was last night.

"Do you still want to play football for the Baylor Bears?" he asked.

My response was an easy one. "Yes, I sure do."

"Hold on," Cotton said, "let me get someone on the phone who can do more about that than anyone." I heard Coach Teaff's voice on the phone, and he offered me a scholarship to play football at Baylor University. I was ecstatic.

During my official on-campus visit, there were a lot of recruits from lots of different places. Several of them talked about how many visits they had made and how many offers they had from different colleges. I did not have the courage to tell them how I pursued Cotton and Baylor. There is nothing I can do about that now. But it is regrettable.

Playing football at Baylor was not easy for me. In my freshman year, I tore up my left knee and spent that year rehabbing it. In my sophomore year, I was redshirted. In my junior year, I was on the scout team and never saw the playing field.

The next spring, I was at a very low point in my career at Baylor. Cotton must have sensed it. He came to me one afternoon after practice, and we sat down outside the locker room and talked. During practice that day, he said he saw me beat a double team block and make a tackle on a running back. He said that that was as good a play as one can make, and with a continued effort like that, my time would come, and I would be on the playing field.

That one observation and compliment from Cotton gave me the confidence to keep working hard. There is no doubt in my mind that our conversation gave me just the boost I needed to keep fighting the fight. I went on to have a great spring and was voted by my teammates as the most improved defensive player.

When I look back on life, many people have done a great deal for me. However, the one person who gave me direction taught me the value of obtainable goals, genuinely cared for me, and wanted the best for me was Cotton Davidson.

I love the man!

Ty Newton

Baylor baseball; Graduated 1954; Air Force instructor pilot in Viet Nam; Flight instructor at Air Force Academy; 30-year service in Air Force; Personal pilot for Congressman Lyndon Johnson in late 1950's

Cotton and I had known each other since September 1949, when we entered Baylor University. We became friends from the day we met as he was leaving football practice at the old Baylor Dutton Street Stadium. He had a smile on his face from ear to ear, and he still has that same smile every time I see him. I soon found the source of that smile and his friendly manner when he invited me home for the weekend. His father, mother, brother, Hy, and sisters Anita and Sandra had the same smile. I had never seen such a happy family. I had many occasions to visit with them over the years, and they always treated me as part of the family. He was blessed by being raised in a strong Christian home, and those Christian values have remained a central part of his life through the years.

Cotton's uncle had a cabin near Inks Lake in the Hill Country, and we went there several times to fish. On our first visit there, he said he would cook pancakes for breakfast. I was really impressed that he could do that – that is until I stuck my fork into the first pancake and dough squirted out. I have not let him forget about it to this day.

One other experience from our freshman year stands out because I was afraid I had ruined his football career early on. One evening he was studying at his desk in Kokernot Hall, a circumstance that was likely one of the few times it happened. I quietly opened the door, dropped a Baby Giant firecracker in the wastebasket next to his desk, and then slammed the door shut. The deafening explosion was immediately followed by the door bursting open with Cotton sprinting hot on my heels. Down the hallway, I went through two double glass doors (the kind that has mesh wire between the two glass panes). I slammed the last door shut after going through and didn't slow down. A few minutes later, I realized that Cotton had given up the pursuit, and I went back to find him. At the last door, I had gone through, I found broken glass and blood. I followed the blood trail to the dispensary that was in our building. Sure enough, Cotton was sitting on a table with a big grin on his face. A doctor was stitching up a cut on the wrist of his throwing arm. It healed quickly, and a very successful football career followed.

Cotton and I roomed together for the next three years, and I don't recall ever having a cross word. However, I do have some rope burns on my neck from him lassoing me when I came into the room. I got even, though, because I was on the top bunk, and he was below me. The window shade by our bed was rolled up during the day, so I would come in from the chow hall and fill the rolled-up shade with salt and pepper. When he went to bed, he would pull the shade down, and all of the salt and pepper would dump into his bed. Then I would have to hold on for dear life because he was going to push with his feet against my mattress and send me for a ride.

One of our roommates had a pet squirrel. Being academic types, we decided to do a research project to see if we could bleach a stripe down its back to make it look like a skunk. After two bottles of bleach, we finally decided that a squirrel's hair would not absorb bleach.

During the summer of 1952, we had the opportunity to play on the same baseball team at Weimar, Texas. We lived in a hotel in a room so small we had to walk across the bed to get to the other side of the room. We made many trips in my old 1941 Chrysler to Smithville and La Grange to visit a couple of girls who came to our baseball games. The one in Smithville had a swimming pool, so it was worth the 50-mile roundtrip for a swim after a ball game. My car got to where it would not shift into first gear, so when we came to a stoplight, we would get out and push to get it going. It was quite a sight as we pushed it down Seawall Boulevard at each stoplight in Galveston.

On one of our visits, we had weeks of fun with a bag of confetti that Cotton's cousin gave us. We would put confetti under the covers of our suitemate's beds, always with a good alibi so they would not suspect us. We even put some in our beds and complained about it. It nearly drove them crazy trying to figure out who was doing it. Fortunately for us, they never did.

These are just some of the fun things we did during college. I cannot imagine anyone having more fun or having a stronger friendship. I asked Cotton to be the best man in Ruth's and my wedding in December 1953, but he was selected to play in the East-West All-Star Game, which conflicted with the wedding. In June 1954, I was the best man in Cotton and Carolyn's wedding in Breckenridge.

Although we went in different directions after college, we stayed in touch enough to share in the growth of our families and the excitement of our children's accomplishments. After our families were grown, Cotton, Carolyn, my wife Ruth, and I, along with good friends Mitch and Charlene Isenberg, traveled together for many years and had just as many good and funny experiences as we had in college. We feel fortunate to still talk frequently and take short trips together. Because of our strong friendship, our children feel a common bond and always ask how Cotton and Carolyn are doing. We can only hope our children have the good fortune to have such close friendships as the Davidsons' and Newtons'.

Randy Sage

Senior Vice President, Investments, Wells Fargo Advisors
Baylor Graduate 1980

Cotton became my father-in-law in 1984 when I married his youngest daughter, Tracy. Like many of his family and friends, I have so many great stories and memories with Cotton that there might not be enough paper to print them. But, here is just one fond memory.

In deer hunting season during the winter of 1985, Cotton was going to take me, Tommy, and Ty out to his land for an early morning hunt. It was near New Year's Eve, and Ty had bought some fireworks. He bought one type of explosive device that we connected to Cotton's pickup truck battery. Once the truck started, the firecracker was to explode. The next morning, the three of us made sure we were in the truck before Cotton in anticipation of what we hoped would be a good prank.

The truck started, warmed up, and Cotton began the short drive to where he was going to place his three hunters. We remained quiet but kept cutting our eyes toward each other, shaking our heads and shrugging our shoulders, trying to figure out why the device never ignited.

A few short hours later, Cotton began picking each of us up. This was a time prior to pickups having back seats and four doors. As each of us climbed into the truck, our eyes were diverted to the object lying on the dashboard. It was the explosive firecracker. It was spread out with its wires exposed and fully intact. How had he discovered this when nothing ever happened? As we all stared forward without talking, Cotton broke the silence. He told us he felt the truck was running a bit rough that morning, so he popped the hood after dropping us off. He noticed that the distributor cap had loosened, and there was a mysterious foreign object attached to his battery.

We all had a good laugh at our failure, but Cotton had the best laugh in the end.

I have been blessed beyond words to have such an honorable man leading the Davidson family. He is a fine Christian, mentor, hunting guide, and fishing partner. Also, he is an understanding and loving man. Those are just a few characteristics I freely use when describing Cotton. I am truly thankful each and every day that he is in my life.

James Ray Smith

Baylor Guard/Defensive End No. 84, 64; Graduated 1954; Cleveland Browns (1956-1962); Dallas Cowboys (1963-1964); Baylor University Athletics Hall of Fame 1968; College Football Hall of Fame 1987; Texas Sports Hall of Fame 2008

My friend, Cotton Davidson, is one of the good men in this world today. Also, he is a good friend from my early days at Baylor University. In Cotton's senior year at Baylor, he was the starting quarterback for Baylor's football team. We were not ranked as one of the top teams in the nation, but we did have a good team. Our first game was with the University of California (Cal) at Berkley. We were the underdogs by 25 points which gave us an incentive to beat the hell out of them. And, we did, by 25 to 0. This was the first year the NCAA ruled all players on university and college teams had to play both ways. That meant all players had to play the whole game with few substitutions. Under that rule, most teams would pick on quarterbacks with their running and passing game, believing that was the place of weakness in the defense. That was the way Cal played. Cal's first pass play was to their tight end, going over the middle and running right at Cotton. Oh my, I thought if he hit Cotton, Cotton would be out of the game, and maybe for the season. Well, Cotton lowered his shoulder to take him on, and the tight end lowered his head to run over Cotton, oh my. Well, just at the last second, Cotton took a step to his right and bulldogged him to the ground right there in front of all those 90.000 people in the stands. Cotton did it just like he did as a teenager at Gatesville, Texas, bulldogging young steers out in the barnyard. What a tackle that was, and Cotton stayed on the field to play many more downs for the whole game. Cotton had a great year that year and went on to be a number one draft choice in the NFL.

Now, on the other side of the coin, both Cotton and I had been at Baylor for a few years and had not found a life-long mate. Well, the Good Lord saw our needs and solved them that fall. About the middle of December that year, Cotton pulled me to the side one day and asked me what he should do about a gift he had gotten from Carolyn, his girlfriend and wife-to-be. I asked him what she had given him. He said it was a 30-30 rifle. Now, there is not an old country boy who would not want a 30-30 rifle. I said, "That's simple. She wants an engagement ring. Now, go get it and give it to her for Christmas." He did, and what a wonderful life they have had.

Cotton, we love you both and pray that you have many more wonderful years.

Your friend in Christ, James Ray Smith.

Ricky Thompson

Baylor wide receiver; Graduated 1976; Baltimore Colts (1976-1977); Washington Redskins (1978-1981); St. Louis Cardinals 1982; Sideline Reporter for the Baylor Radio Network

I have had the privilege of knowing Cotton for most of my life since we share the same hometown of Gatesville, Texas. Growing up, I knew Cotton as the professional football quarterback for the Oakland Raiders and, later, as a Raiders coach. I had always admired him from afar, but it was later in high school and then in college at Baylor that I had the opportunity to get to know Cotton personally. He is the first person that told me he thought I had a great opportunity to play college football. Then, when I was playing at Baylor, he told me that he thought I could play in the NFL. It had always been just a dream of mine until Cotton told me he thought it could become a reality.

Not many players are lucky enough in college to have an individual from their hometown, who is an NFL veteran, coach them in college as their position coach. I was one of the lucky ones. Cotton had forgotten more about football and what it took to be a wide receiver than most ever knew in the first place. From him, I learned the game, how to run routes, how to read defensive coverages, and how to get open. All I had to do was play the game the way that we practiced every day. And, of course, being a former quarterback, Cotton threw passes to us on a daily basis. And, I mean, he threw missiles at us! I still have a scar from a compound fracture of my little finger to prove it. At the time, I told Cotton, "I think I've broken my finger," to which he replied, "Nah, you just jammed it." He then grabbed my hand and said, "Gosh, I think you broke your finger!!!" It didn't take a "rocket scientist" to figure that one out! Thereafter, I thought of Cotton in every game because I never played another football game at Baylor, or in the NFL, without taping my fingers together to hold my little finger in place.

In 1974, Baylor had a special year by winning its first Southwest Conference Championship in 50 years. Cotton and I often talked of the 54-yard touchdown reception that I had in the 1974 game against the University of Texas. That game became known as "The Miracle on the Brazos." He said he would never forget that play. I can't express in words what his saying that meant to me.

I could go on, but I'm just going to make a couple of comments about Cotton's impact on my NFL career, although he was no longer my coach. In my first NFL training camp, I knew that I was way ahead of most of the rookie receivers because of what I had learned from Cotton at Baylor. Most of my "rookie" teammates couldn't read defenses. But, for me, it was automatic. I had learned at Baylor what to look for coming off of the ball and, in most cases, knew what the coverage was as quickly as a quarterback could read the defense. I wonder why that was? Maybe, because I had a quarterback named Cotton Davidson as my college receiver coach!!! Without a doubt, Cotton played a huge role in my ability to achieve a childhood dream and have a 7-year career in the NFL. I will be forever grateful.

Trey Weir

Baylor kicker and punter No. 17; Graduated 1993

Not unlike many of the guys who played football at Baylor University from the early seventies to the early nineties, I have been privileged to call Cotton Davidson "coach." However, in the years since graduating, it has been one of my greatest honors to call him "friend."

Most people, who know his name, remember him to be a great college and NFL player whose accomplishments are too numerous to list. Although very important, it merely scratches the surface of this quintessential Texas gentleman.

Even today, a single handshake with Coach is all that you need to understand why he was such a great quarterback. His strong grip pales in comparison to his strength of character. It would be understandable for someone, who has accomplished so much to have an enormous ego, but that's not Coach Davidson.

Not once in the last thirty years of knowing him have, I heard him brag about his successes or make a disparaging remark about someone. Instead, he has proven to be a humble man who is most proud of his family and friends. Always quick with a smile, Coach enjoys remembering the best of his former teammates and the players he has coached.

The legacy of all great men is the ability to make a positive impact on people and their lives, and I proudly stand as one whose life is better for knowing Coach Davidson.

Albert Witcher

Baylor linebacker No. 88; Graduated 1959; Houston Oilers 1960, AFL Champions 1960

Cotton and I grew up in neighboring counties. Although both of us played high school football, I was a few years younger, and we never played each other. However, I knew of his good character and outstanding ability, and talent as a football player. He was well recognized and appreciated in our part of the world.

My first experience with Cotton was at Baylor in 1959. I was a senior end and linebacker on Baylor's football team, and Cotton coached there that year. That was a great year for me as a player because of what I learned from Cotton and his friend, Raymond Berry. Raymond came to Baylor during our training camp as a favor to Cotton. Cotton's outstanding knowledge and skills as a play-caller, passer, runner, and punter, plus Raymond's exceptional capabilities with running routes and catching passes, were huge benefits for our whole team. Both Cotton and Raymond were very effective teachers and coaches.

My next experience with Cotton was in competition on opposing AFL teams in 1960. He was with the Dallas Texans, and I was with the Houston Oilers. The Oilers won the AFL Championship that year. I am confident that what I learned from Cotton and Raymond had a major positive impact on my ability to play professional football.

Through the years since 1960, I have had the pleasure of keeping up with Cotton and his lovely wife,

Carolyn, and their family. It has also been satisfying to witness Cotton's continual support for charitable organizations in his Gatesville community. He was instrumental in helping establish the Gatesville Boys and Girls Club. Fundraising programs were essential to the club's survival in its early days, and Cotton's contributions were critical. Proceeds from his popular Celebrity Golf Tournaments made a huge difference. I was always eager to join my pro football friends at those events and enjoy an evening of entertainment, a round of golf, and a delightful reunion.

Dr. Greg Wood

Baylor quarterback; Two-year Letterman; Graduated 1979

I met Cotton Davidson when I was in high school. He recruited me to Baylor University to play football. I was unaware at the time that he would become a greater role model in my life than football would.

He not only was my coach, but he became a wonderful father-in-law to me, and a beloved PaPa to my children. Through him, I have been blessed beyond measure to have my wife and children. They are an important part of his life too.

He has supported my family with unwavering love, exhibited through words and actions. I can see in his eyes the evidence of pride and unconditional love when the grandchildren are in his presence. He has been a calm, patient, and humble influence in my life. He is slow to speak and slow to anger. Rarely have I heard a negative word from him.

I also appreciate his sense of humor. Each year, he would tell the incoming freshmen about the time he was in the Army and jumped on a grenade. The story was told to explain the depression in his chest. The real explanation was that he has a condition called "pectus excavatum" that develops over time. That story always produced astonished looks in the young athletes' eyes.

I do take pride in telling his football stories and exploits, but the blessings I have received because of his love outside of football are a much greater treasure. My family and I love PaPa.

You have just read very complimentary remarks from some of the people I have "rubbed elbows with." They certainly are treasures. However, I expected at least a few "gigs." I hope those folks didn't have their fingers crossed behind their backs when they were doing the writing.-Cotton

Appendix 2 - Children's Notes

My Note:

Carolyn and I have been blessed beyond all expectations with our four children. We are exceedingly proud of them and their accomplishments. Also, blessings from them have grown and grown with the grandchildren and great-grandchildren they have brought into our lives. Their commentaries below are invaluable to me.

Dr. Tommy Davidson

Baylor wide receiver; Graduated 1978; Three-year letterman in football

Francis, Cotton, Dad, Coach, and finally, Papa are all the titles that my father has carried at different ages and stages. I watched him be all of them. Having been a part of his life more than anyone, except Carolyn, I can say, without hesitating, that he was a champion at all the stages he took on. Football was his passion, and he was a pioneer in that sport for many years. But, Papa is where his heart was best and most appreciated. His love for grandkids and great-grandkids will never be outdone. Many have enjoyed and benefitted by knowing him at one or more stages, but I have been blessed to appreciate them all.

Kelly Davidson Wood

Baylor Graduate 1980

There are so many memories I have of my dad, and all of them are good. He always worked hard, whether it was with his ranch, oil company, or football. Those activities often took long days, and many times, he was away from home, but Mom always filled the gap. Their teamwork was exceptional. However, whatever Dad was doing, he did his best to make time to spend with his children. I remember loving to ride in the back of his pickup at the ranch to help him pen sheep, or just watch the sheep shearers, or hear him call the cows. I knew he was in his happy place out on his land. That plainly showed as he tended ranching activities and coordinated work with Bus and Dean Barton, who lived on our land, and Hy, Dad's brother, who covered for Dad when he was away with football. Dean Barton was an exceptional lady and a Godsend to our family, as was Hy. Daddy and Hy were very close. Family has always been very important to Dad. After retirement, Dad would spend every morning at the hospital with his dad, whose health was in decline.

Dad is a man of many talents. When he started coaching at Baylor, I knew it was a great learning curve for him. The speaking engagements were not something that came easy with his personality, but he made it seem easy. As I look back on the Raider days, I am so proud of how he handled the notoriety and the pressures that came with the job. There were all kinds of personalities to influence us and "avenues" we could have gone down during our time in California, but he and Mom made sure we were going to church every Sunday morning. We never missed church, even after very late nights from Saturday ball games.

I admire Dad for his perpetual positive attitude and for never giving up. When his shoulder was almost destroyed, I remember his rehab routine of hitting a punching bag in the garage and the sounds that it made. I think the whole garage shook! I vividly remember how he dealt with disappointments and unfair situations. He never let adversity get him down. He was always able to dismiss distressful issues without burdening anyone around him. No matter what is happening in his life, he keeps a splendid attitude.

Also, I remember hearing that, later in life, he recommitted his life to Christ at a Cowboy church in Gatesville, and that's the kind of life he lives. Staying true to his soul and living life his way, he didn't jump on fads or pressures from the world. He is an example I will gladly follow.

Tracy Davidson Sage

Baylor Graduate 1983

Finding words to adequately describe my relationship with my daddy is no easy task. I guess I will start with the obvious. He is so very kind. He always remains true to his upbringing and his faith, even when he has been given many reasons to not be kind. He has faced those situations much more often than a few times. Yet, he remained steady as a rock, consistent at every turn of his life. Most of the time, his response of, "You don't say," is enough. Somehow, he manages to say the right things when needed and takes action only when necessary. But, in the case of grandchildren, he always goes with the choice of "no action" and just tends to laugh and love his time with each of them, always allowing them to do things we were never allowed to do. Good ol' PAPA. Another thing about Daddy is, no matter where I go, somehow, his name comes up (okay, I sometimes mention it), and there are always good, positive remarks about his career and character. It's funny that so many people of his generation can recall certain series of big games that he played in like it was yesterday. They remember exactly where they were when Daddy threw a TD or handed off to win the game. He is such a big part of the glory of football, not only locally but throughout the pros too.

He handles life with grace. He always chooses kindness, even when it is not called for. I believe he is responsible for turning the lights on in the church every Sunday, and he never misses. He lives his life by a few solid, tried, and true rules; never complicated, just Coryell County common sense.

Here's to my daddy! May a little of him rub off on me ----- and the world!

Ty Davidson, D.D.S., General Dentist

Baylor Graduate 1987

When I was asked to contribute experiences regarding my father, many stories came to mind. However, predominant memories were of weekends spent on our ranch, working with livestock or mending fences in the Texas sweltering heat. Those experiences stood out because they were significant influences in my choice for a career. At a young age, I was convinced that a career indoors was what I wanted, and I chose dentistry.

Ranch work involved its own unique hazards. In one instance, Dad and I were working on a fence near a creek on the backside of the ranch. After spending a few hours in the hot sun, we went down to quench our thirst straight from the creek. That might seem like a bad idea to some, but it was something we did regularly. As I finished drinking and stood up, I realized that Dad was coughing and choking. Having never performed the Heimlich maneuver, I improvised as best I could. It worked, but I broke his rib in the process!

Both of us were more than a little shaken by the event. We took a break to calm our nerves and sat down in the shade of a small limestone shelter. As we were sitting there recovering from the choking episode, I gazed down and saw a perfectly formed arrowhead in the dirt, exposed for all to see.

Growing up we sought these elusive arrowheads in trails, caves, and along the river as they signaled good luck. What I have learned is that arrowheads are more likely to find you at the right time. No doubt, that shelter had been used by Native American tribes inhabiting the land for generations before us. I picked it up and showed it to Dad. While we were not entirely sure this find was worth a broken rib, we believed it was a good sign and a remarkable find. With that, I stuck the arrowhead in my pocket, and we went back to toiling in the hot sun. Dad and I continued to work side by side, and he never once complained about his broken rib. We did however quit a little early before we had to take another drink from the creek though. I still have that arrowhead and it reminds me of the moments dad and I had working together on the ranch and how they shaped my outlook and my life.

Appendix 3 - Carolyn's Notes

Before Cotton joined the Baltimore Colts in 1954, he told me that he would not play football unless I went with him wherever he went. That decision didn't change as our family grew. Cotton would not play without his family being where he was. That was easy for me before we had children. However, moving became just a little more complicated as each of our four children was born. By the time Cotton joined the Oakland Raiders in 1962, we had three children, Tommy, Kelly, and Tracy. Their ages were six, four, and one-and-a-half. In 1964, Ty was born. He was only a couple of months old when the children and I flew from Texas to join Cotton in California. Needless to say, that year was a bit more of a challenge. I had to have a baby bed, and bless assistant coach John Madden's wife, Virginia, for loaning me hers for the '64 season. Virginia's generosity was an example of so many other acts of kindness among players' families. Team families were like a neighborhood with neighbors helping neighbors.

During our seven years with the Raiders, we moved twice a year. We spent the first half of the year in Texas and football season in California. Cotton would go to California for spring training and arrange for our living quarters. Near the end of spring training, the children and I would pack up and fly to Oakland to see what kind of lodgings we would have for the next five or six months. Every year, we lived in a different place, and our kids attended a different school. Some of our living accommodations were good, but some were just barely okay. However, that was never a "show stopper." We made the best of our situations, and no one complained. We were together. That was most important.

Looking back at those days, sometimes I wonder how we managed to get by for five or six months on the small amounts of bags and baggage we were limited to on the plane. However, at the time, I didn't agonize over difficulties. I knew what had to be done, and I did it. I never wasted time on considering any "what ifs" about things going wrong. Cotton was doing his part for the family, and I would do mine. Not all of our travels were trouble-free, but we "got by" and managed the problems we had. Perhaps, we were lucky to have avoided the really big ones.

Why did I do it? Cotton and I were partners, a team, and he was the man I loved. I was proud of him. While we were both at Baylor, he impressed me before I even knew him. As his accomplishments, awards and honors continued down through the years, I was full of admiration for him on each and every occasion. The list is long. He was the MVP of the 1954 East-West Shrine game. He was the Baltimore Colts' first-round draft pick in 1954. He played in the 1954 Chicago College All-Star Classic Game. He was named All-Army Quarterback in 1955. He was the MVP of the very first American Football League (AFL) All-Star Game in 1961. He was inducted into the Baylor Hall of Fame in 1982. He was inducted into the Southwest Conference (SWC) Hall of Fame in 2015. In 2017, he was selected as "One of the Ten Best All-Time Baylor Assistant Coaches." The city of Gatesville, Texas, proclaimed "April 30, 1994, as Cotton Davidson Day in recognition of his significant and distinguished contributions, dedication and service to the City."

Carolyn and I – courtesy of the Davidson family

Cotton always had a keen interest in helping to further improvements in our esteemed Gatesville community. He lent a hand in many projects. Starting our city museum was one notable project that significantly involved him. The fledgling museum needed money, and city elders had an idea for Cotton. They proposed to organize an evening featuring him at a gathering in our community center. The evening would include a dinner and entertainment. The entertainment would be a "Cotton Roast." His friends, including so many from Baylor, would be invited to attend and have a go at putting Cotton on the "hot seat." That evening turned out to be one of the most humorous and interesting events that I can remember. The building was filled with people, and the "roast" went on and on. The young men, who Cotton had coached, really gave him fits. They were the "stars." My sides hurt from so much laughing. I learned a few things too. Unquestionably, everyone got their money's worth, and the museum received a huge contribution.

Interestingly, Cotton's connection to the museum didn't end with the "roast." Due to generous donations of antiques and artifacts, the museum has developed into an establishment that Gatesville is very proud of. It is the reason for Gatesville to have been named "Spur Capital of Texas" by the State Legislature in 2001. That designation is in recognition of the Lloyd and Madge Mitchell collection of over 5,000 spurs. Coach Mitchell spent decades gathering that rare collection which his family generously donated to the museum. Cotton and I have always had close ties and friendships with the Mitchell family, and Cotton was involved in the "Spur Capital" saga. Several Gatesville citizens pursued getting some kind of state-wide recognition for the remarkable spur collection, and they needed a name for that citation. They accepted Cotton's "Spur Capital" idea. After months of preparation with state representatives, Cotton accompanied a group of Gatesville citizens who met in Austin for the official proclamation of Gatesville being "Spur Capital of Texas." A Texas flag was flown over the capital for the occasion, and the flag was given to Cotton. It was another of his honors that, if asked, he would say someone else deserved.

Awards and honors are one thing, but I love and appreciate Cotton for the honorable person he is.

Carolyn and I at the front of our house, December 2020
– photo by Carole Corgill

Appendix 4 - Wayland's Notes

From childhood, Cotton could out-run, out-jump, out-throw, out-maneuver, out-last, and out-think essentially everyone around him. His exceptional athletic abilities propelled him to headlines in the sports world through high school, college, the Army, pro football, and Baylor coaching. In every sport, he was an "all-heart" competitor. However, throughout nearly a half-century of competing in so many different arenas, his splendid character and attitude constantly equaled or outshone his athletic talents – and still does.

An old West Texas maxim goes something like, "the best recommendation a man can have is by the people where he comes from." Without a doubt, Cotton has that recommendation. On the 30th day of April 1994, city government officials in Gatesville issued a proclamation declaring that date to be Cotton Davidson Day. Credits listed in the proclamation make no mistake about what people in his hometown think of him. Those credits are examples of how he was, and is, thought of, wherever he has been.

Cotton is my neighbor and friend. This book is "His Story." It is a distillation of hundreds of pages of notes from scores of conversations with Cotton. My contribution was only to organize the information and formulate sentences and paragraphs to copy what he said.

Talking to Cotton is always a pleasure. I have been privileged to learn much of his remarkable story and help record it.

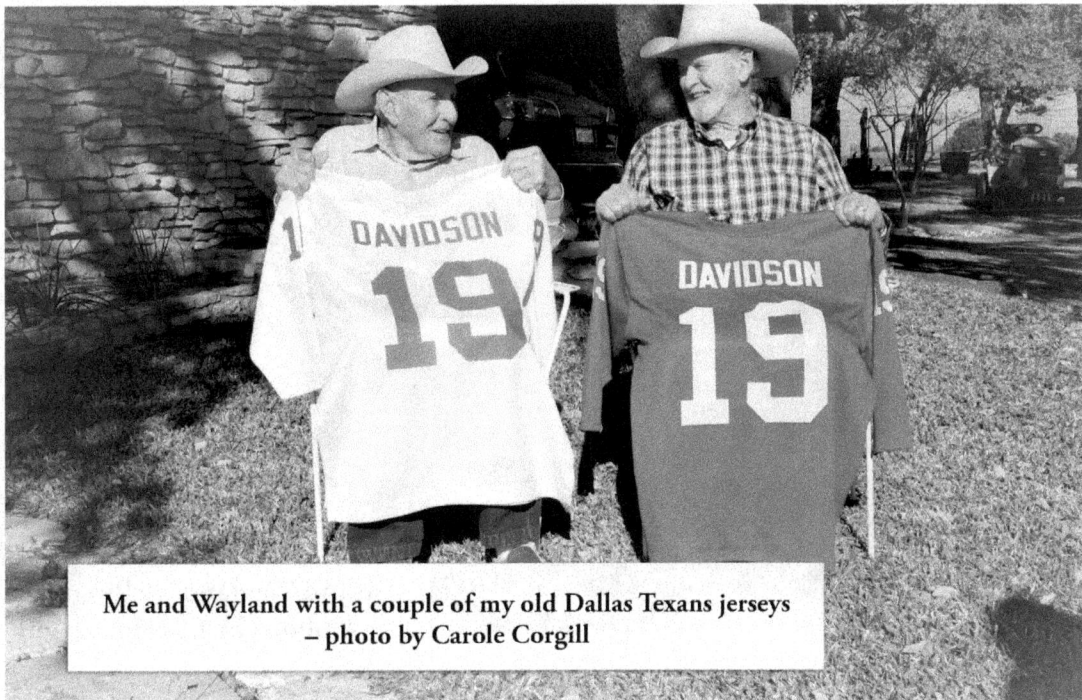

Me and Wayland with a couple of my old Dallas Texans jerseys – photo by Carole Corgill

Acknowledgments

The authors owe many thanks to the friendly and helpful people who graciously researched their files to provide pictures for this book. Our sincere thanks go out to Trisha Kirk and Jacqueline Belloso of the Las Vegas Raiders, Mike Davidson and Bob Moore of the Kansas City Chiefs, Pete Ward and Jon Scott of the Indianapolis Colts, and Geoff Hunt of Baylor University. Also acknowledged are Gale Galloway and Kent Hance for their extraordinary, timely support. Special thanks go to Carole Corgill whose editorial skills were put to use throughout the writing of this book.

To those who generously contributed their stories to this book, we are forever grateful.

It was a fruitful undertaking and a pleasure to correspond with such pleasant, professional and helpful people.

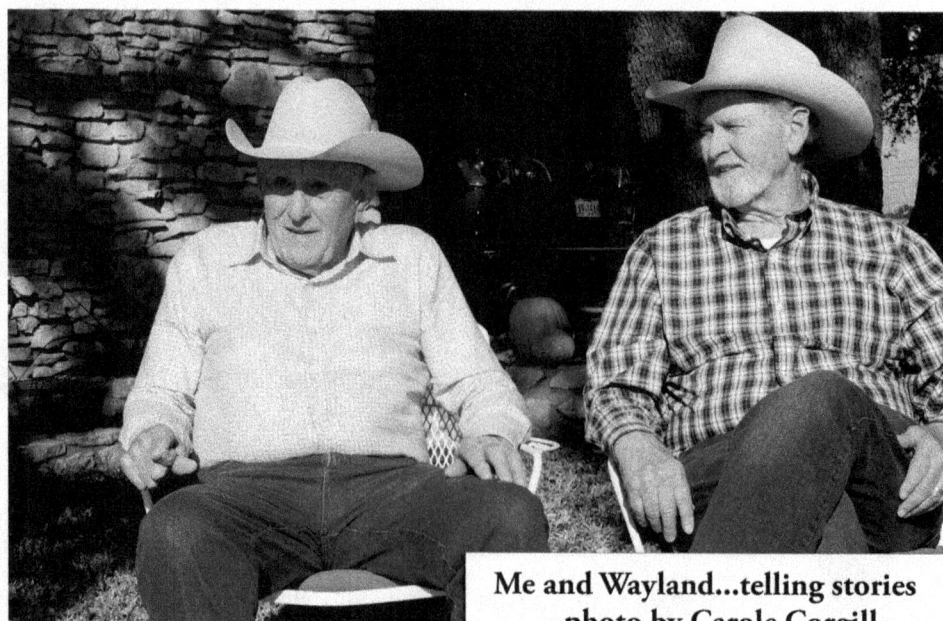

Me and Wayland...telling stories
– photo by Carole Corgill

Author Wayland Corgill

Wayland Corgill is an electrical engineer. He has a BS degree from Southern Methodist University. He engaged in engineering and engineering management throughout his professional career. A large part of that work involved writing technical specifications for equipment and construction projects. After retirement, writing about other subjects proved to be a satisfying hobby. One book recently published is about life on a small West Texas sharecropper cotton farm. Three more books about experiences in Saudi Arabia are near completion. His wife, Carole, has a journalism degree from The University of Texas and that is unquestionably fortunate for Wayland.

Carole & Wayland

COTTON DAVIDSON DAY PROCLAMATION

WHEREAS, Cotton Davidson is a native of Coryell County, Texas and was born in the Pecan Grove Community, and

WHEREAS, Cotton Davidson graduated from Gatesville High School in 1949, and

WHEREAS, Cotton Davidson was an outstanding athlete lettering in 4 sports his Senior Year at Gatesville High School, and

WHEREAS, Cotton Davidson continued to participate in sports while attending Baylor University, graduating in 1954, and

WHEREAS, Cotton Davidson served his country from 1955 until 1957 in the U.S. Army, and

WHEREAS, Cotton Davidson played professional football until 1969, and

WHEREAS, Cotton Davidson coached football at Baylor University from 1972 until 1993, and

WHEREAS, Cotton Davidson has contributed significantly to Gatesville and Coryell County, and

NOW THEREFORE I HEREBY PROCLAIM SATURDAY, APRIL 30, 1994 AS COTTON DAVIDSON DAY IN GATESVILLE, TEXAS in recognition of his significant and distinguished contributions, dedication, and service to City.

IN WITNESS THEREOF, I have set my hand and caused the seal of the City of Gatesville to be affixed this 30th day of April, 1994

_____
Wyllis H. Ament
Mayor
City of Gatesville